# Pictures of Belonging:
## Miki Hayakawa, Hisako Hibi, and Miné Okubo

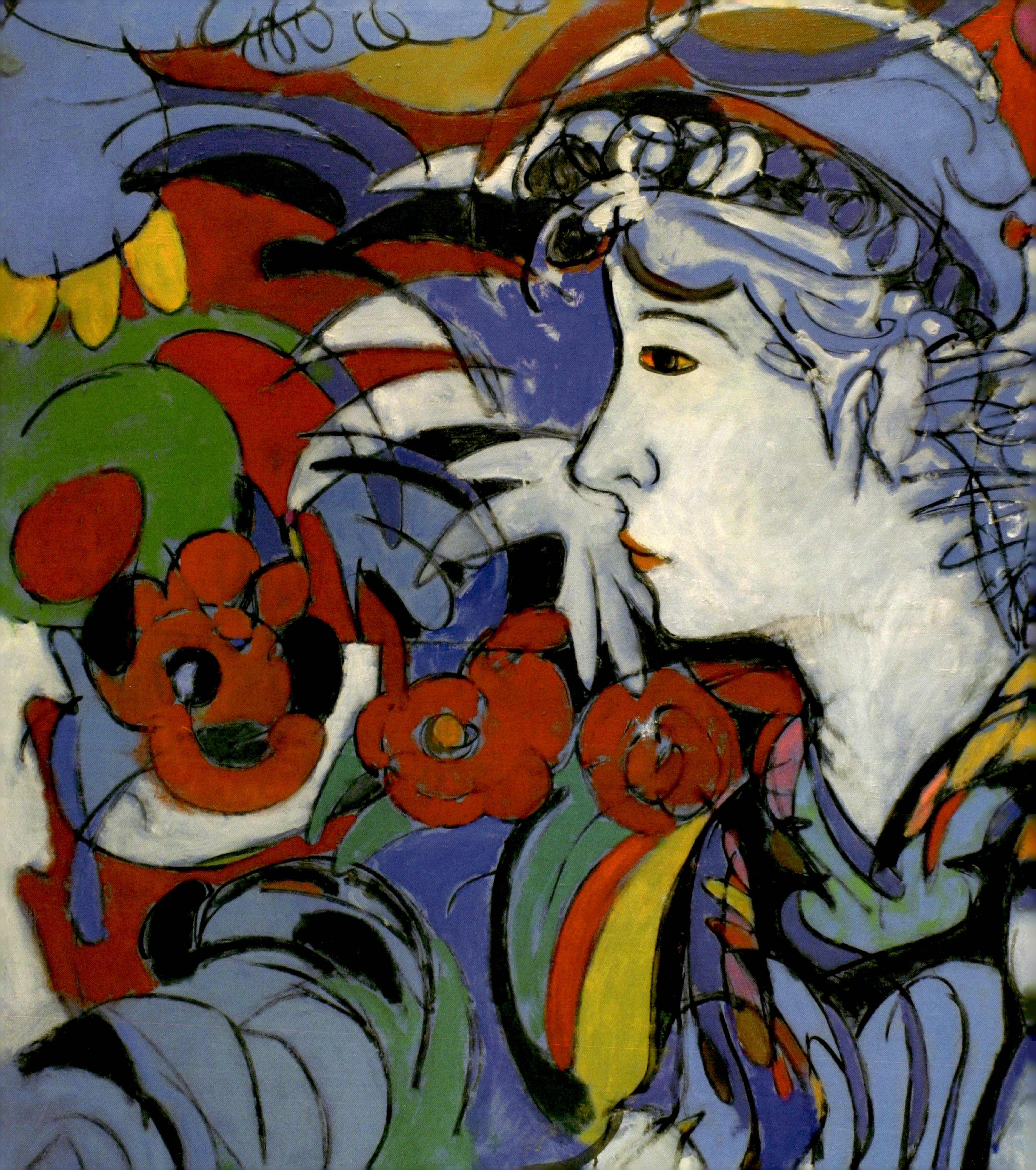

# Pictures of Belonging

# Miki Hayakawa, Hisako Hibi, and Miné Okubo

Edited by
ShiPu Wang

Contributors
Becky Alexander
Melissa Ho
Rihoko Ueno
Patricia Wakida
Cécile Whiting

Japanese American National Museum, Los Angeles
University of California Press, Oakland

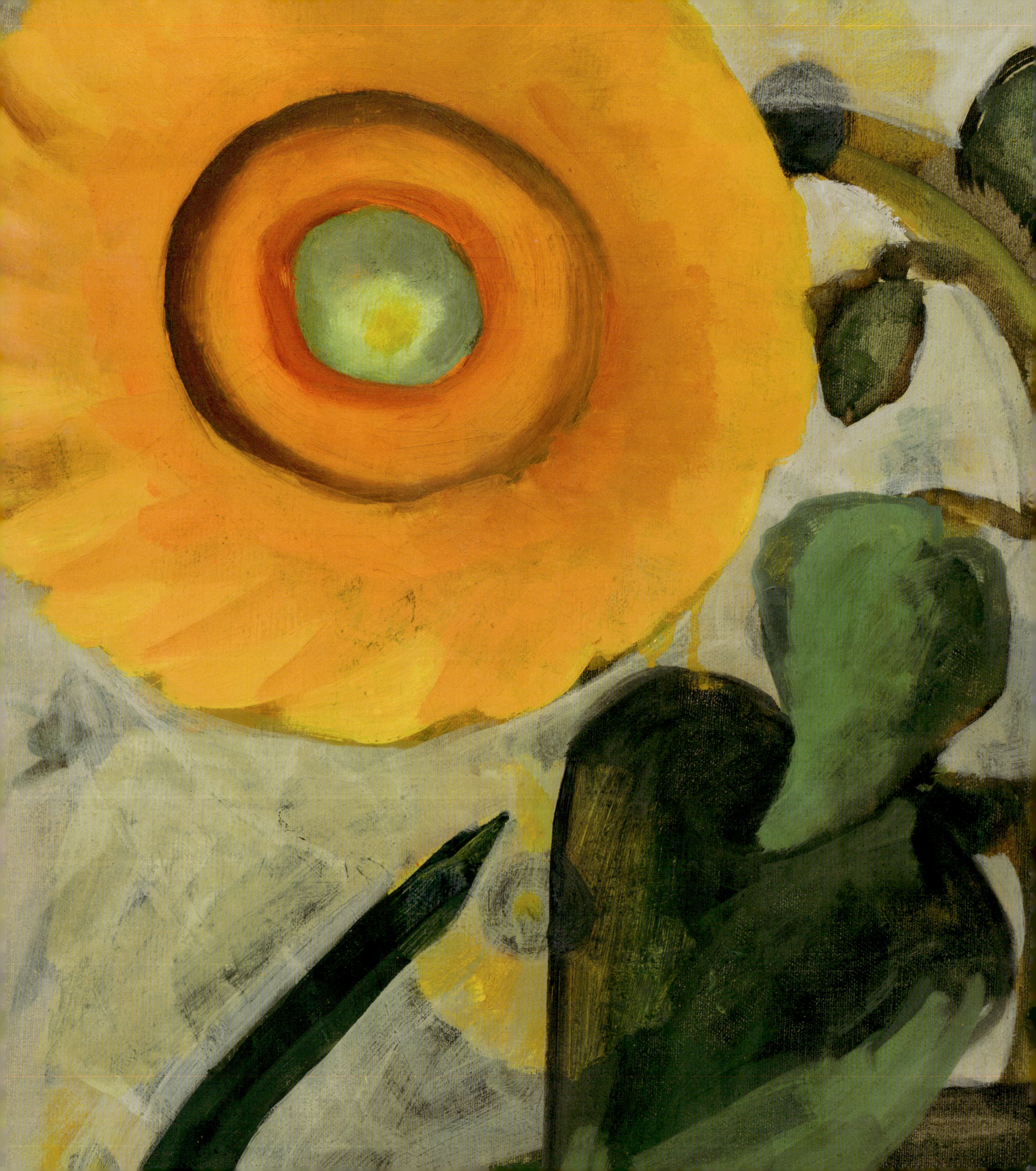

# Contents

## Foreword

The Japanese American National Museum is delighted to collaborate with the Terra Foundation for American Art to present *Pictures of Belonging: Miki Hayakawa, Hisako Hibi, and Miné Okubo*. Curated by Dr. ShiPu Wang, of the University of California, Merced, and commissioner of the Smithsonian National Portrait Gallery, *Pictures of Belonging* showcases nearly one hundred works created by Miki Hayakawa, Hisako Hibi, and Miné Okubo. These trailblazing American women of Japanese descent—part of the pre–World War II generation of artists in California—were committed to exploring art as a productive means of storytelling, but their achievements are rarely recognized in the pages of American history.

Sharing these and other experiences of Japanese Americans to promote the understanding and appreciation of America's diversity is central to the Museum. We are fortunate to have works by all three artists in the Museum's permanent collection, and we are proud to co-organize this exhibition with Dr. Wang so that a broader audience can consider how the overlooked legacies of these artists illuminate the beauty, connections, turmoil, and resilience in their remarkable lives and work. *Pictures of Belonging* also puts the artists' works in dialogue with one another for the first time—creating new conversations on citizenship, community, and agency in the historical record during an era of exclusion for Japanese Americans in particular and Asian Americans as a whole.

Moreover, touring this exhibition to five museums across the country invites the art world to consider how these trailblazers created monumental records of their prewar, wartime, and postwar experiences that were also commentaries on democracy and U.S. immigration history. In doing so, they brought their artistic achievements, unique perspectives, and lessons from Japanese American history to the forefront of American art.

Ann Burroughs, President and CEO
Japanese American National Museum

## A Note on Terminology and the Japanese American Experience by the Japanese American National Museum

"The present procedure of keeping loyal American citizens in concentration camps on the basis of race for longer than is absolutely necessary is dangerous and repugnant to the principles of our Government."
—Attorney General Francis Biddle, Memorandum to President Roosevelt, December 30, 1943

"They were concentration camps. They called it relocation but they put them in concentration camps, and I was against it. We were in a period of emergency but it was still the wrong thing to do."
—Harry S. Truman, quoted in Merle Miller, *Plain Speaking: An Oral Biography of Harry S. Truman* (New York: Berkley, 1974)

The words and phrases used to describe this history vary considerably among scholars, government officials, and even those directly affected by Executive Order 9066: "relocation," "evacuation," "incarceration," "internment," "concentration camp." There is no general agreement about what is most accurate or fair.

Officially, the camps were called "relocation centers." Many now acknowledge that "relocation center" and "evacuation" are euphemisms used purposefully by the government to downplay the significance of its actions. It is an unequivocal fact that the government itself, including the president, used the term "concentration camp" during World War II in speeches and written documents.

A concentration camp is a place where people are imprisoned not because of any crimes they committed, but simply because of who they are. Although many groups have been singled out for such persecution throughout history, the term "concentration camps" was first used at the turn of the century in the Spanish-American and Boer Wars. In recent years, concentration camps have existed in the former Soviet Union, Cambodia, and Bosnia.

During World War II, America's concentration camps were clearly distinguishable from Nazi Germany's. Nazi camps were places of torture, barbarous medical experiments, and summary executions; some were extermination centers with gas chambers. Six million Jews and many others, including Romani, Poles, homosexuals, and political dissidents, were slaughtered in the Holocaust.

Despite the difference, all had one thing in common: the people in power removed a minority group from the general population, and the rest of society let it happen.

The Japanese American National Museum uses "concentration camp" not in an effort to bear comparisons to the atrocities of the Holocaust, but to express the veritable magnitude of what was done to Japanese Americans.

This language came out of the Japanese American National Museum's conference "Whose America? Who's American? Diversity, Civil Liberties, and Social Justice," part of the Museum's "Enduring Communities: The Japanese American Experience in Arizona, Colorado, New Mexico, Texas, and Utah" initiative, which began in 2008. It was adapted from a 1994 joint statement written by the Japanese American National Museum and the American Jewish Committee that appeared in Karen Ishizuka, *Lost and Found: Reclaiming the Japanese American Incarceration* (Chicago: University of Illinois Press, 2006), 163.

# Acknowledgments

There are a plenitude of joys in realizing a curatorial project like *Pictures of Belonging*. One comes from the thrill of pursuing, locating, and seeing previously unknown works of art, through which a fuller picture of these little- or lesser-studied artists' rich oeuvres is revealed, one painting at a time. Another lies in the tremendous generosity and trust that I have received in the past decade, from artist estates and from a wide range of individuals, including collectors who shared their treasures, archivists and registrars, and researchers who preserved and organized historical objects and documents to facilitate archival research.

My deep gratitude thus must go, first and foremost, to the four collections from which most works in *Pictures of Belonging* have been drawn: the Hisako and Matsusaburo George Hibi estate—namely Ibuki Hibi Lee, the artists' daughter, and her family, especially Amy Lee-Tai, Eric Lee, and Michio Aoyagi; Richard Sakai and his impressive, one-of-a-kind collection of Japanese American art; the Miné Okubo Charitable Corporation—Seiko Buckingham, the estate's trustee, along with Tracy Fisher, director of the Center for Social Justice & Civil Liberties of the Riverside Community College District, where more than two thousand Okubo works reside; and the Japanese American National Museum (JANM), whose holdings of work by American artists of Japanese descent are unparalleled. I greatly admire and appreciate these people's and institutions' dedication and profound sense of responsibility toward cherishing and preserving the artists' legacies. The same appreciation goes to other lenders, as well: the Smithsonian American Art Museum; the Los Angeles County Museum of Art; the New Mexico Museum of Art; the Oakland Museum of California; the Hayward Area Historical Society; Sandra and Bram Dijkstra; David and Shirley Astilli; Melinda McCrossen and Katrina Egger Fearn; Michael De Grazzio; and Stephanie S. Lawrence and Elizabeth L. Divekar.

Organizing an original exhibition, not to mention a national tour, is nearly impossible without institutional support. I am more than grateful for JANM's unwavering belief in this project, and it has been a pleasure working with its staff, led by Ann Burroughs, JANM's president and chief executive officer. My heartfelt acknowledgments go to Doug Van Kirk, chief financial officer, and Kristen Hayashi, director of collections management and access and curator, for being such collaborative partners in realizing this curatorial vision. Thanks are also due to Clement Hanami, vice president of exhibitions and art director; Karen Ishizuka, chief curator; Kelli-Ann Nakayama, chief development officer; Nadiya Conner, philanthropy officer; and Sherrill Ingalls, director of marketing and communications; as well as Mia Russell, Tori Ishikawa, Dance Aoki, Coffee Kang, Maria Kwong, Jamie Henricks, and other staff who help keep the Museum running. And I must recognize Karin Higa (1966–2013), a longtime curator at JANM, who is credited with recovering and preserving numerous works by Japanese American artists of the earlier generations, and whose trailblazing work has been our guiding light throughout the process of putting together this exhibition.

The generous exhibition grant from the Terra Foundation for American Art is a much-appreciated boost of confidence and support that enables us to bring this exhibition to a broader audience and to produce a publication that will share the artists' work and stories for years to come. My gratitude extends to the museums that believed in *Pictures of Belonging* and agreed to participate in the national tour. To the directors and staff at the Utah Museum of Fine Arts, the Smithsonian American Art Museum, the Pennsylvania Academy of the Fine Arts, and the Monterey Museum of Art: thank you for going on this special journey with us.

In addition, the exhibition catalogue is made possible by the valuable research and scholarship of the essay contributors, and I am thankful to these friends and colleagues for joining me: Cécile Whiting, Patricia Wakida, Melissa Ho, Rihoko Ueno, and Becky

Alexander. I can say on all our behalves that we could not have written our essays if not for the herculean efforts of archivists, librarians, registrars, and assistants in preserving and cataloguing works of art and historical materials over many decades. Special acknowledgments go to Joyce Davis and Tom Callas, who volunteered to organize and document the immense Miné Okubo Collection in Riverside for many years, for so generously sharing with me their invaluable records; and to Hillary Jenks, former director of Riverside's Center for Social Justice & Civil Liberties, and Hal Fischer, guest curator of the inaugural Okubo retrospective, whose work serves as an inspiration. Many thanks to Jeff Gunderson, Marian Yoshiki-Kovinick, Dillon Kennedy, and Ben Morse for indulging my endless requests to examine artworks and documents for more than a decade; to all the museum staff who provided access and oversaw conservation: Diane Curry, Meredith Patute, Ruth LaNore, John Rexine, Jayne Manuel, and their colleagues; and to the many librarians/archivists who took the time to track down historical documents, including Tami Suzuki, Diana Godwin, Nancy Brown-Martinez, and Abby Smith.

The production of this exhibition catalogue would not have been possible without the editorial and design teams at Marquand Books and University of California Press, in particular Adrian Lucia, Kestrel Rundle, Tom Eykemans, Jayme Yen, Kristin Kearns, and Leah Finger at Marquand Books and Kim Robinson and Archna Patel (former editor) at UC Press. I received indispensable support from the administrative staff at the School of Social Sciences, Humanities and Arts at the University of California, Merced, my home institution, as well as research funding from the Isabel Coats Endowed Chair in the Arts, a position I have held since 2018. The endowment also enabled me to employ and mentor an undergraduate assistant, Memphis Despain, who performed essential tasks for *Pictures of Belonging* and this accompanying catalogue.

I am fortunate to have many friends and colleagues who have generously offered their intellectual and emotional support and guidance since the inception of this project. Among them are Bruce Robertson, Mary K. Coffey, Carrie Haslett, Virginia Mecklenburg, Luke Kelly, Anna O. Marley, Leah Lehmbeck, Amelia Goerlitz, Juliet Sperling, Margo Machida, Nadine Little, Kathy Wong, Yinshi Lerman-Tan, Dennis Carr, Charles C. Eldredge, Betty Kano, William Maynez, Mark D. Johnson, Matthew Simms, Kay Sekimachi, Kimi Kodani Hill, and Mia Kodani, to name only a few.

Finally, and as always, I am grateful to have a supportive partner and family members in the United States and Taiwan. I dedicate this exhibition to my mother, Lin-Dai Tsai (1944–2021), a painter/music teacher/choir conductor/dressmaker whose wistful reflection, before dementia ravaged her brilliant brain, on her unfulfilled artistic career as a wife/mother in a patriarchal society compelled me to share the work and stories of these trailblazing women.

ShiPu Wang
Exhibition Curator

ShiPu Wang

# Introduction: Pictures of Belonging

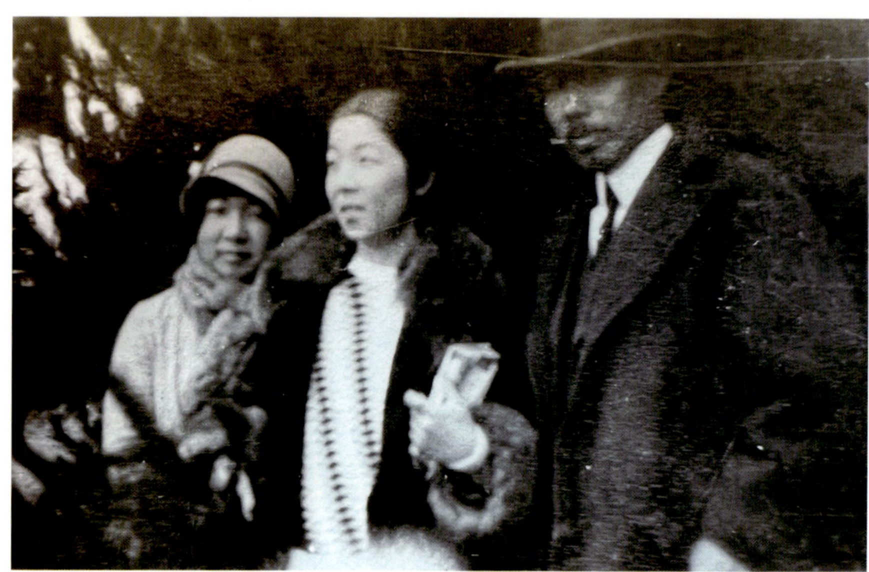

1.1

In 1929, Miki Hayakawa (1899–1953) seemingly burst onto the art scene with a solo exhibition of some 150 paintings at San Francisco's Golden Gate Institute (Kinmon Gakuen, or 金門学園). The word "genius" was used to describe her talent in a positive review by the *San Francisco Examiner*'s Gobind Behari Lal. Praising the artist's tremendous industry, keen observation, and "supple fingers," Lal asserted that Hayakawa "feels and conveys beauty through her brush in irrepressible flashes." Informing his readers that Hayakawa was a "very young woman" and an immigrant from northern Japan who studied at the California School of Fine Arts (CSFA, later renamed the San Francisco Art Institute, now the San Francisco Art Institute Legacy Foundation), Lal further proclaimed that the artist's work "represents the full blossom of the Occidental art of painting."[1]

Lal—himself an immigrant from Delhi, India; a science reporter who had written about arts and culture for the *Examiner* since 1925; and an eventual co-winner of the 1937 Pulitzer Prize for distinguished reporting—acknowledged Hayakawa's artistic acumen without attributing it to an essentialized assessment based on her race, nationality, or gender.[2] He instead offered that Hayakawa's sophisticated artwork "excellently answers the question, 'What are the younger women painters of California doing worth particular recognition?'" In Lal's view, Hayakawa's accomplishments proved San Francisco to be a place where people of divergent backgrounds could converge and flourish: "The prophets of a new renaissance have said so often that here, if any where, the East and the West will meet and pool their talents and begin new creative romances in cultural history." Hayakawa and her art in effect evidenced the arrival of that multicultural "renaissance."

Hayakawa was not exactly the kind of undiscovered ingénue that Lal presented her to be, however. An excavation of historical exhibition records shows that Hayakawa had in fact been exhibiting her

1.1
Hisako Shimizu (Hibi), Miki Hayakawa, and Matsusaburo George Hibi (left to right), 1927. Courtesy of the Hibi Estate.

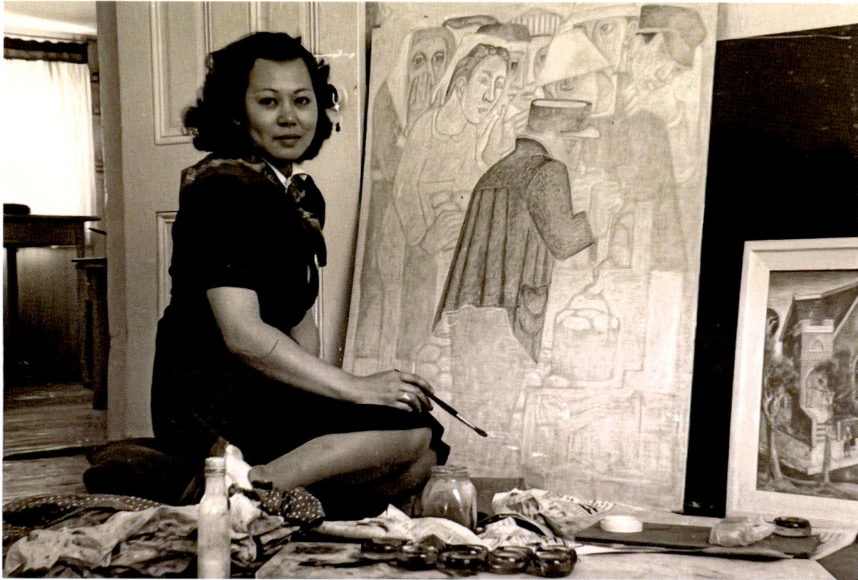

1.2

work, to critical acclaim, for years before 1929. Since commencing her formal art education, first at the California School of Arts and Crafts (now California College of the Arts) around 1920 and then at the CSFA in 1923, Hayakawa had won a series of honors, including becoming the first student in the CSFA's fifty-six-year history to have been awarded both the Virgil Williams and the Anne Bremer scholarships in the same year (1927). In addition to the 150 works in her solo show, Hayakawa had paintings in the annual exhibitions of the Oakland Art Gallery/Oakland Art League and the San Francisco Art Association (SFAA), as well as the first San Francisco Japanese Art Association exhibition, to which she submitted eight works, all in 1929.[3] She followed this banner year by becoming the only female artist of Japanese descent (there were twelve other artists of Asian descent, all men) in the opening exhibition of the San Francisco Museum of Art (now SFMOMA) in 1935. Among her four submitted paintings were *One Afternoon* (ca. 1935; Plate 12) and *From My Window* (1935; Plate 53)—the latter was exhibited in the Golden Gate International Exposition (GGIE) in 1939. As my archival research has revealed, between 1925 and 1953, when Hayakawa passed away at age fifty-three, she had participated *every year* in art exhibitions in prewar California, and in wartime/postwar Santa Fe, New Mexico.[4]

Hayakawa might appear to be an outlier in the early twentieth-century American art world, where the overwhelming majority who received most critical (and commercial) attention were male and white. She was, but not alone. Hayakawa, Hisako Hibi (1907–1991), and Miné Okubo (1912–2001) would become the three most visible and critically acclaimed female artists of Japanese descent of the pre–World War II generations in the San Francisco Bay Area and the entire United States.[5] All three pursued their art training in California: Hayakawa and Hibi at the CSFA in the 1920s and Okubo at the University of California, Berkeley, where she earned both a bachelor and a master of fine arts in the late 1930s (Figs. 1.1 and 1.2). All three artists consistently showed works and received honors in juried exhibitions by the SFAA, the Oakland Art Gallery, and other artist collectives throughout California; Okubo, for example, won prizes from the SFAA in 1941 and 1945. And all three shared the distinction of being the only female artists of Japanese descent to represent the United States in the GGIE in 1939–40.

When President Franklin D. Roosevelt issued Executive Order 9066 on February 19, 1942, in response to Japan's attack

1.2

Miné Okubo in her studio in Berkeley painting *Grocer Weighing Produce*, 1940. Japanese American National Museum, Los Angeles, 2007.62.557_3.

on Pearl Harbor, more than 120,000 first- and second-generation Japanese Americans (Issei and Nisei, respectively) were forced to abandon their homes on the West Coast. They had to either give up everything they had earned over decades to leave the so-called Western Defense Zone, or be moved into incarceration camps hastily established in several inland states. All three artists experienced displacement: Hayakawa had to abandon her Northern California residency of more than three decades and relocated to Santa Fe in 1942; Hibi and Okubo were incarcerated first at the Tanforan Assembly Center in San Bruno, California, and later at the Central Utah Relocation Center, also known as Topaz, between 1942 and 1944/45.

None of them ever stopped making art, however. Hayakawa regularly exhibited in Santa Fe between 1943 and 1953 (Fig. 1.3), and one of her later paintings (*Angie* [ca. 1948–51; Plate 46]) won the First Premium Prize at the Santa Fe State Fair in 1951.[6] Hibi became an active and respected member of the San Francisco art circles for nearly forty years following her return to California in 1954, after moving from Topaz to New York City in 1945; losing her husband, the artist Matsusaburo George Hibi (1886–1947), to cancer; and raising her two children alone. She was an early supporter of the San Francisco Women Artists Association (Fig. 1.4) and received a U.S. congressional tribute (courtesy of Rep. Robert T. Matsui), a commendation from the Arts Commission of San Francisco, and a declaration of June 14 as "Hisako Hibi Day" by then-mayor Dianne Feinstein, all in 1985, at age seventy-nine (Fig. 1.5). Okubo also moved to New York, but earlier, in 1944, for special assignments at the invitation of *Fortune* magazine's editors, and she stayed in the city for nearly six decades, until she passed away in 2001. She built a prolific career as an illustrator and fine artist, creating works numbering in the tens of thousands. Her graphic memoir *Citizen 13660*, a first-person account of the Japanese American incarceration experience, won the American Book Award in 1984, an honor that followed her invited testimony

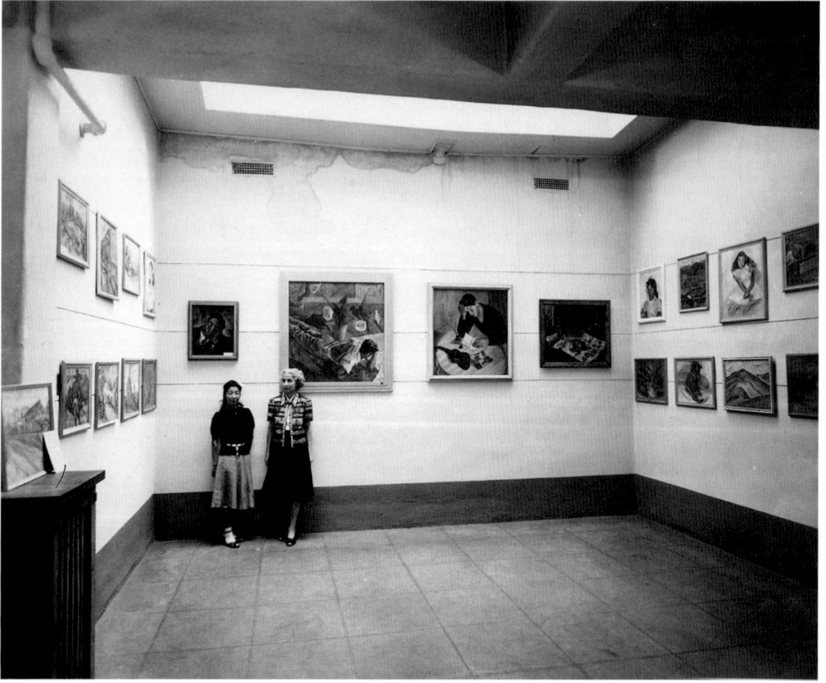

1.3

1.3

Miki Hayakawa (left) at her Alcove Show at the Museum of New Mexico, November 1944. On the wall behind Hayakawa, from left to right, are *Portrait of a Young Man* (Plate 11), *One Afternoon* (Plate 12), and *Music*. On the wall to the right, *Untitled (Female Nude)* (Plate 45) is the second painting from the left in the bottom row. Courtesy of Shirley and David Astilli, Santa Fe, New Mexico.

1.4

Moving out of the old San Francisco Women Artists Gallery at 451 Hayes Street, October 1, 1985. Lori Waterman (left) and Hisako Hibi (front). Photo by Lynda Robinson. Courtesy of the Hibi Estate.

1.5

Hisako Hibi flanked by Ruth Asawa (right) and Kimi Kodani (granddaughter of Chiura Obata) at Hibi's *Floating Clouds* exhibition and an award ceremony honoring Hibi, organized by the Northern Japanese American Historical Society, San Francisco, June 14, 1986. Courtesy of the Hibi Estate.

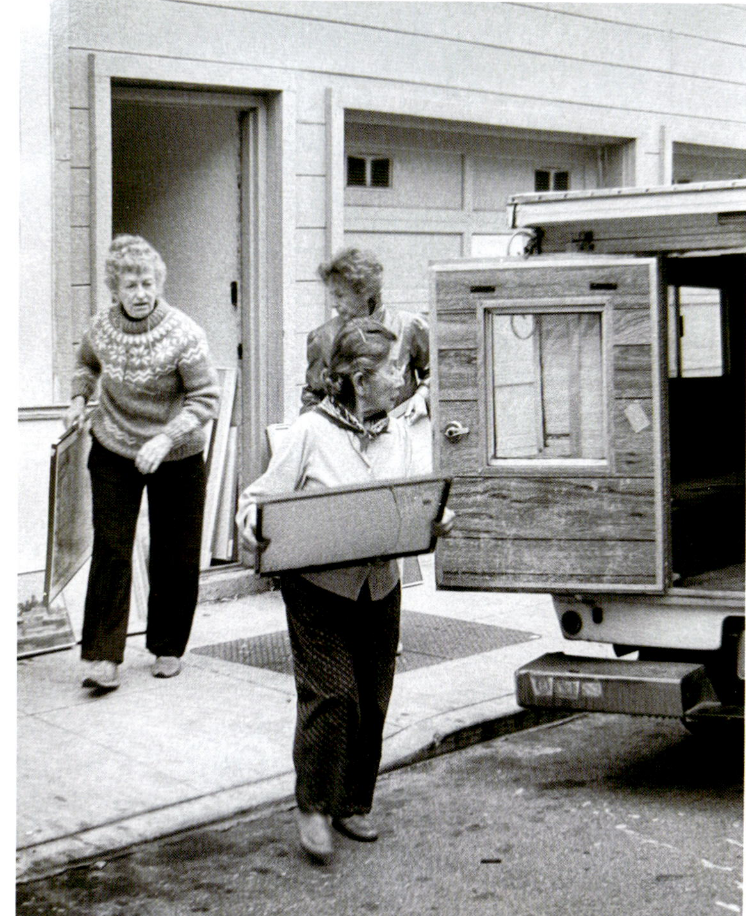

1.4

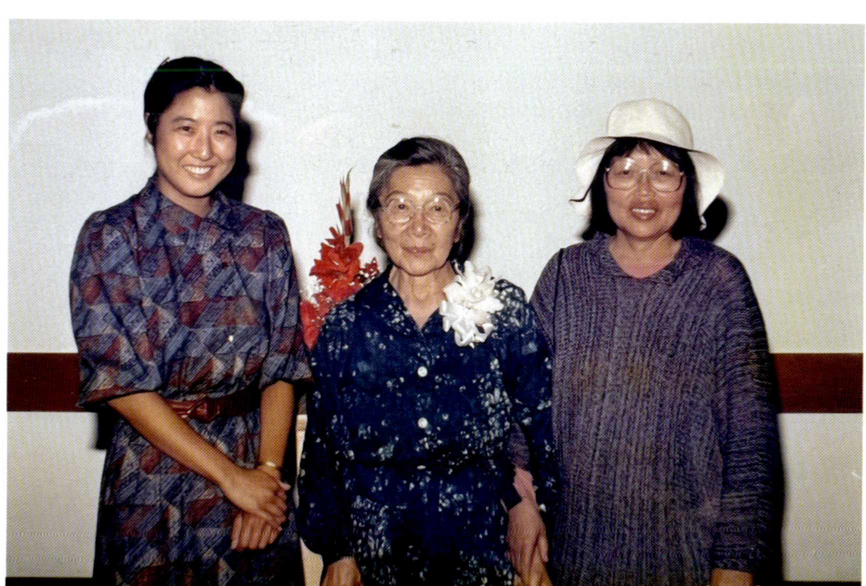

1.5

before the U.S. Congress's Commission on Wartime Relocation and Internment of Civilians in 1983, during which she urged the government to apologize to those who were unjustly imprisoned and displaced during World War II. The College Art Association's Women's Caucus for Art gave her a Lifetime Achievement Award in 1991 to recognize her vital role as both a lifelong artist and an advocate for righting historic wrongs (Fig. 1.6).

Today, the full extent of these trailblazers' oeuvres is largely unfamiliar to American art specialists and the general public alike, save for Okubo's better-known *Citizen 13660*. With such long and active careers, why have Hayakawa, Hibi, and Okubo remained peripheral, if not invisible, in accounts of twentieth-century American art? Why has these artists' original and varied work not garnered substantial attention in studies or exhibitions in the past decades? Few surveys of American art or modernism in California have included these artists in any substantive way. Even fewer museums in the United States or elsewhere have actively acquired their work—the Oakland Museum of California was gifted a number of Okubo artworks after the artist's death, and the Hibi estate donated dozens of her wartime paintings to the Japanese American National Museum, the organizing institution for Hibi's retrospective in 1999 and for *Pictures of Belonging*.[7] Might the lack of representation in museum collections have to do with a residual effect of the Exclusion Era (1885–1965), a period in U.S. history that saw promulgations of anti-immigration and anti-Asian laws that affected generations of Asian Americans? And what can the art and life stories of Hayakawa, Hibi, and Okubo tell us about diasporic Japanese Americans' effort and conviction in becoming full-fledged American artists, in affirming that they belonged?

*Pictures of Belonging* thus aims to (re)introduce the three artists by bringing representative works from each together in dialogue for the first time. The exhibition retraces and reimagines a more heterogenous and inclusive story of twentieth-century American art from the perspectives of these artists of Japanese descent. With nearly a hundred divergent artworks spanning eight decades, many of which have never been on public display, the exhibition showcases the range and depth of their artistic output in three loosely chronological sections: "Faces & Communities," "Belongings & (dis)Locations," and "Explorations & Rediscoveries." From portraiture and figurative works to landscapes, still lifes, and abstractions, the exhibition's groupings correspond to the artists' sustained engagement with and contributions to various artistic movements, such as realism, American Scene, muralism, Synchromism, and Abstract Expressionism, to name only a few. *Pictures of Belonging* invites the viewer to appreciate and learn about these artists' work, and to reflect on what (and who) defined American art in specific historical moments, while considering reasons for the omission of these artists from accounts of twentieth-century art in the United States.

The exhibition highlights the artists' now-forgotten personal connections, as well, making it a reunion of sorts. Hayakawa and Hibi, both Issei who immigrated to the United States as teenagers, were good friends in the 1920s. They appeared in the same exhibitions on several occasions in prewar California, as did Okubo, a Nisei born in Riverside, California. Both Okubo and Hibi taught classes at the Topaz Art School, established by fellow incarcerees Chiura Obata and Matsusaburo Hibi.[8] And both Okubo and Hisako Hibi moved to New York from Topaz; while they did not form a close friendship, they stayed in touch through the postwar decades (Fig. 1.7).

Furthermore, *Pictures of Belonging* is an intersectional presentation that

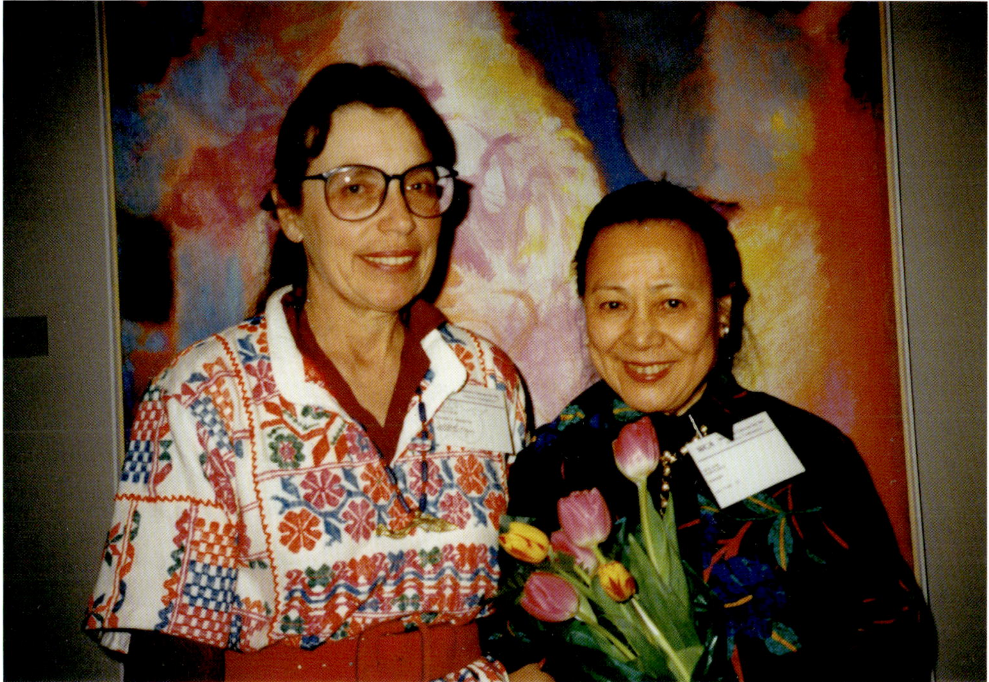

1.6

1.6
Miné Okubo with artist Betty LaDuke at the Women's Caucus for Art Lifetime Achievement Award exhibition, 1991. The Miné Okubo Collection, Center for Social Justice & Civil Liberties, Riverside Community College District, California, b88f20 88-1-6.

acknowledges these artists' multifaceted, at times precarious and conflicting identities: as immigrant/alien/American, Issei/Nisei, and women (daughter/wife/mother/grandmother), among others. The exhibition resists constructing a "master narrative" about (Asian) American art or "women artists," both contestable categories that carry their own historical and ideological baggage. It tells, instead, interrelating stories of three trailblazers who managed to become acclaimed artists despite, or perhaps motivated by, conventional expectations and restrictions for women of Japanese heritage at the time. The presentation highlights, for example, the artists' shared but diverse life paths: Hayakawa was married at least twice but did not have any offspring,[9] Hibi was a married/widowed mother of two and grandmother of five, and Okubo never married nor had children. Early Issei women emigrated as spouses or daughters or, as scholars have shown, "picture brides" for Issei bachelors. Many had to work as domestic servants, factory and farm workers, or even prostitutes.[10] Hayakawa and Hibi were thus outliers among Issei women in their pursuit of art as their vocation. But they also had to sustain their livelihood by taking on other jobs; Hayakawa, for example, worked as a caterer, and Hibi worked as a seamstress and live-in maid. Okubo largely earned an acceptable living as an illustrator in New York. See Cécile Whiting's and Patricia Wakida's essays in this book for more biographical information.

Acknowledging the Exclusion Era and the mass incarceration and displacement as the historical backdrop, *Pictures of Belonging* further broadens the existing, almost exclusive spotlight on Japanese Americans' wartime trauma toward illuminating what "American experience" looks like through these artists' work made before, during, and after the war. It explores the myriad ways in which art

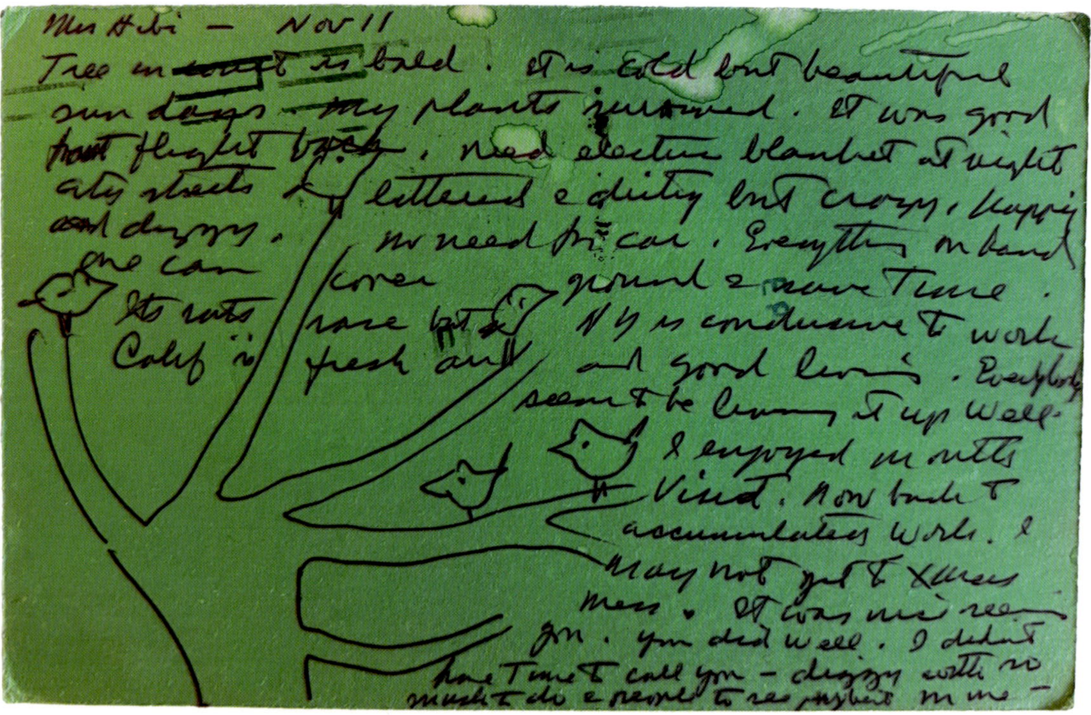
Mrs Hibi — Nov 11
Tree in [illegible] is bald. It is cold but beautiful
sun days — my plants survived. It was good
[illegible] flight back. Need electric blanket at night
city streets littered & dirty but crazy, happy
and dizzy. No need for car. Everything on hand
One can cover ground & save time.
Its rats race but NY is continuing to work
Calif is fresh and good living. Everybody
seems to be living it up well.
I enjoyed my little
visit. Now back to
accumulated work. I
may not get to Xmas
mess. It was nice seeing
you. You did well. I didn't
have time to call you — dizzy with so
much to do & people to see [illegible]

1.7

for these artists served as a vital means to capture lived experiences, navigate through good times and bad, and build relationships in diverse communities. Most crucially, it asks the viewer to consider how Hayakawa, Hibi, and Okubo leveraged art-making as a productive way to take control of the power of representation in an era when anti-Asian imagery had proliferated since the nineteenth century.[11] In other words, their artistic production enabled them to "take up space" (to use its positive connotation), to make their presence and existence visible, to assert that they belonged.

*Pictures of Belonging* is an incomplete project, to be sure, as much future work awaits. Through making previously unknown artworks available, the exhibition and this accompanying catalogue aim to direct more curatorial and scholarly attention toward these and, by extension, other artists who blazed the trail. This project will hopefully encourage curators, scholars, and art enthusiasts to rediscover the work of these artists, give them due attention, and incorporate them into relevant accounts of American art in the future.

Dr. ShiPu Wang is the Coats Endowed Chair in the Arts and professor of art history at the University of California, Merced. The winner of the 2018 Georgia O'Keeffe Museum Book Prize for *The Other American Moderns: Matsura, Ishigaki, Noda, Hayakawa* (Penn State University Press, 2017), he is a former editorial board member of the Smithsonian American Art Museum's *American Art* and now serves on the Smithsonian National Portrait Gallery's Board of Commissioners. He curated the internationally touring retrospective *Chiura Obata: An American Modern* and edited its exhibition catalogue (University of California Press, 2018).

1.7
Postcard from Miné Okubo to Hisako Hibi, November 11, 1976. Courtesy of the Hibi Estate.

NOTES

1 Gobind Behari Lal, "Japanese Girl's Paintings Challenge Attention. Work of Four Years Proves Her Genius," *San Francisco Examiner*, June 2, 1929, 10E.

2 Another review stated, for example: "Her paintings are sincere and direct recreations of reality as she sees it tinged with the sensitive poetry of her race." "Miki Hayakawa Art Work on Exhibition," *San Francisco Chronicle*, June 2, 1929, D-5:5.

3 By 1929 she had won first prize in a poster contest at the California School of Arts and Crafts (1920), First Award in the portrait painting class at the CSFA (1925), and third prize at the Berkeley League's annual exhibition (1926) for her *Japanese Tea House* (ca. 1925; Plate 48), among other awards. She was in the SFAA's Forty-Eighth through Fifty-First Annual Exhibitions (1925–29), in addition to appearing in the Oakland Art Annual (1926); the Los Angeles Museum of Art's *Painters and Sculptors of Southern California* (1927); the Oakland Art Gallery/Oakland Art League's annual exhibit (1929); and both Japanese Art Association shows in 1929 and 1930.

4 For a rediscovery of Hayakawa's career and life, see ShiPu Wang, "In Search of Miki: A California Cosmopolitan," in *The Other American Moderns: Matsura, Ishigaki, Noda, Hayakawa* (University Park: Penn State University Press, 2017), 97–126.

5 For Hibi's life and art, see her memoir, edited by her daughter, Ibuki Hibi Lee, *Peaceful Painter: Memoirs of an Issei Woman Artist* (Berkeley: Heyday Books, 2004). Shirley Sun's short book for Okubo's retrospective in 1972, *Miné Okubo: An American Experience* (Oakland, Calif.: Oakland Museum, 1972), contains some coverage of Okubo's oeuvre beyond her wartime graphics. And historian Greg Robinson published two volumes, co-edited with Elena Tajima Creef, that continue to be valuable sources for learning about Okubo's life: *Miné Okubo: Following Her Own Road* (Seattle: University of Washington Press, 2008); and "A Tribute to Miné Okubo," special issue, *Amerasia Journal* 30, no. 2 (2004).

6 This is likely *Little Angie*, a painting that Hayakawa first submitted to the *Thirty-Fifth Annual Fiesta Exhibition*, held at the Museum of New Mexico Art Gallery in 1948.

7 *A Process of Reflection: Paintings by Hisako Hibi* was on view at the museum from July 27, 1999, through January 30, 2000. The most recent effort to acquire Hibi's art came from the Smithsonian American Art Museum in 2022; two of its new acquisitions are in *Pictures of Belonging*, which served as a catalyst for the museum to approach the Hibi estate about representing both Hibis' art in its collection.

8 See the exhibition catalogue *Chiura Obata: An American Modern* (Berkeley: University of California Press, 2017) for more information about the art school and the East West Art Society, which Obata and Matsusaburo Hibi co-founded in 1921.

9 I was able to locate a San Francisco marriage certificate between Hayakawa (age eighteen) and Kiyoshi Okuye (twenty-three) in 1917, but the marriage was dissolved in 1919, with Hayakawa seeking a divorce due to Okuye's alleged "cruelty" and Okuye also filing for divorce on the ground of "desertion," according to announcements in the *Merced Sun-Star*, November 1, 1917, and January 16, 1919, respectively. Hayakawa married Preston Elmer McCrossen in 1947, according to the records in the Santa Fe County Clerk's Office. Thanks to Laura Hernandez, the office's records manager, for locating the marriage certificate in June 2022.

10 For the history and surveys of Issei women, see Yuji Ichioka, "Amerika Nadeshiko: Japanese Immigrant Women in the United States, 1900–1924," *Pacific Historical Review* 49, no. 2 (1980): 339–57; Yuji Ichioka, *The Issei: The World of the First Generation Japanese Immigrants, 1885–1924* (New York: Free Press, 1988); Evelyn Nakano Glenn, *Issei, Nisei, War Bride: Three Generations of Japanese American Women in Domestic Service* (Philadelphia: Temple University Press, 1986); and Eileen Sunada Sarasohn, *Issei Women: Echoes from Another Frontier* (Palo Alto, Calif.: Pacific Books, 1998), among others.

11 See, in particular, John Kuo Wei Tchen and Dylan Yeats, *Yellow Peril! An Archive of Anti-Asian Fear* (London: Verso, 2014).

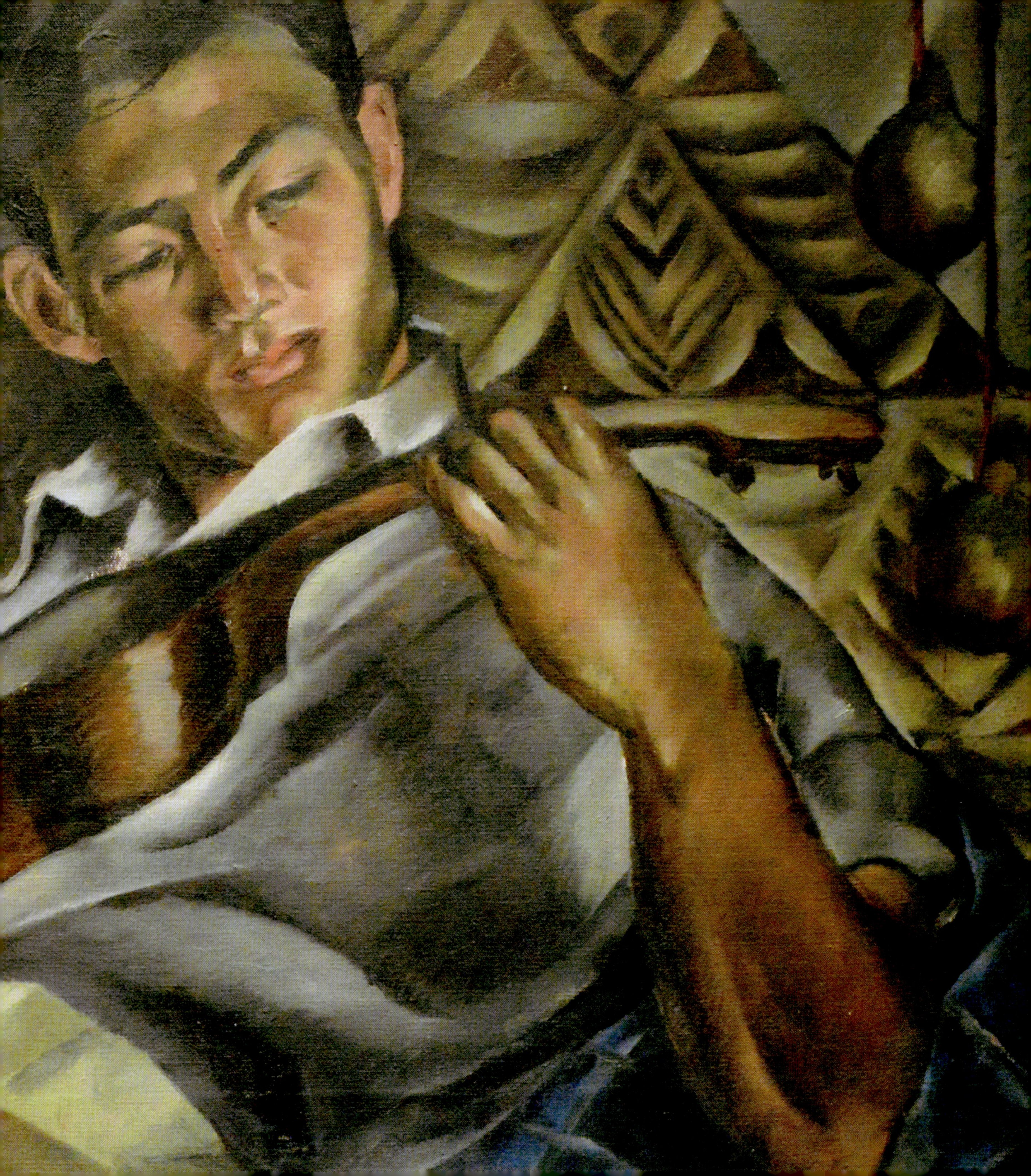

# I

# Faces & Communities

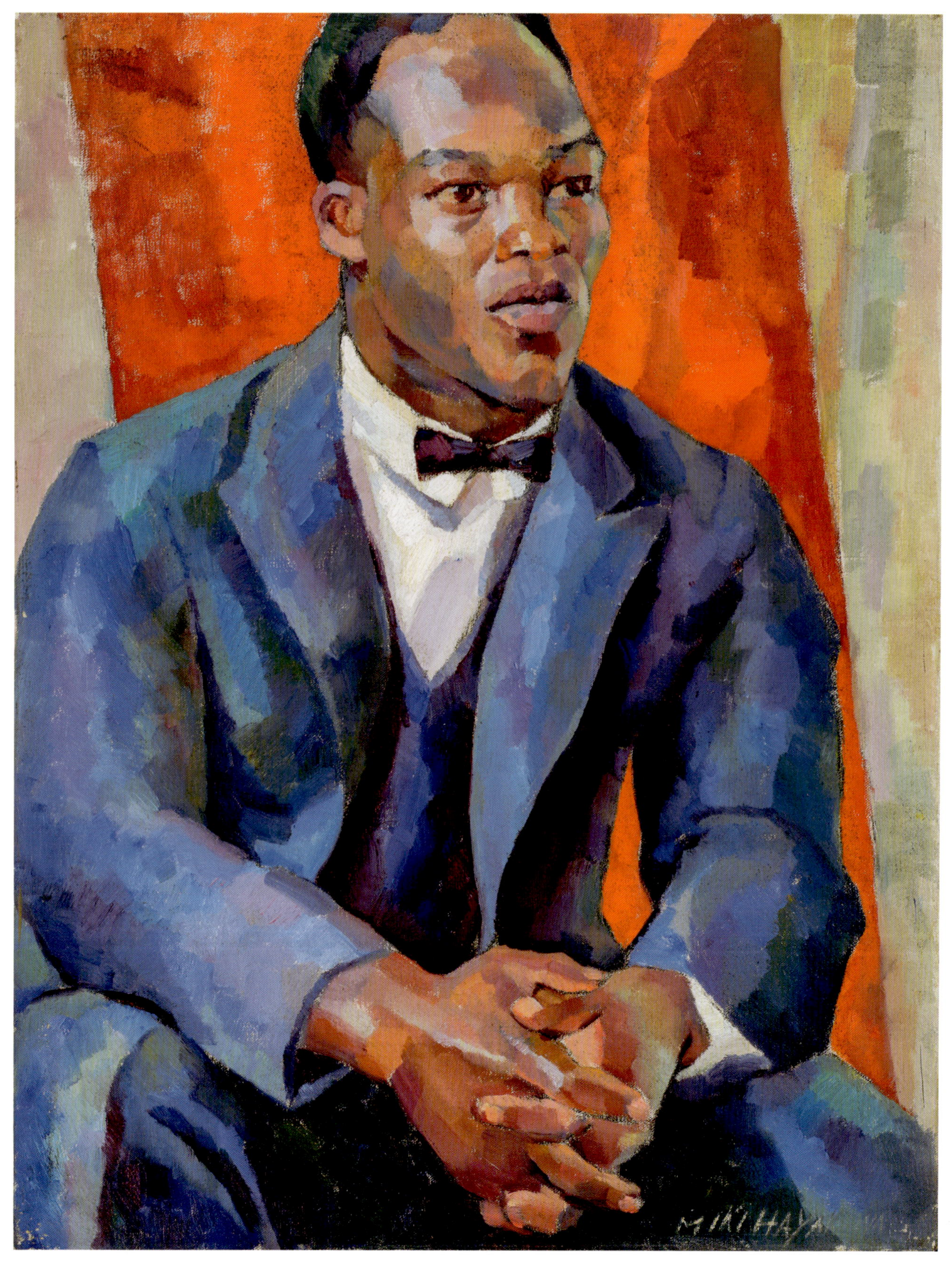

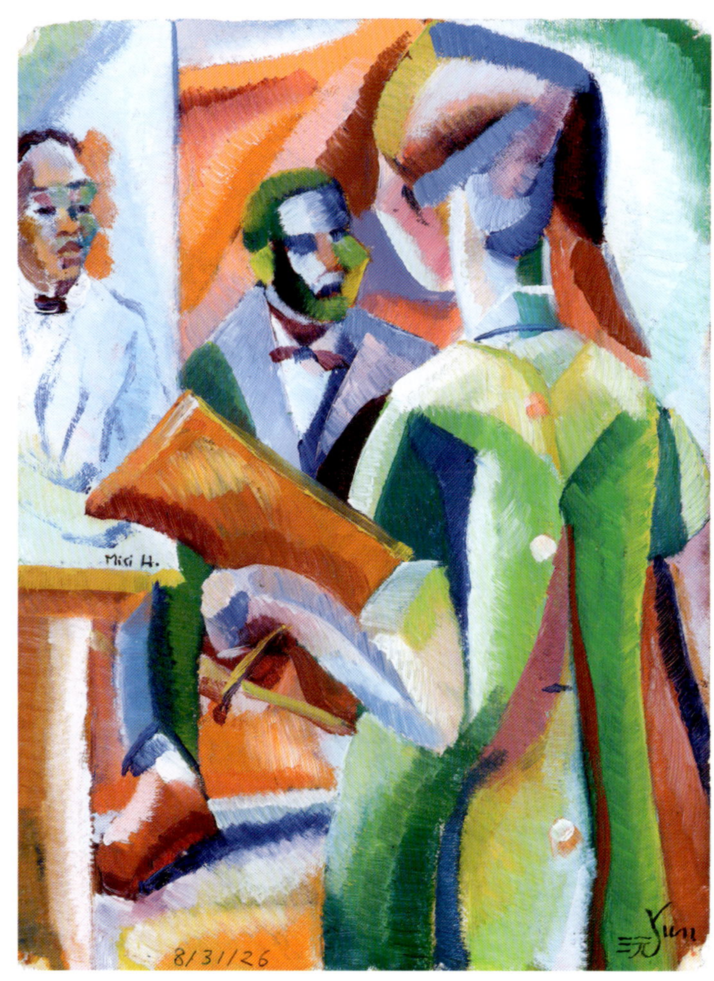


1
Miki Hayakawa
*Portrait of a Negro*
1926

Oil on canvas, 26 × 20 in. (66.04 × 50.8 cm); frame, 36 × 29½ × 4 in. (91.44 × 74.93 × 10.16 cm). Los Angeles County Museum of Art, Purchased with funds provided by Mrs. James D. Macneil, M.2004.27.2. Photo © Museum Associates/LACMA

2
Yun Gee
*Artist Studio*
1926

Oil on paperboard, 12 × 9 in. (30.48 × 22.86 cm); frame, 19¼ × 16 × 2¼ in. (48.9 × 40.64 × 5.72 cm). Los Angeles County Museum of Art, Purchased with funds provided by Mr. and Mrs. Robert B. Honeyman, Jr., and Mrs. James D. Macneil, M.2004.27.1. Photo © Museum Associates/LACMA

Gee likely depicts Hayakawa, a fellow California School of Fine Arts student, creating *Portrait of a Negro* in a shared studio or classroom, as both artists attended a few of the same classes at the CSFA in early 1926. The late Michael D. Brown, a dedicated collector of Asian American artists' work, was responsible for finding and pairing these paintings, which were both acquired by the Los Angeles County Museum of Art in 2004.

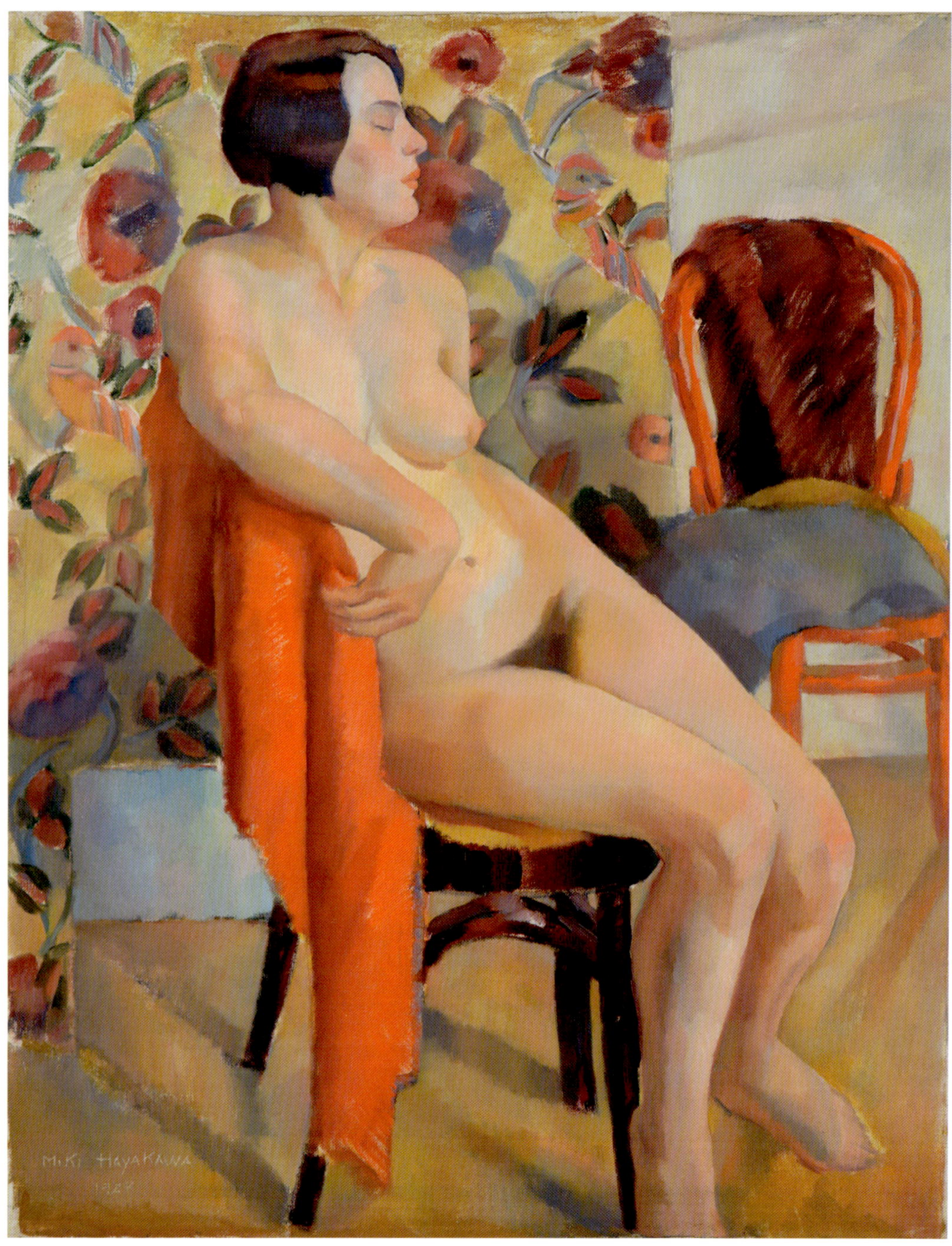

3
Miki Hayakawa
*Untitled (Seated Female Nude)*
1928

Oil on canvas, 36 × 28½ in. New Mexico Museum of Art, Santa Fe, Gift of Bessie A. Hurt, 1986, 1986.103.1

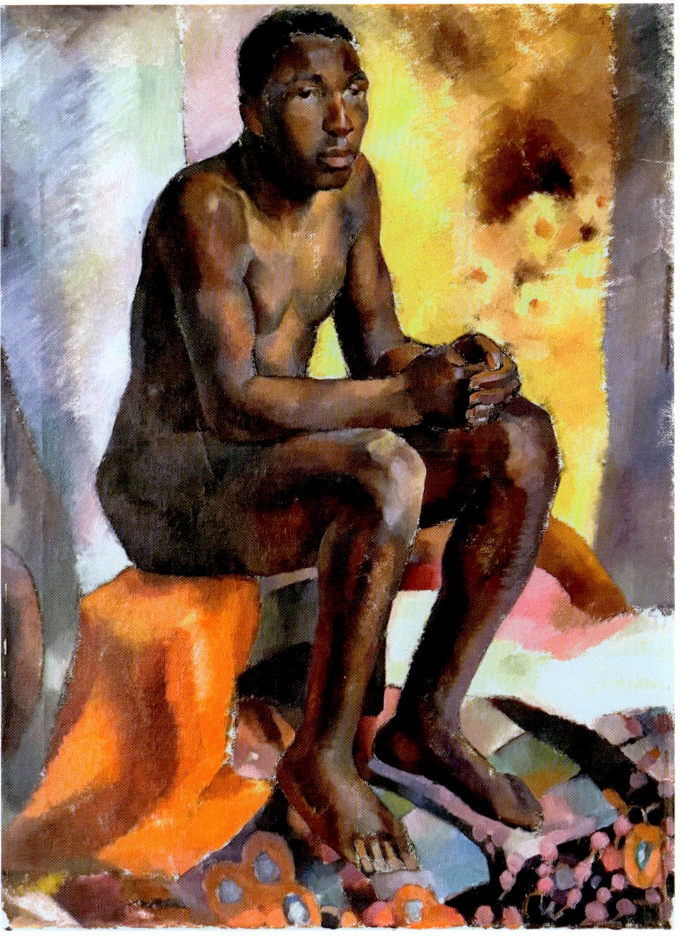

4

Miki Hayakawa

*Untitled (Male Nude)*

ca. 1928

Oil on canvas, 36 × 27 in. Collection of the De Grazzio Family

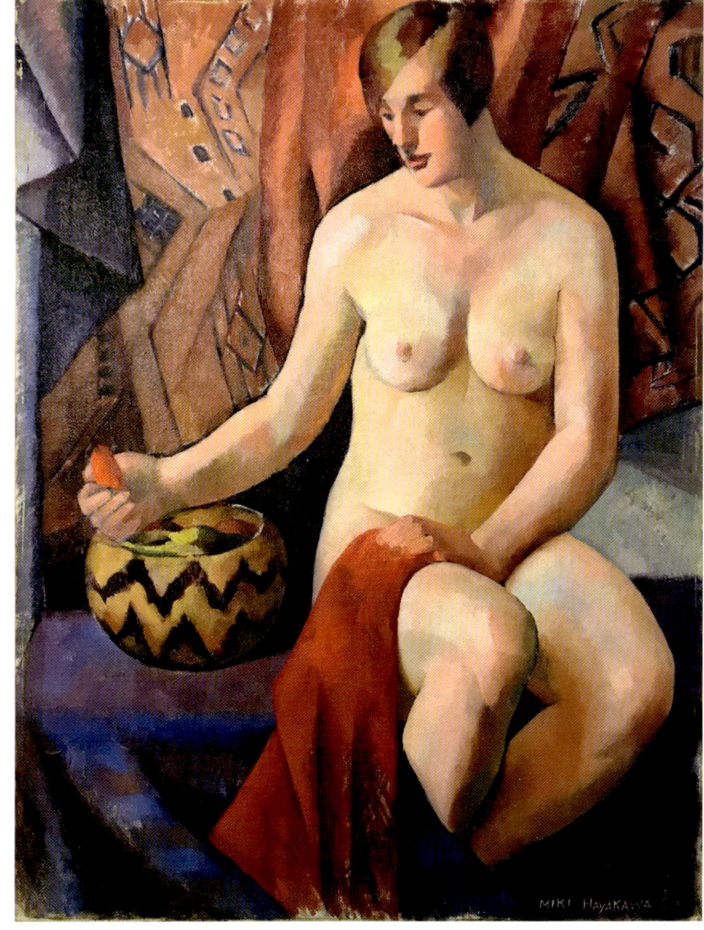


5

Miki Hayakawa

*Untitled (Seated Female Nude with Pottery)*

ca. 1927

Oil on canvas, 36 × 27 in. Collection of the De Grazzio Family

A reproduction of Hayakawa's seated female nude with pottery appeared in the California School of Fine Arts 1927–28 catalogue. See Fig. 2.2 in this volume.

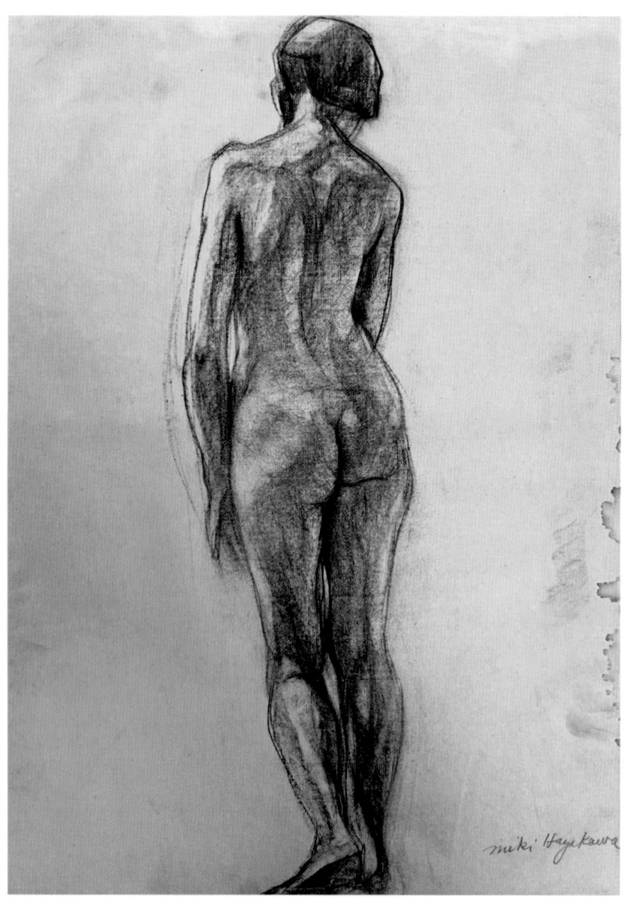

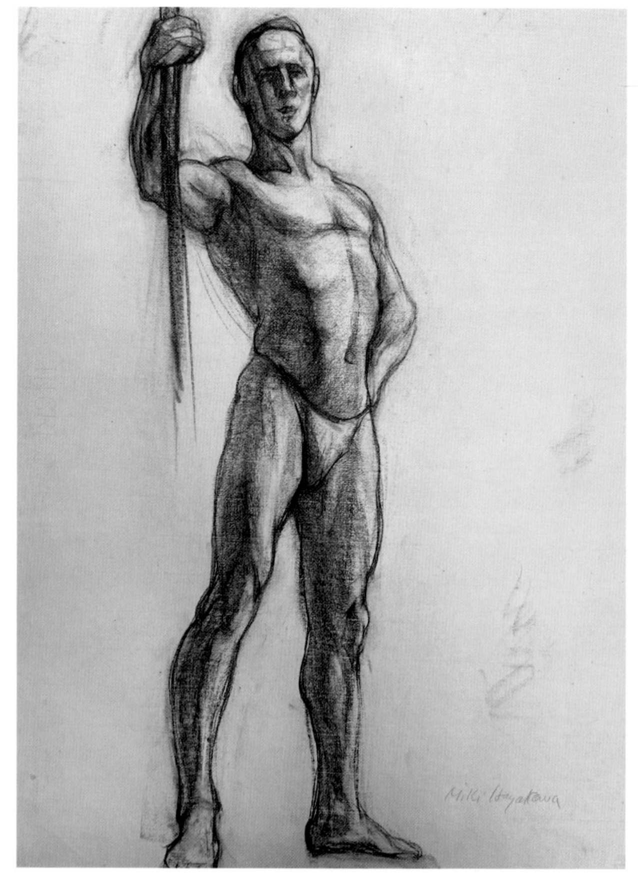

6
Miki Hayakawa
*Nude Study*
ca. 1930s

Charcoal on newsprint, 24 × 17½ in. Collection of Richard Sakai. Photo by ShiPu Wang

These nudes represent only a fraction of Hayakawa's output; based on her enrollment records at the CSFA, she showed a special interest in portraiture and figurative drawing and painting techniques as a student. Her teachers included Constance Macky and Eric Spencer Macky, Gertrude Partington Albright, and Lee Randolph, all of whom gave Hayakawa high marks for her work in their classes.

7
Miki Hayakawa
*Nude Study*
ca. 1930s

Charcoal on newsprint, 24 × 18 in. Collection of Richard Sakai. Photo by ShiPu Wang

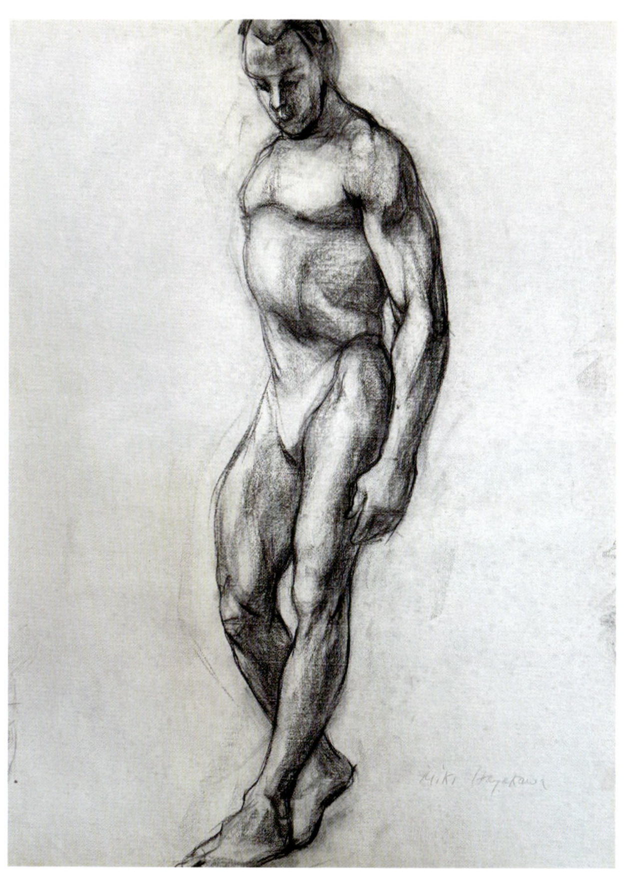



8
Miki Hayakawa
*Nude Study*
ca. 1930s

Charcoal on newsprint, 24 × 18 in. Collection of Richard Sakai. Photo by ShiPu Wang

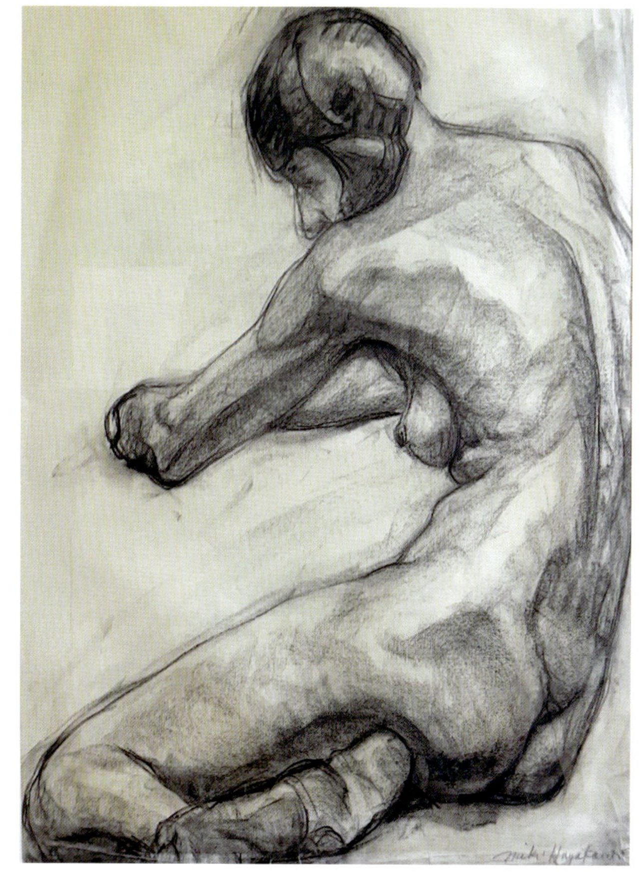



9
Miki Hayakawa
*Untitled (Seated Female Figure Study)*
ca. 1924–25

Charcoal on paper, 23½ × 18 in. Collection of Richard Sakai. Photo by ShiPu Wang

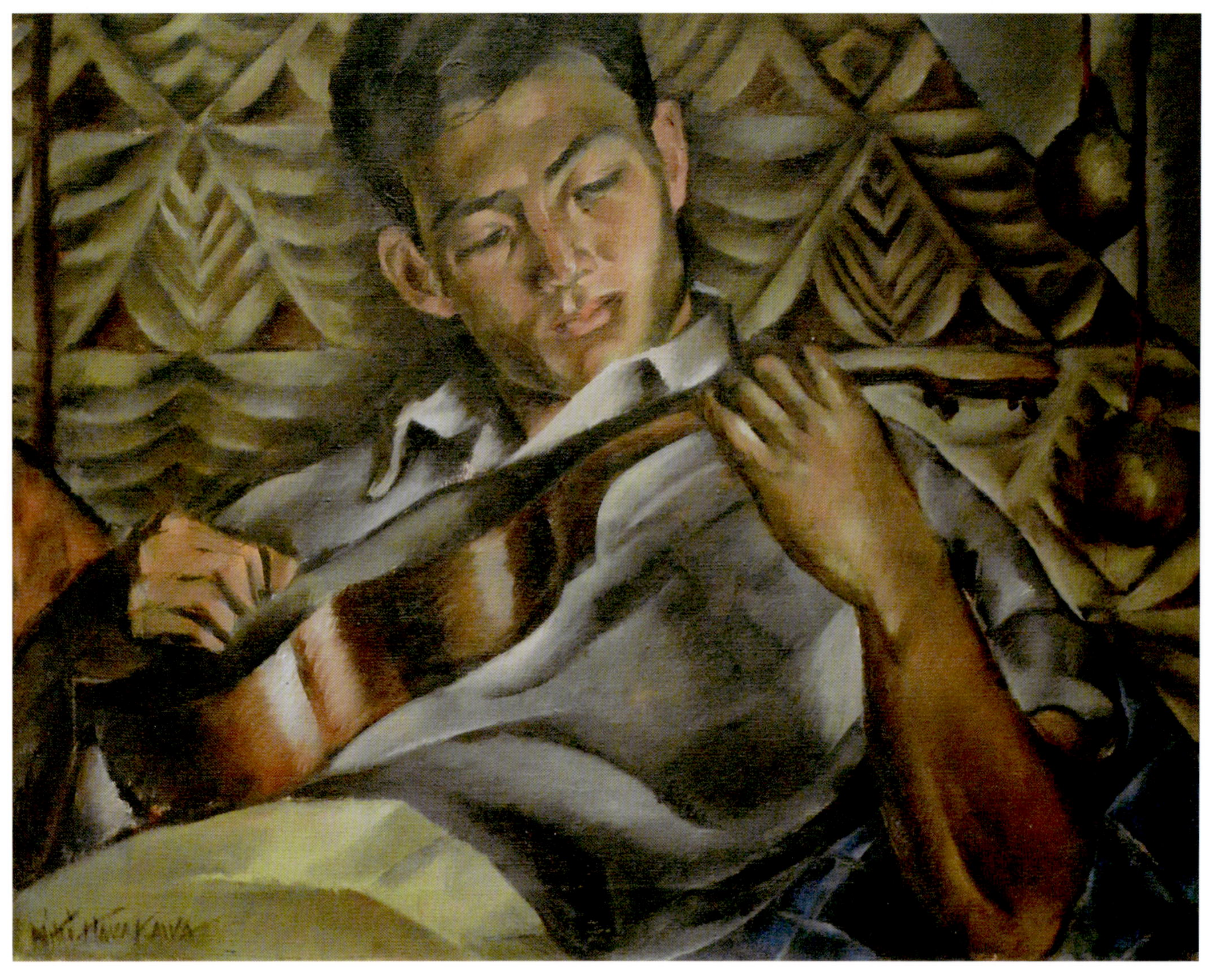

10
Miki Hayakawa
*Untitled (Young Man Playing Ukulele)*
ca. 1934–36

Oil on canvas, 20 × 26 in. (50.8 × 66.04 cm). Monterey Museum of Art, California, Gift of Mateo Lettunich, 2004.062

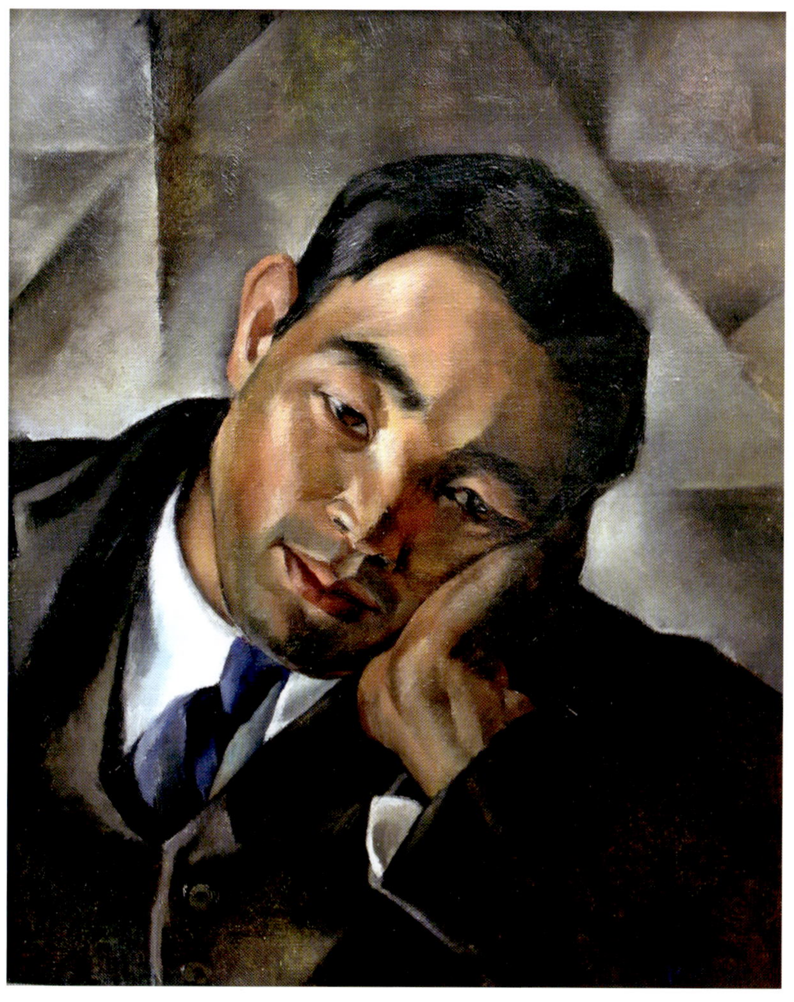

11
Miki Hayakawa
*Portrait of a Young Man*
ca. 1930s

Oil on canvas, 18½ × 15½ in.
Collection of Richard Sakai. Photo
by ShiPu Wang

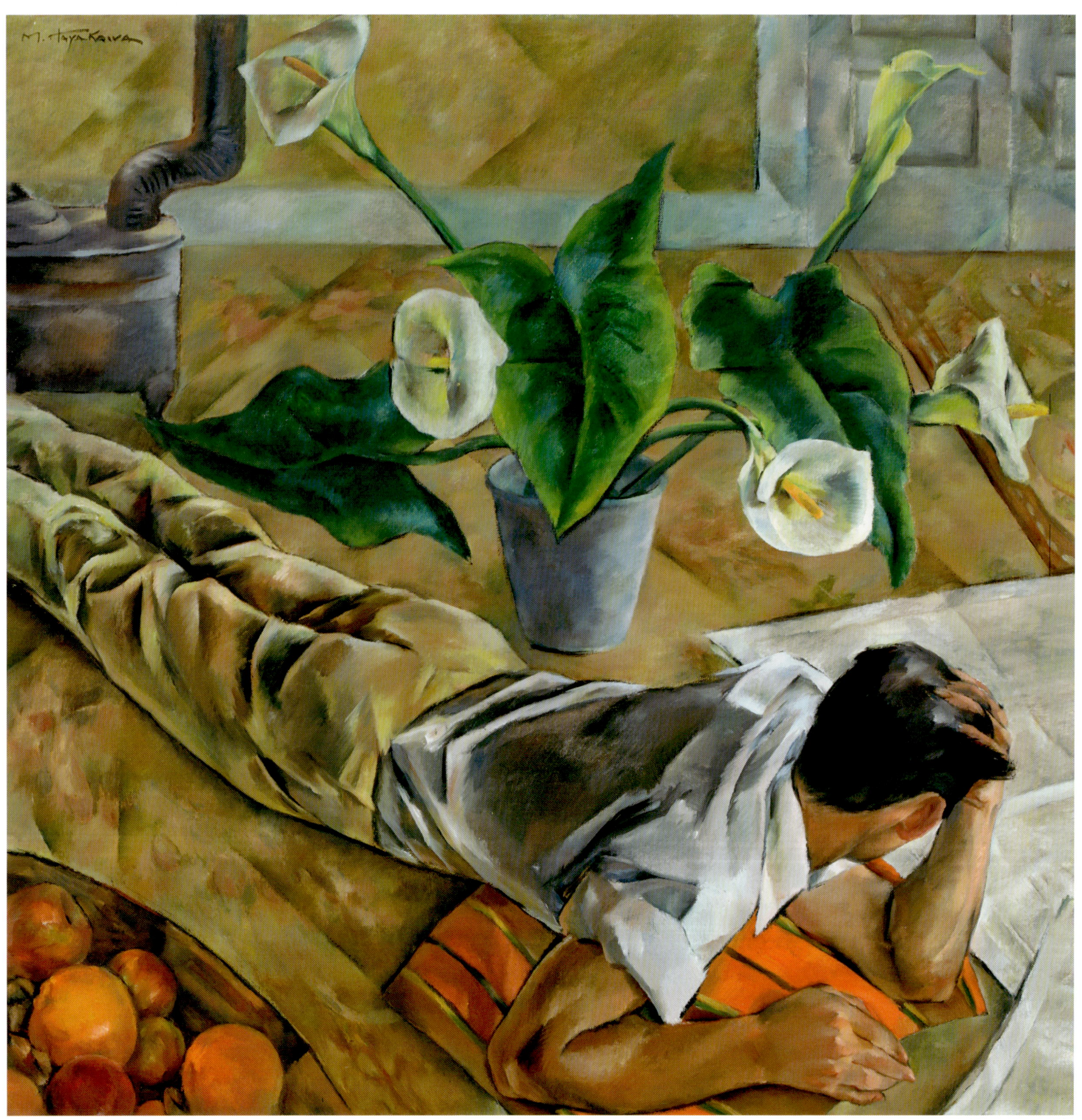
M. Hayakawa

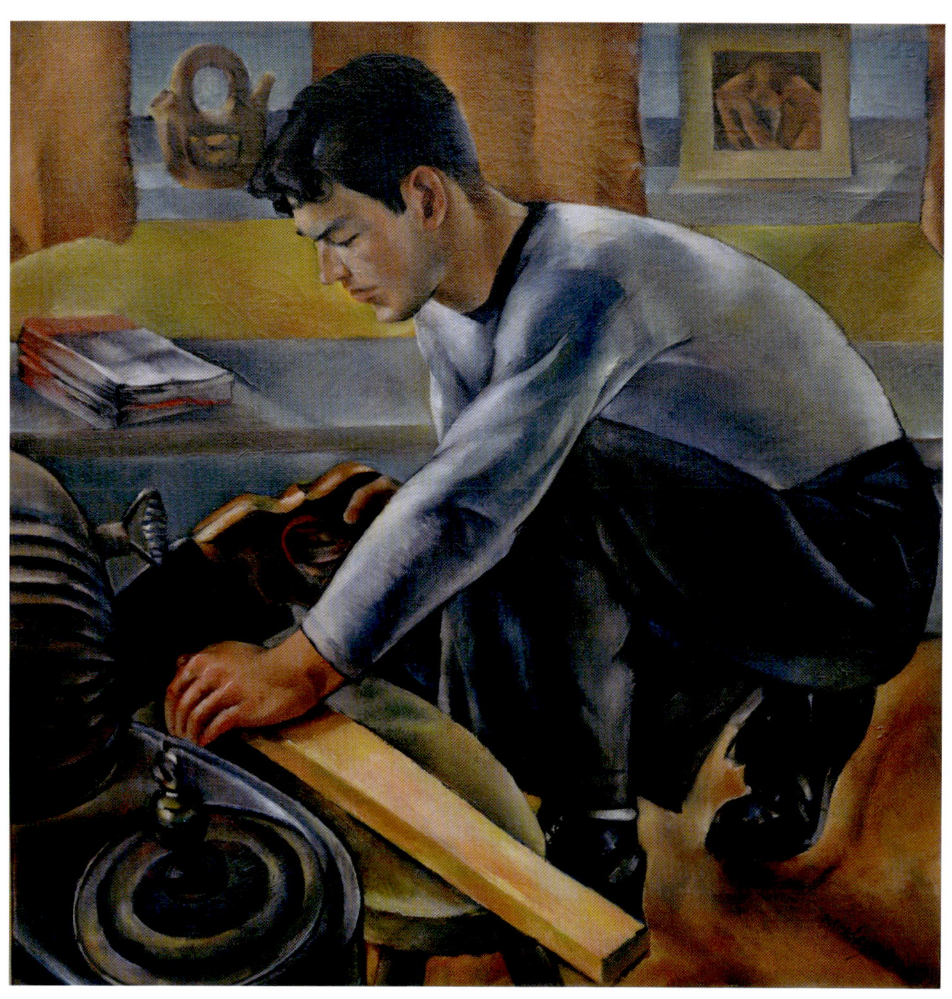

12
Miki Hayakawa
*One Afternoon*
ca. 1935

Oil on canvas, 40 × 40 in. New Mexico Museum of Art, Santa Fe, Gift of Preston McCrossen in memory of his wife, the artist, 1954, 520.23P. Photo by Blair Clark

One of Hayakawa's most treasured and displayed works, this painting appeared in a few landmark exhibitions, such as the opening exhibition of the San Francisco Museum of Art (now SFMOMA) in 1935. Hayakawa kept the canvas with her when she moved to Santa Fe, New Mexico, at the onset of the forced relocation and incarceration of Japanese Americans in early 1942. She continued to showcase this painting in several local exhibits, including her solo show at the Museum of New Mexico (now the New Mexico Museum of Art) in 1944. Preston Elmer McCrossen, Hayakawa's husband since 1947, gave the work to the museum after she passed away at the age of fifty-three in 1953.

13
Miki Hayakawa
*Worker (Boy Sawing)*
ca. 1936

Oil on canvas, 26 × 26 in. Collection of Richard Sakai. Photo by ShiPu Wang

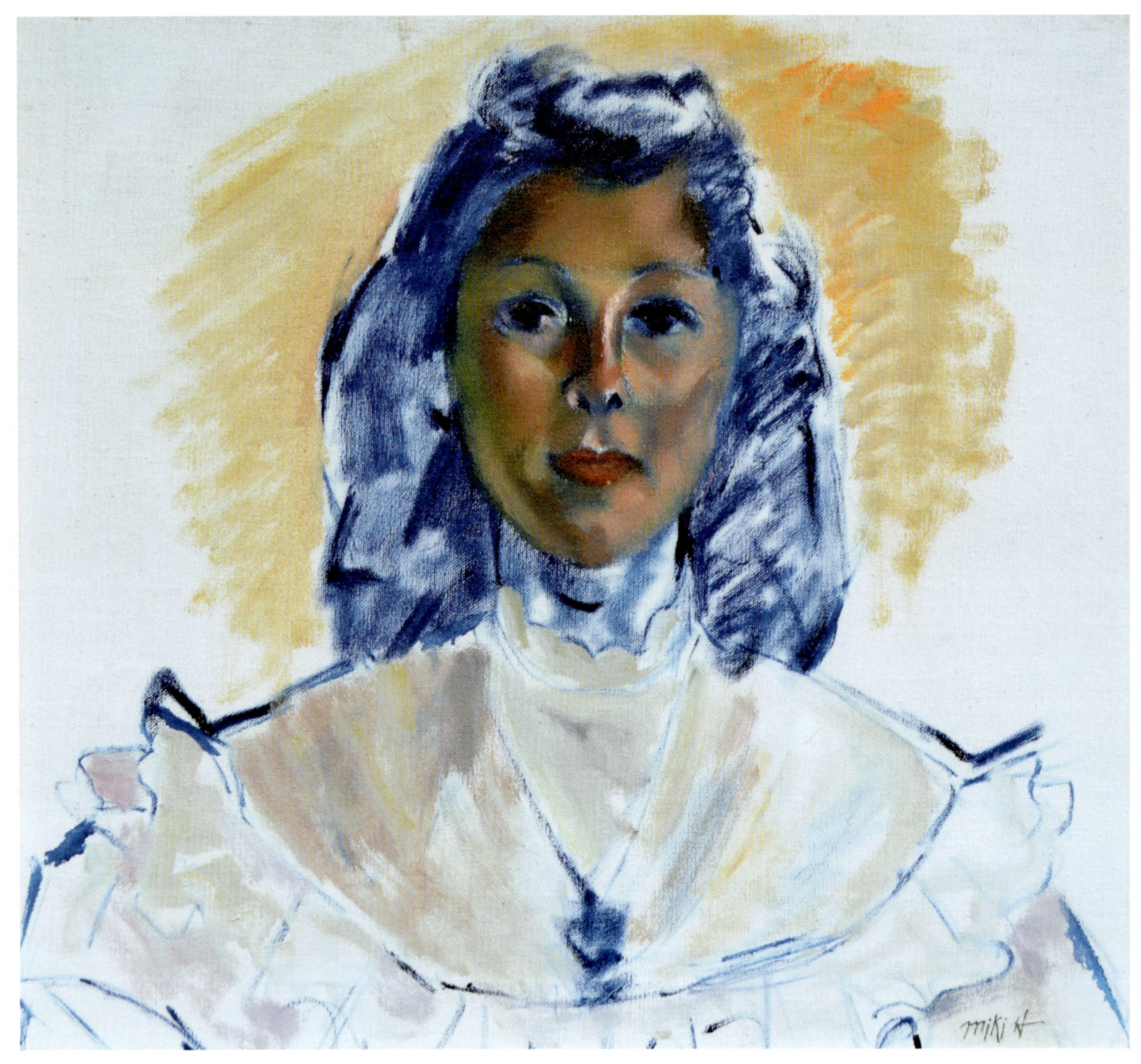

**14**
Miki Hayakawa
*Untitled (Woman with Blue Hair)*
ca. 1930s

Oil on canvas, 18 × 19¾ in.
Collection of Richard Sakai. Photo by ShiPu Wang

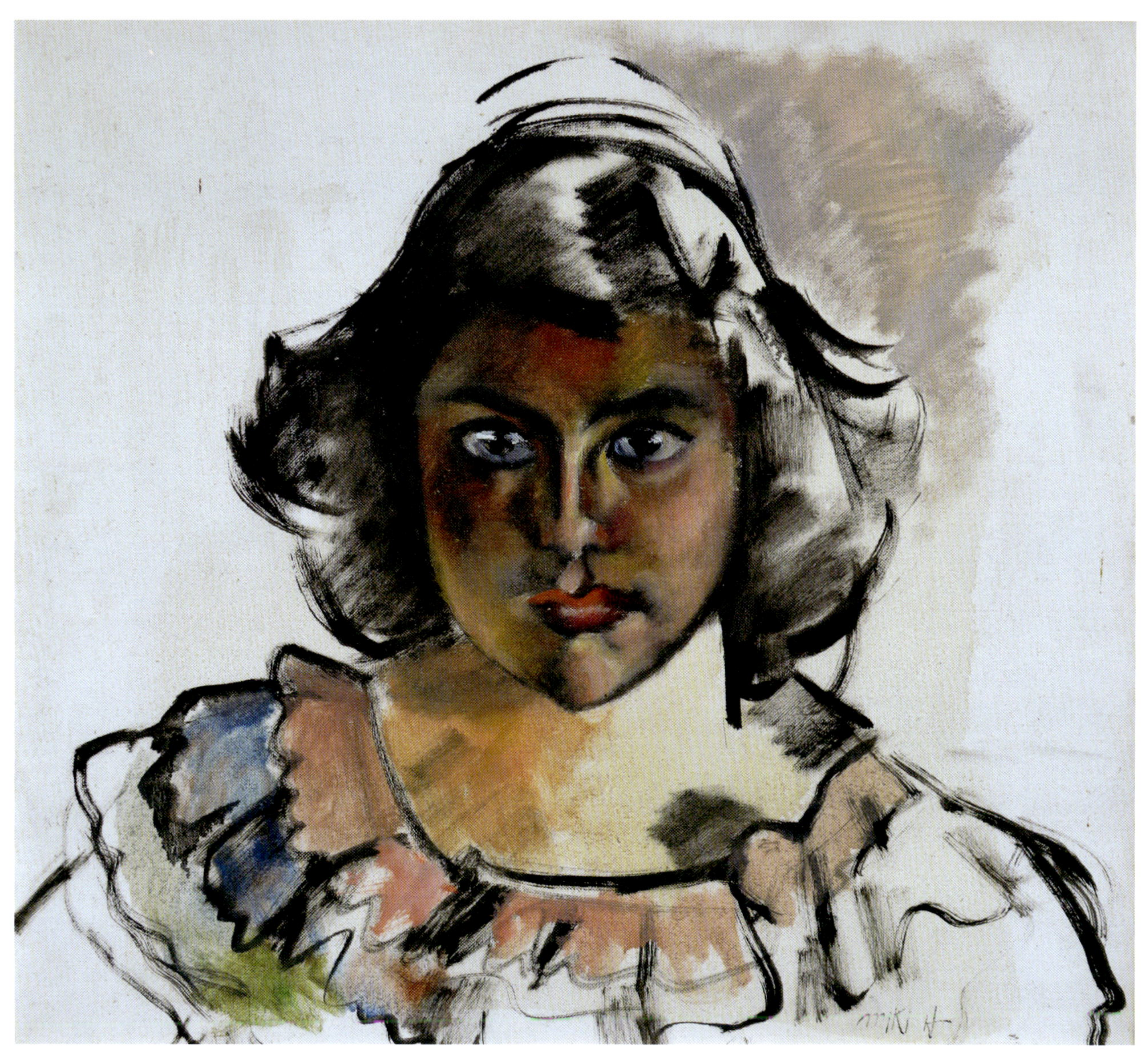

15
Miki Hayakawa
*Portrait (Petulant Girl)*
ca. 1930s

Oil on canvas, 17½ × 20 in.
Collection of Richard Sakai. Photo by ShiPu Wang

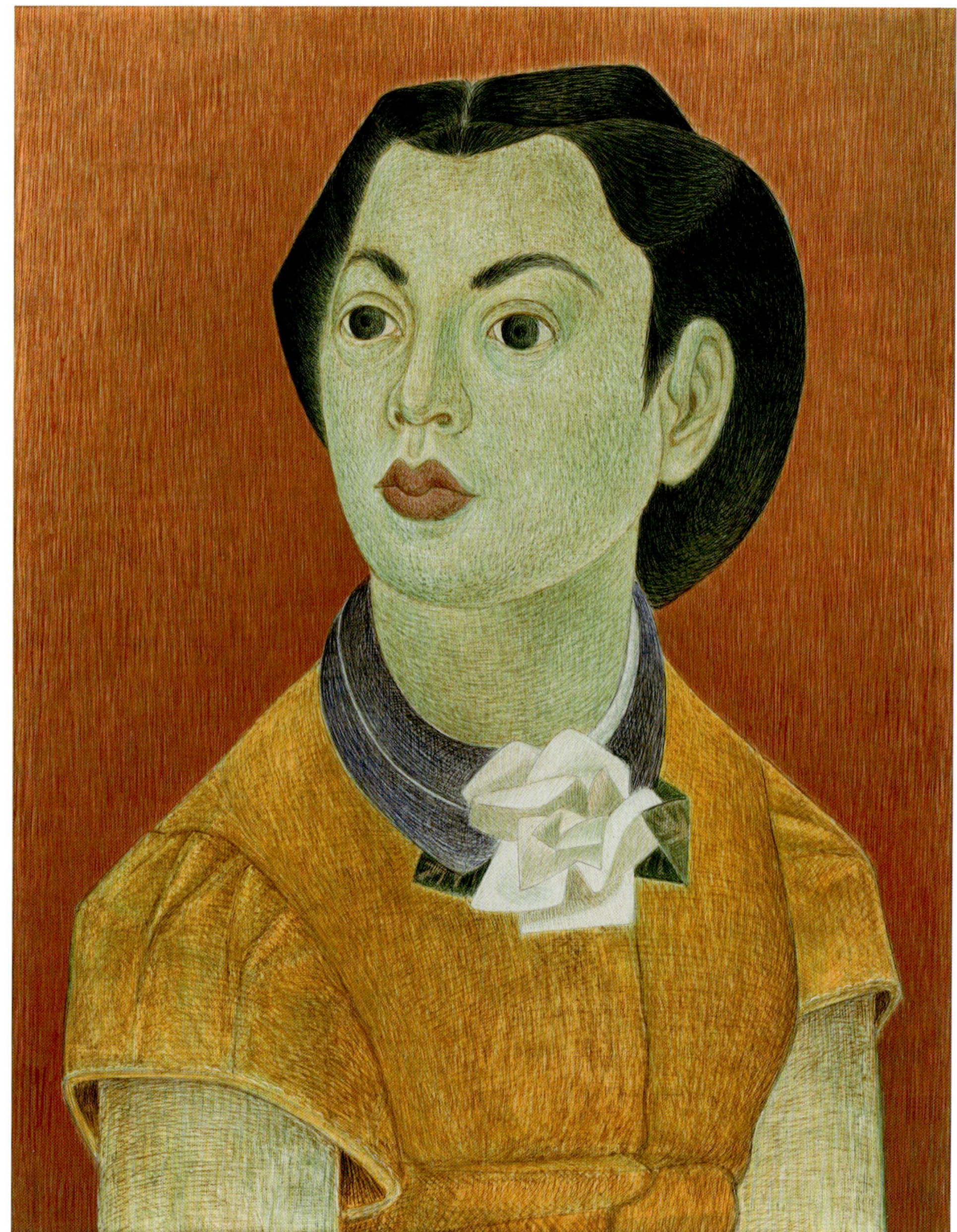

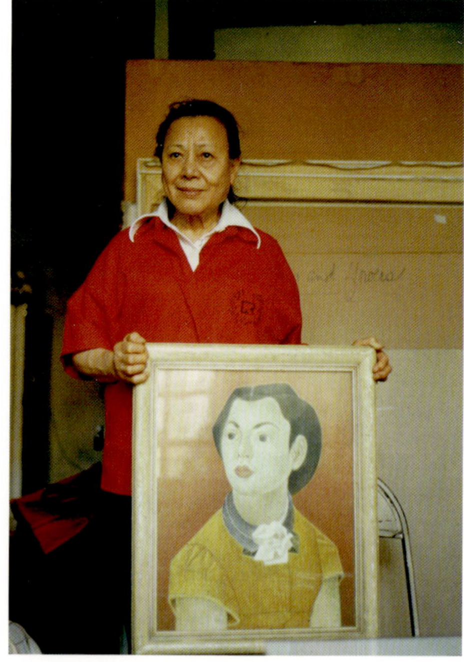

16
Miné Okubo
*Portrait Study*
ca. 1937

Tempera on hardboard, 20 × 16 in. (50.8 × 40.6 cm). Smithsonian American Art Museum, Museum purchase. © The Miné Okubo Charitable Corporation. Photo by Lucia RM Martino. Courtesy of the Smithsonian American Art Museum

17
Miné Okubo photographed with *Portrait Study* in her Greenwich Village apartment in New York City
ca. 1980s

The Miné Okubo Collection, Center for Social Justice & Civil Liberties, Riverside Community College District, California, b89f6 89-6-27

Okubo kept some of her prewar paintings with her in a small rent-controlled apartment, where she remained for the rest of her life after leaving Topaz (Central Utah Relocation Center) in 1944 to relocate to New York City.

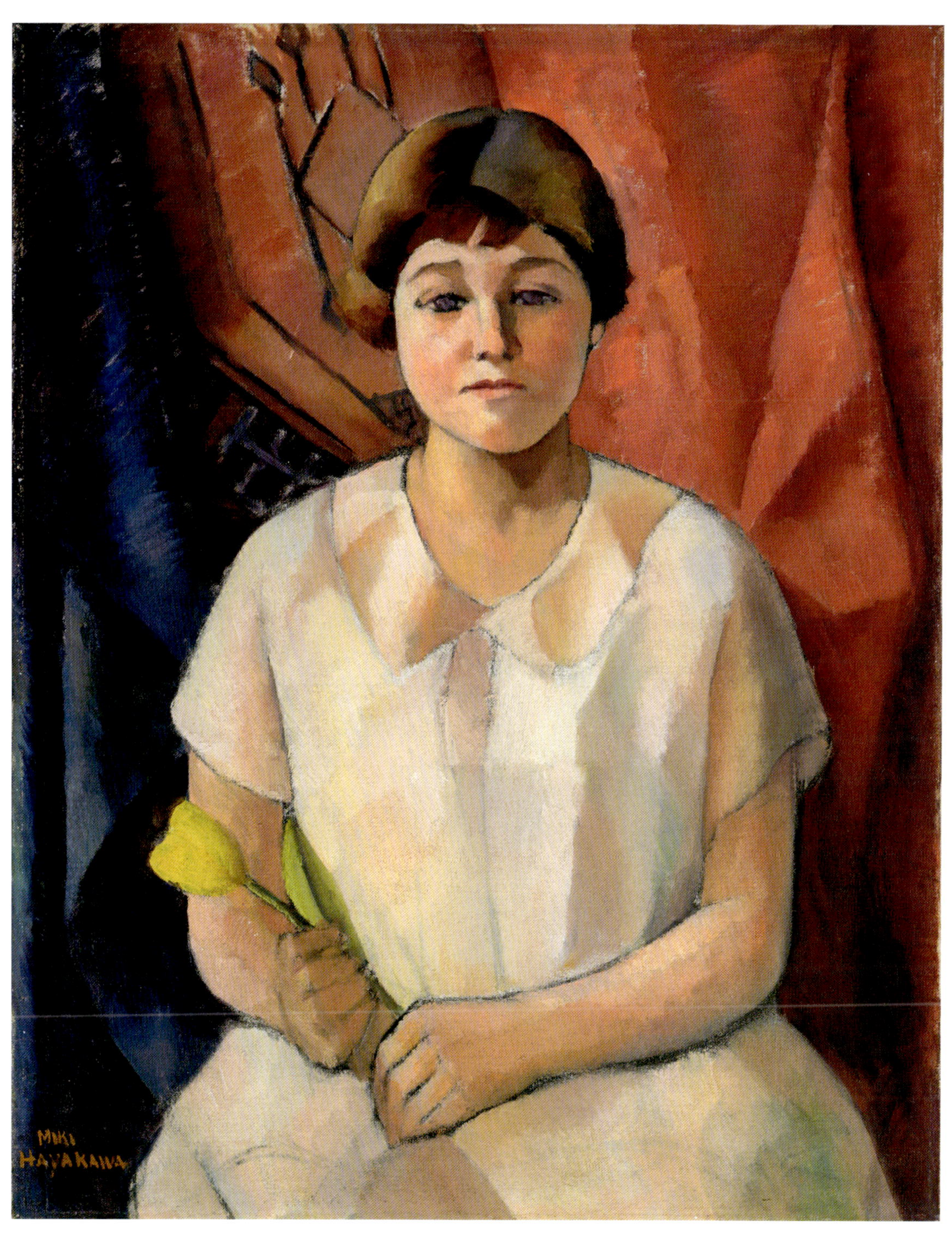


18
Miki Hayakawa
*Portrait (The Yellow Tulip)*
ca. 1940

Oil on linen, 29 × 23½ in.
Collection of Elizabeth L. Divekar
and Stephanie S. Lawrence

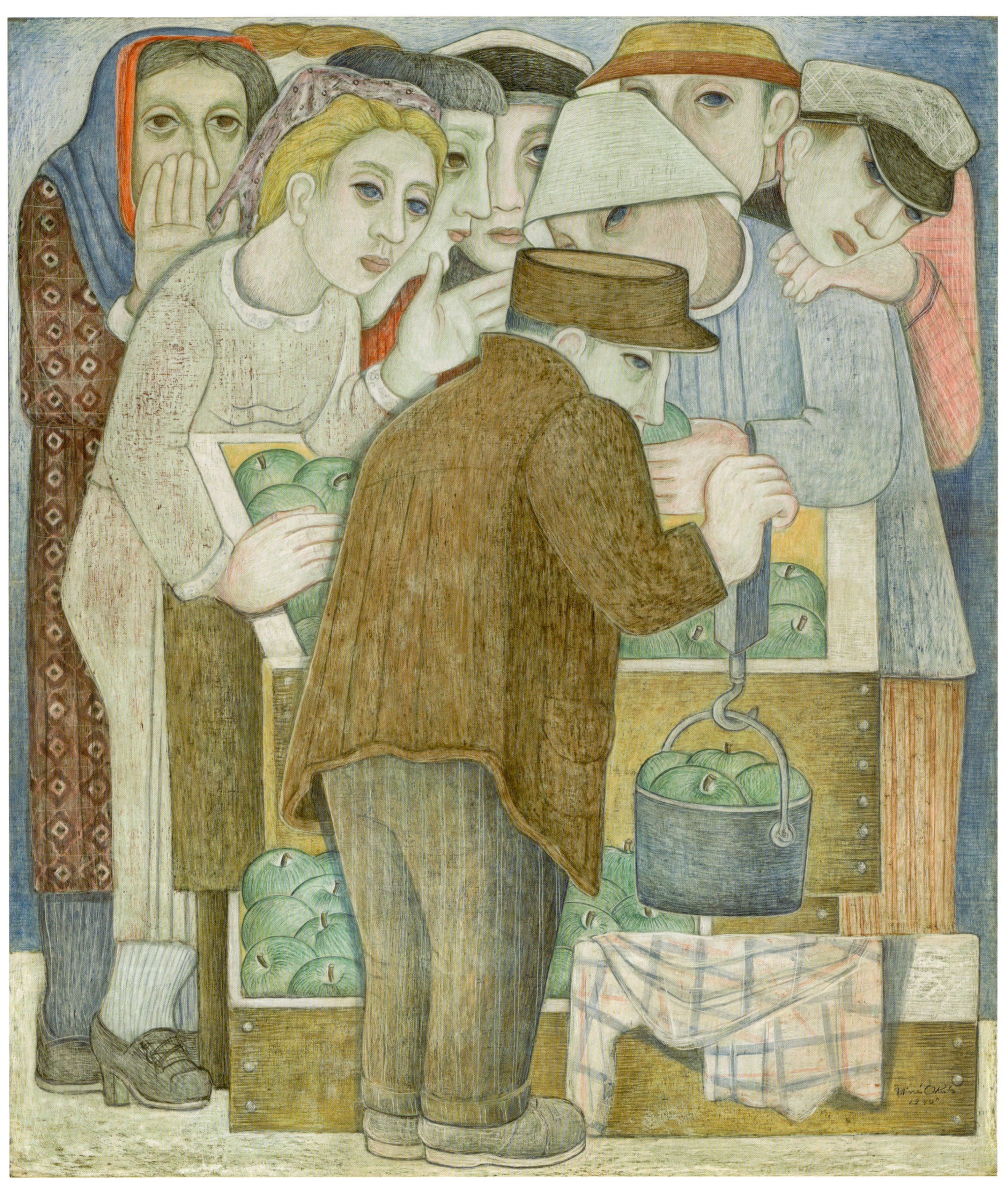

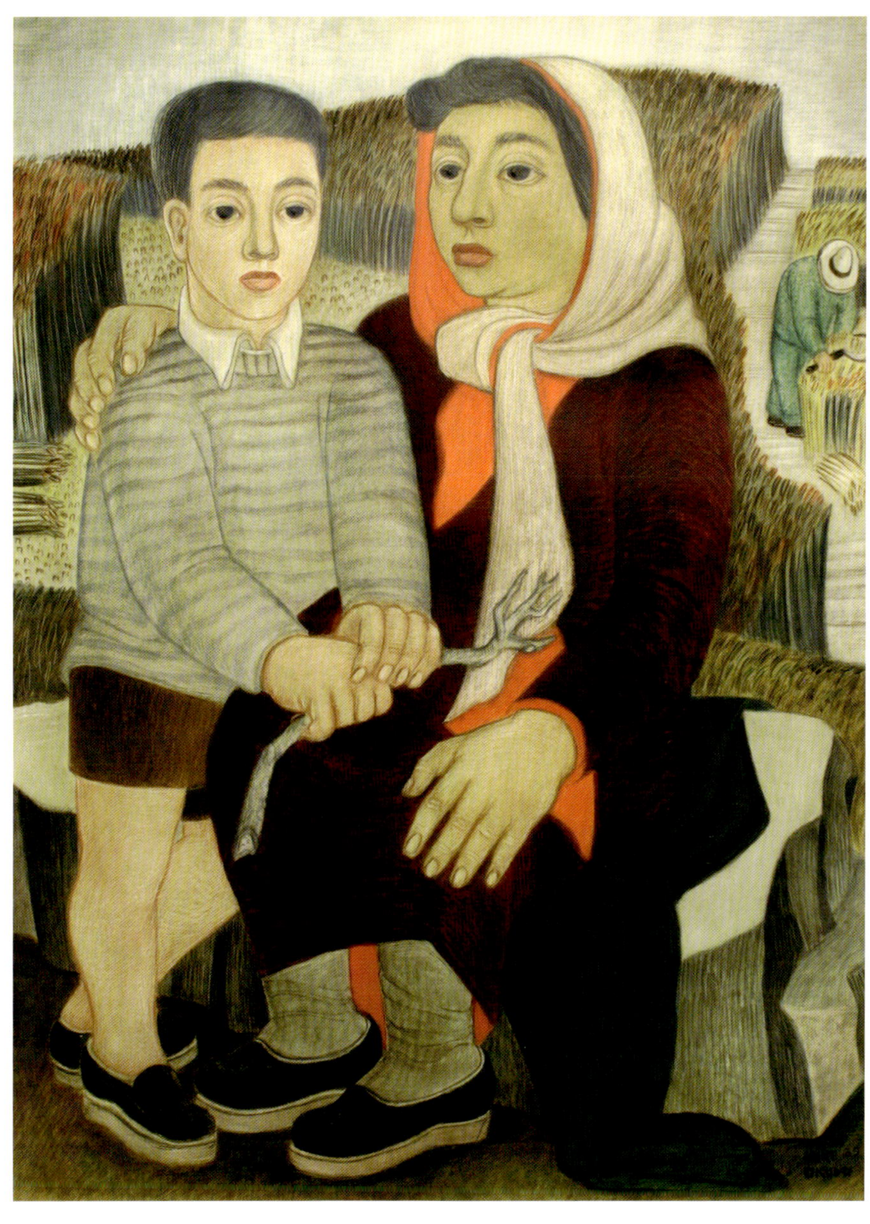

**19**

Miné Okubo

*Grocer Weighing Produce*

1940

Tempera on hardboard, 40 × 35 in. (110.6 × 88.9 cm). Smithsonian American Art Museum, Museum purchase. © The Miné Okubo Charitable Corporation. Photo by Lucia RM Martino. Courtesy of the Smithsonian American Art Museum

This painting, along with *Untitled (Mother and Boy)*, *Portrait Study*, and *Self-Portrait*, shows Okubo's exploration of her own style as an artist following her recent return from European travels, during which she briefly studied with French artist Fernand Léger. Her admiration for Mexican muralists José Clemente Orozco and Diego Rivera is evident in these works as well. See Fig. 1.2 in this catalogue's introduction for a photo of Okubo creating this painting in her studio in Berkeley.

**20**

Miné Okubo

*Untitled (Mother and Boy)*

1939

Oil on paper, 36 × 28¼ in. The Miné Okubo Charitable Corporation, EL 2012.1.19. Photo by Tom Callas

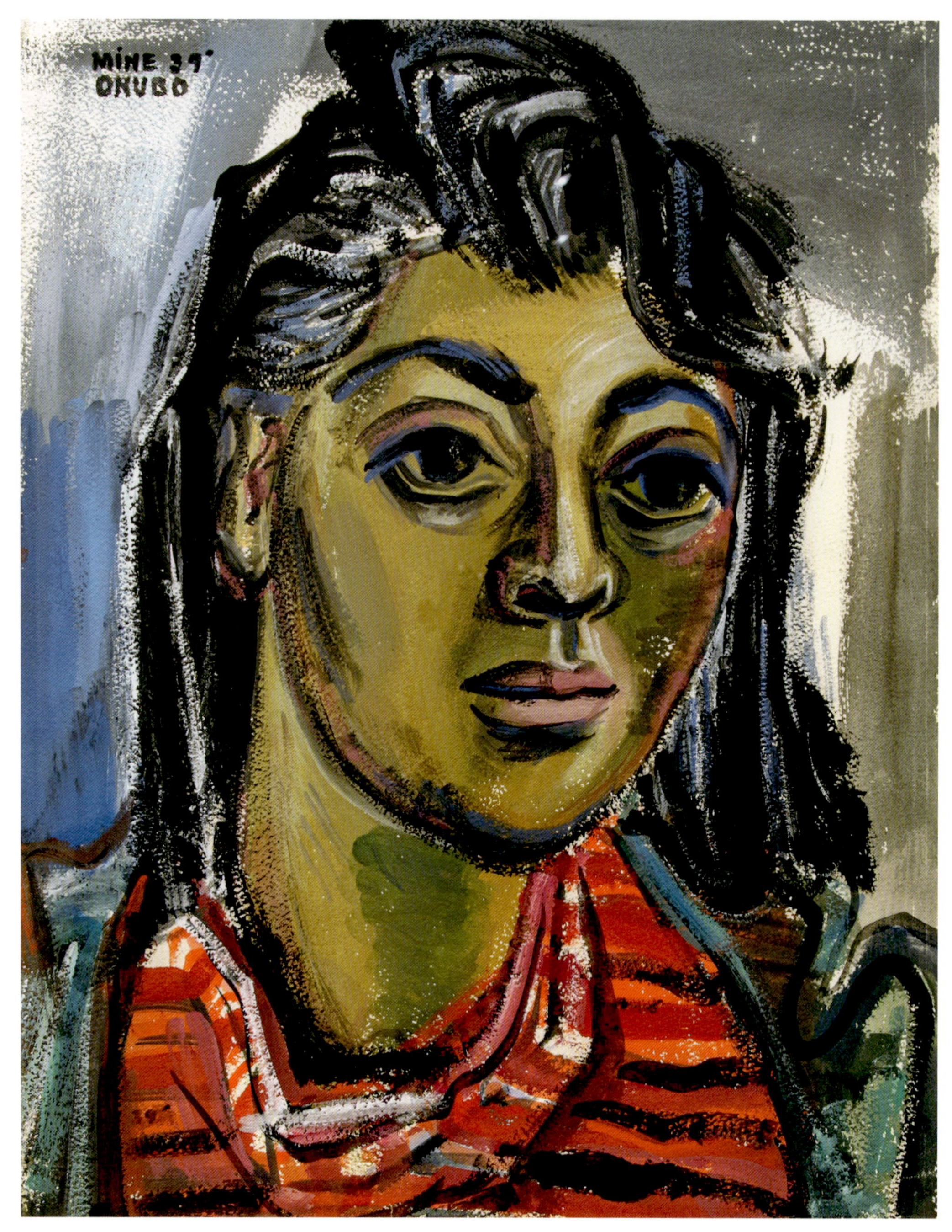


**21**

Miné Okubo

*Untitled (Portrait of Young Woman)*

1939

Gouache on paper, 25¼ × 21¼ in. The Miné Okubo Charitable Corporation, EL 2012.1.13. Photo by Giovanni Cardenas, Chief Photographer Strategic Communications Riverside Community College District, 2023

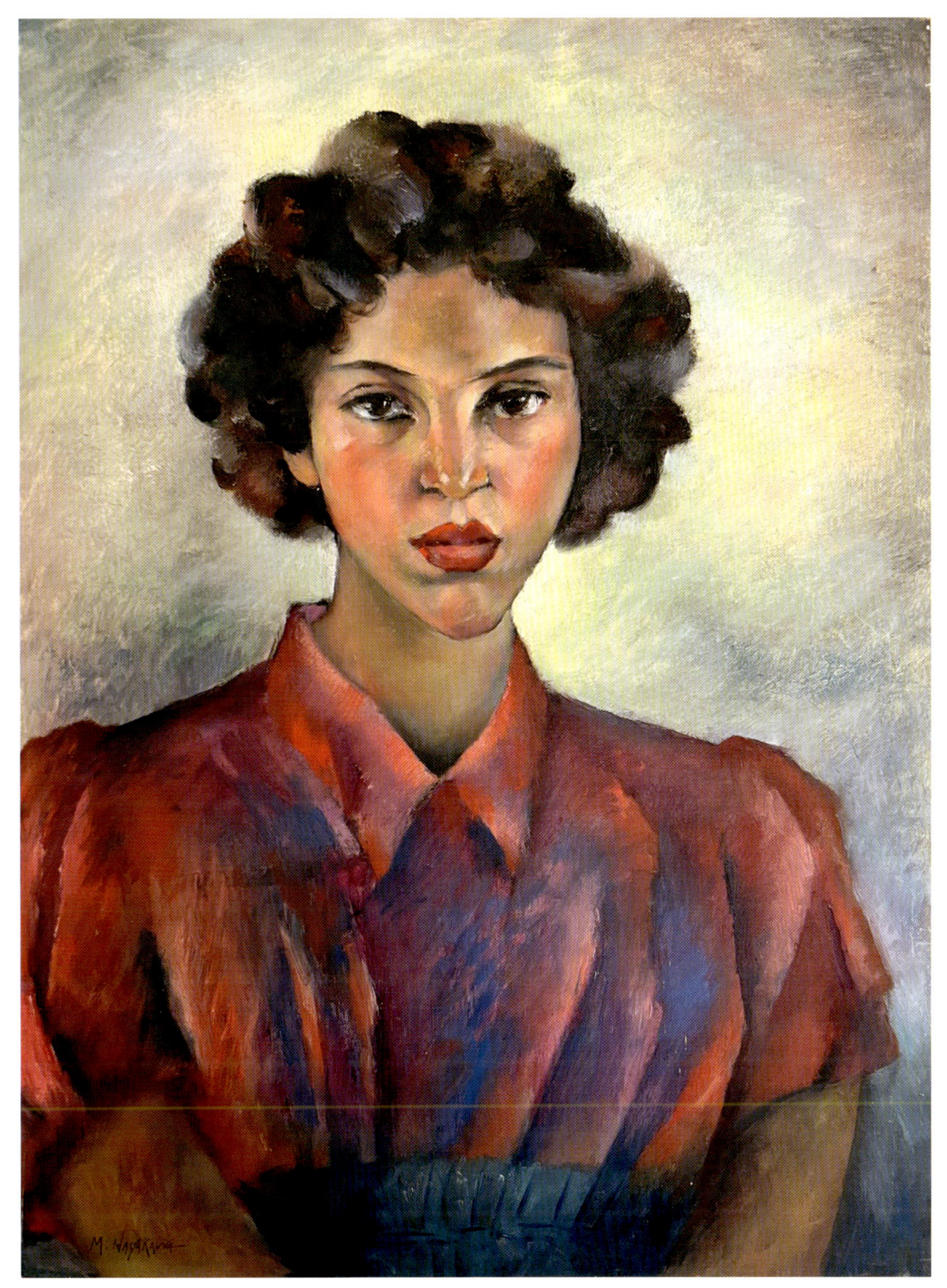

**22**
Miki Hayakawa
*Brown Eyes*
ca. 1940s

Oil on canvas, 24 × 18 in. Collection of Richard Sakai. Photo by ShiPu Wang

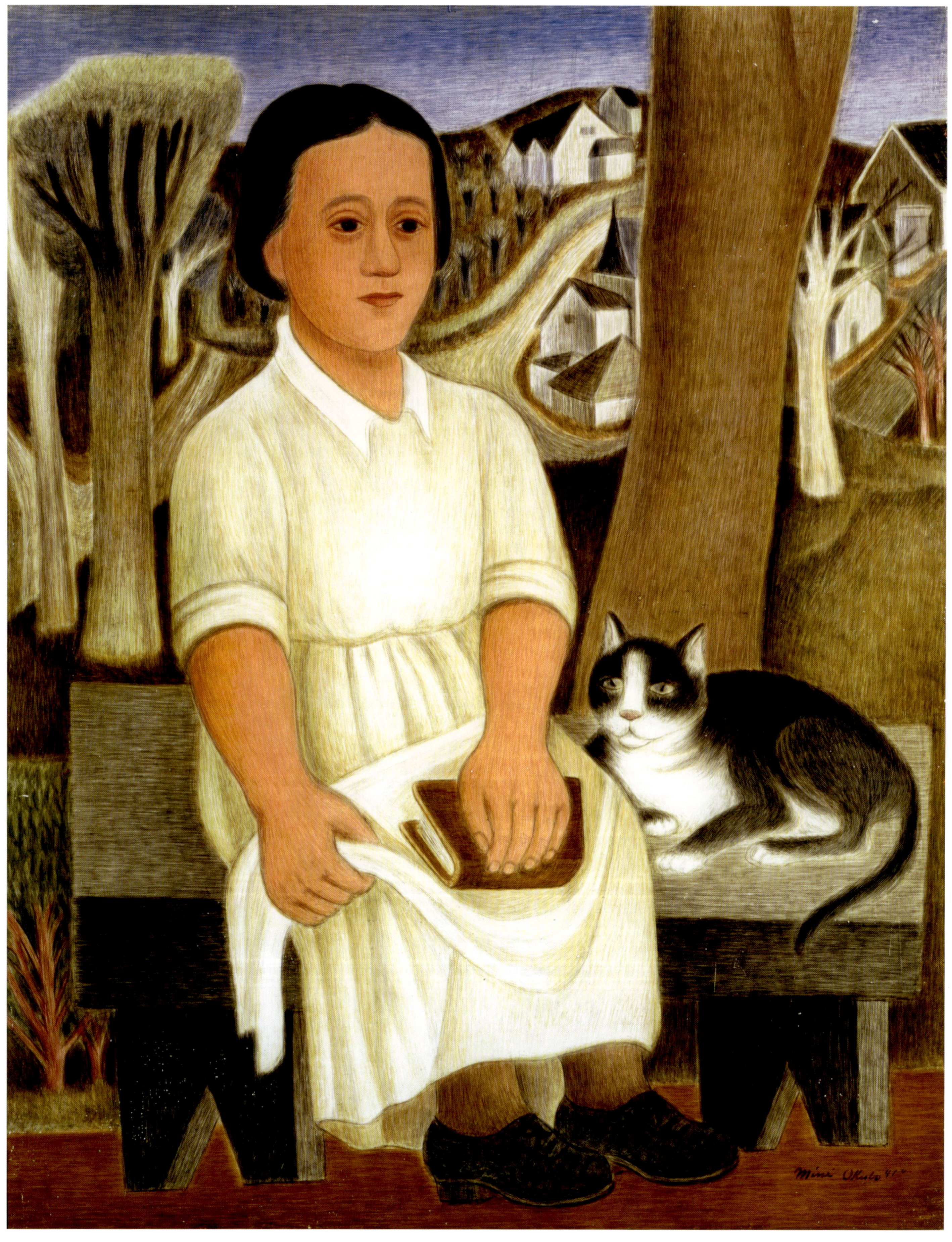

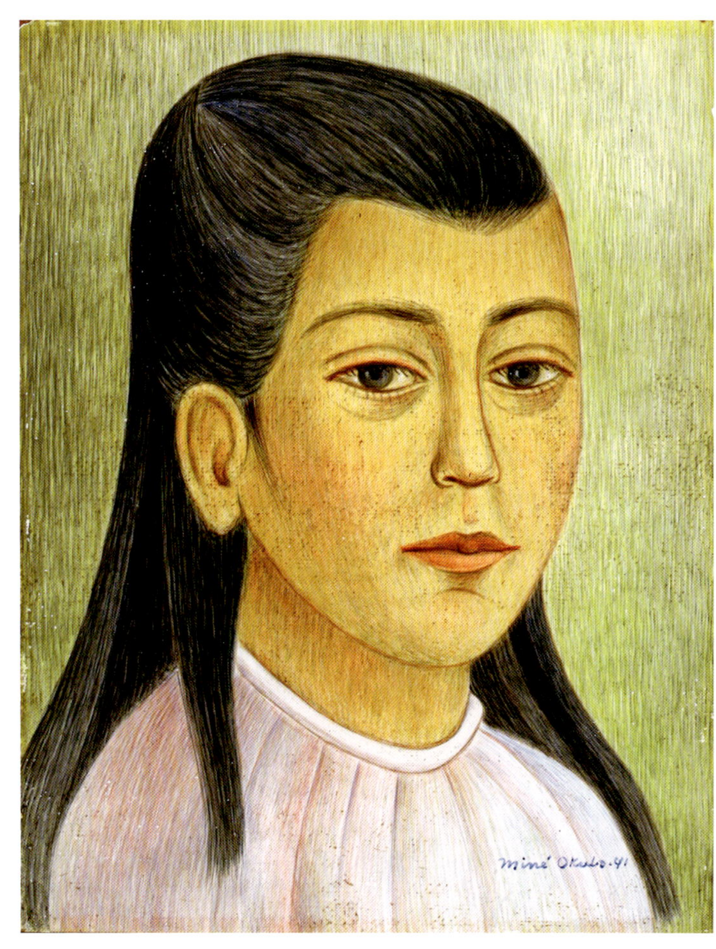

**23**
Miné Okubo
*Mother and Cat*
*(Miyo and Cat)*
1941

Tempera on Masonite, 29¾ × 24 in. Collection of the Oakland Museum of California, Acquired through funds provided by the Collectors Gallery, A72.74. © The Estate of Miné Okubo

This painting, originally titled *Miyo and Cat*, won the Anne Bremer Memorial Prize at the Sixty-First San Francisco Art Association Annual Exhibition in 1941. Okubo kept this work with her throughout wartime dislocation and featured it in her 1972 retrospective at the Oakland Museum of California and in *Into the Light*, a retrospective sponsored by the Japan Society of Boston in 1993.

**24**
Miné Okubo
*Self-Portrait*
1941

Tempera on board, 12 × 9½ in. Collection of the Oakland Museum of California, Gift of Roy Leeper and Gaylord Hall, A98.5. © The Estate of Miné Okubo

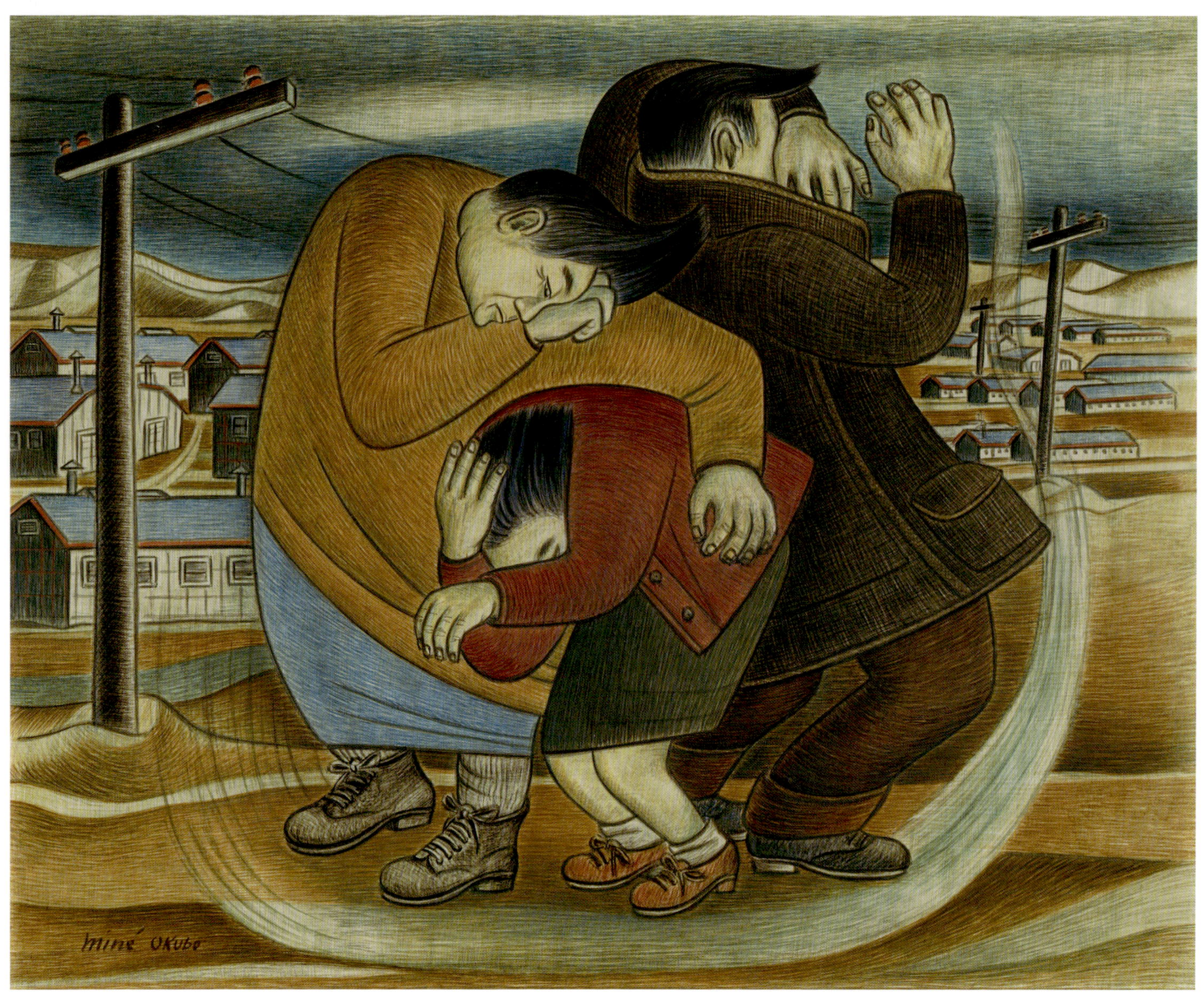


**25**

Miné Okubo

*Wind and Dust*

1943

Opaque watercolor on paperboard, 19 × 24 in. (48.3 × 61 cm). Smithsonian American Art Museum, Museum purchase.  Photo by Lucia RM Martino. Courtesy of the Smithsonian American Art Museum

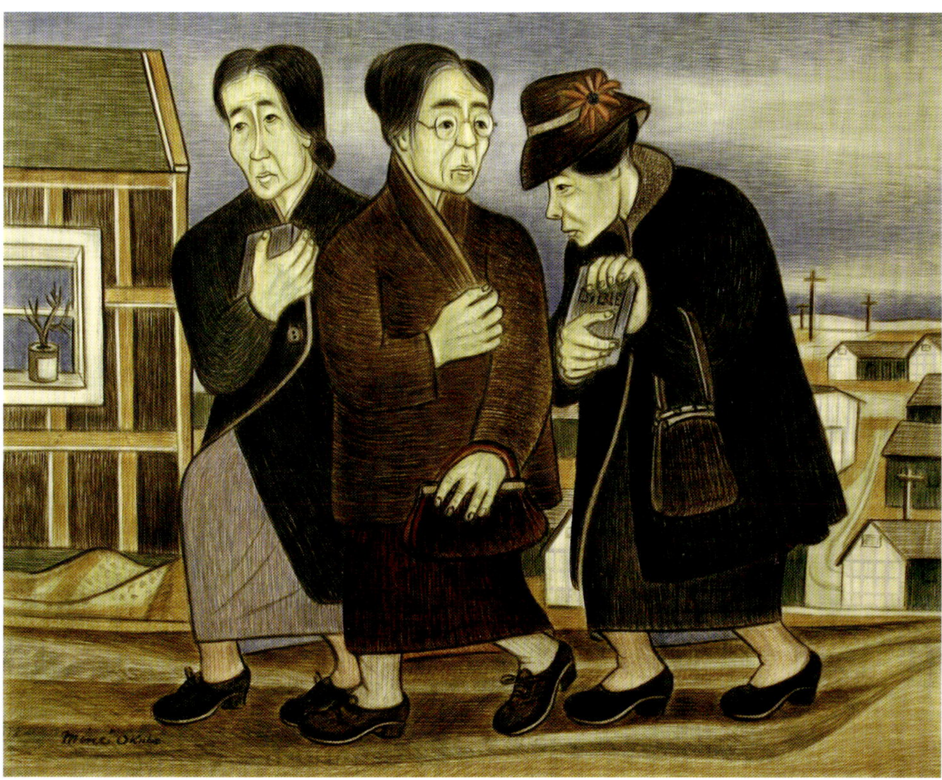

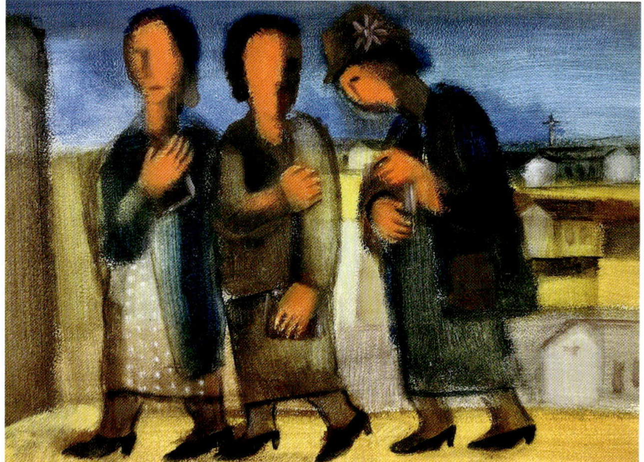

**26**
Miné Okubo
*Sunday*
1943

Watercolor on illustration board, 23¼ × 29¼ in. The Miné Okubo Charitable Corporation, EL 2012.1.5. Photo by Tom Callas

**27**
Miné Okubo
Preparatory sketch for *Sunday*
1943

Gouache on paper, 9½ × 13¾ in. Japanese American National Museum, Los Angeles, 2007.62.238

Okubo created *Sunday* at Topaz and sent it to the Fifty-Fifth Annual American Exhibition of Water Colors and Drawings at the Art Institute of Chicago in 1944.

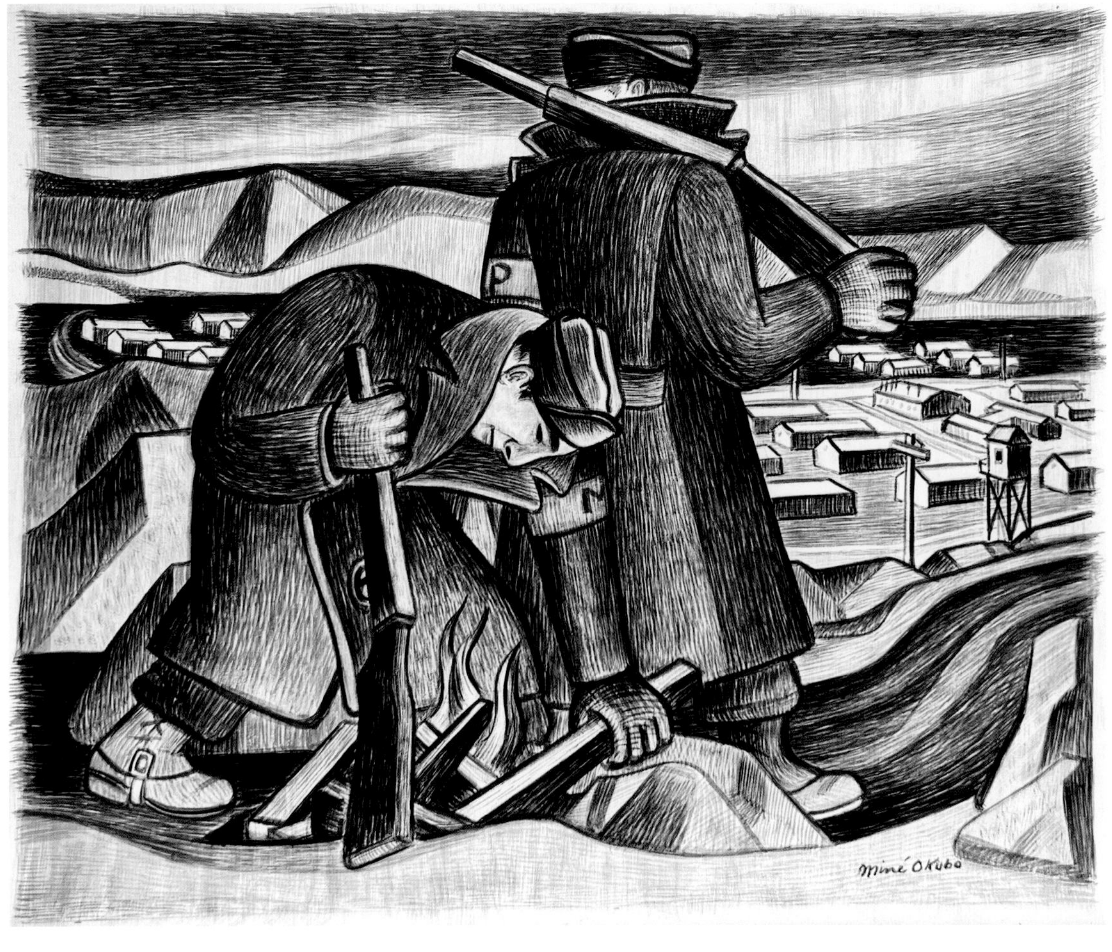


**28**
Miné Okubo
*On Watch*
1943

Tempera on paper, 15 × 20 in. The Miné Okubo Charitable Corporation. Photo by ShiPu Wang

While incarcerated, Okubo maintained her creative productivity and professional connection by sending artworks to various exhibitions. She submitted *On Watch* to the San Francisco Art Association's 1943 drawings and prints show, where the work attracted *Fortune* magazine's attention; this led to a commission for the magazine's special "Japan" issue in 1944 and an invitation to work on other illustration projects, for which Okubo moved to New York City in 1944.

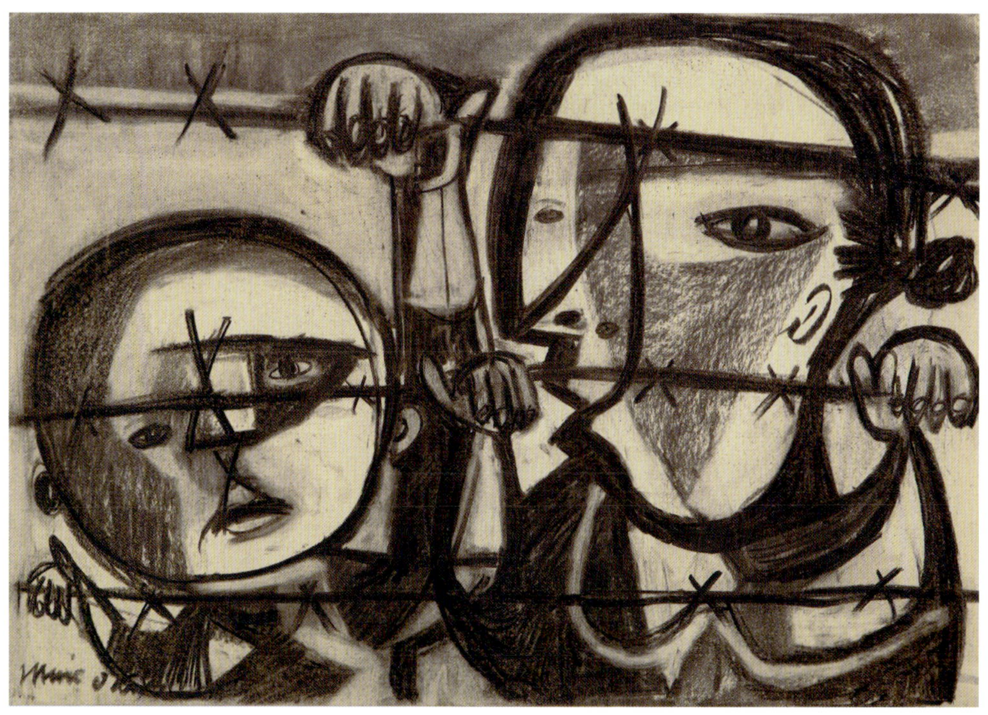

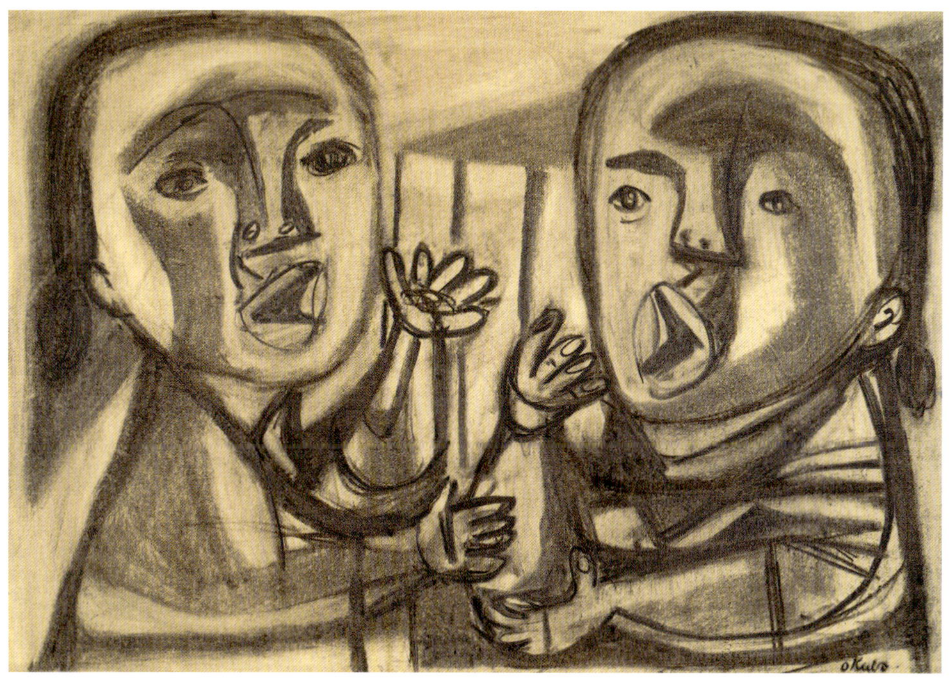

29
Miné Okubo
*Untitled*
ca. 1942–44

Charcoal on paper, 13¾ × 20 in.
Japanese American National Museum, Los Angeles, Gift of the Miné Okubo Estate, 2007.62.5

30
Miné Okubo
*Untitled*
ca. 1942–44

Charcoal on paper, 13¾ × 20 in.
Japanese American National Museum, Los Angeles, Gift of the Miné Okubo Estate, 2007.62.208

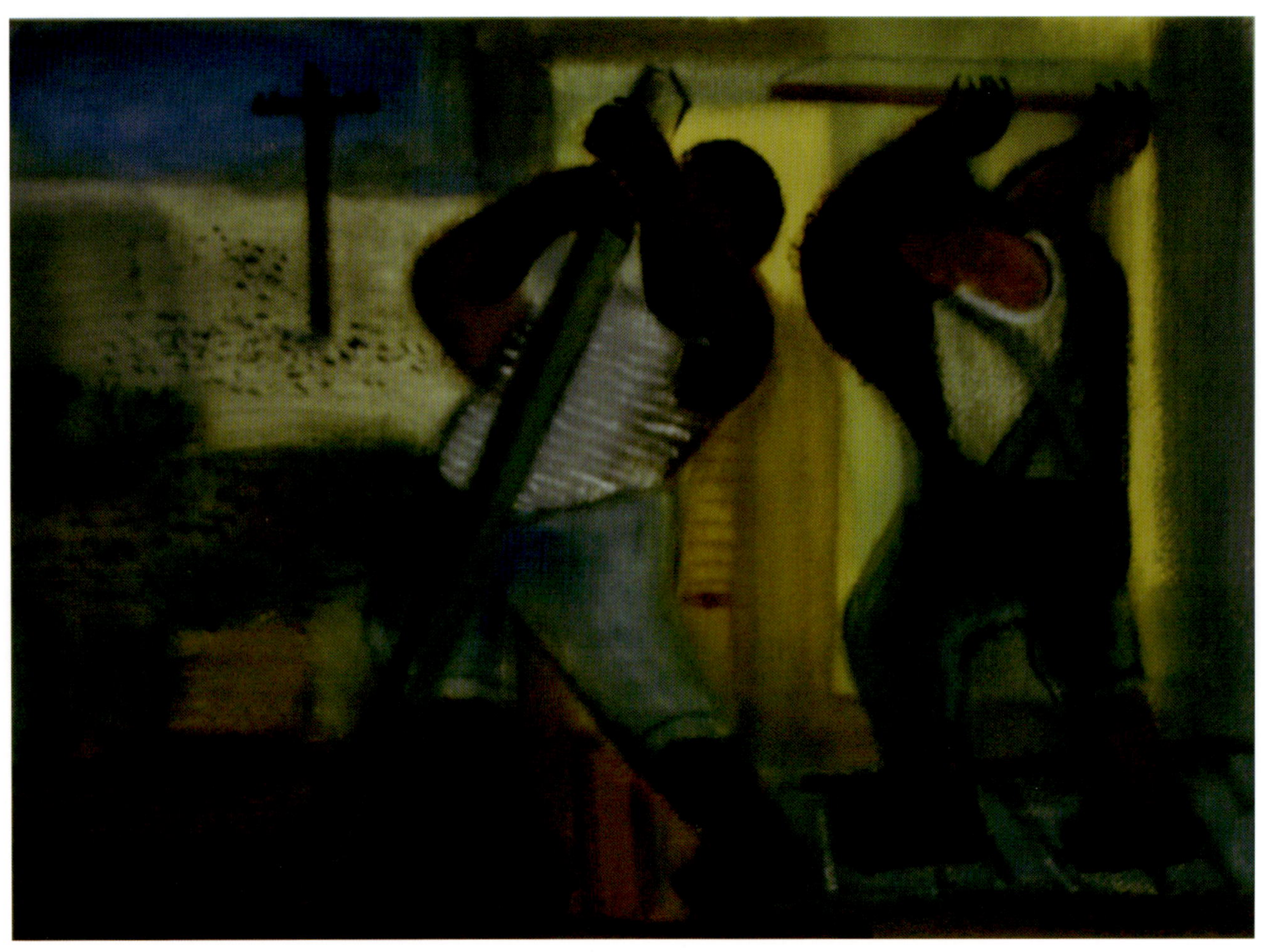

31
Miné Okubo
*The Camps Were Unfinished so the Evacuees Had to Prepare for Living There*
1943

Gouache/tempera on paper, 23¼ × 29¼ in. The Miné Okubo Charitable Corporation, EL 2010.1.717. Photo by Tom Callas

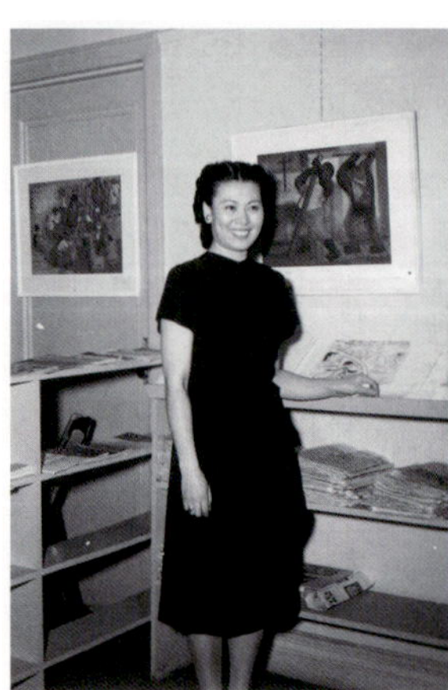

32
"Miss Mine Okubo, Nisei, who resettled to New York from the Topaz Center, paused to have this picture taken while greeting friends at a tea in her honor at the opening of an exhibit of her drawings and paintings of center life at the American Common in New York City on March 6, under the auspices of the Common Council for American Unity"
1945

War Relocation Authority Photographs of Japanese-American Evacuation and Resettlement, 1942–45, BANC PIC 1967.014—PIC, The Bancroft Library, University of California, Berkeley, WRA no. G-828. Photo by Toge Fujihira. Courtesy of Wikimedia Commons

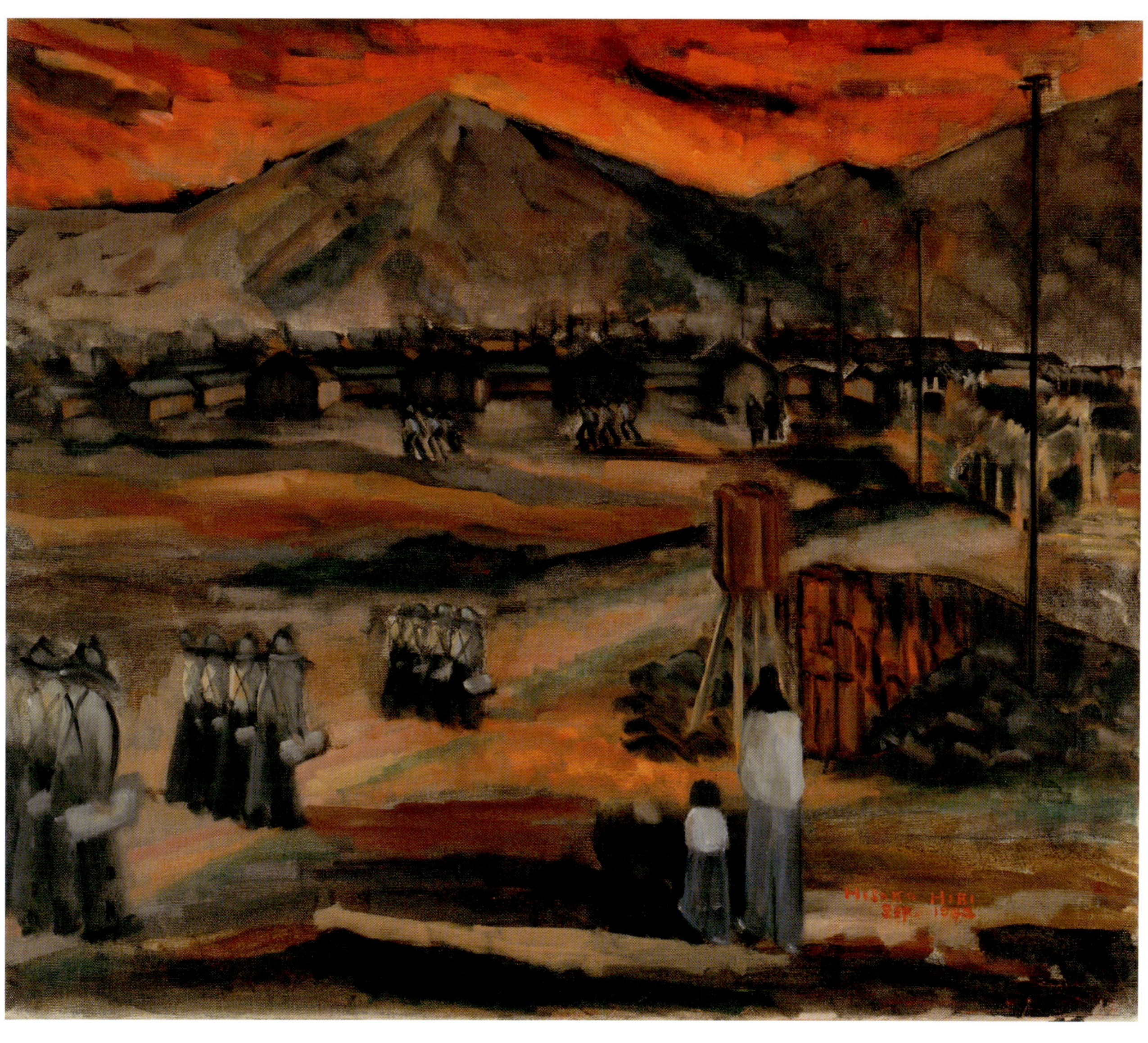

33
Hisako Hibi
*Morning*
September 1942

Oil on canvas, 22 × 26 in. Japanese American National Museum, Los Angeles, Gift of Ibuki Hibi Lee, 96.601.8

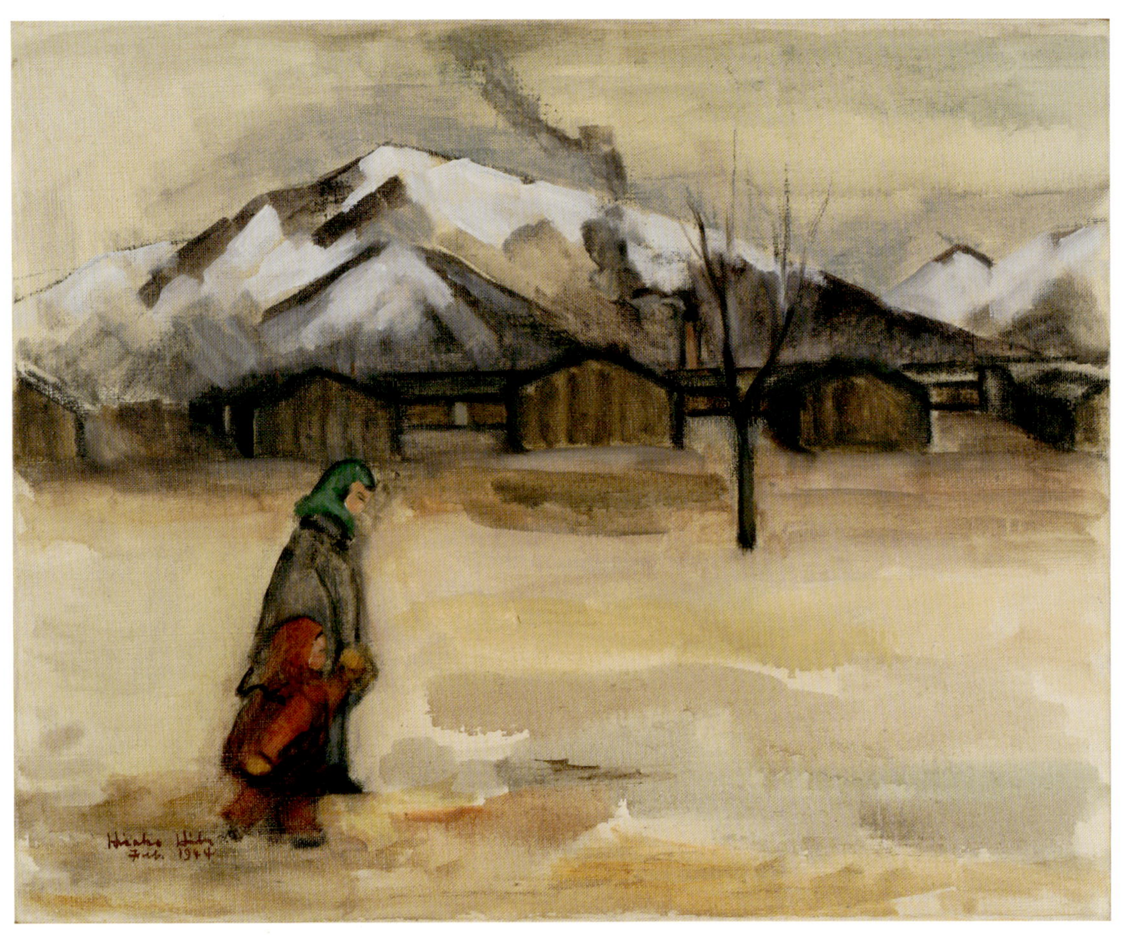

**34**
Hisako Hibi
*With Mother*
1944

Oil on canvas, 16 × 20 in. Japanese American National Museum, Los Angeles, Gift of Ibuki Hibi Lee, 96.601.35

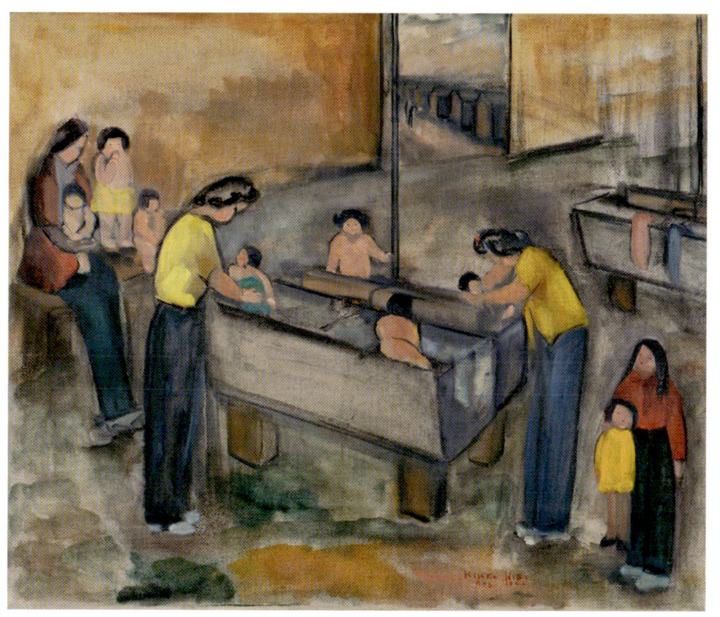

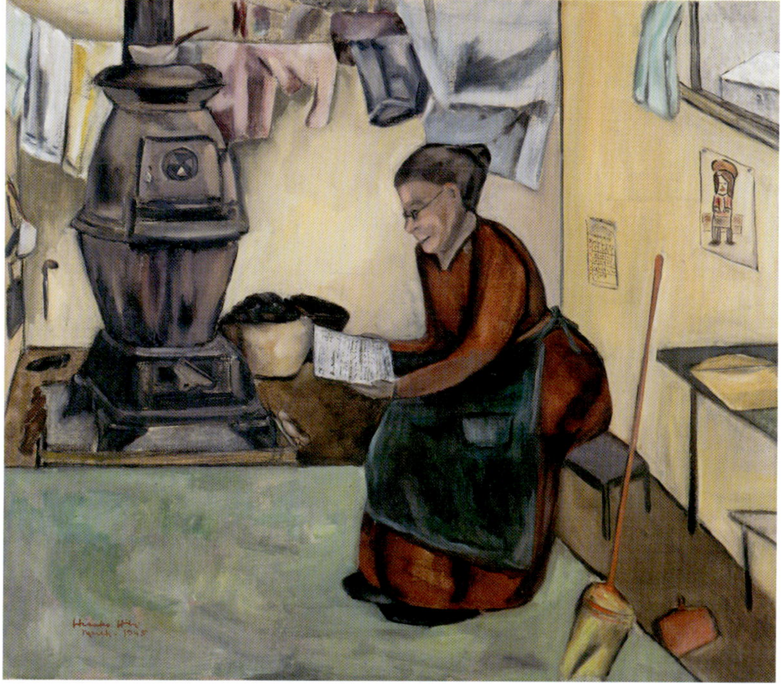

35
Hisako Hibi
*Laundry Room*
August 1943

Oil on canvas, 20 × 24 in. Japanese American National Museum, Los Angeles, Gift of Ibuki Hibi Lee, 96.601.15

36
Hisako Hibi
*A Letter*
March 1945

Oil on canvas, 22 × 26 in. Japanese American National Museum, Los Angeles, Gift of Ibuki Hibi Lee, 96.601.51

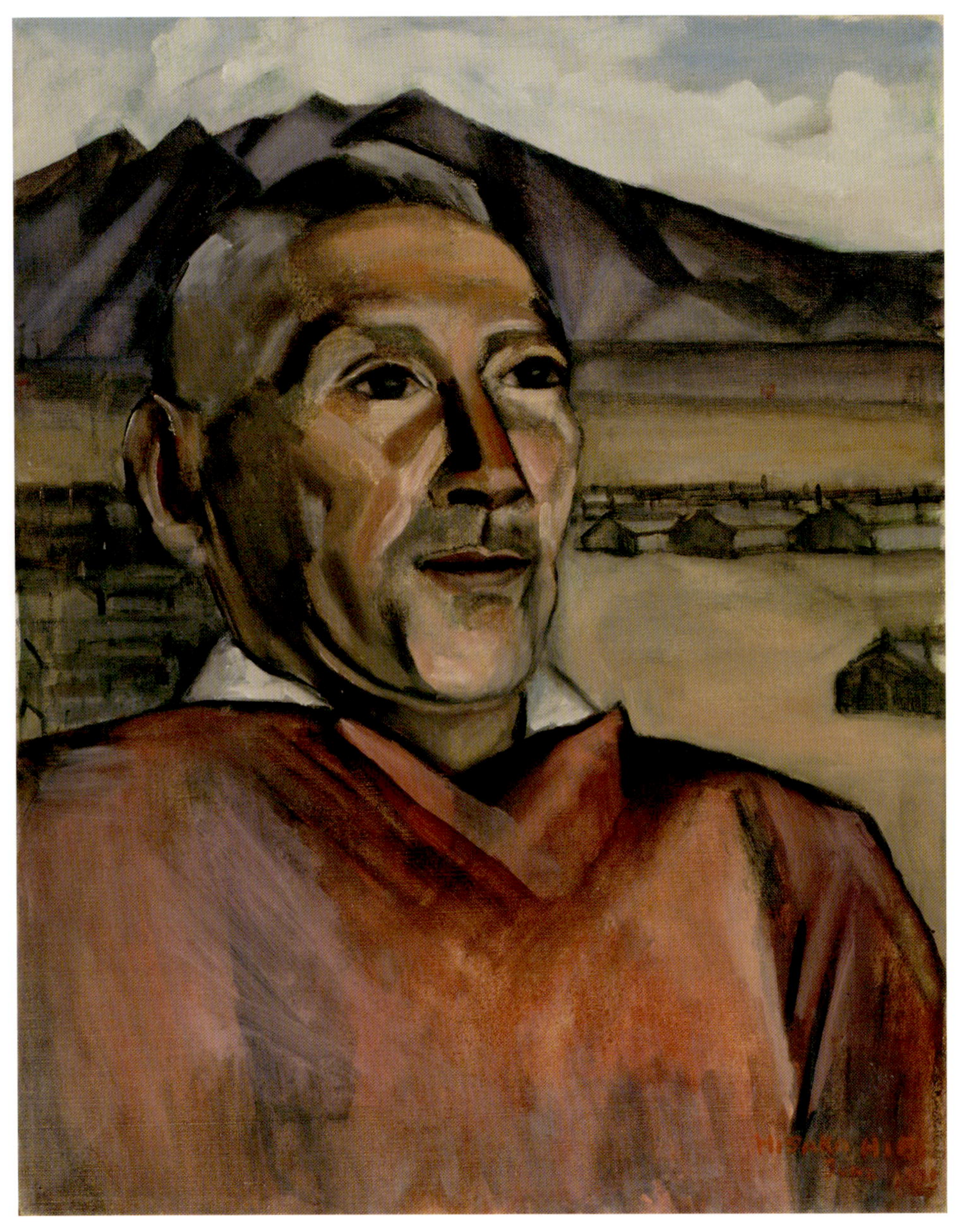

**37**

Hisako Hibi
*A Study #1*
June 1944

Oil on canvas, 20 × 16 in. Japanese American National Museum, Los Angeles, Gift of Ibuki Hibi Lee, 96.601.42

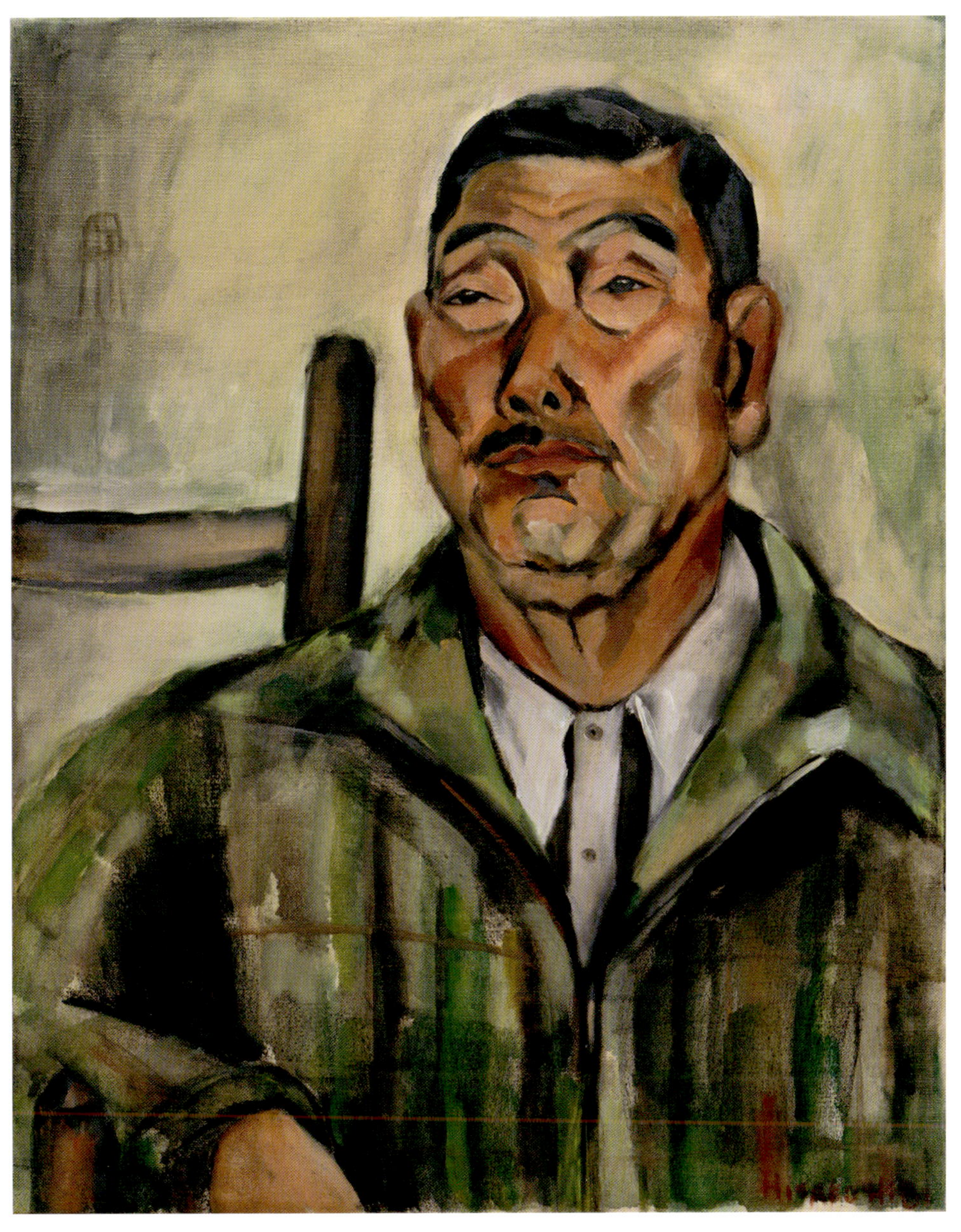

38
Hisako Hibi
*A Study #2*
June 1944

Oil on canvas, 20 × 16 in. Japanese American National Museum, Los Angeles, Gift of Ibuki Hibi Lee, 98.138.6

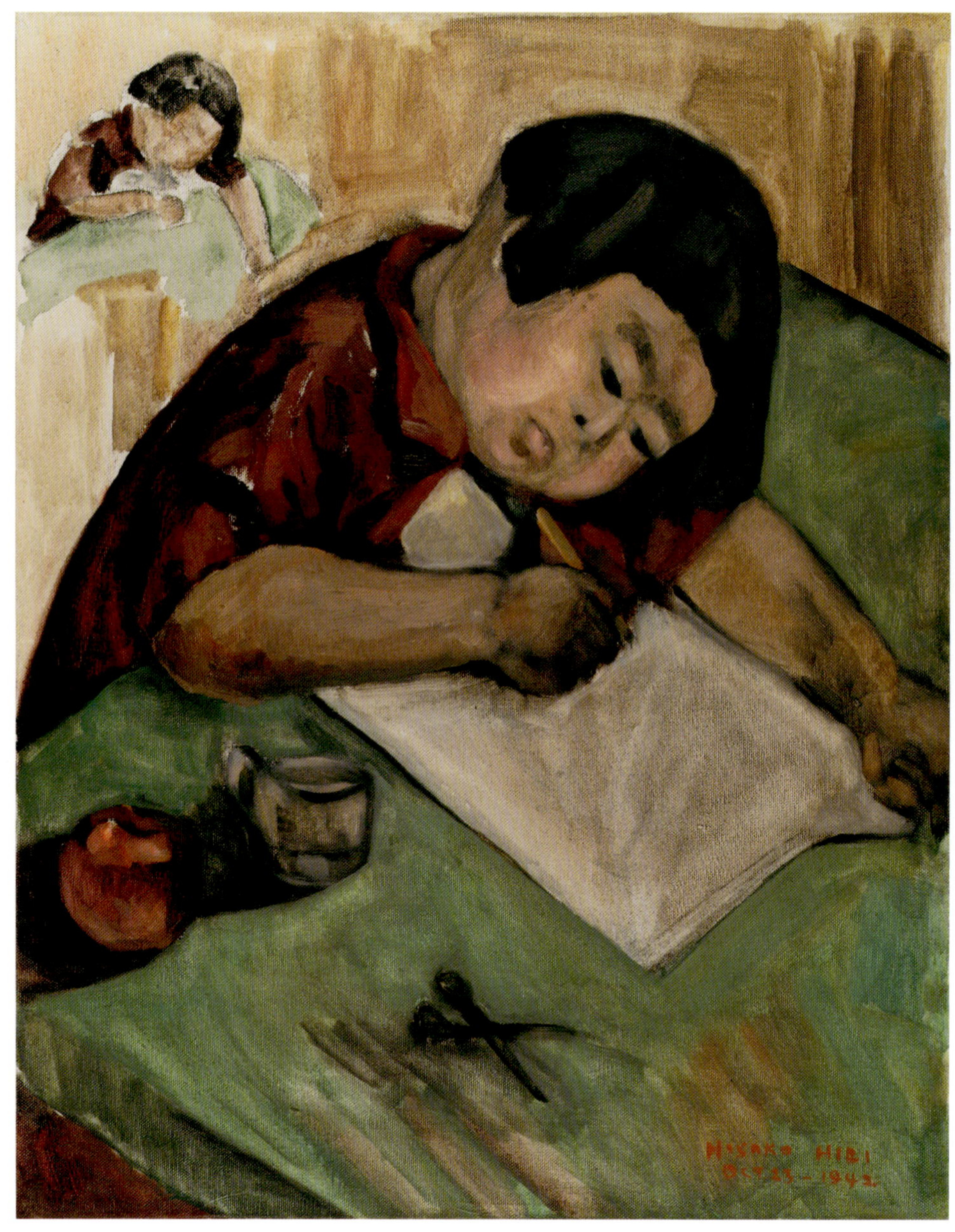


**39**

Hisako Hibi
*Study (Ibuki)*
Topaz, Utah, October 1942

Oil on canvas, 20 × 16 in. Japanese American National Museum, Los Angeles, Gift of Ibuki Hibi Lee, 98.138.2

Ibuki Hibi Lee is the younger of the two children of Hisako and Matsusaburo George Hibi; Ibuki's older brother is Satoshi. The family of four was incarcerated at Tanforan and Topaz from 1942 to 1945, before relocating to New York in September 1945.

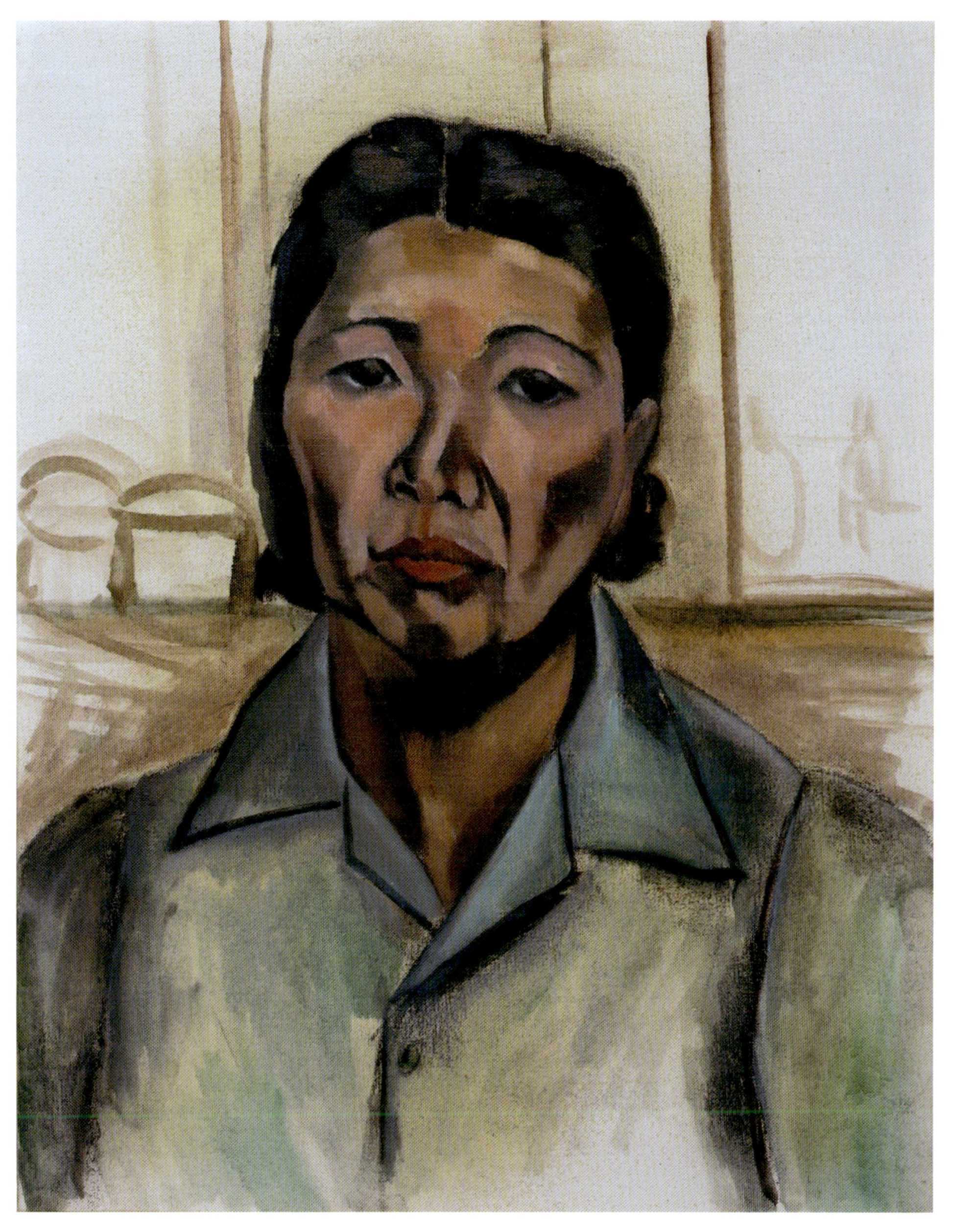

40
Hisako Hibi
*Study for a Self-Portrait*
ca. 1944

Oil on canvas, 21¾ × 17½ in.
Japanese American National Museum, Los Angeles, Gift of Ibuki Hibi Lee, 99.63.1

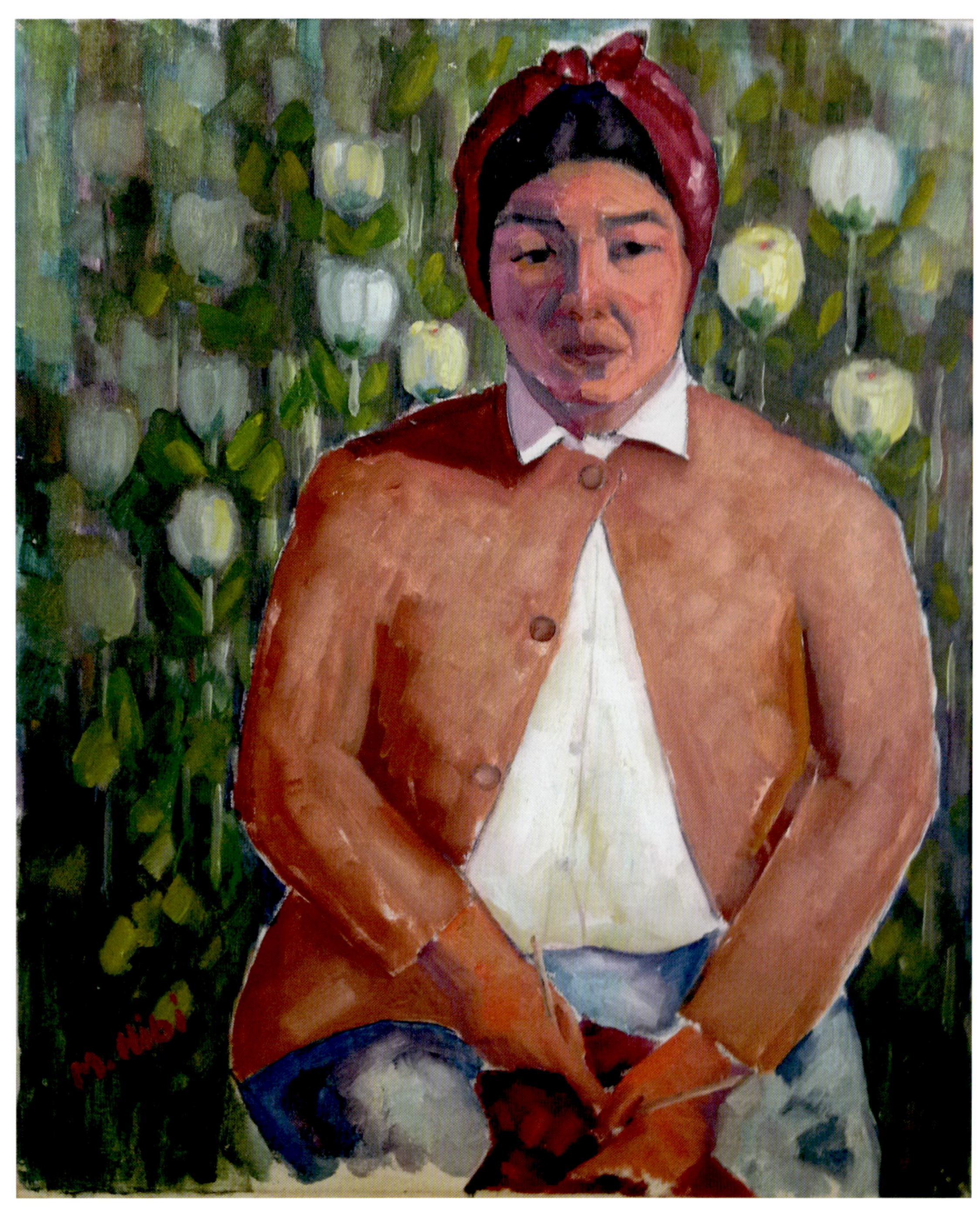

**41**

Matsusaburo George Hibi

*Hisako, Wife*

1943–44

Oil on canvas, 26 × 22 in. The Hibi Estate. Photo by ShiPu Wang

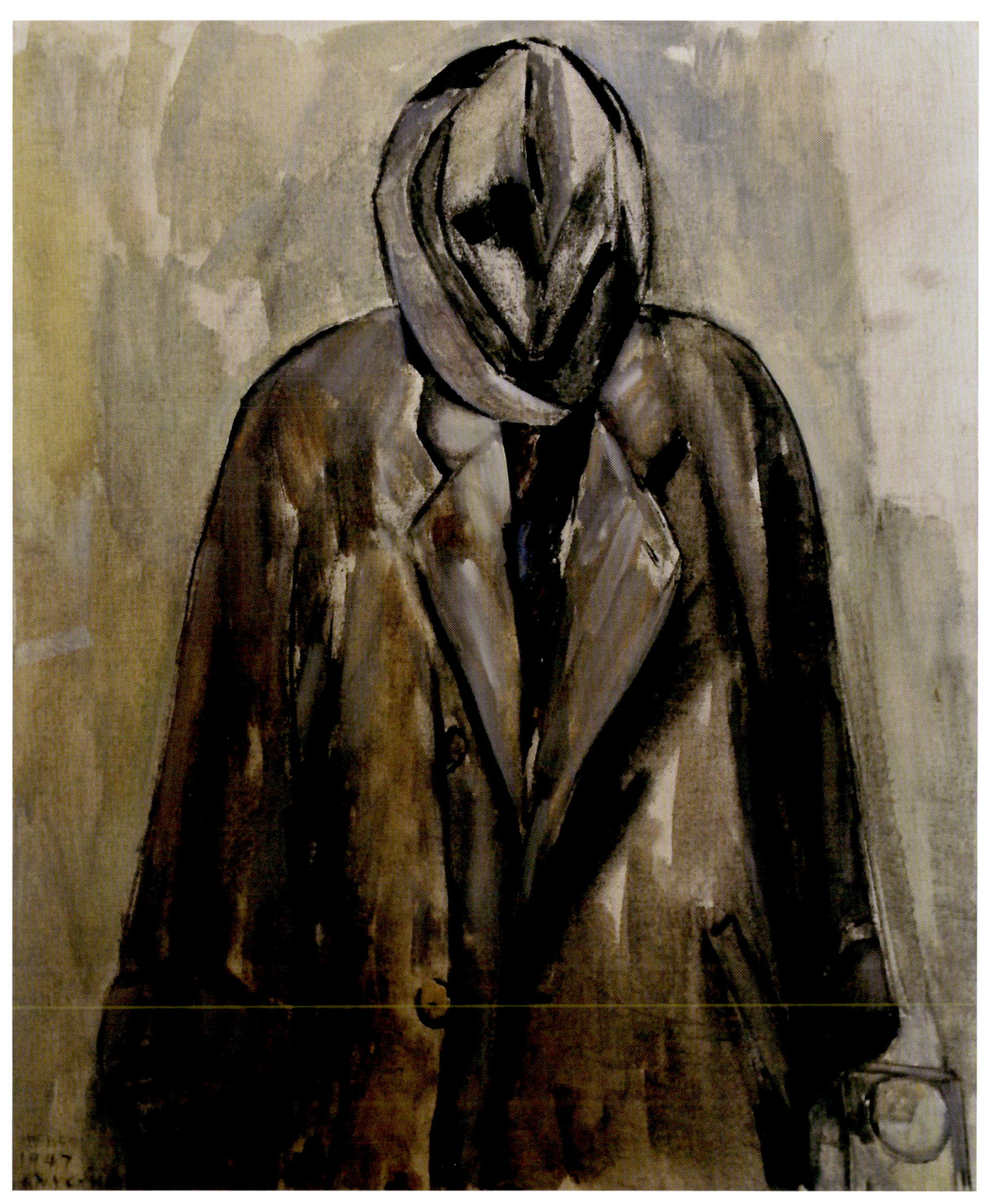

**42**
Hisako Hibi
*As Usual . . . Still Hanging*
New York, August 1947

Oil on canvas, 26 × 22 in. The Hibi Estate. Photo by ShiPu Wang

This is a posthumous portrait of Matsusaburo George Hibi, who passed away from cancer in June 1947, less than two years after the Hibis were released from Topaz and moved to New York City to rebuild their life. Hisako Hibi wrote on the painting's verso: "His hat and overcoat were hanging on a nail on the kitchen door as usually [*sic*], August 1947 NYC."

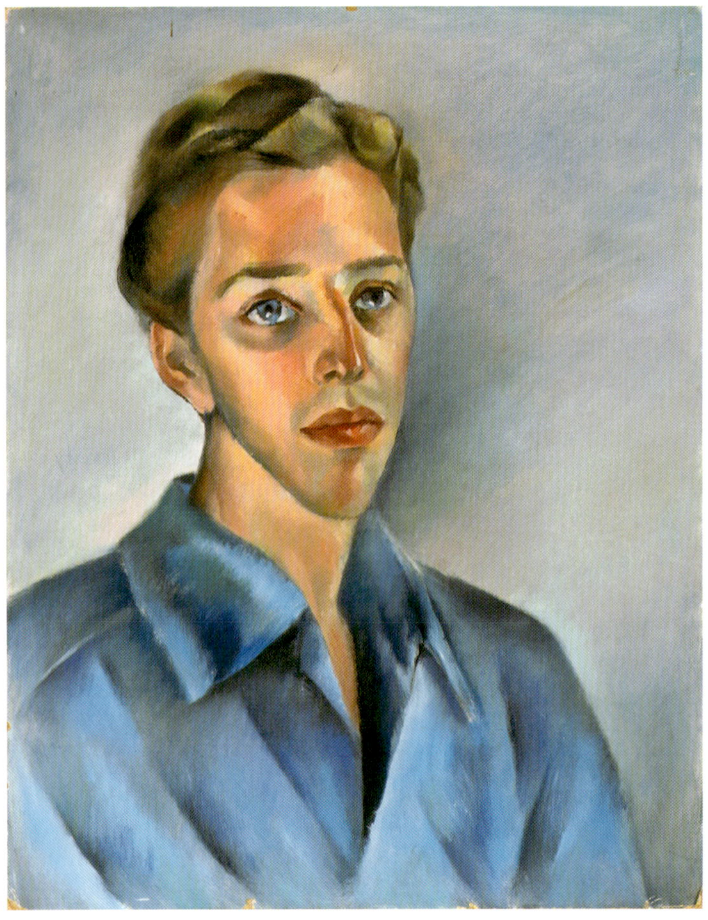

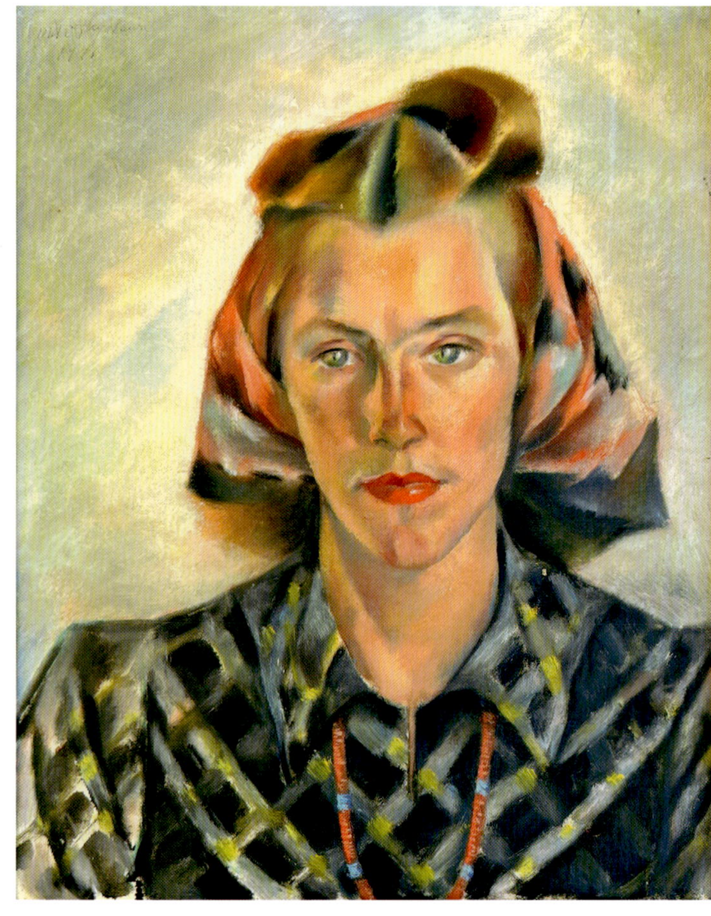

43
Miki Hayakawa
*Portrait of Bill Ford*
1946

Oil on canvas board, 19½ × 15½ in. Collection of Shirley and David Astilli, Santa Fe, New Mexico

Bill Ford (1920–2009), an artist who moved from New York to Santa Fe in 1959, had been visiting the city on a regular basis since 1942, when he likely first met Hayakawa, who had relocated from California to New Mexico earlier that year. The two stayed in touch throughout wartime, when Ford was stationed at Fort Myer, Virginia, with Hayakawa writing long letters detailing her creative endeavors, health challenges, and seemingly endless drama/gossip among their mutual artist friends in Santa Fe. This is one of several portraits that Hayakawa painted of her dear friend during his annual visits.

44
Miki Hayakawa
*Joanne*
1946

Oil on canvas, 20 × 16 in. Collection of Cindie Johns Christiana. Photo by ShiPu Wang

Joanne was Hayakawa's stepdaughter-in-law from the family of Preston Elmer McCrossen, whom she married in Santa Fe, New Mexico, in 1947.

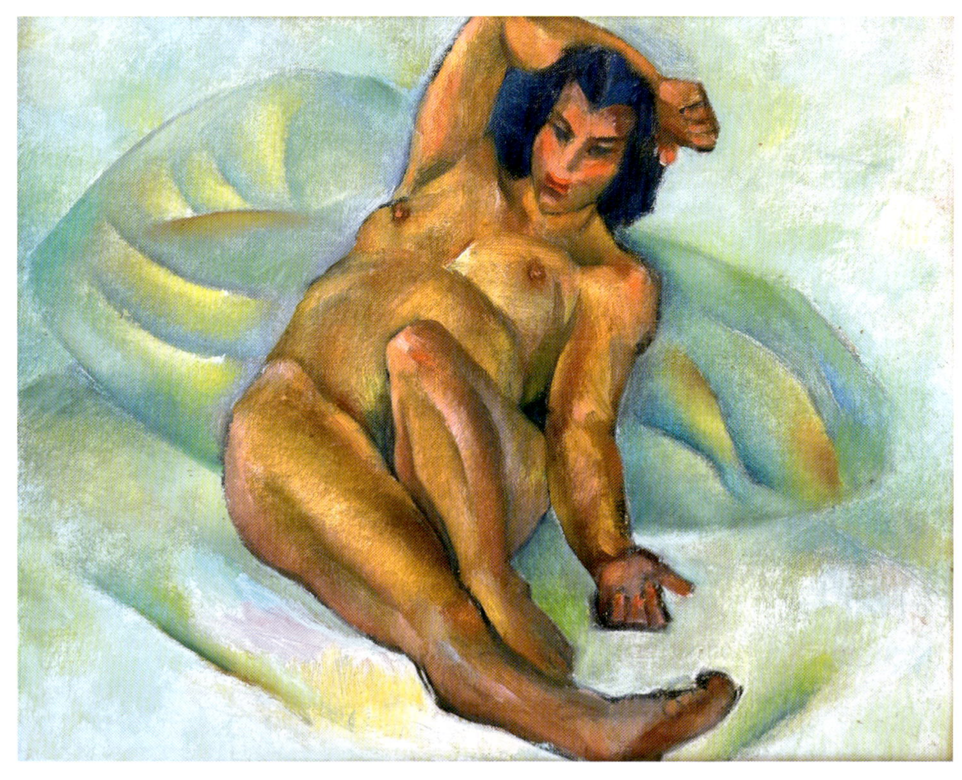

**45**
Miki Hayakawa
*Untitled (Female Nude)*
ca. 1940s

Oil on canvas, 16 × 20 in. Collection of the McCrossen Family. Photo by ShiPu Wang

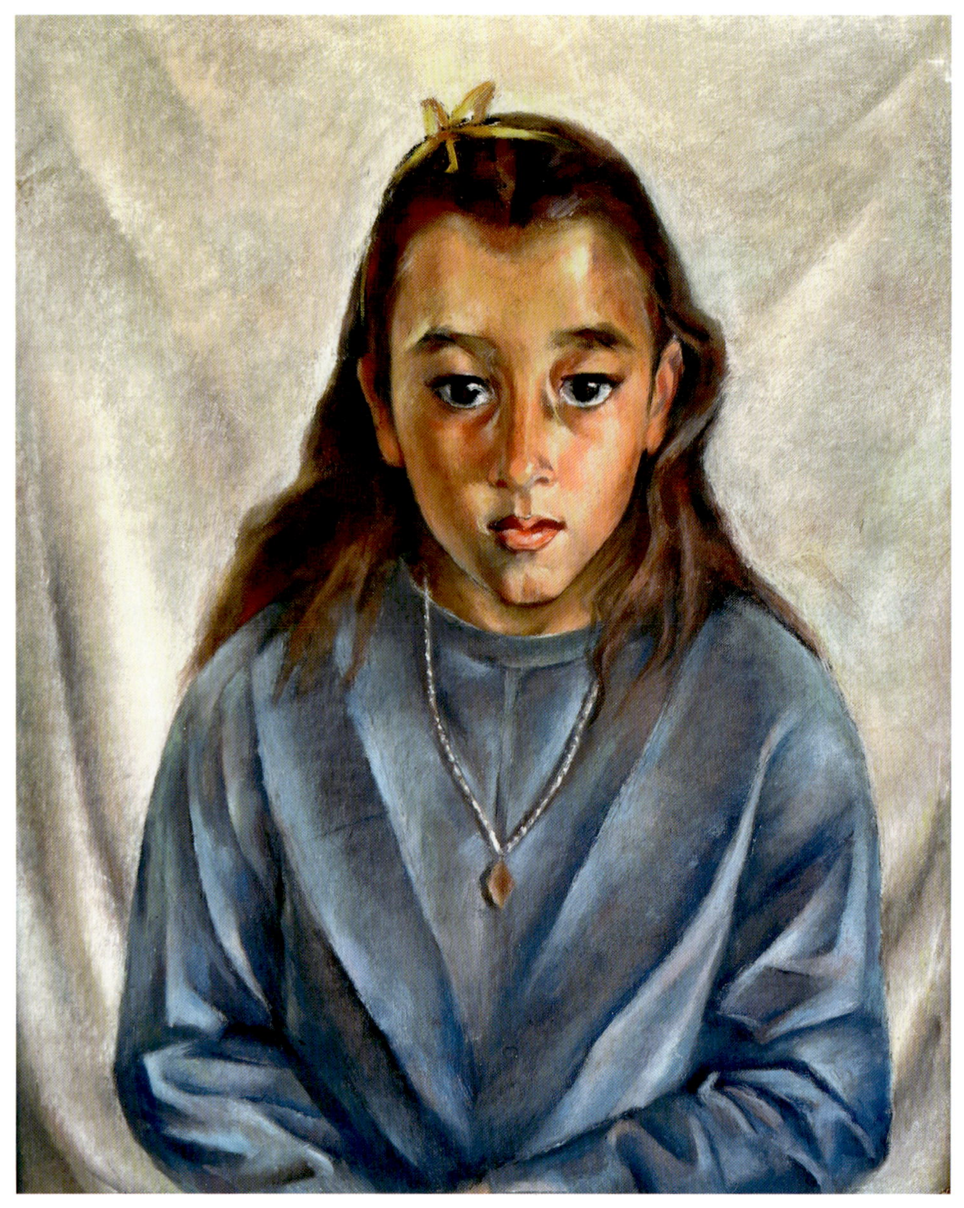

**46**
Miki Hayakawa
*Angie*
ca. 1948–51

Oil on canvas, 24 × 20¾ in. Collection of the McCrossen Family. Photo by ShiPu Wang

Winner of the First Premium Prize at the New Mexico State Fair in 1951, this is likely the same painting that Hayakawa called *Little Angie* and submitted to the *Thirty-Fifth Annual Fiesta Exhibition: Painters, Sculptors and Craftsmen of New Mexico*, held at the Museum of New Mexico Art Gallery in Santa Fe in August/September 1948.

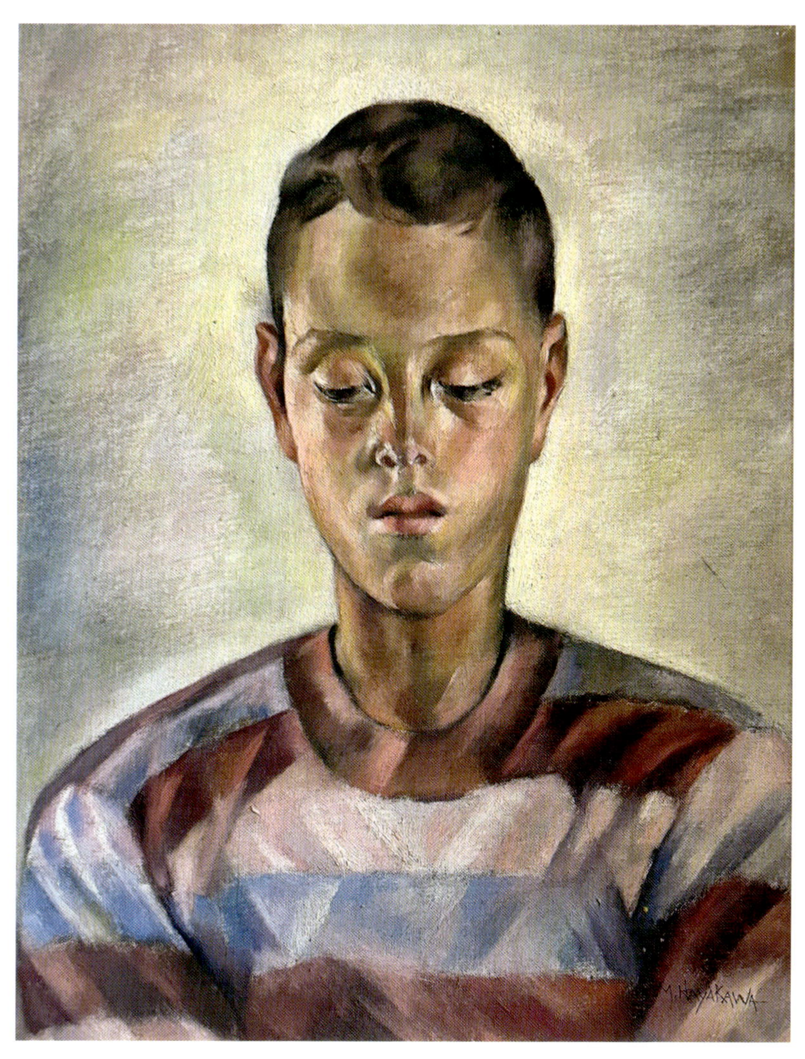


**47**

Miki Hayakawa

*Boy in Striped Shirt*

ca. 1953

Oil on canvas, 19 × 15¼ in.
Collection of Richard Sakai.
Photo by ShiPu Wang

Becky Alexander

# The California School of Fine Arts in Interwar San Francisco

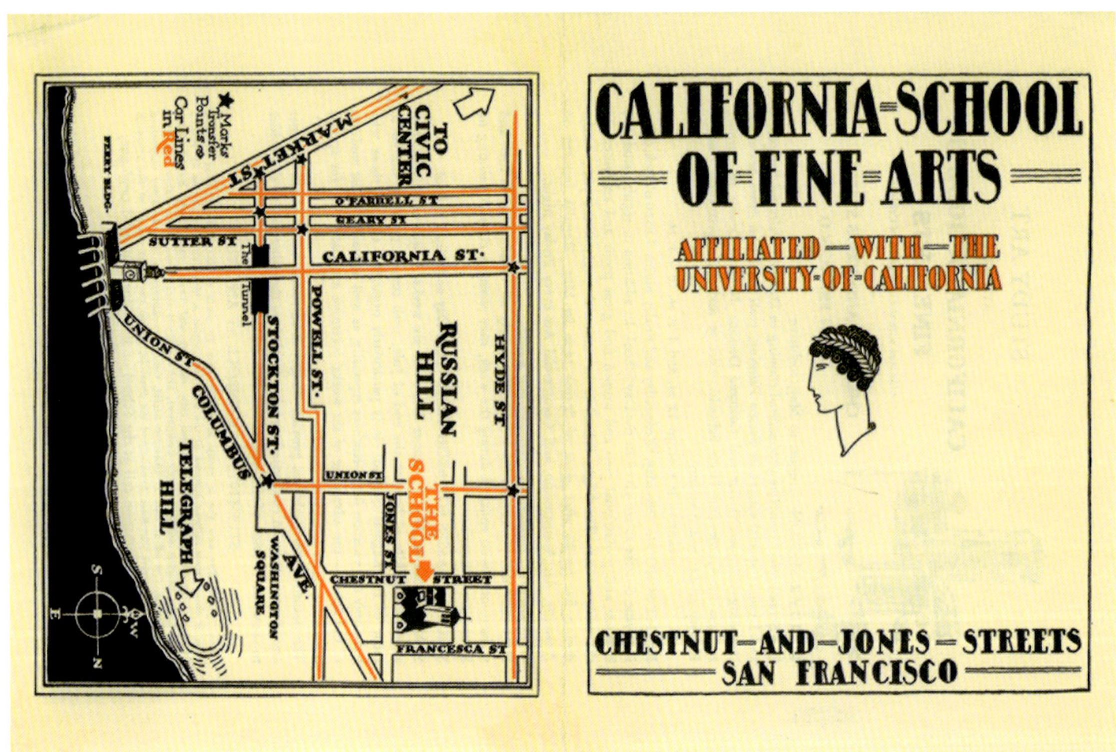


2.1

2.1

Map showing the location of the school on the back of a California School of Fine Arts flier, 1928. San Francisco Art Institute Legacy Foundation + Archive.

The San Francisco of Miki Hayakawa's 1935 painting *From My Window* is a peaceful one. Through the artist's open window we see the southern slope of Telegraph Hill, its buildings and rocky outcroppings gold and brown in the afternoon light (Plate 53). From here, the hustle and bustle of the city is nowhere to be found. Yet *From My Window* situates Hayakawa at the center of a time and place that must have been anything but quiet, pinpointing her location a handful of blocks south of the foot of Telegraph Hill, in the beehive of activity that was San Francisco's bohemian enclave. Here, just minutes from Italian North Beach, Chinatown, and Market Street's busy commercial district, San Francisco's artists lived and worked, in and around the "Montgomery Block," a hulking, four-story, city-block-sized building named for its 628 Montgomery Street location and nicknamed the "Monkey Block" for its rabble-rousing inhabitants.

*From My Window* suggests—and city directories of the time confirm—that Hayakawa painted here in San Francisco's "art colony," a tight-knit community heavily populated by her former classmates and instructors from the California School of Fine Arts (CSFA, later renamed the San Francisco Art Institute, now the San Francisco Art Institute Legacy Foundation), which was itself only a twenty-minute walk away (Fig. 2.1).[1] Just across the street, the sculpture studio and stone yard of CSFA instructor Ralph Stackpole was very much a center of activity—Henri Matisse attended a party in his honor there when he stopped briefly in San Francisco on his way to Tahiti in 1930, and famed Mexican muralist Diego Rivera stayed there while working on murals at the CSFA and the Pacific Stock Exchange building in 1930–31. CSFA painting instructor Otis Oldfield married his wife, Helen Clark—herself a painter and CSFA alumna—there in 1927. For the occasion they commandeered both the stone yard and the studio, which was at the time being rented out to CSFA instructor-to-be Dorothea Lange. The evening ceremony took place under an arch formed by two excavated ribs of a Gold Rush–era ship, illuminated by Chinese lanterns and bricks that had been soaked in kerosene and set on fire. Helen's tradition-defying dress was black, sewn from fabric that Oldfield's student Yun Gee had received in the mail from his mother in China, who had woven it herself as a wedding gift for her son's mentor.[2] In other words, it was a small world.

Yet this small world was an expansive one, one that drew in artists from around the globe, often for the purpose of studying at the CSFA. An announcement of the school's 1927 fall season in the *Argus*, a local "journal of art criticism"—which was itself published out of an office in the Monkey Block at the time—boasted of "pupils from practically every state in the Union, and from many foreign countries."[3] San Francisco was still a city of immigrants, one in which nearly three in ten residents were born outside of the United States,[4] and the art world still took its cues from Europe in general and Paris in particular. Nearly all the school's fine arts faculty had studied abroad, with Paris's leading art schools lending particular prestige to a résumé.

Within the context of this cosmopolitan community, language barriers were not seen as insurmountable. Italian sculptor Giovanni Portanova, "who couldn't speak a word of English," was nevertheless hired to fill in for Ralph Stackpole while Stackpole was overseas in 1921 and 1922.[5] Letters sent in the 1920s and 1930s by the school to U.S. consulates in support of accepted international students' visa applications stated explicitly that "knowledge of the English language is not considered necessary for a student of the fine arts."[6] International students had in fact been a constant presence at the school from the start, with the names of Japanese students in particular appearing in some of its earliest existing records. The school's founding, in 1874, had coincided with the post-isolationist period in Japan, a time that fostered cross-pollination between Japanese and Western artists. It took longer for Chinese names to appear in the roll books, but the large influx of Chinese immigrants who had arrived in California, many recruited as laborers to build the western portion of the transcontinental railroad, meant that Chinese artists certainly had an early presence in the city, and eventually in the art school as well.

It was within this energetic, tight-knit, yet cosmopolitan San Francisco arts community that Hayakawa, Hisako Hibi, and Miné Okubo all spent formative years, to varying degrees. Hayakawa and Hibi both studied at the CSFA, although Hayakawa did so much more extensively, attending classes every year from 1923 through 1929 (Fig. 2.2). Hibi started taking summer and evening classes in 1926, while still in high school, having moved to the United States from Japan with her family as a teenager. (These classes may have been a bright spot in a difficult time. Whereas in high school Hibi "did not know how to talk with teachers and [her] classmates" and could "only accept their orders," at the CSFA she experienced the "great joy" that it was to "carry a paint box for the first time" while wandering the hills of Marin County with Gottardo Piazzoni's landscape painting class.)[7] Hayakawa and Hibi both made important personal and professional connections at the CSFA, including with each other and with the men they would go on to marry, with Hayakawa marrying classmate Preston Elmer McCrossen years later, in 1947, and Hibi (Shimizu at the time) marrying Matsusaburo George Hibi in 1930 (Matsusaburo started out as a CSFA student and ended up becoming a staff member in the 1920s). While Okubo studied art across the bay at the University of California, Berkeley, she was certainly part of the same small Bay Area art scene, joining the San Francisco Art Association (SFAA) in 1937 and participating regularly in its exhibitions.

The SFAA was a major force in San Francisco's art world at the time. It was not only the founding and governing body of the CSFA but also an active association of working artists, and its highly anticipated annual exhibitions brought the CSFA together with the wider Bay Area arts community. Hayakawa, Hibi, and Okubo all exhibited repeatedly in the annuals, which were often held at the art museum run by the SFAA, first out of the Palace of Fine Arts—the only building of the 1915 Panama-Pacific International Exposition to be saved from demolition after the fair—and later out of a new veterans building downtown. The SFAA's active presence in the local art scene added to the sense of the CSFA as not just a school, but a community. CSFA students and faculty members sometimes pooled resources to help each other out of financial trouble, and the school offered financial assistance to students in need.[8] In a 1925 letter from CSFA director Eric Spencer Macky to then-student Hayakawa ("My Dear Miki") during her extended absence due to illness, Macky writes with obvious fondness and familiarity, telling Hayakawa that she "may be sure that [she has] been missed," and offering her an enclosed check "as a small mark of our appreciation of your loyal work for the School and help in many things" (Fig. 2.3).[9]

The school's curriculum was highly flexible, and Hayakawa, Hisako Hibi, and

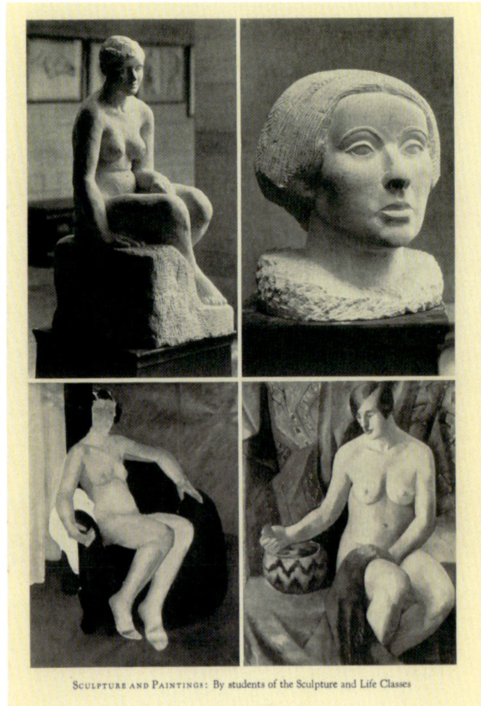


2.2

2.2

Spread from the California School of Fine Arts 1927–28 catalogue featuring student artwork. Hayakawa's painting of a seated female nude with pottery is in the bottom right-hand corner. San Francisco Art Institute Legacy Foundation + Archive.

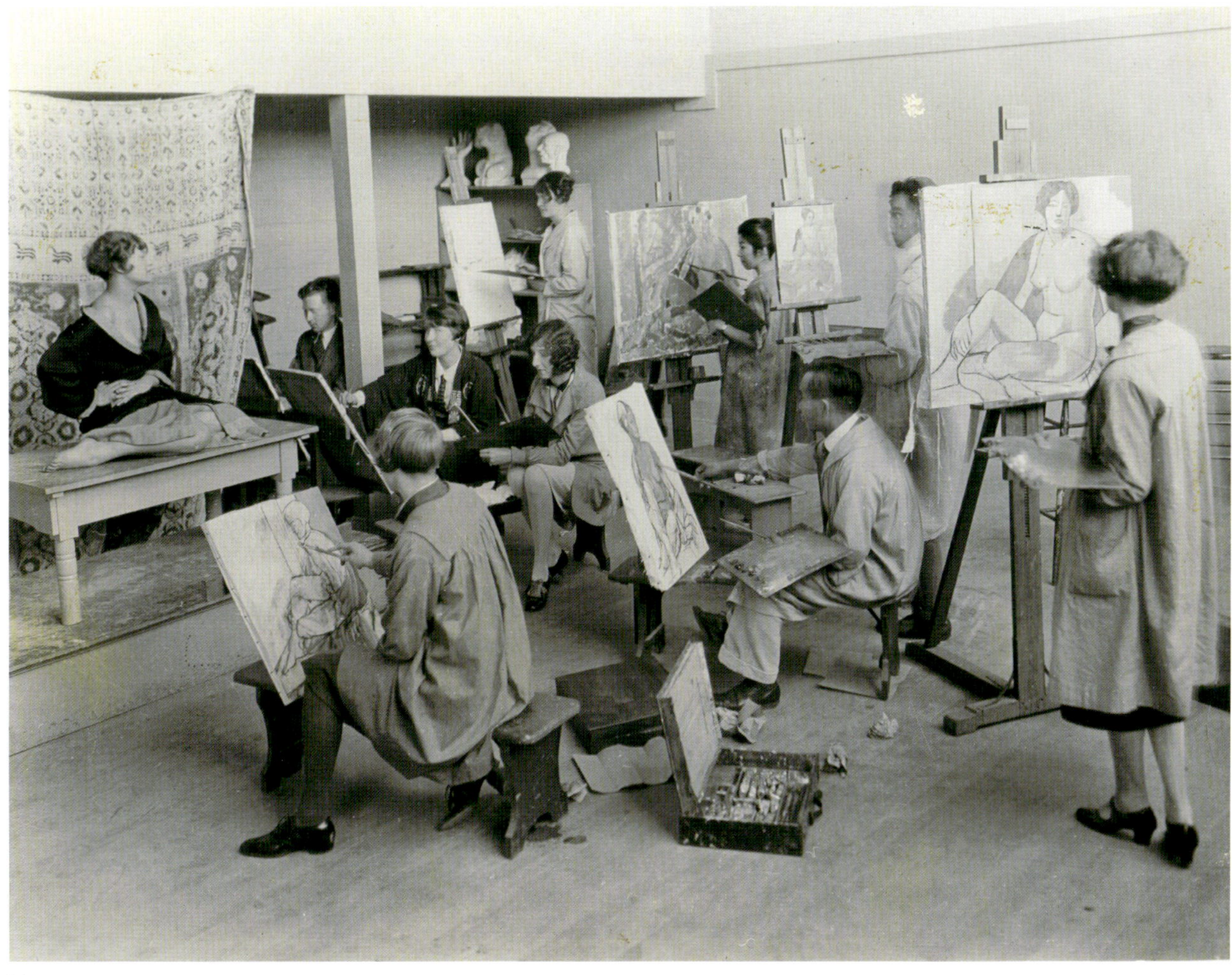

2.3

2.3

Photograph of a life painting class from the California School of Fine Arts 1927–28 catalogue. Hayakawa is the third standing painter from the right. San Francisco Art Institute Legacy Foundation + Archive.

Matsusaburo Hibi took advantage of this flexibility to determine their own course loads and durations of study, coming and going as they saw fit over the months and years of their time there. While it did offer a more structured, four-year "Normal Course" for students looking to earn teaching certification, for the "Fine Arts and professional courses of study" the school did not offer degrees nor impose any but the most minimal curricular requirements. No "examination or previous instruction" was required to enroll, and students could begin taking classes at any time.[10] This level of unstructured freedom gave it a reputation as a place for serious, self-directed, practicing artists.[11] Those who felt drawn to a particular faculty member could take that instructor's classes as often as they liked, sometimes forming strong mentor/mentee relationships. Oldfield's mentorship of Gee, for example, developed into a lifelong friendship. The two spent time camping and painting together in the Sierras, and Gee, on his last day in town before leaving for Paris in 1927, donned Oldfield's trademark outfit of a suit and beret pulled low over his forehead, accessorized with a cane and a pipe, in affectionate tribute to his mentor.[12]

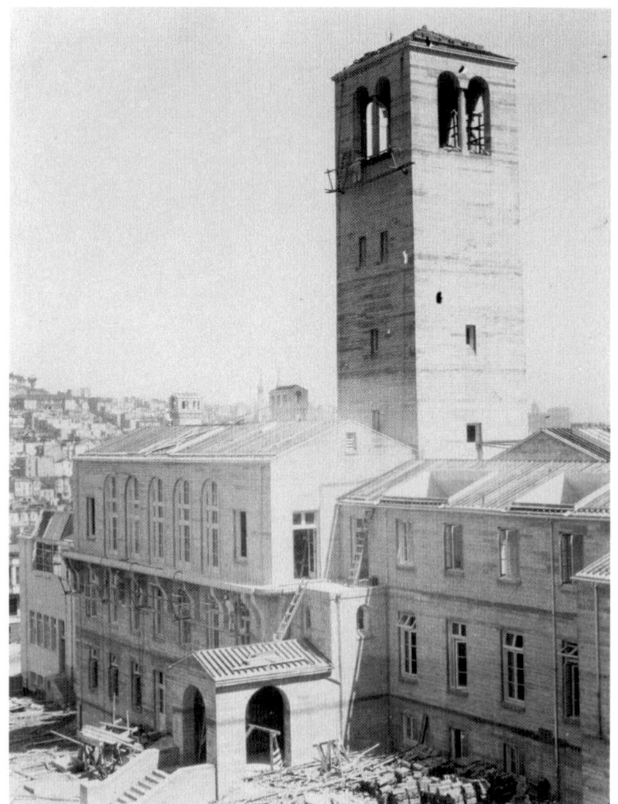

2.4

The CSFA's artists benefited from a San Francisco art scene that was coming into its own during the 1920s, when post–World War I enthusiasm and financial resources brought renewed energy to San Francisco's cultural institutions, as well as the Depression-era 1930s, as New Deal programs provided many artists with both a living wage and opportunities to create works of art for the city's schools, parks, and municipal buildings. With enrollment strong at the CSFA, the SFAA sold its Nob Hill property and used the proceeds to fund the construction of a new building on the northeastern slope of Russian Hill, just past North Beach (Fig. 2.4). The spacious new school, with its large, light-filled studios and gallery arranged around a picturesque central courtyard and tower, was a point of pride for the SFAA, one worthy, as its *Bulletin* newsletter was quick to point out, of Matisse's "hearty approbation" when he visited in 1930 and declared that he "had never seen such magnificent lighting and working conditions in Europe" (Fig. 2.5).[13]

For artists of Asian descent living and working in San Francisco, the 1920s and 1930s offered unprecedented opportunities for professional recognition within a receptive arts community, despite the larger context of widespread racism and progressively draconian anti-Asian/anti-immigrant laws. In 1924, the Johnson-Reed Act effectively halted immigration from Asia altogether while imposing strict numerical quotas on immigration from other parts of the world. While international students were still able to attend American universities on student visas, new application procedures were put in place for "non-quota immigrant students" and the schools that wanted to host them.[14] Nevertheless, artists of Asian descent were able to thrive in San Francisco, with their

2.4
The California School of Fine Arts building under construction in 1926. San Francisco Art Institute Legacy Foundation + Archive.

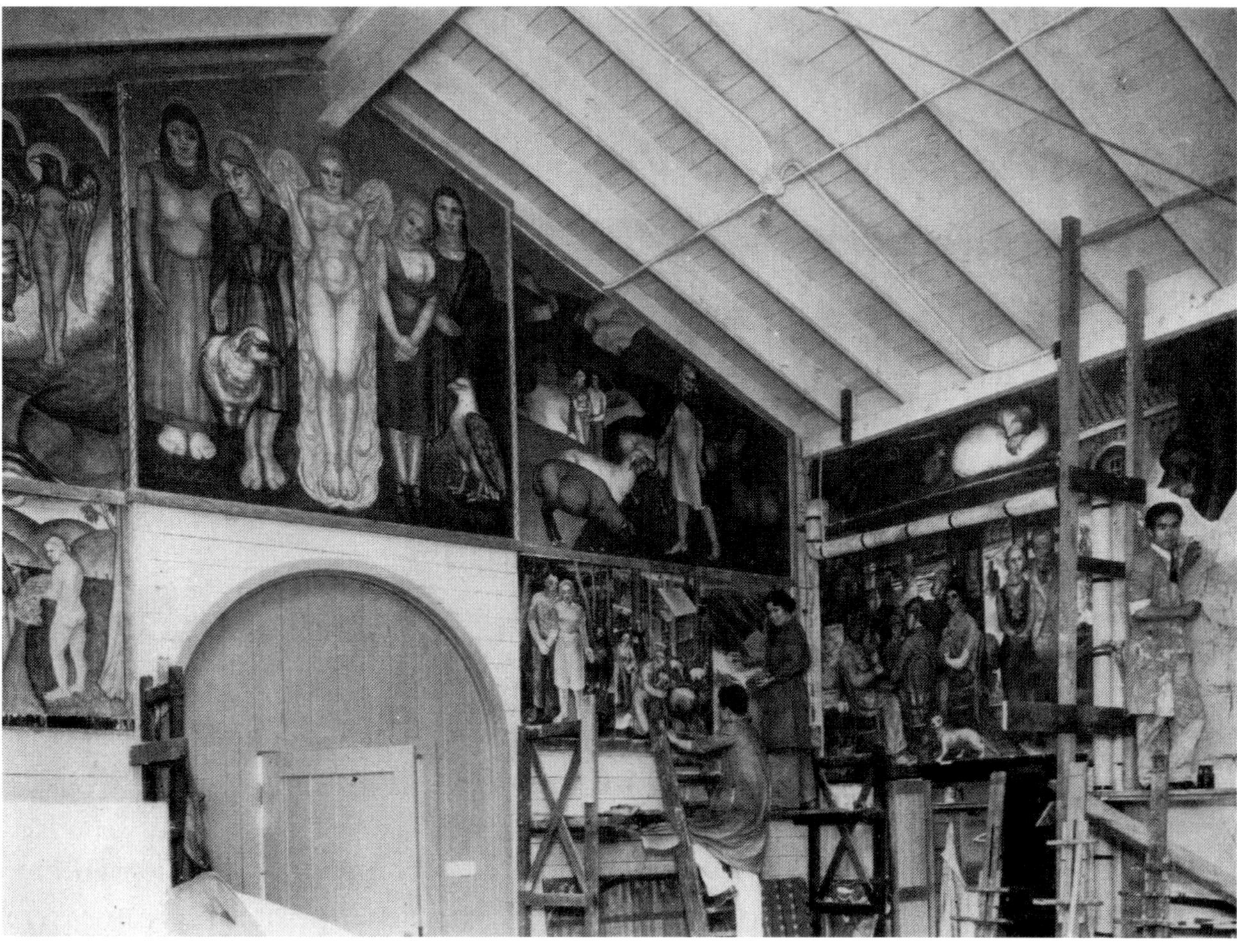

2.5

2.5

Photograph from the California School of Fine Arts 1931–32 catalogue of CSFA students at work in a classroom outfitted with removable wall panels for fresco painting. San Francisco Art Institute Legacy Foundation + Archive.

work exhibited and reviewed both by Chinese and Japanese cultural associations and venues and in the broader art scene.[15] They not only were well represented in group shows like the SFAA annuals but also were featured in solo exhibitions in the city's prominent galleries and museums. The California Palace of the Legion of Honor, for instance, staged solo exhibitions by Chiura Obata, Yoshida Sekido, Noboru Foujioka, Isami Doi, Isamu Noguchi, and Henry Sugimoto, all between 1931 and 1933.[16]

As the 1930s came to a close, the Golden Gate International Exposition on San Francisco's Treasure Island provided an opportunity for local artists to see their work featured on a world stage. In its second year, an "Art in Action" attraction was added, which showcased artists at work in real time, including Diego Rivera, who climbed scaffolding each day to complete an enormous fresco on ten large panels as visitors looked on from below, and Okubo, who demonstrated fresco painting techniques nearby. The fair's theme, "Pageant of the Pacific," celebrated the interconnected arts and cultures of the Pacific Rim. Hibi, Hayakawa, and Okubo all showed paintings at the fair, alongside a long list of CSFA-affiliated artists.

Yet within just three years this vibrant, inclusive art scene would be all but dismantled. The CSFA's enrollment would fall by half between 1941 and 1942 alone, as the country's entry into World War II sent its young adults into military service or to factories. The empty classrooms of the school's east wing would be repurposed as a blood bank by the Red Cross.[17] In 1942, the lives of the Japanese Americans of California would be upended and permanently reshaped by President Franklin D. Roosevelt's Executive Order 9066. A year later, the cover of the catalogue for the Annual Exhibition of Drawings and Prints of the San Francisco Art Association would feature a drawing by Okubo titled *On Watch* (1943; Plate 28), depicting two armed guards in long coats stationed in the hills above the Topaz War Relocation Center, where Okubo and the Hibis were imprisoned. By placing this drawing on the cover, the SFAA made Okubo's work the representative image of an annual event that itself had come to be representative of the Bay Area arts community. The San Francisco artists seem to be saying to Okubo, *You are still one of us*. Yet for Okubo and the Hibis, surrounded by barbed wire and surveilled by armed guards in a camp seven hundred miles away, in a practical sense this was simply not the case. The acceptance of a community of fellow artists was meaningful, but it could only go so far.

An ongoing discussion within the arts community of 1920s–30s San Francisco was one of regional artistic identity. What did it mean to be an American artist, or a Californian artist? How could artists move beyond the "obedient repetition of European formulas," as artist Maynard Dixon put it in a 1927 issue of the *Argus*, to create a "vital American Art" from "forms that are our own"? The mass incarceration of Japanese Americans sheds a different light on this line of inquiry. Who is included in Dixon's "our," and who is excluded? Executive Order 9066 provided one answer to that question. Through their work and active engagement in the artistic communities with which they surrounded themselves throughout their careers, Miki Hayakawa, Hisako Hibi, and Miné Okubo gave a better one. Far from the East Coast's artistic centers and even farther from Europe, Californian artists were creating something new out of the unique amalgamation of cultural forces that made up the West Coast, shaped in no small part by the vitality of its Asian immigrant communities. By exploring their full artistic trajectories, including their prewar creative development during this rich yet under-studied interwar period in San Francisco, *Pictures of Belonging* helps us see how these artists were beginning to answer Dixon's question even as he asked it.

Becky Alexander is an archivist at the San Francisco Art Institute Legacy Foundation + Archive.

NOTES

1 The 1931, 1932, and 1934 editions of *Polk's Crocker-Langley San Francisco City Directory* include Hayakawa's name and address (one in the Monkey Block and one in a nearby building) alongside many of her fellow Montgomery Street denizens under the heading "Artists," in a section of the directory organized by profession.

2 Helen Oldfield, "Helen Oldfield: Otis Oldfield and the SF Art Community, 1920s–1960s," interview by Ruth Cravath and Michaela DuCasse, 1981, Oral History Center, Bancroft Library, University of California, Berkeley.

3 "Here and There," *Argus* 1, no. 6 (September 1927): 4.

4 Campbell Gibson and Kay Jung, "Historical Census Statistics on the Foreign-Born Population of the United States: 1850 to 2000" (U.S. Census Bureau, Population Division Working Paper No. 81, February 2006).

5 Ruth Cravath, "Oral History Interview with Ruth Cravath," by Mary McChesney, September 2, 1965, Archives of American Art, Smithsonian Institution.

6 1924–35 Immigrant Students Correspondence, San Francisco Art Institute Legacy Foundation + Archive. The school's early Asian students often faced extreme racism in San Francisco. In his 1910 memoir *A Japanese Artist in London*, Yoshio Markino, who came to study at the school in 1893, describes being spit on, pelted with pebbles and bricks in the street, and snubbed in public by a fellow art student (London: Chatto & Windus, 1910), 6.

7 Hisako Hibi, *Peaceful Painter: Memoirs of an Issei Woman Artist*, ed. Ibuki Hibi Lee (Berkeley: Heyday Books, 2004), 6.

8 This atmosphere of mutual aid is a theme shared by various oral histories with students and faculty of the time. Otis Oldfield, describing the help he and others gave to German and Russian art students, said, "That was the old school, you see, and of course, maybe it's not a profitable way to do [it]. Maybe you don't build up a school, but that was the way it . . . worked there." "Oral History Interview with Otis Oldfield," by Lewis Ferbranché, May 21, 1965, Archives of American Art, Smithsonian Institution.

9 Miki Hayakawa, Artist's File, San Francisco Art Institute Legacy Foundation + Archive.

10 College Catalog Collection, San Francisco Art Institute Legacy Foundation + Archive.

11 While some, like Helen Oldfield, were attracted to the CSFA specifically for the freedom it offered, others saw downsides. Sculptor Ruth Cravath came to the CSFA from the School of the Art Institute of Chicago and appreciated the latter's more structured curriculum, despite the fact that drawing, painting, and design requirements precluded her from taking sculpture altogether in the program's first year. Ruth Cravath and Dorothy Wagner Puccinelli Cravath, "Two San Francisco Artists and Their Contemporaries, 1920–1975," transcript of a series of oral history interviews conducted by Ruth Teiser and Catherine Harroun, Regional Oral History Office, Bancroft Library, University of California, Berkeley, 1974–75, 11.

12 Oldfield, "Helen Oldfield: Otis Oldfield and the SF Art Community."

13 "Personal," *San Francisco Art Association Bulletin* 1, no. 1 (April 1930).

14 The CSFA's ability to navigate this system was aided by its affiliation with the University of California, which applied and received approval for UC schools to serve as host institutions within months of the law's enactment. 1924–35 Immigrant Students Correspondence, San Francisco Art Institute Legacy Foundation + Archive.

15 Cultural associations and venues included the East West Art Society, founded by Matsusaburo Hibi and Chiura Obata in 1921 with a mission of cross-cultural pollination; CSFA student Yun Gee's Chinese Revolutionary Artists' Club; and the CSFA student–founded Chinese Art Club of California, later ambitiously renamed the Chinese Art Association of America. In addition, the Kinmon Gakuen (Golden Gate Institute), a Japanese community center, put on various large-scale exhibitions during this time, including a 1927 show of fifty-two panels of CSFA alumnus Henry Kiyama's cartoons (later compiled and published as a groundbreaking work of autobiographical manga) and Miki Hayakawa's solo exhibition in 1929. See ShiPu Wang, *The Other American Moderns: Matsura, Ishigaki, Noda, Hayakawa* (University Park: Penn State University Press, 2017); and Mark Dean Johnson, "Uncovering Asian American Art in San Francisco, 1850–1940," in *Asian American Art: A History, 1850–1970*, ed. Gordon H. Chang, Mark Dean Johnson, and Paul J. Karlstrom (Stanford, Calif.: Stanford University Press, 2008), for more on these and other venues and associations. For more on the Chinese Revolutionary Artists' Club, see Anthony Lee, *Yun Gee: Poetry, Writings, Art, Memories* (Seattle: University of Washington Press, 2003).

16 Johnson, "Uncovering Asian American Art," 15.

17 *San Francisco Art Association Bulletin* (November 1942): 1.

ShiPu Wang

# Faces of Belonging

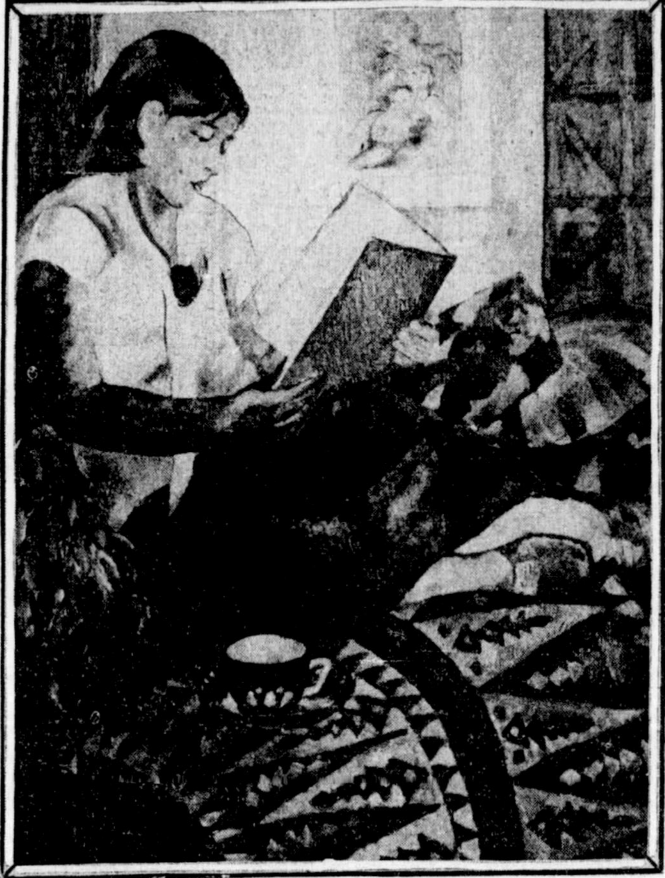

**By Miki Hayakawa**

*"READING POSE of Miss Shimizu," painting by Miki Hayakawa, Japanese girl artist. This picture was purchased by General Consul of Japan, Morizo Ida, at the exhibition ow being held by the artist.*

3.1

3.1
Miki Hayakawa's *Reading Pose of Miss Shimizu* (n.d.) reproduced in Gobind Behari Lal's *San Francisco Examiner* review, 1929.

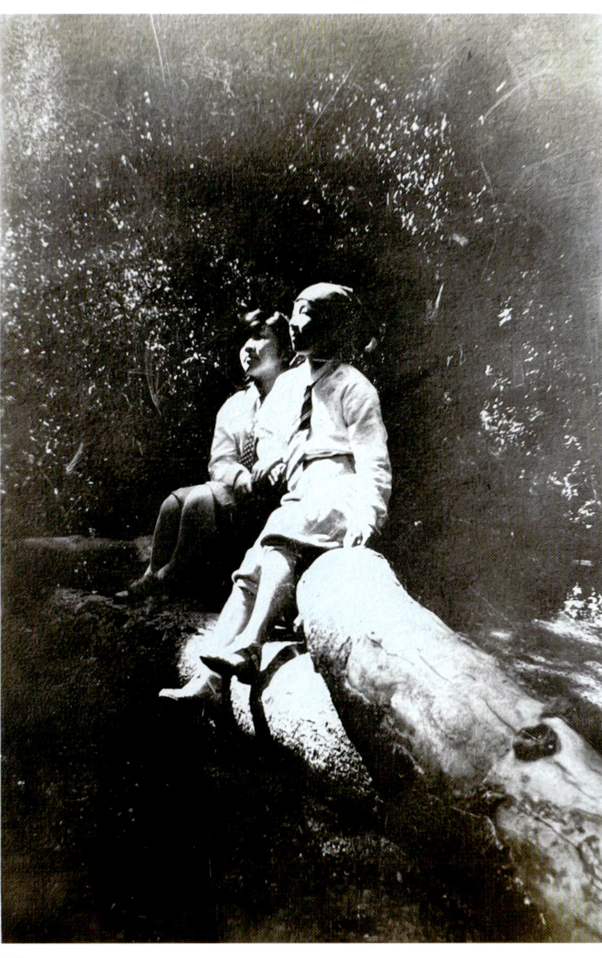

3.2

3.2
Miki Hayakawa (front) and Hisako Shimizu (Hibi) at California's Muir Woods National Monument, ca. 1927–28. Photo by Matsusaburo George Hibi. Courtesy of the Hibi Estate.

Gobind Behari Lal's review of Miki Hayakawa's 1929 exhibition in the *San Francisco Examiner* contains a treasure that I admittedly missed when I first encountered the clipping a decade ago.[1] Illustrating the review is a reproduction of Hayakawa's painting *Reading Pose of Miss Shimizu* (n.d.), of a young woman in a richly filled interior (Fig. 3.1). It dawned on me, when I began curating *Pictures of Belonging*, that this "Miss Shimizu" was none other than Hisako Hibi, whose last name was indeed Shimizu before she married Matsusaburo George Hibi in 1930. This turns out to be a rare painterly record of the friendship between Miki and Hisako from their pre–World War II days—"rare" because there appears to be a curious absence of Hayakawa from the Hibis' otherwise extensive archives, save for a few precious photographs from the late 1920s (Fig. 3.2). Incidentally, Matsusaburo had also painted a portrait simply titled *Miki*, which was among the five works he submitted to the Forty-Seventh Annual Exhibition of the San Francisco Art Association (SFAA) in 1924; that, along with Hayakawa's portrait of Hisako, has not been rediscovered.[2]

The Shimizu portrait, singled out from some 150 works, served additional functions other than illustrating the review. It is reasonable to argue that the newspaper's choice to reproduce this particular painting had a geopolitical consideration. As the image's caption notes, the consul general of Japan purchased the work, and the acquisition was newsworthy because it happened during a period of fraught international and racial relations. The landmark Immigration Act of 1924 (Johnson-Reed Act), which in effect stopped all immigration from Asia and prevented Asian immigrants from becoming naturalized U.S. citizens, had been in place for five years by then. The Japanese consul's acquisition of a Japanese citizen's portrait of another Japanese citizen, both living in the United States, from an exhibition at a Japanese school in San Francisco, could be interpreted as a gesture of solidarity with Japan's diasporic communities.[3]

Furthermore, the portrait served to illustrate Lal's multicultural proclamation of San Francisco as a place where "the East and the West will meet and pool their talents and begin new creative romances in cultural history." By calling Hayakawa's exhibition an excellent example of "the full blossom of the Occidental art of painting," Lal (an immigrant reporter from India) repudiated xenophobic views toward Asians by exalting the perceived assimilationist virtues in Hayakawa's artistic accomplishments. In other words, Lal viewed 1920s San Francisco as an incubator for immigrant and female artists like Hayakawa to pursue their art education and flourish, even against an exclusionary backdrop that Lal did not acknowledge in his review.[4]

Hayakawa's *Miss Shimizu* and other portraits that her fellow diasporic artists created point to the multivalent and distinct role that portraiture played for immigrants and racioethnic minorities. Many of these portraits would not be regarded as "honorific" in the traditional sense, for they differ from imagery of canonical figures that art history and institutions have amply preserved and celebrated—for example, the many portraits of politicians or royal and aristocratic figures from the Renaissance through the Gilded Age and into the modern era. Identity—who those sitters are—is critical to understanding the significance and value of such honorific portraits, for many of them were created to valorize, if not flatter, a certain echelon of American society, contributing, in turn, to a visual history of the privileged.[5]

In contrast, portraits created by Hayakawa and her fellow émigré artists are visual representations of their moments of intense connection with people they encountered. This kind of portraiture allows minority artists (in terms of race and gender) to use visual means to affirm their place in a society that, by and large, relegates them to the margins vis-à-vis legal, social, or even artistic status. After all, painting a portrait is an immersive and intimate experience: one must engage with another person through attentive observation and analysis. Artists then have to translate their understanding of another human being into visual forms, and such translation requires internalization, an empathetic convergence of self and other through an eye-mind-hand connection. For diasporic artists, creating portraits, including self-portraits (Plates 40 and 24), enables them to, in effect, capture that deep engagement with another person, memorialize their relationship and shared experience, render their own existence visible, and, most crucially, affirm a sense of belonging for both the model and the artist.

Hayakawa, Hibi, and Okubo all produced many portraits and figurative paintings, with Hibi focusing more on landscape paintings throughout her life. As the oldest and the earliest to make a name for herself, Hayakawa showed a sustained passion for portraiture in her three-decade-long career. My review of Hayakawa's attendance records at the California School of Fine Arts (CSFA, later renamed the San Francisco Art Institute, now the San Francisco Art Institute Legacy Foundation) between June 1923 and May 1927 shows, for instance, her dedication to taking almost exclusively portrait and life/figure classes taught by Constance Macky and Eric Spencer Macky, Gertrude Partington Albright, and Lee Randolph—renowned artists and teachers in interwar San Francisco. Hayakawa's work earned top marks from her instructors, based on the school's grade books, and was featured in the school's catalogues, including a charcoal figure sketch in the 1924–25 season and a female nude in the 1927–28 season (Plate 5 and Fig. 2.2).[6]

Hayakawa's extant portraits enable us to chart her journeys and relationships in divergent communities in the absence of archival records.[7] And she approached her models of different stripes with equal care and empathy. Leaving visible her deliberate brushwork and interweaving colors, the artist imbues her paintings with a sense of fluidity that enables the viewer to see the models' energy pulsating on the surface of the canvas. It is as if Hayakawa were trying to deploy an intricate play of tonality and shapes that reveals, or at least

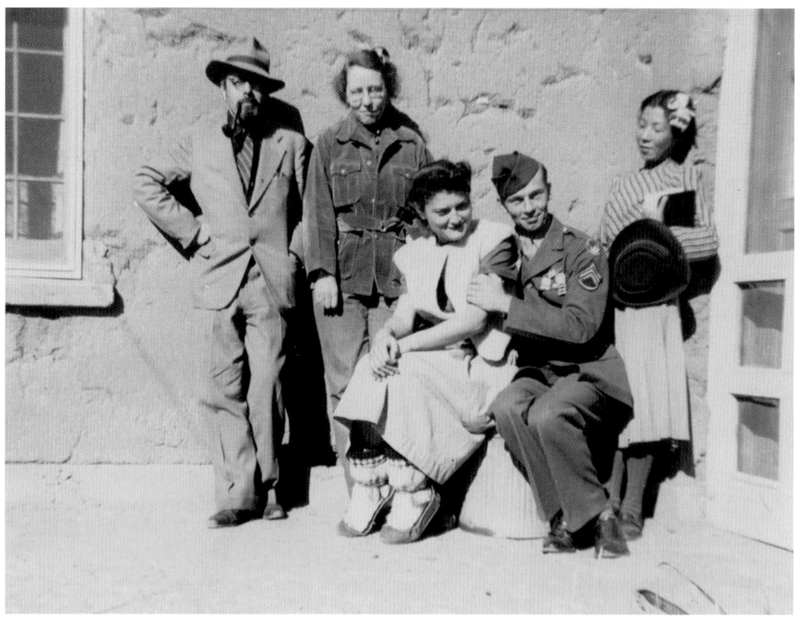

3.3

3.3

Alfred and Dorothy Morang, Mary Hunsaker and friend, and Miki Hayakawa, November 1943. Courtesy of Shirley and David Astilli, Santa Fe, New Mexico.

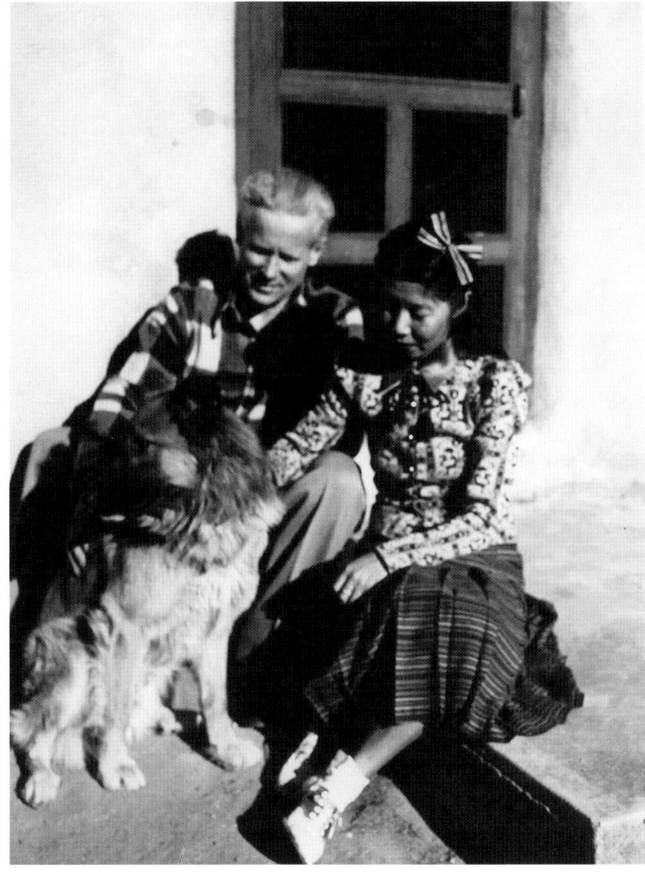

3.4

3.4
Miki Hayakawa and Preston Elmer McCrossen in Santa Fe, New Mexico, ca. 1940s. Courtesy of Shirley and David Astilli, Santa Fe, New Mexico.

suggests, the inner qualities of her sitters. Her *Portrait of a Negro* (1926; Plate 1), for example, uses patches of colors to build up a face with reflective skin and glinting eyes. The man depicted exudes vitality and intensity from within. The portrait's luminous quality is also evident in *Portrait of a Young Man* (ca. 1930s; Plate 11), *Boy in Striped Shirt* (ca. 1953; Plate 47), *Brown Eyes* (ca. 1940s; Plate 22), and a portrait of her friend Bill Ford (1946; Plate 43), among others. These works show Hayakawa's genuine interest in not only studying the human form in a meticulously painterly way, but also leveraging portraiture to make deep connections with members of various communities (Fig. 3.3).

Created in two places and two decades apart, *Portrait of a Negro* and *Portrait of Bill Ford* illustrate the diverse communities that Hayakawa built for herself, as well as her effort in pursuing new painterly techniques and expressions. In the earlier portrait, saturated and graduated color planes build forms and give the body volume and musculature. The later work adopts feathery, interweaving brushwork to endow Ford with a soft, almost ethereal quality. The former, made when Hayakawa was a student, suggests a more analytical approach, which shifted toward a looser construction of the human form in the latter, with both exhibiting Hayakawa's signature layering of undertones to illuminate the nuance and diversity of human complexions. Furthermore, *Portrait of a Negro* pairs with Yun Gee's *Artist Studio* (1926; Plate 2) to highlight the artistic dialogue and multi-ethnic milieu of San Francisco in 1926, while *Portrait of Bill Ford* can be regarded as the companion piece to Ford's portrait of Hayakawa, pointing to the home that Hayakawa was able to find despite wartime displacement and challenges.[8]

Some of Hayakawa's portraits also offer tantalizing glimpses of the artist's relationships, such as her portraits of the same man in the 1930s. Larger in scale among her extant canvases, *One Afternoon* (ca. 1935; Plate 12) is more than a portrait or an interior scene; it depicts an experience, albeit an emotionally ambiguous one. Warm, soft hues blanket the stillness of a private moment. Hayakawa's careful variation of values and edges conveys the physicality of the figure. Yet the artist's intricate brushwork, along with a generous use of foreshortening that brings everything up to the picture plane, gives the scene an ethereal quality, as if everything slightly hovers in space. Her delicate, interweaving brushstrokes imbue the scene with multilayered, shimmering tones, from the bowl of fruits and the prone man to the woodstove and the pot of calla lilies in full bloom, whose outstretched green leaves, white spathes, and yellow spadices punctuate the room's quietness with animated gesticulation.

Tonally luscious and texturally alluring, *One Afternoon* is nevertheless enigmatic due to its deceptive straightforwardness and mixed messages. It is compositionally open while appearing to be closed off in its depiction of the subject's interiority.

For as rich and inviting as the painting appears, the man's obscured face and prone body refuse the viewer access to his facial features or expressions. The image is thus simultaneously intimate and distant, accessible yet inscrutable.

The male model in *One Afternoon* appears in several portraits and was said to have been "Edward," the artist's companion at the time.[9] Yet Hayakawa chose to depict this subject of affection absorbed in his own world, as seen in *Worker (Boy Sawing)* (ca. 1936; Plate 13), her portrait of a ukulele player (ca. 1934–36; Plate 10), and *Music* (ca. 1934).[10] Depicted in various states of concentration, the man exhibits a kind of disengagement from the viewer and, by implication, the artist, and thus resists any easy reading of the artist-model relationship. The consistent inscrutability of the same male figure also marks a curious phase in Hayakawa's oeuvre, which is full of open and engaging portraits.

The emotionally private *One Afternoon* turned out to be Hayakawa's most public work, however—one that she was apparently proud to exhibit on multiple occasions. In addition to the landmark opening exhibition of the San Francisco Museum of Art in 1935, she sent it to the Los Angeles Museum of Art's and the Santa Cruz Art League's exhibitions in 1937. Hayakawa kept *One Afternoon* with her even as she was forced to leave California in 1942, and she prominently displayed it at the Museum of New Mexico in 1944 (see Fig. 1.3)—the museum was gifted the painting by the artist Preston Elmer McCrossen, her husband since 1947, after she passed away in 1953 (Fig. 3.4).[11]

One can also see an emotionally charged portrait of an intimate partner in a painting by Hisako Hibi (Hayakawa's "Miss Shimizu") that was created under very different circumstances. In *As Usual . . . Still Hanging* (New York, August 1947; Plate 42), Hibi depicts a large coat and small hat hanging behind a door. The image appears unremarkable at first glance, like a painter's sketch of everyday objects. The quick brushstrokes and a few untouched areas give the canvas an unfinished quality, perhaps hinting at something amiss.

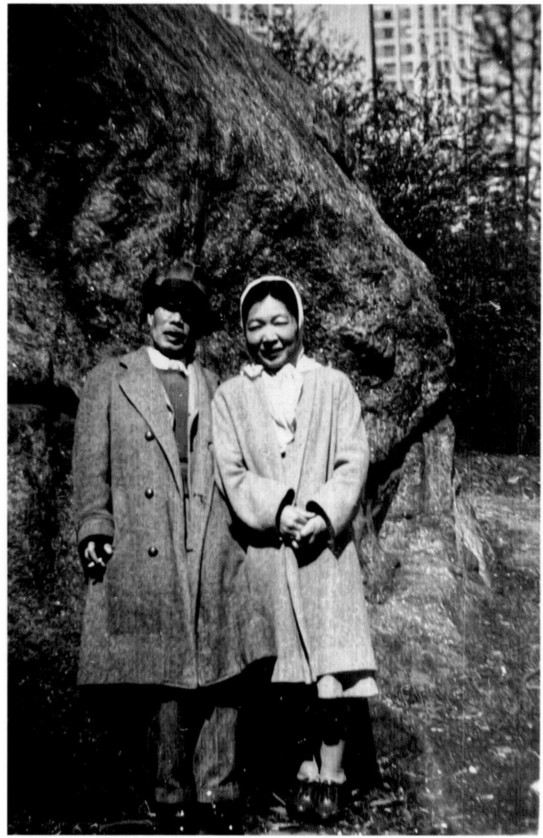

3.5

This, indeed, is more than a still life. Hibi's title refers to the personal objects of her husband of seventeen years, Matsusaburo George Hibi, who died of cancer on June 30, 1947—barely two years after the Hibi family was released from Topaz and moved to New York City. Hibi painted her husband's hat and coat hanging behind the door, less than two months after his passing, as if he could at any moment reappear to use them. The faint wash in the phantasmal background only reinforces a wistful (and perhaps wishful) depiction of an empty shell—a memorial of what remains and of that which is lost (Fig. 3.5).

Hibi created a loving portrait of her deceased husband by letting those objects stand in for the body and convey a sense of intimacy. Imagine, for example, the smells of Matsusaburo lingering on the clothes, among other sensorial memories

3.5

Hisako Hibi and Matsusaburo George Hibi (wearing the same coat and hat) in New York City's Central Park, ca. 1946–47. Courtesy of the Hibi Estate.

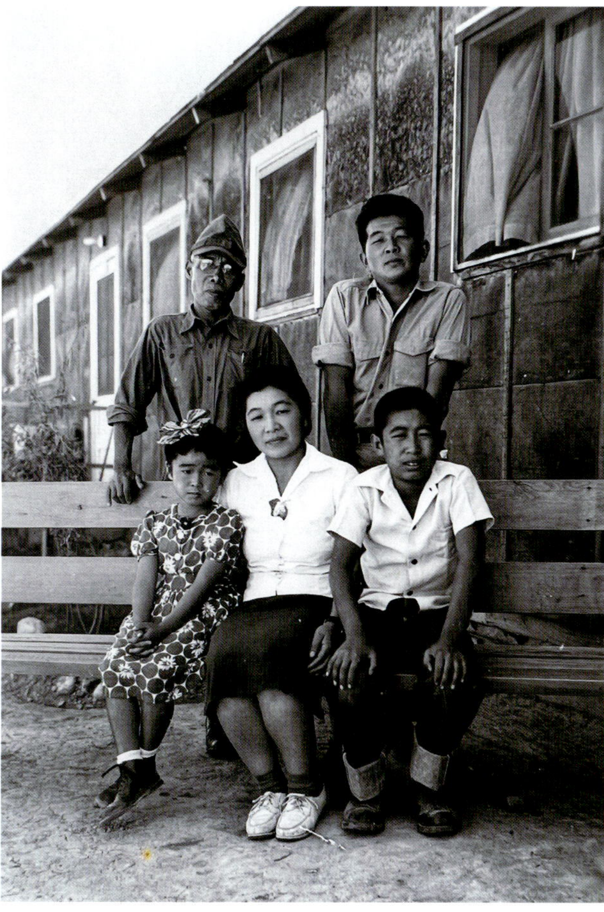

3.6

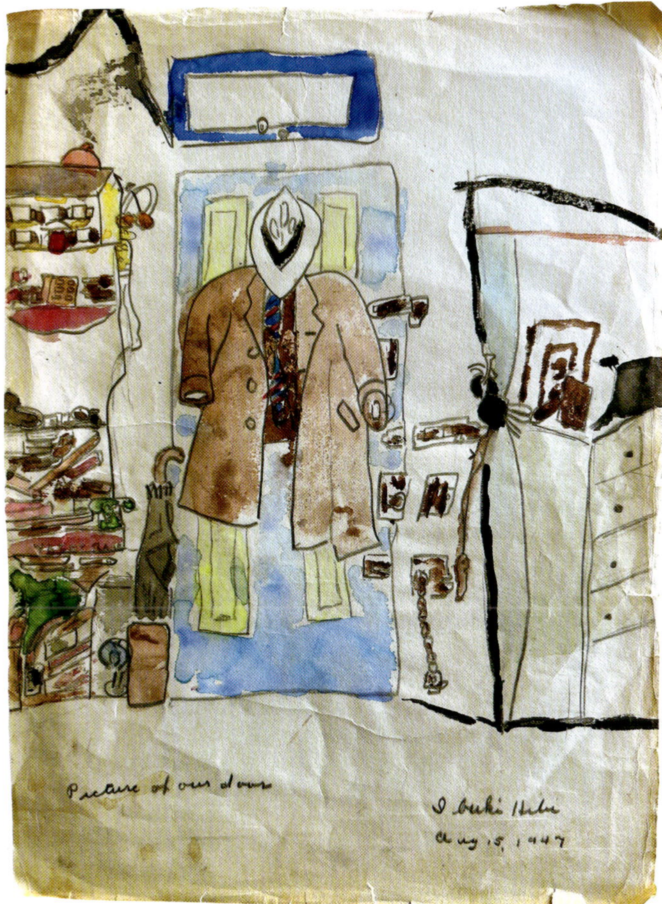


3.7

3.6

The Hibi family at Topaz: Hisako (front/center) flanked by daughter Ibuki and son Satoshi; Matsusaburo with glasses in the back, next to Hisako's brother, Hisao Shimizu, ca. 1945. Courtesy of the Hibi Estate.

3.7

IbukI HIbI, *PIcture of Our Door*, August 15, 1947. Watercolor on paper, 10 × 8 in. Courtesy of the Hibi Estate.

associated with him, which could elicit reactions as visceral as seeing his likeness. By capturing the hat and coat, Hibi in effect memorialized and preserved her husband's presence in physical paints. And the painting also stands as a poignant companion piece to Matsusaburo's portrait of Hisako (Plate 41) painted only three years prior at Topaz. The Hibis never stopped making art, even as they lived under difficult circumstances. Matsusaburo later became the director of the Topaz Art School, after its founder, his good friend Chiura Obata, was discharged from the camp in 1943, and oversaw an art program that provided hundreds of incarcerees with technical training and a vital source of emotional outlet and moral uplift. Hisako helped and taught at the school as well, drawing on her art training at the CSFA, where she had met Matsusaburo.[12]

Considering the challenging environment of the incarceration camp and her responsibility of caring for two children, Hisako Hibi was determinedly prolific (Fig. 3.6). Her more than one hundred paintings and drawings made while incarcerated depict subjects as diverse as family members and fellow incarcerees (Plates 37–39), the punishing climate in the desert and spectacular views of the sky (Plates 62 and 66), and daily activities and everyday objects (Plates 35, 36, and 70). As Kristine Kim, curator of the Hibi retrospective in 1999, reminded us, the produce and other items depicted in Hibi's paintings were in many cases cultivated by imprisoned Japanese Americans, who grew life out of nothingness in an inhospitable land.[13] In this context, her imagery can be understood as collective portraits of community, displacement, and *gaman*—a Japanese term conveying perseverance, patience, and an acceptance of the reality of the moment.

Hibi's *As Usual . . . Still Hanging* could be understood in a similar vein, for her image of everyday objects takes on the character of an emotional portrait because the objects were intimately connected to her husband. The straightforward, seemingly unsentimental depiction—which is also evident in her ten-year-old daughter Ibuki's painting that gives us a broader view (Fig. 3.7)—belies what Hisako must have experienced, having survived the wartime trauma and regained freedom to build a new life in a faraway city, only to be confronted by the devastating loss and the crushing responsibility of raising children as a widow in the overwhelming metropolis of New York (Plates 75 and 76). The painting marked the beginning of Hibi's more than decade-long "gray painting period," as she called it, before her art blossomed into a rich repertoire of striking colors, fluid movement, and vibrant imagination (Plates 93, 102, and 103).

In *Mother and Cat (Miyo and Cat)* (1941; Plate 23), Miné Okubo similarly deployed portraiture to memorialize a loved one without emphasizing likeness and realism. Made after Okubo's mother, Miyo, passed away in 1940, the painting depicts a plain-clothed, seated Miyo, whose blocky figure and simplified face give her a kind of sculptural monumentality—Okubo's visible, vertical brushstrokes seemingly simulate traces of carving of wood or stone. The forced perspective of the uptilted bench is more severe on her end than that on which the curious cat sits. Everything else is pushed toward the picture plane, such as the trees and the road that leads to the white barn houses on the hills. The overall flatness reflects Okubo's interest at the time in the painterly techniques of Mexican muralists and early Renaissance frescoes (think Piero della Francesca), as seen in *Portrait Study* (ca. 1937; Plate 16), *Grocer Weighing Produce* (1940; Plate 19), and *Untitled (Mother and Boy)* (1939; Plate 20).

The choice to create an iconography of commemoration, instead of focusing on mimesis or realism, enabled Okubo to produce a portrait that is rooted in real life but offers broader symbolism. The Bible in Miyo's hand references, perhaps, the Union Church to which she and her husband belonged in Riverside, California, and, as such, brings into the picture her Issei father, Tametsugu Okubo, whose

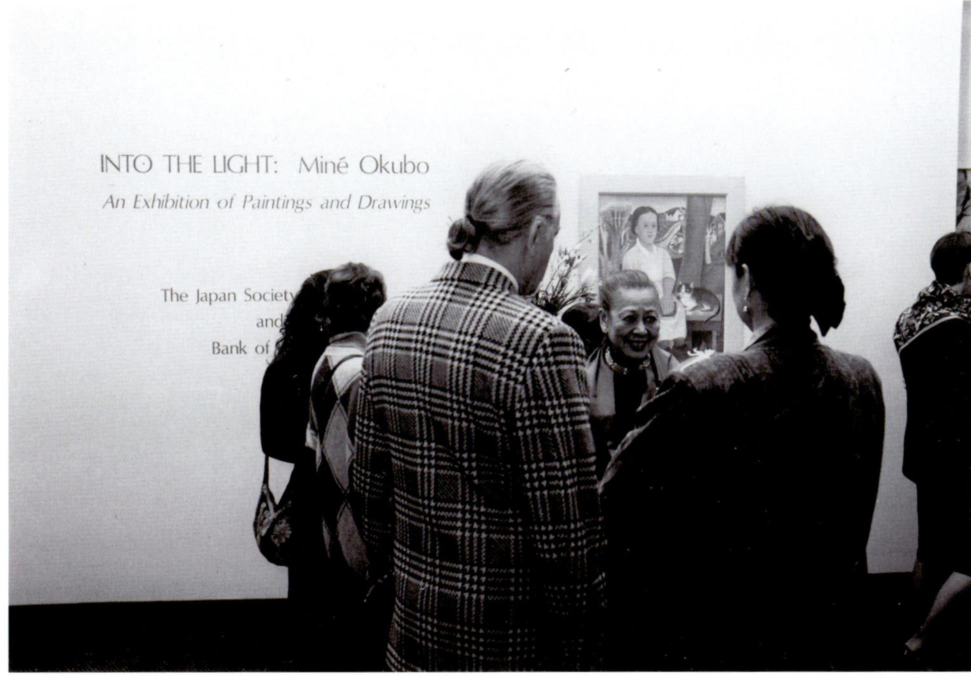


3.8

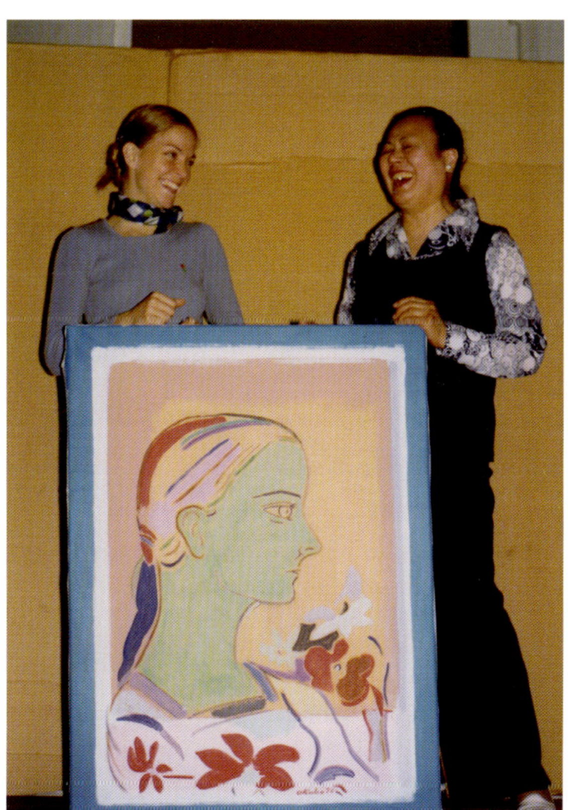

3.9

3.8

Miné Okubo at the reception for her retrospective *Into the Light*, sponsored by the Japan Society of Boston, 1993. The Miné Okubo Collection, Center for Social Justice & Civil Liberties, Riverside Community College District, California, 89-3-50.

3.9

Miné Okubo with Kristine Elliott Schwabacher and her portrait, 1976. The Miné Okubo Collection, Center for Social Justice & Civil Liberties, Riverside Community College District, California, a3 p13-1.

active role in the community would later lead to his undue imprisonment at the Justice Department–run Fort Missoula detention center in Montana after Pearl Harbor. The idyllic background, supported and protected by solid trees, reinforces the central importance of the mother figure, whose sculptural form and features render her an unwavering, statuesque presence that presides over and in effect guards the entire community. And the cat by Miyo's side seems to take on anthropomorphic features and becomes another figure in the picture (community), as its big, knowing eyes engage the viewer and beckon their attention. Cats would indeed become a motif throughout Okubo's oeuvre and a main character in many of her visual narratives and portraiture.

Like Hayakawa's *One Afternoon*, Okubo's *Miyo and Cat*, an intimate portrait, became one of her most public works almost as soon as it was created. She sent it to the SFAA's Sixty-First Annual Exhibition in 1941 and won its Anne Bremer Memorial Prize. It appeared on the cover of the Oakland Museum's pamphlet for Okubo's first retrospective, in 1972,[14] and the painting was acquired by the museum in the same year. The Japan Society of Boston also displayed the painting on the title wall of its Okubo exhibition in 1993 (Fig. 3.8). Being an artist who exercised meticulous control over how her art should be seen and received, Okubo likely had a say in the decision to feature her mother's portrait in a prominent way, further reinforcing the work's significance in the artist's oeuvre.

Even as Okubo's art shifted toward simplification and total abstraction, she continued to produce a prodigious number of figure-based paintings. More than straightforward portraits, her imagery of real and imaginary figures served as her means of connecting with people in her life and, in many cases, as motifs through which to reiterate and reinvent her colorful vision of this world. Okubo's recurring models included her longtime supporters Roy Leeper and Gaylord Hall, whose papers were donated to the Smithsonian Archives of American Art and are referenced in Rihoko Ueno's essay in this catalogue.

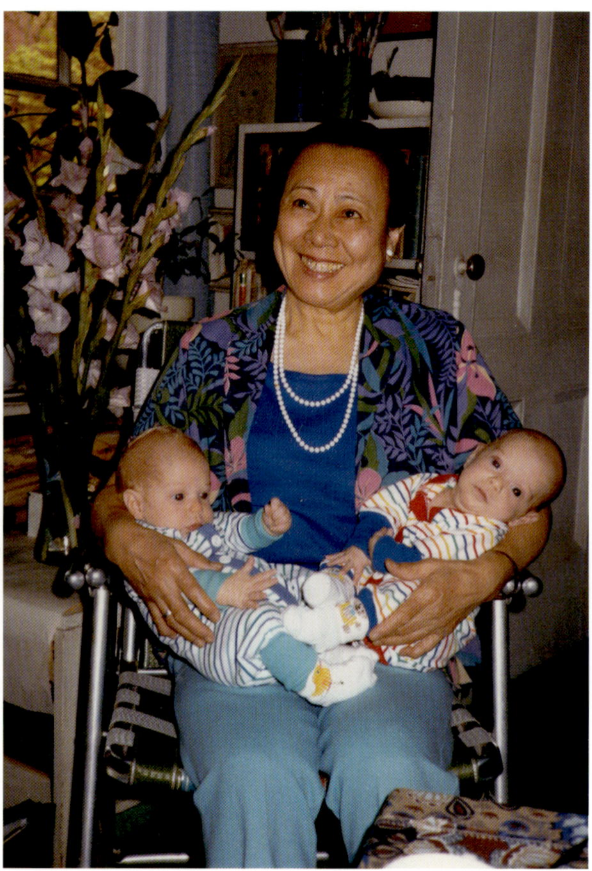

3.10

There was also Kristine Elliott Schwabacher, a principal dancer at New York's American Ballet Theatre in the mid-1970s, whose friendship with Okubo resulted in many vibrant portraits (Fig. 3.9).[15] And judging by the photos of a beaming Okubo cradling Schwabacher's newborn sons, the joy in their friendship was evidently mutual (Fig. 3.10).

These personal and emotional connections compelled Okubo, Hibi, and Hayakawa to create portraits that represented their intimate moments with and memories of their loved ones, their friends, and people they encountered. And as these diasporic artists captured and memorialized their lived experiences through visual means, their paintings, in turn, enable us to both retrace their journeys through different times, places, and communities and glean new insights into their lives.

3.10

Miné Okubo with Kristine Elliott and Randall Schwabacher's sons, Tyler (left) and Blake (right), 1984. The Miné Okubo Collection, Center for Social Justice & Civil Liberties, Riverside Community College District, California, 89-21-7a.

NOTES

1. Gobind Behari Lal, "Japanese Girl's Paintings Challenge Attention. Work of Four Years Proves Her Genius," *San Francisco Examiner*, June 2, 1929, 10E. See also the introduction to this volume.
2. Hibi's *Miki* was numbered 162 in the exhibition catalogue; Hayakawa submitted five monotype prints to the same show, including *Night* (ca. 1924), which is in *Pictures of Belonging* (Plate 50). The loss of Hayakawa-related records might have been a casualty of wartime displacement, as the Hibis could not bring all their belongings, and much that was left behind at their home in Hayward, California, including numerous paintings, did not survive. The George Matsusaburo Hibi papers in the Special Collections of the University of California, Los Angeles, contain mostly wartime and postwar materials. I facilitated the donation by the artist's estate of Hisako Hibi's papers to the Smithsonian Archives of American Art in 2022 to encourage future research.
3. The whereabouts of the painting are unknown. The Consulate General of Japan in San Francisco stated that it did not keep pre–World War II records and could not assist in my research. Correspondence with the consulate, February 14, 2022.
4. Lal, "Japanese Girl's Paintings Challenge Attention," 10E.
5. A fascinating exception is Kyohei Inukai, a sought-after society portraitist from Japan who traversed the United States and attracted a divergent clientele. For a biographical study, see Miyoko Davey and John Davey, *Kyohei Inukai (1884–1954)* (New York: 46 WSS Press, 2014).
6. I am grateful to Jeff Gunderson, librarian and archivist at the San Francisco Art Institute since 1981, for his generous guidance in locating archival materials over the years.
7. The fate of Hayakawa's personal documents and effects remains unclear, as some uncorroborated stories suggest that Hayakawa's papers may have been discarded after the Santa Fe East Gallery's closing in the 1990s. Astilli Fine Art Services in Santa Fe, which represented artist William "Bill" Ford's estate, has a few precious letters written by Hayakawa to Ford. Thanks to David Astilli for sharing the documents and photographs.
8. Ford fondly remembered Hayakawa as an excellent artist and gracious person who was beloved: "She was naive yet knowing, a combination of innocence and sophistication." For extended analyses and discussions of these paintings and their historical context, see ShiPu Wang, "In Search of Miki Hayakawa: A California Cosmopolitan," in *The Other American Moderns: Matsura, Ishigaki, Noda, Hayakawa* (University Park: Penn State University Press, 2017), 97–126.
9. The name was offered by Mateo Lettunich, Hayakawa's friend in the Monterey Peninsula in the 1930s, in his donation form for the portrait to the Monterey Museum of Art. Thanks to John Rexine, the museum's collections and exhibitions director, for providing the note.
10. For a reproduction of *Music*, see ShiPu Wang, "Miki Hayakawa: Portraying Interiority," in *The Unforgettables: Expanding the History of American Art*, ed. Charles C. Eldredge (Oakland: University of California Press, 2022), 138–43.
11. The couple married in Santa Fe on October 25, 1947. Hayakawa stated on their marriage license application that she was born on June 7, 1910, and was thirty-seven years old. However, I unearthed another marriage certificate from 1917 that records the union between Kiyoshi Okuye (of Livingston, California) and an eighteen-year-old Hayakawa, with her birth year given as 1899; this matches the biographical information in the 1930 census records. It is reasonable to presume that Hayakawa decided to make herself younger, at least in the official document for the second marriage. Thanks to Laura Hernandez, records manager for Santa Fe County, for locating and providing the certificate.
12. The CSFA attendance records indicate that Hisako or "Mary" Shimizu took life drawing and landscape painting classes in June–July 1928 and June–August 1929.
13. *A Process of Reflection: Paintings by Hisako Hibi*, Japanese American National Museum, July 27, 1999–January 30, 2000.
14. Shirley Sun, *Miné Okubo: An American Experience* (Oakland, Calif.: Oakland Museum, 1972).
15. Schwabacher fondly recalls the influences her "beautiful friend Miné" had on her life, as noted in correspondences with the author, June–July 2022. She thought Okubo's use of green in her 1976 portrait was odd until she later realized that Okubo had in fact astutely captured her physical and emotional state during her grueling tenure as a principal dancer. Kristine Elliott Schwabacher's recollections were recorded by Greg Robinson, "Miné Okubo: The New York Years," *Amerasia Journal* 30, no. 2 (2004): 89–96.

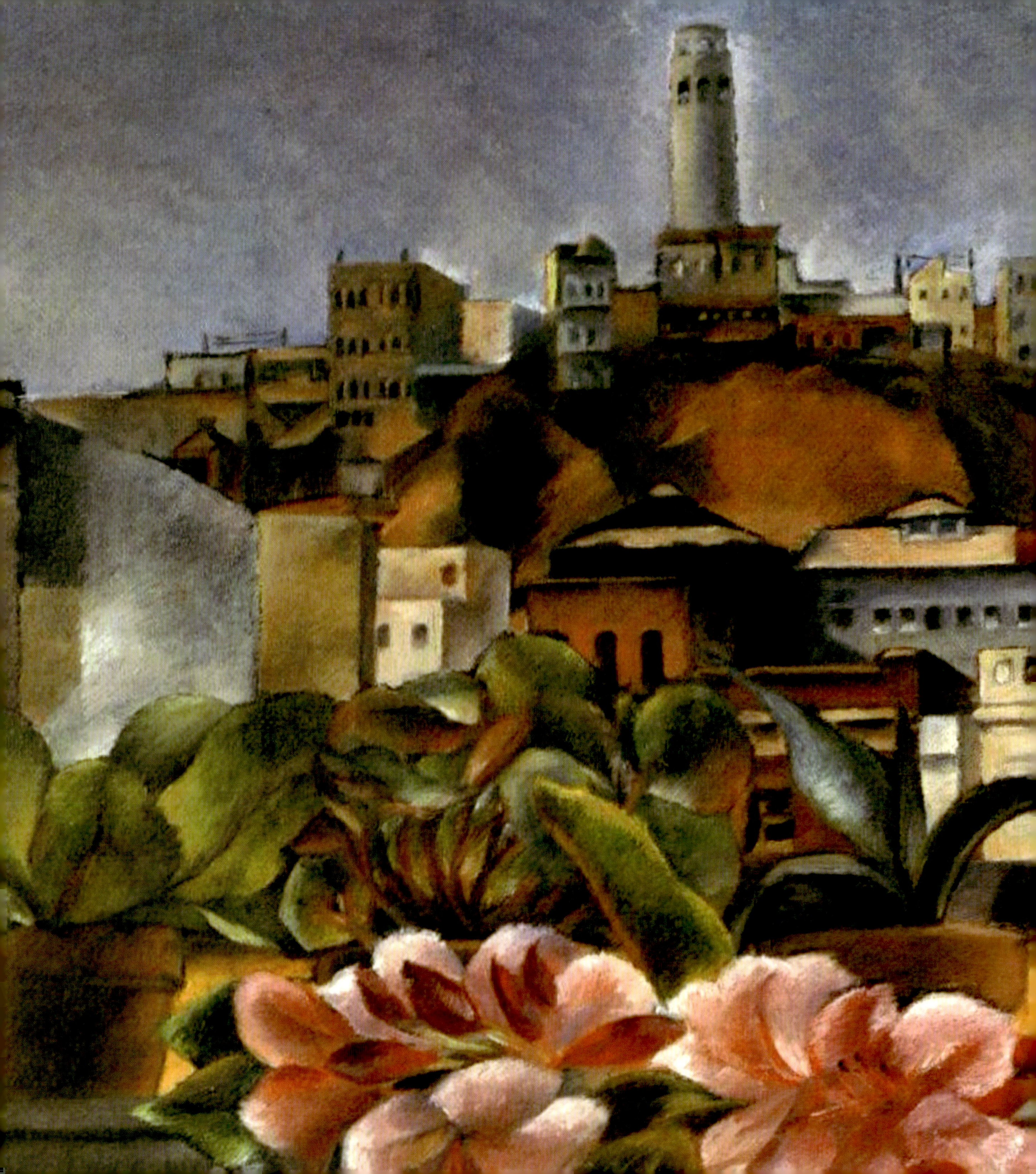

# II

# Belongings & (dis)Locations

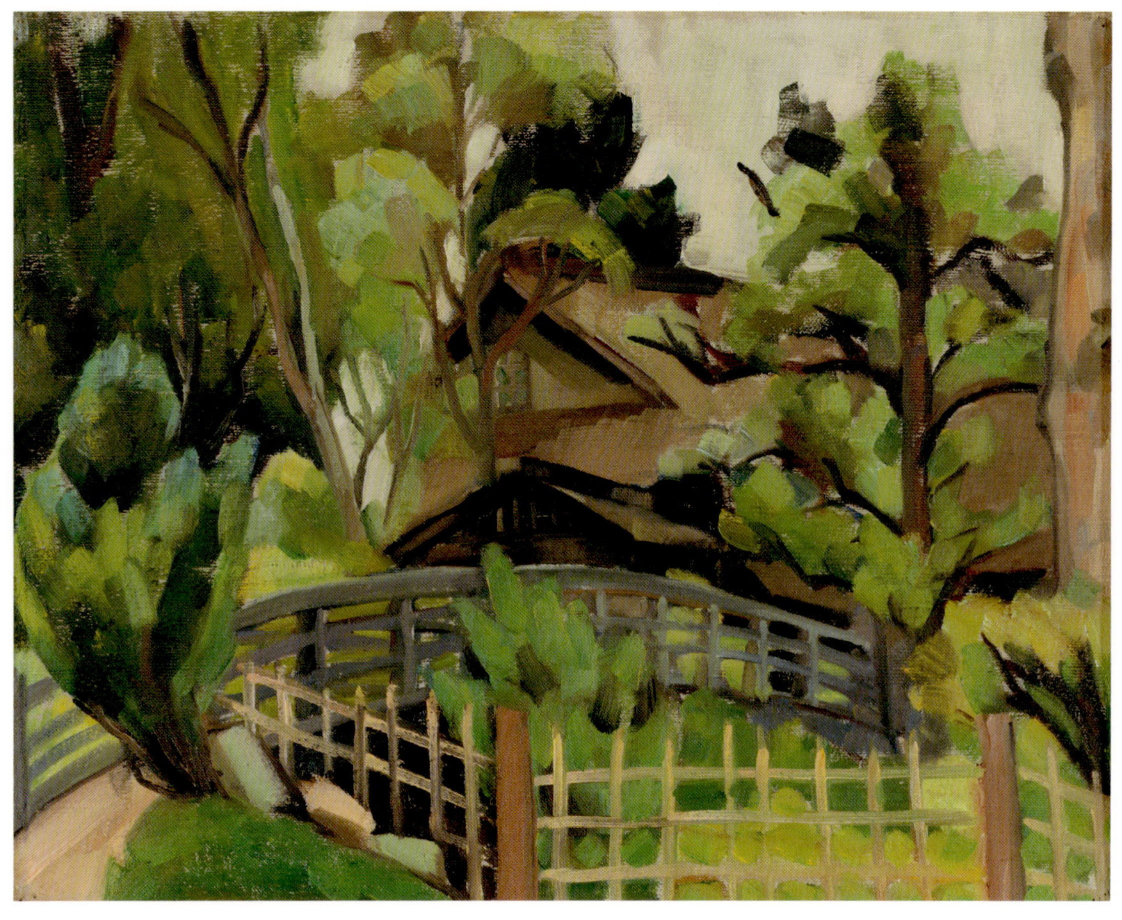

**48**
Miki Hayakawa
*Japanese Tea House*
ca. 1925

Oil on canvas, 19½ × 23½ in.
Japanese American National Museum, Los Angeles, Gift of Yukiyo Hayashi, 99.165.1

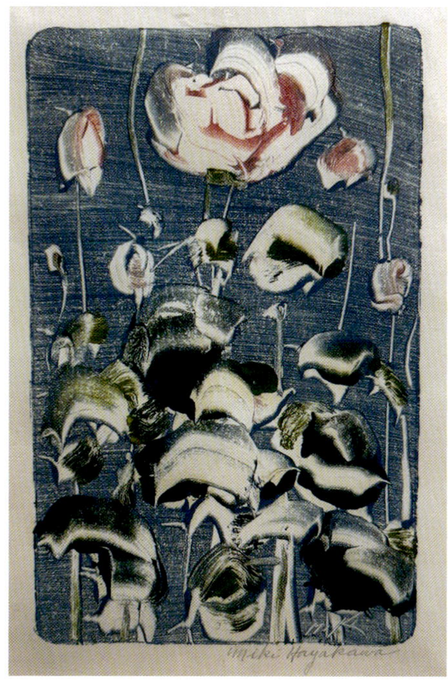

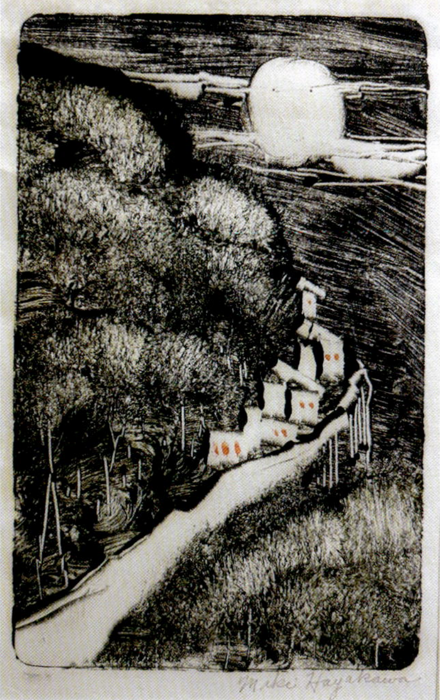

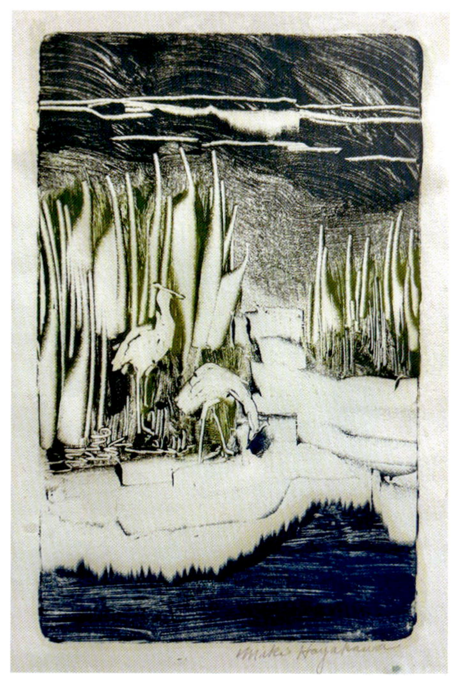

49
Miki Hayakawa
*Flower*
ca. 1924–25

Monoprint, 8¼ × 5¼ in. Collection of Richard Sakai. Photo by ShiPu Wang

50
Miki Hayakawa
*Night*
ca. 1924

Monoprint, 8¼ × 5¼ in. Collection of Richard Sakai. Photo by ShiPu Wang

51
Miki Hayakawa
*Pair Nestling*
ca. 1924–25

Monoprint, 8¼ × 5¼ in. Collection of Richard Sakai. Photo by ShiPu Wang

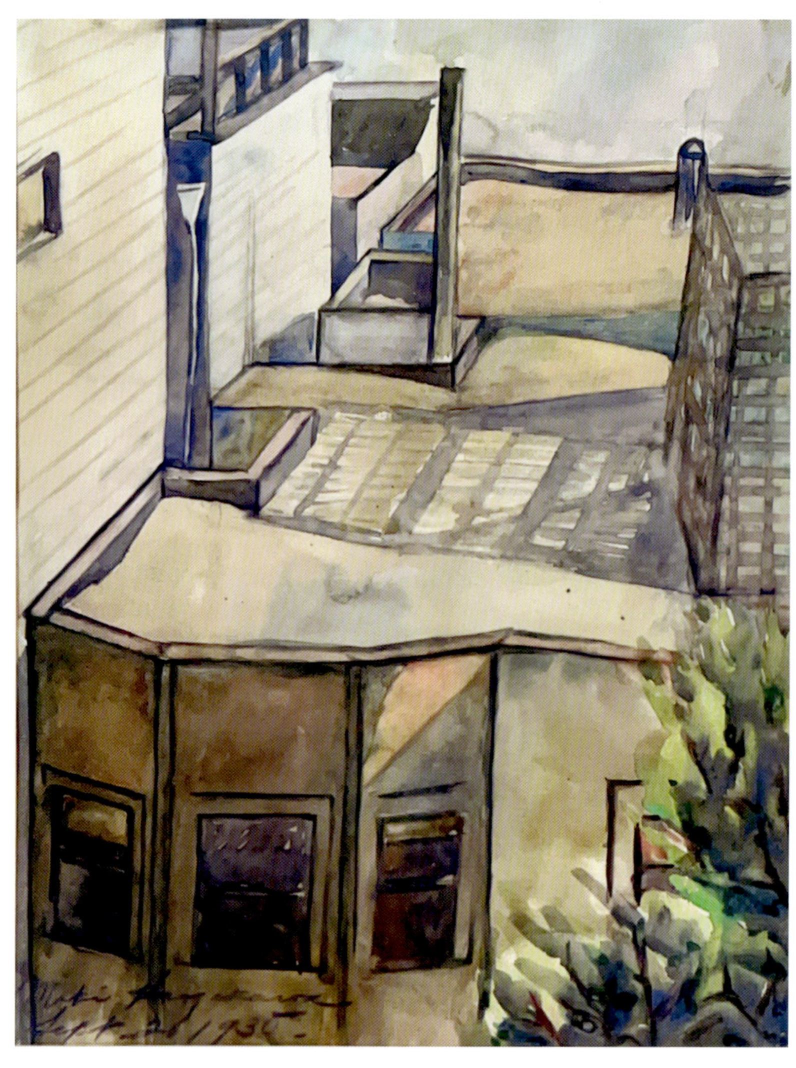

**52**
Miki Hayakawa
*San Francisco Rooftops*
September 26, 1930

Watercolor on paper, 19¼ × 16½ in. Collection of Richard Sakai. Photo by ShiPu Wang

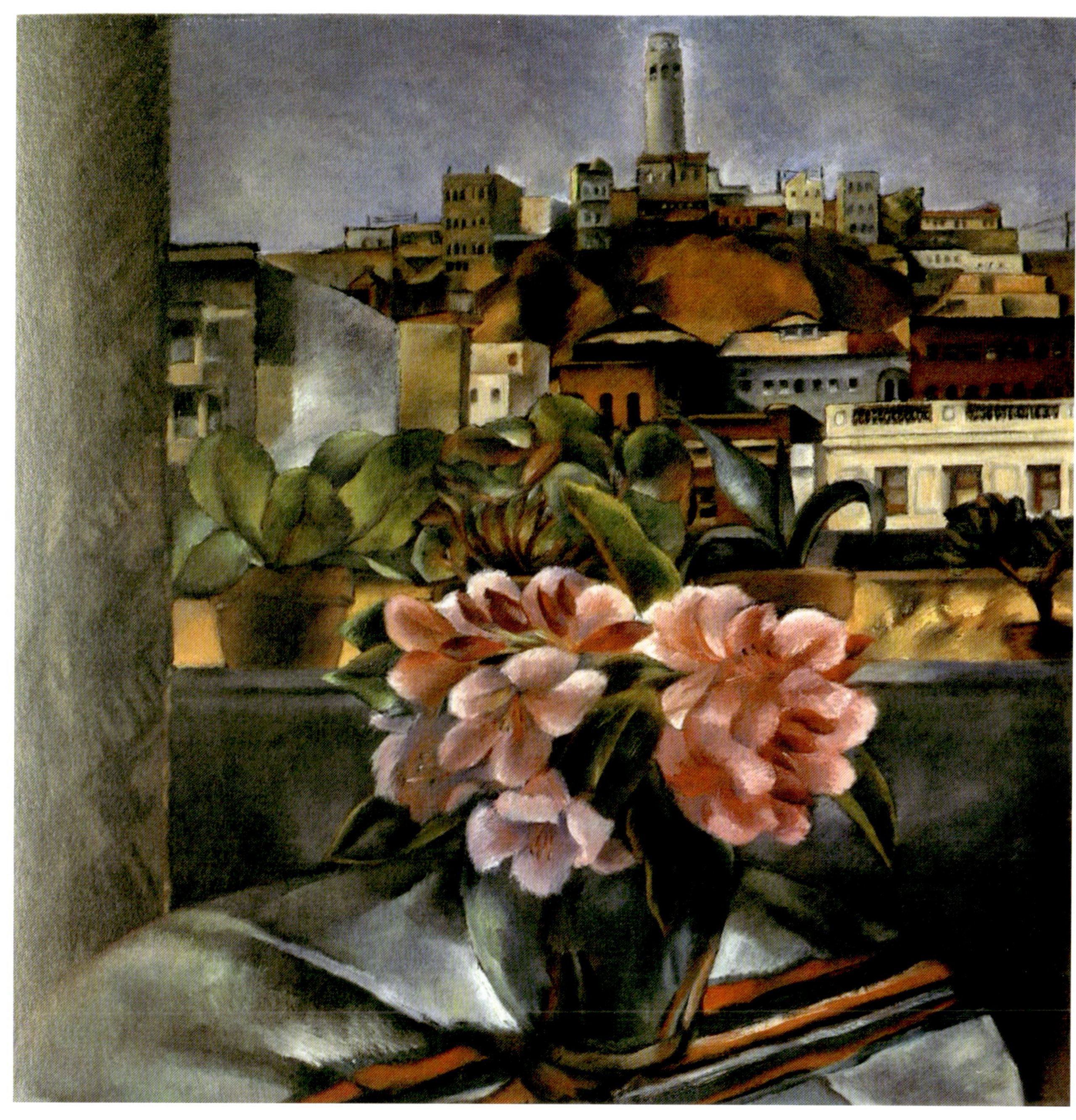

53
Miki Hayakawa
*From My Window*
1935

Oil on canvas, 28 × 28 in. Collection of Sandra and Bram Dijkstra on loan at the Huntington Library, Art Museum, and Botanical Gardens, Pasadena, California

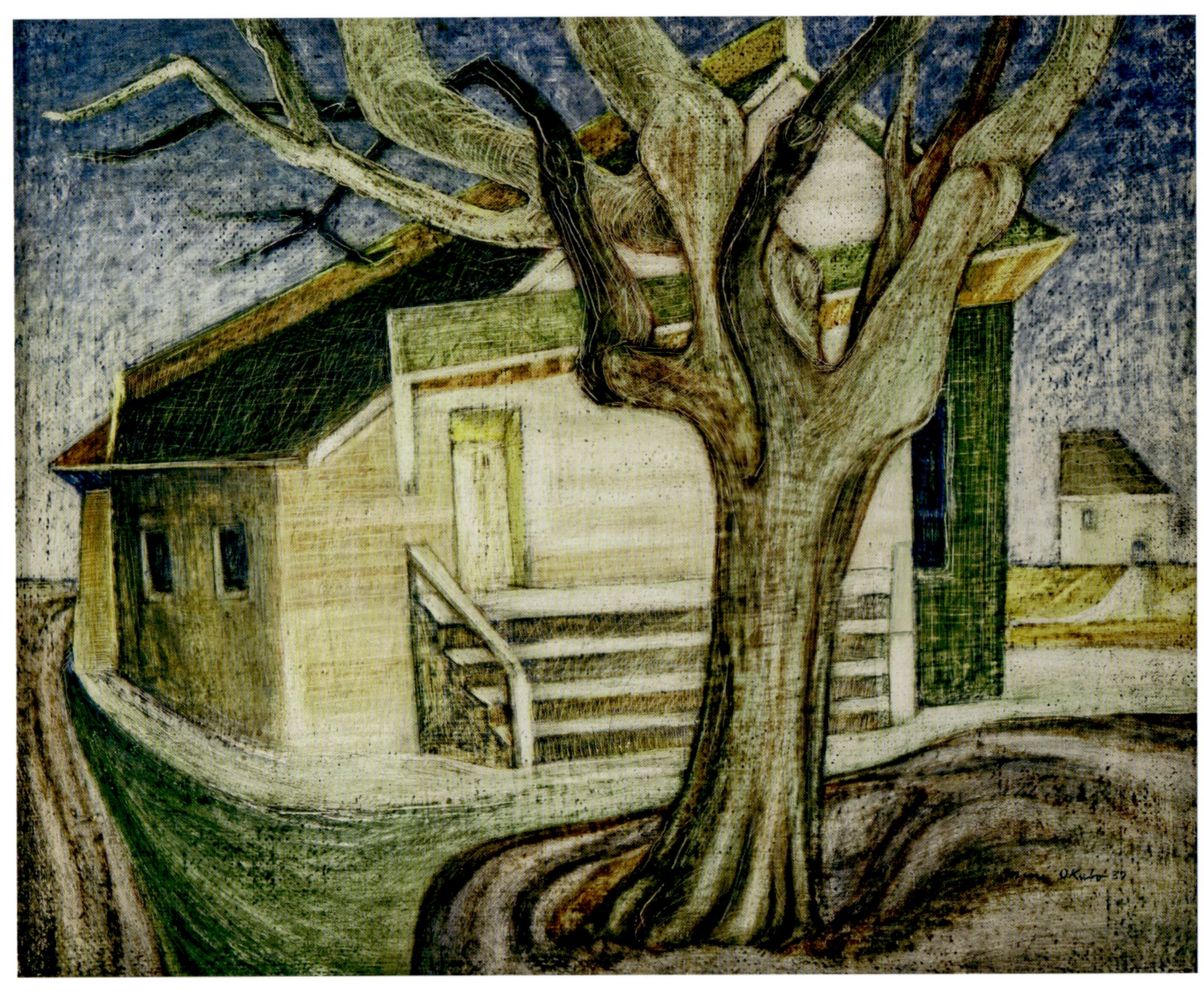

54
Miné Okubo
*Ice House*
ca. 1937

Paint on Masonite, 19¾ × 23¾ in. The Miné Okubo Charitable Corporation, EL 2012.1.23. Photo by Giovanni Cardenas, Chief Photographer Strategic Communications Riverside Community College District, 2023

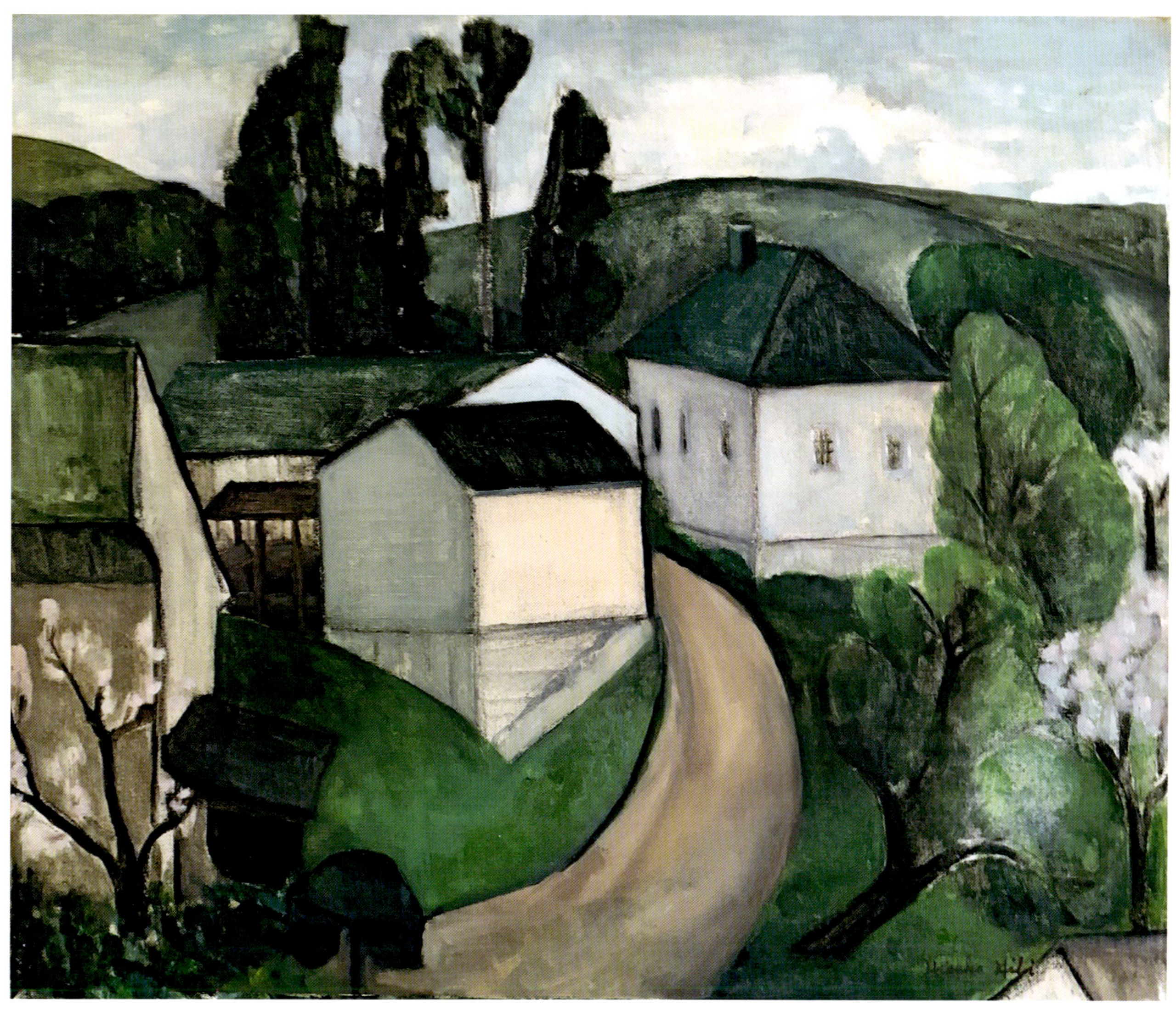

55
Hisako Hibi
*Spring #2, Hayward*
1940

Oil on canvas, 20 × 24 in. The Hibi Estate. Photo by ShiPu Wang

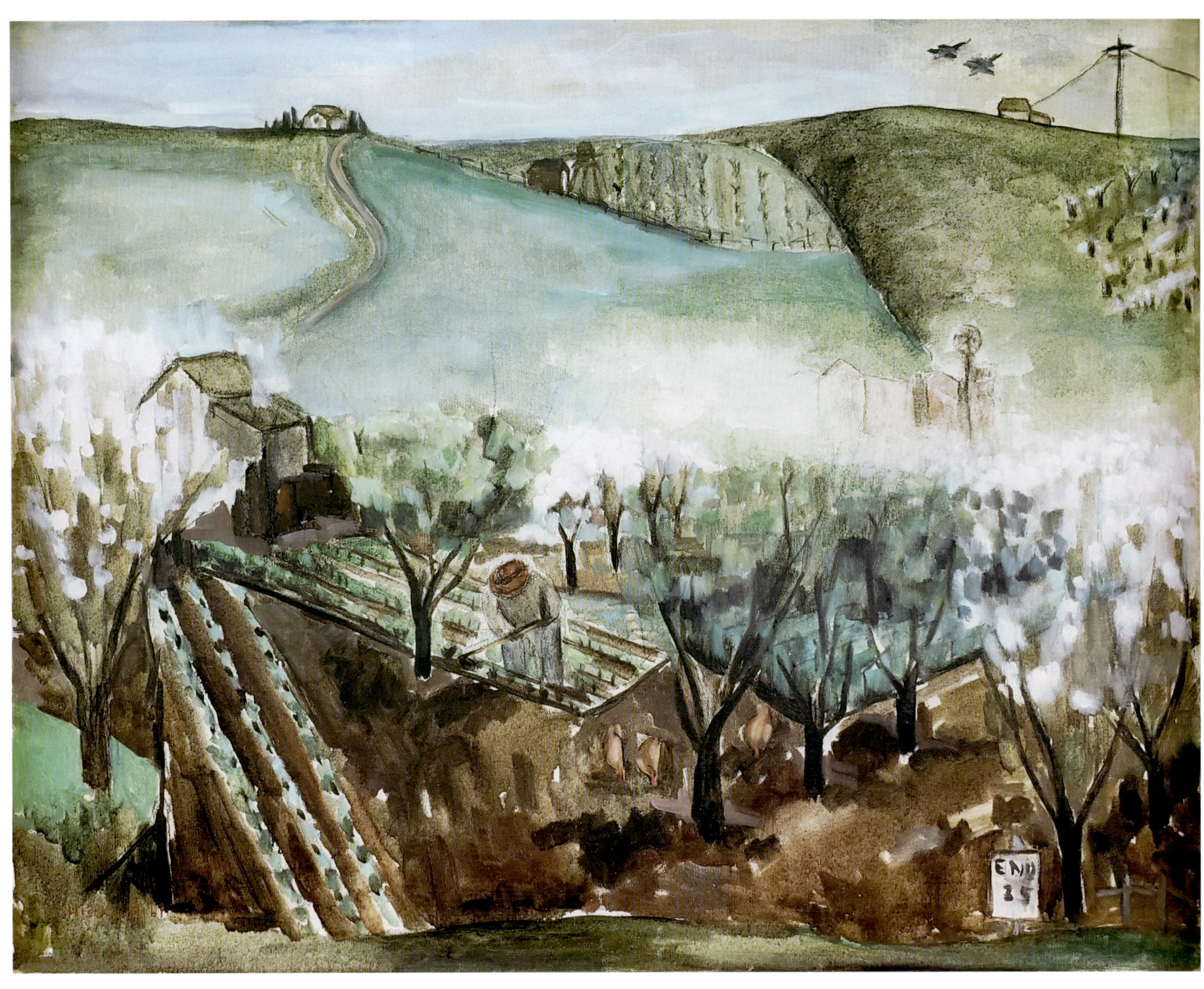


**56**
Hisako Hibi
*Spring II*
ca. 1940

Oil on canvas, 26 × 33 in. Hayward Area Historical Society, California. Photo by ShiPu Wang

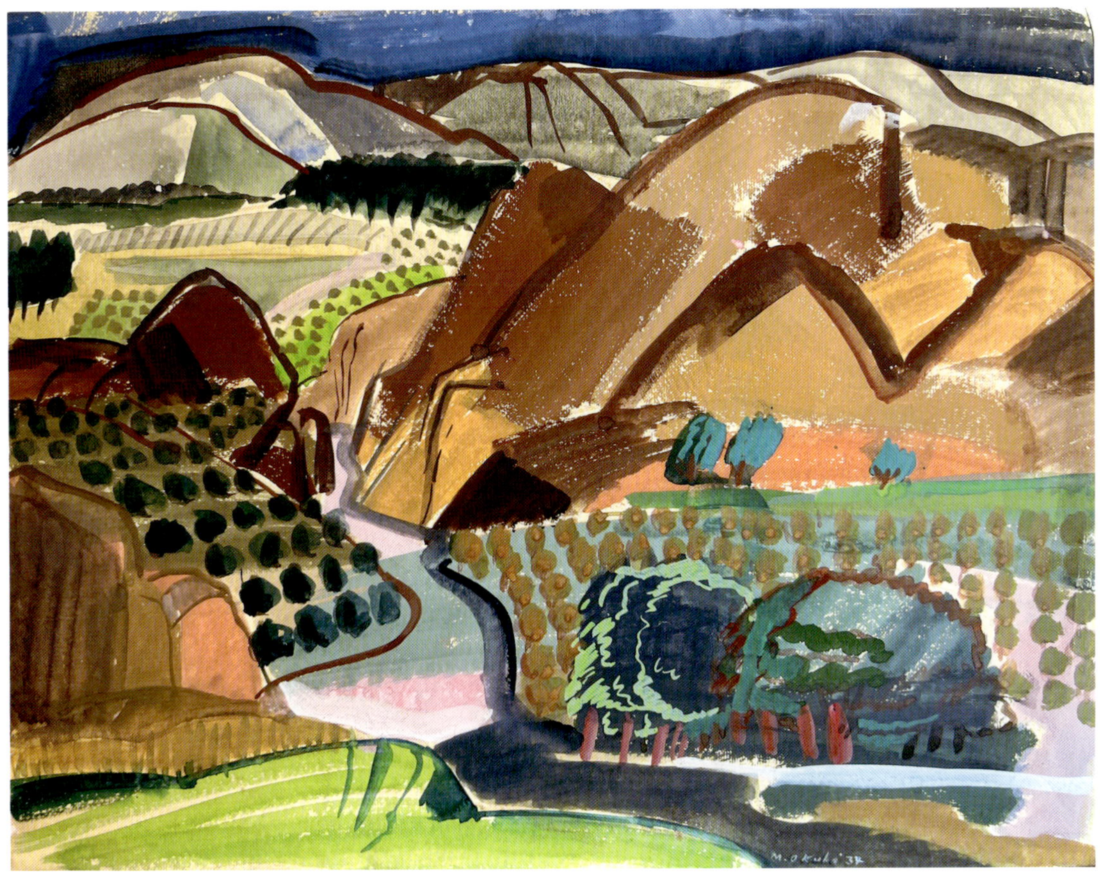

**57**
Miné Okubo
*Riverside*
1934

Watercolor on paper, 16 × 21 in.
The Miné Okubo Charitable
Corporation. Photo by ShiPu Wang

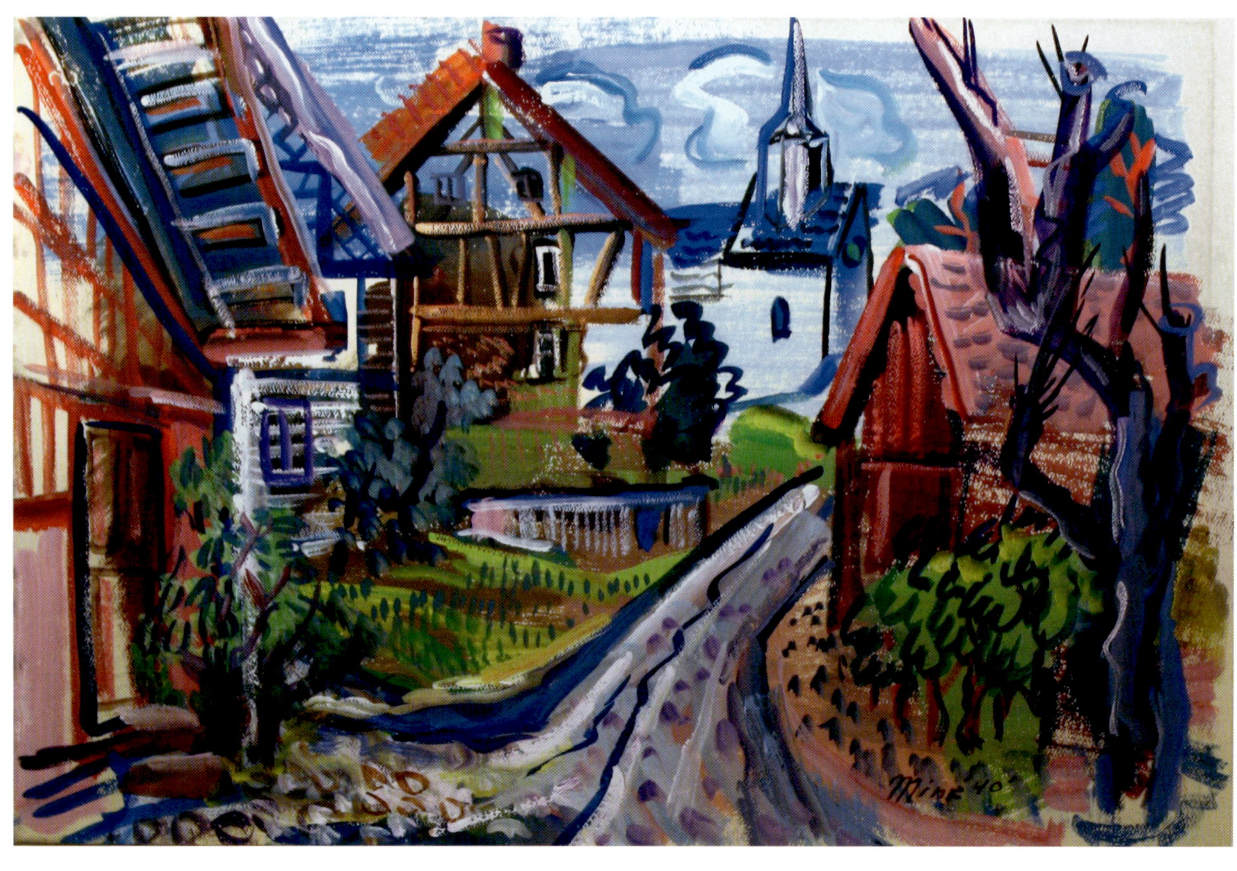


**58**
Miné Okubo
*The Village Street*
1940

Watercolor on paper, 17½ × 20 in. The Miné Okubo Charitable Corporation, EL 2012.1.177. Photo by ShiPu Wang

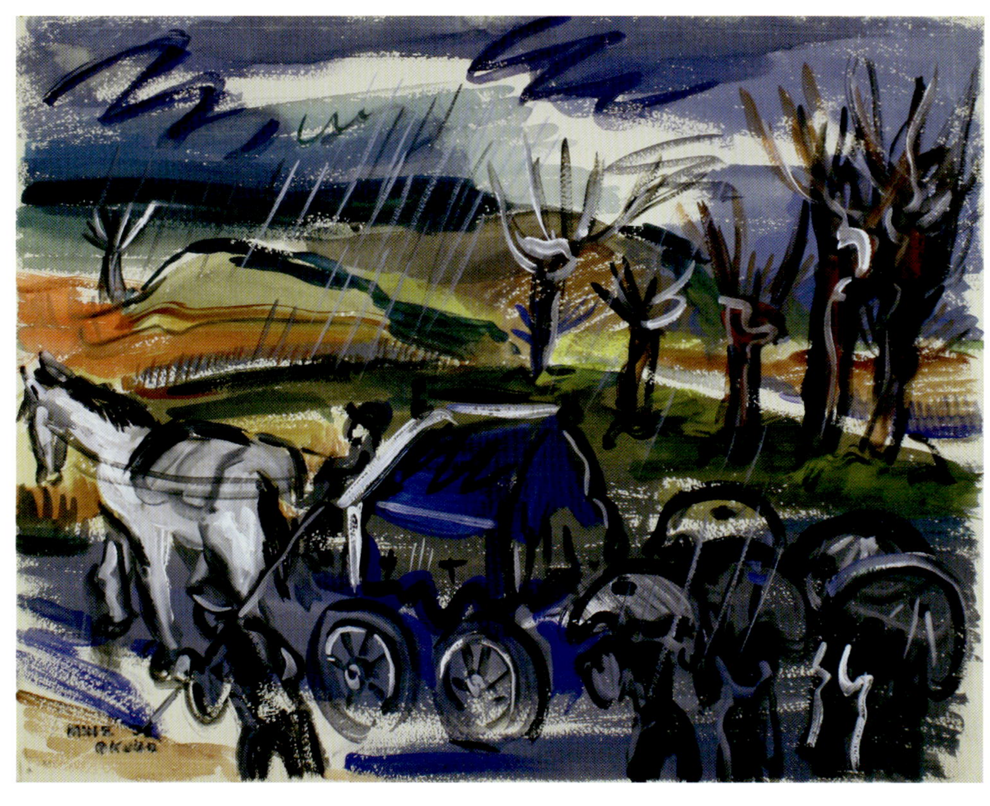

**59**
Miné Okubo
*Funeral Procession, France*
ca. 1938–39

Watercolor on paper, 14¼ × 18½ in. Riverside City College, Riverside Community College District, California, Gift of the Miné Okubo Estate, 2016.1.6. Photo by Tom Callas

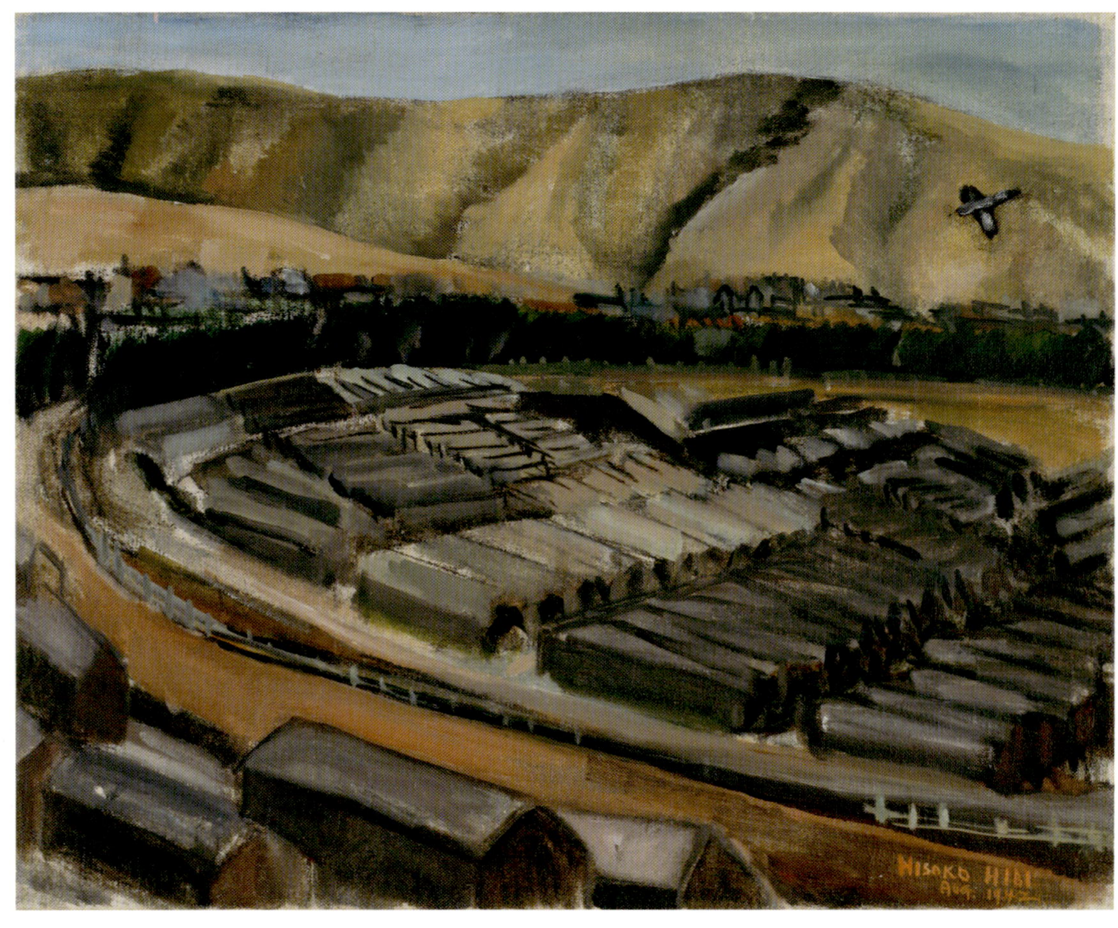


**60**

Hisako Hibi
*Tanforan Assembly Center*
San Bruno, California,
August 24, 1942

Oil on canvas, 16 × 20 in. Japanese American National Museum, Los Angeles, Gift of Ibuki Hibi Lee, 96.601.1

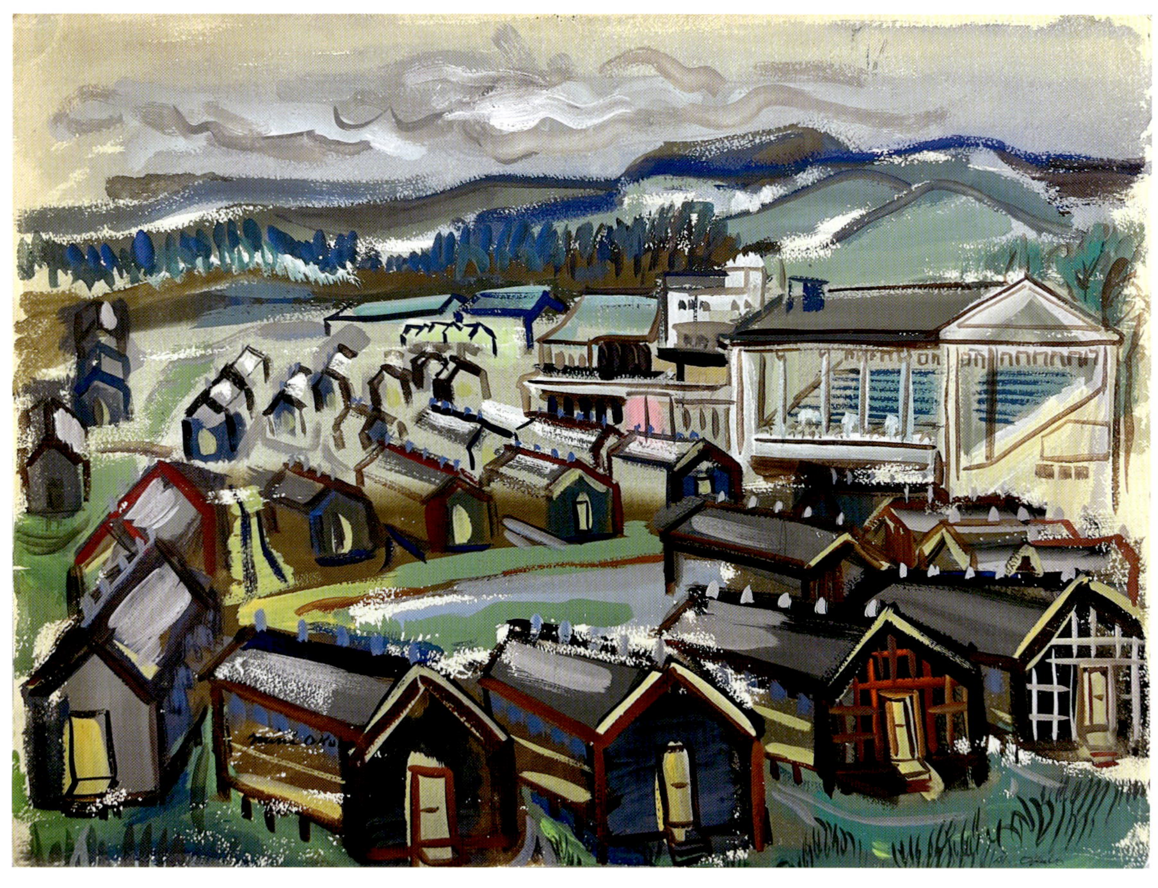

**61**
Miné Okubo
*Tanforan Assembly Center—*
*Grandstand Area*
July 10, 1942

Watercolor on paper, 15 × 21 in
Japanese American National Museum, Los Angeles, Gift of the Miné Okubo Estate, 2007.62.236

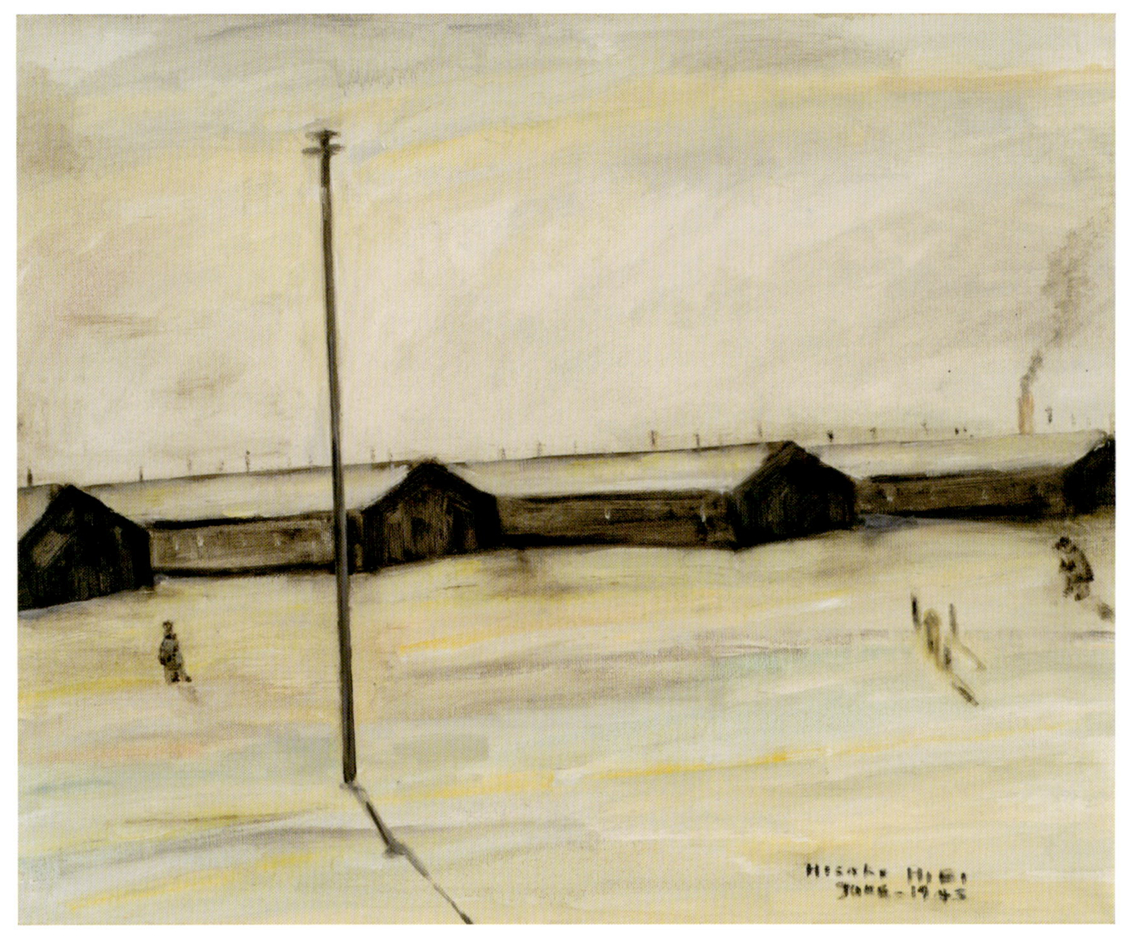

**62**

Hisako Hibi

*White Heat*

June 1943

Oil on canvas, 16 × 20 in. Japanese American National Museum, Los Angeles, Gift of Ibuki Hibi Lee, 96.601.10

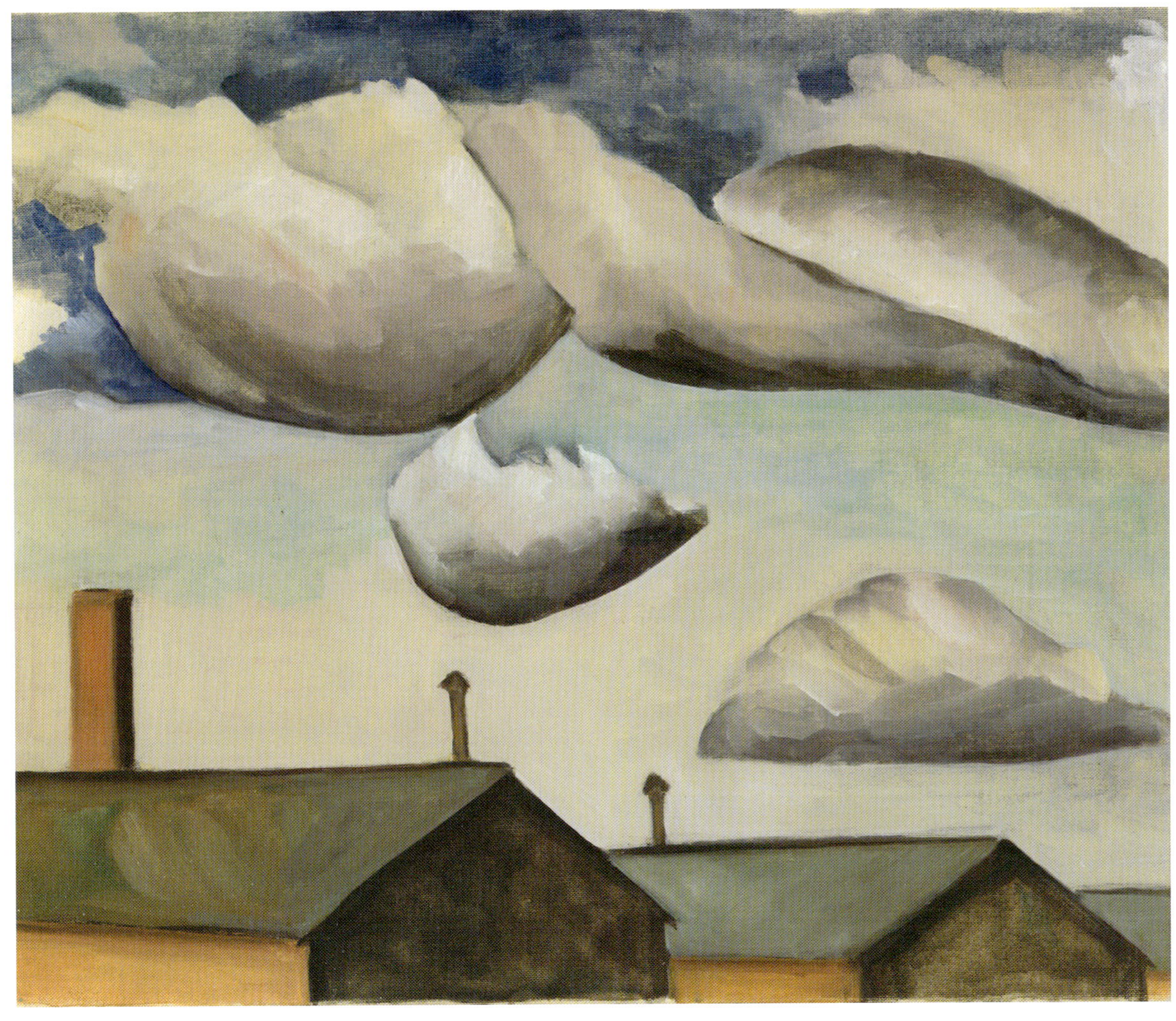

**63**
Hisako Hibi
*Floating Clouds*
April 1944

Oil on canvas, 19¹⁄₁₆ × 23 × 1½ in. (48.4 × 58.4 × 3.8 cm). Smithsonian American Art Museum, Museum purchase through the American Women's History Initiative Acquisitions Pool, administered by the Smithsonian American Women's History Initiative

Hisako Hibi wrote on the verso: "Topaz sky / It was an interesting cloudy day / Floating clouds / フワリ フワリ フワリ [*fuwari, fuwari, fuwari*] / Free, free, freeforme [*sic*] in the spacious sky / I want to be free, as free as that cloud I see up above Topaz." (フワリ, *fuwari*, also ふわり, is a kind of onomatopoeia, meaning "flutter, fluffy, floating.")

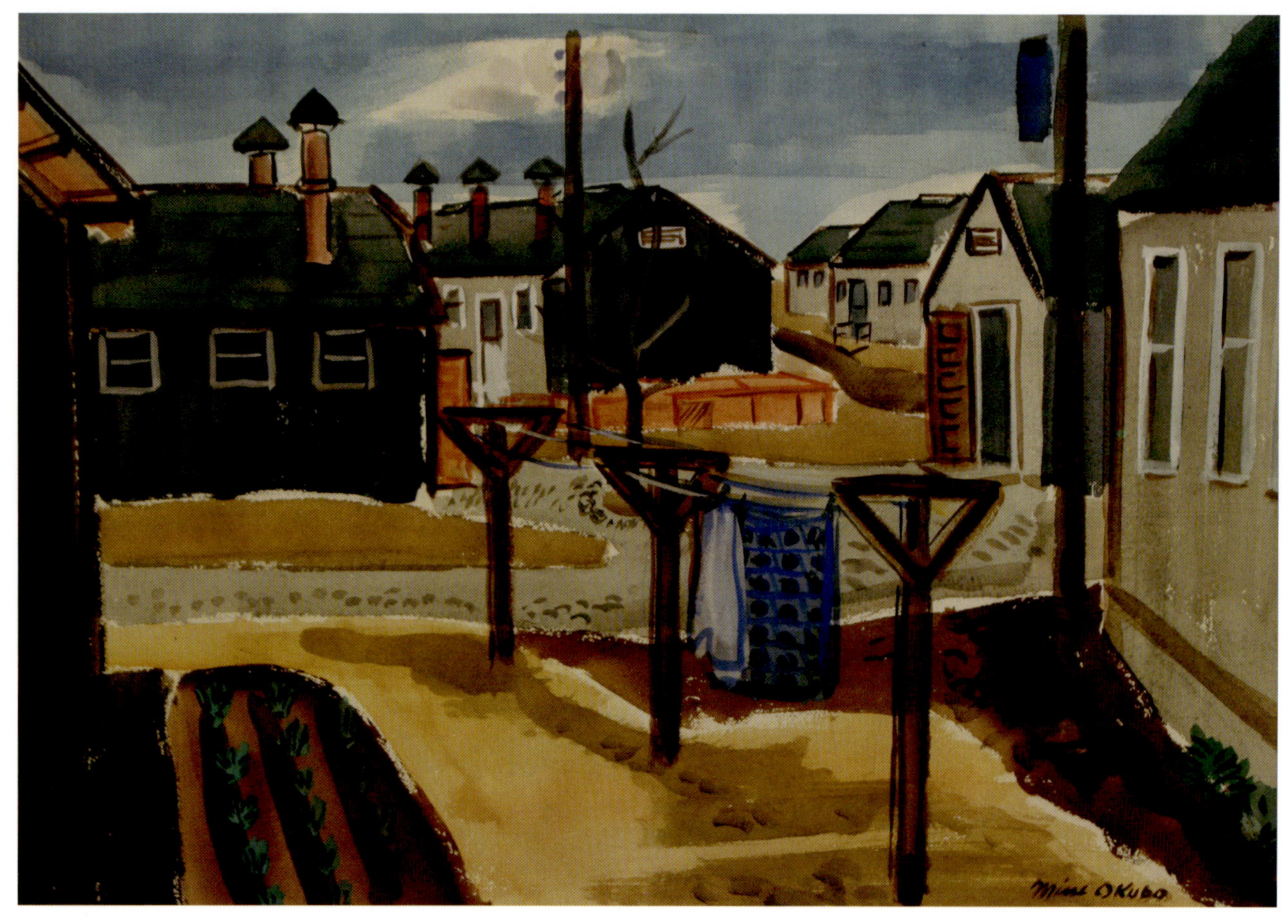


**64**
Miné Okubo
*Untitled (Camp Scene with Laundry)*
ca. 1943

Watercolor on illustration board, 19 × 24 in. The Miné Okubo Charitable Corporation, EL 2012.1.7. Photo by Tom Callas

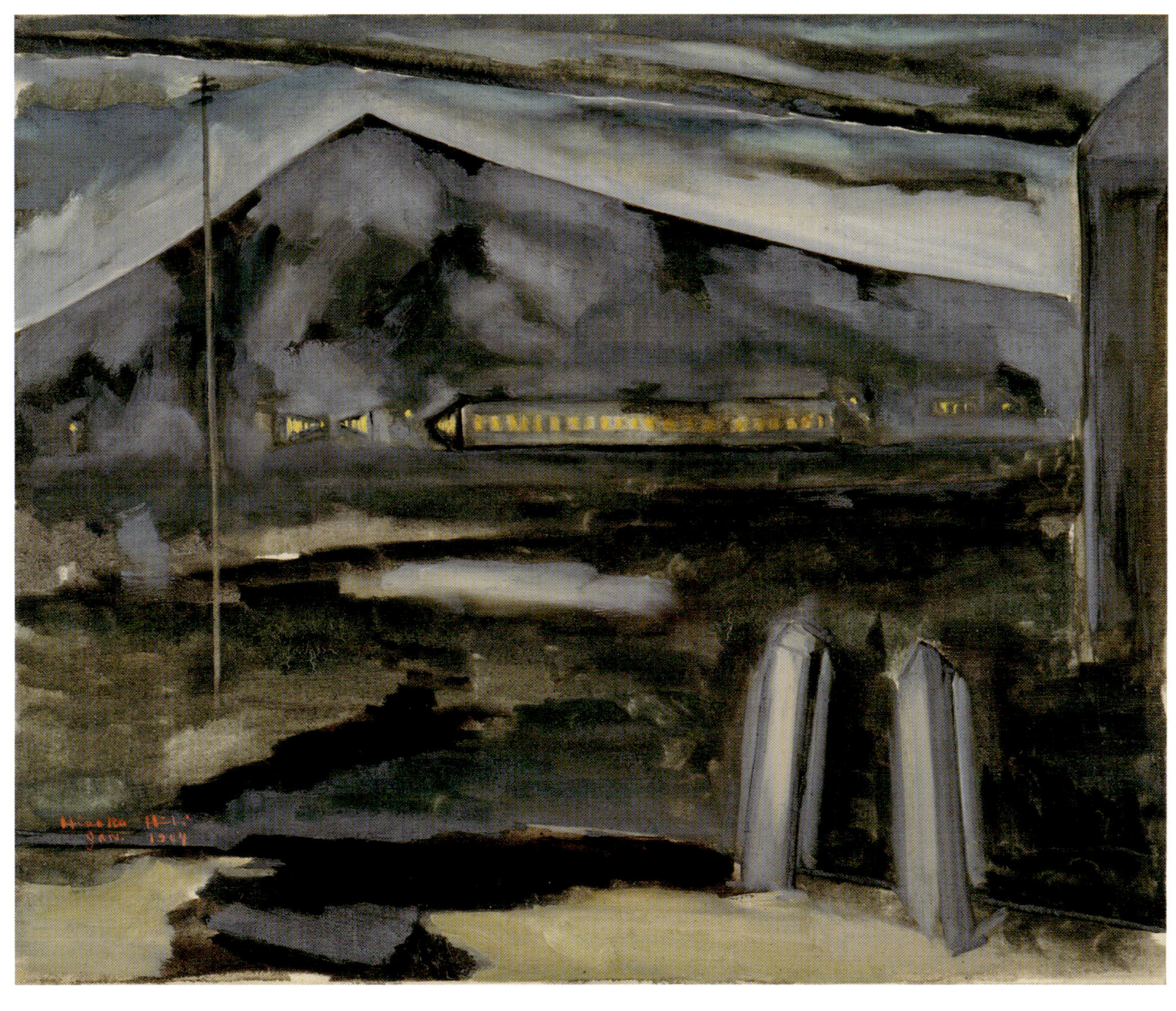

**65**
Hisako Hibi
*A Night*
January 1944

Oil on canvas, 18 × 22 in. Japanese American National Museum, Los Angeles, Gift of Ibuki Hibi Lee, 96.601.22

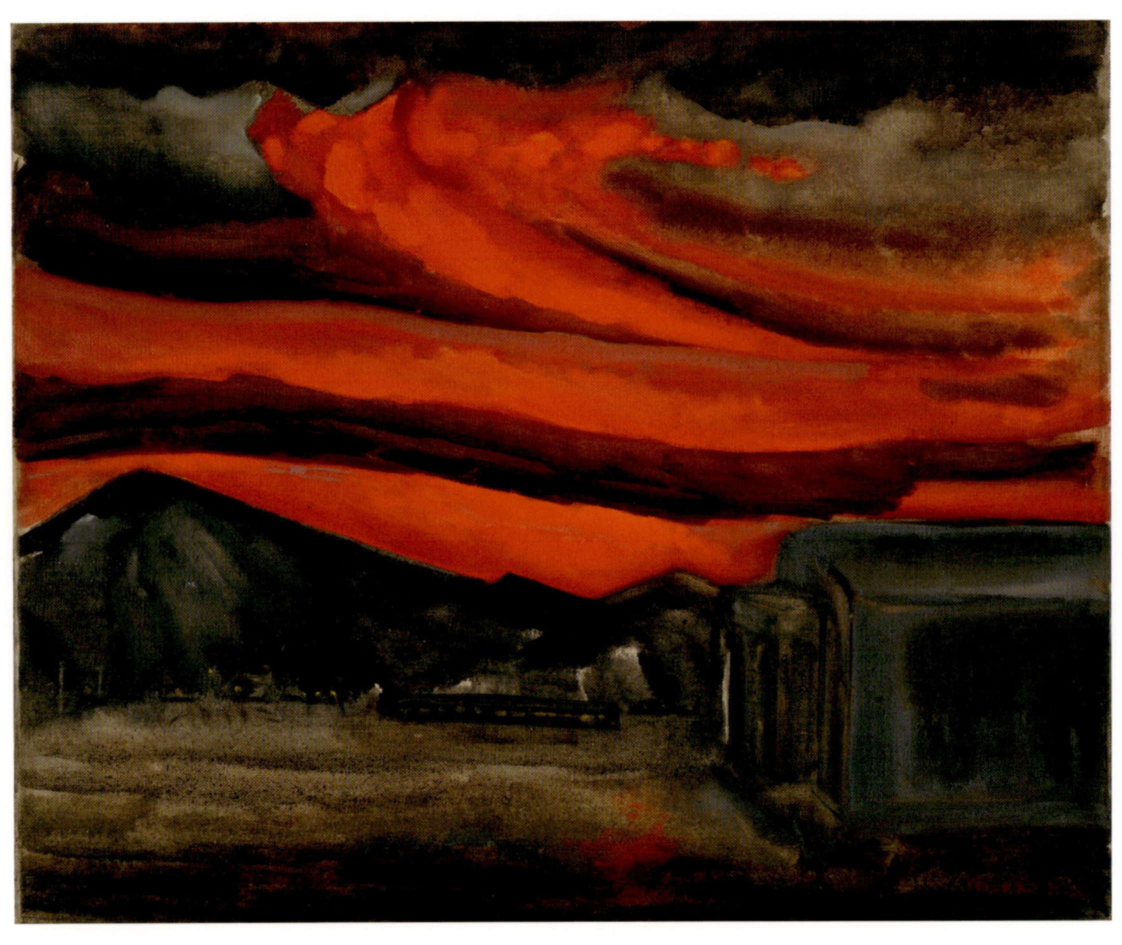

**66**
Hisako Hibi
*Eastern Sky 7:50 A.M.*
February 25, 1945

Oil on canvas, 16 × 20 in. Japanese American National Museum, Los Angeles, Gift of Ibuki Hibi Lee, 96.601.47

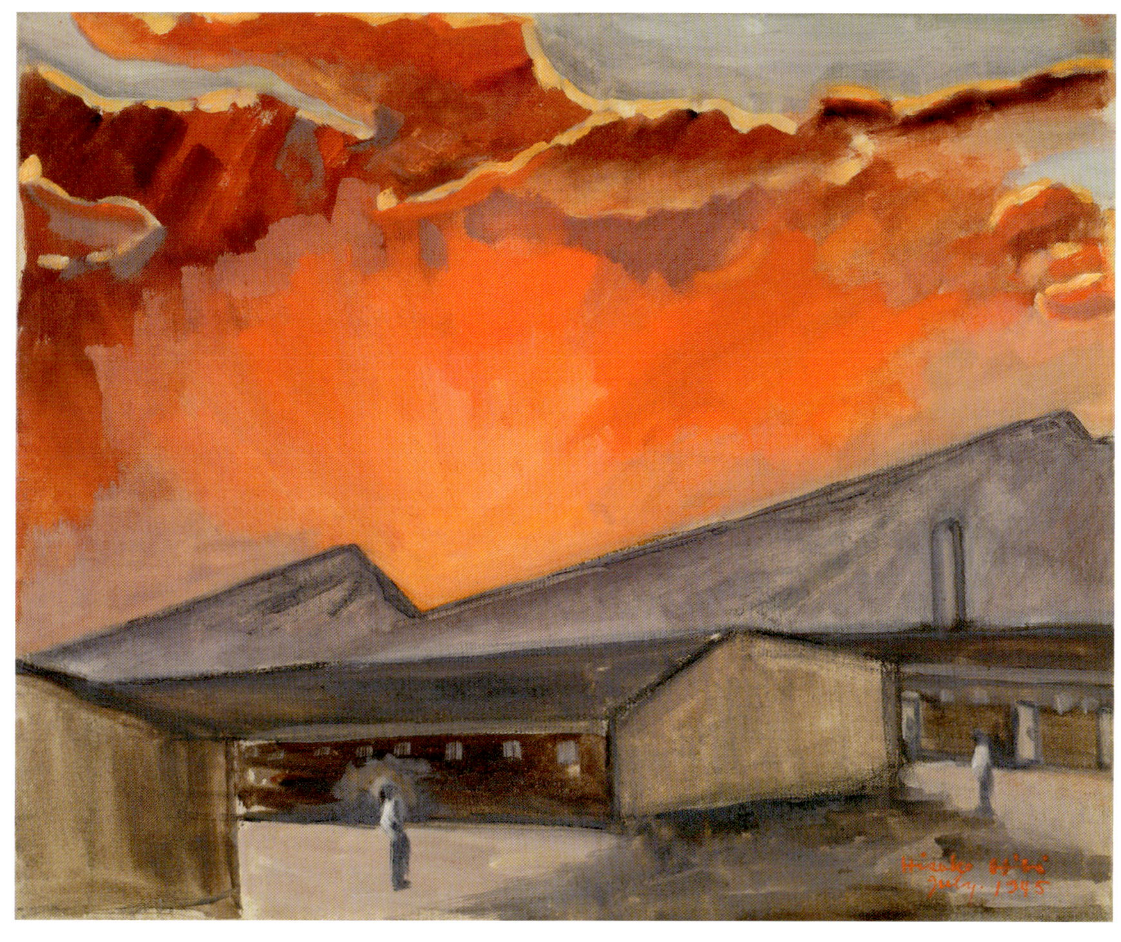

**67**
Hisako Hibi
*Western Sky*
Topaz, Utah, July 1945

Oil on canvas, 16 × 20 in. Japanese American National Museum, Los Angeles, Gift of Ibuki Hibi Lee, 96.601.48

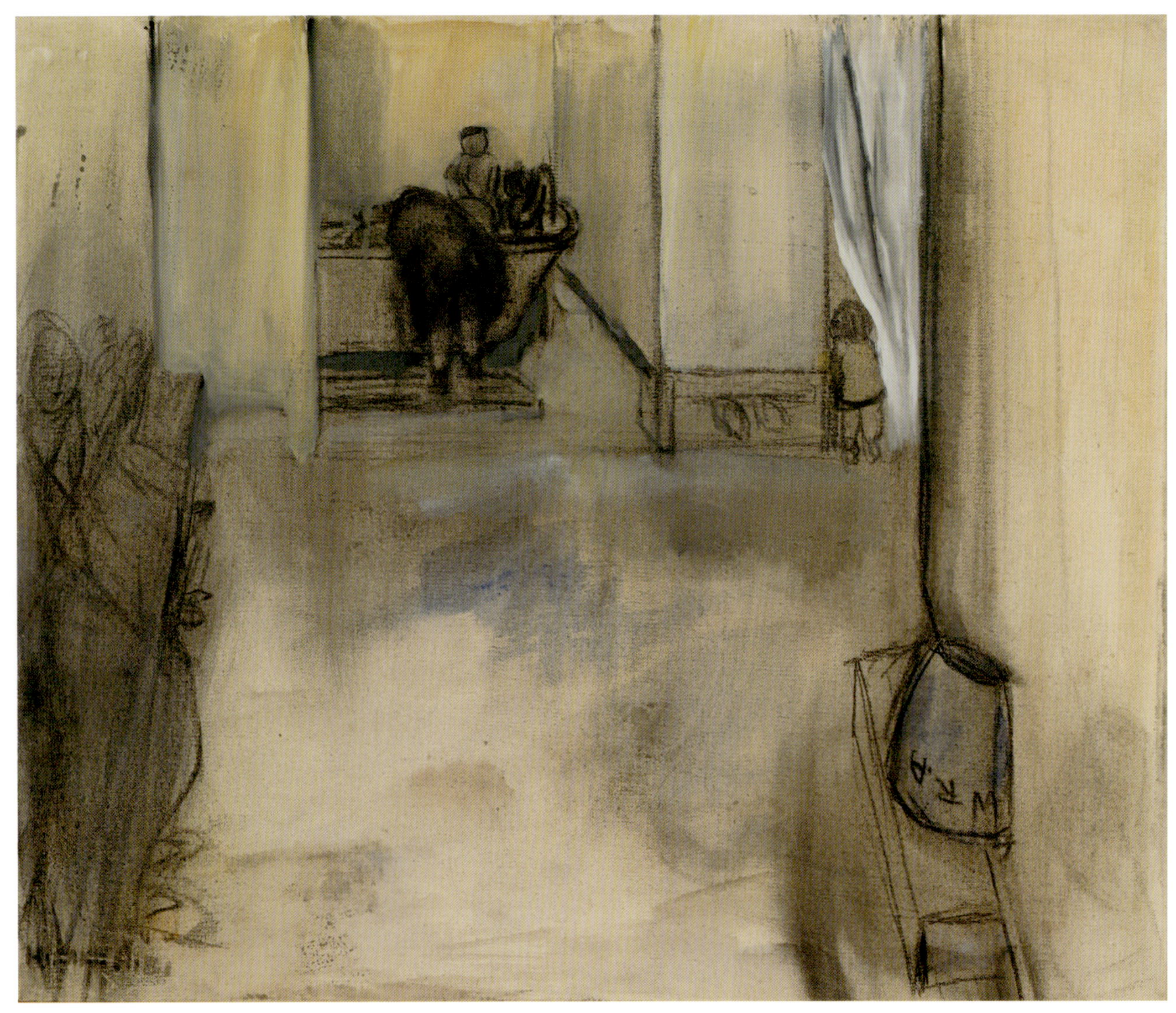

**68**
Hisako Hibi
*A Bathroom*
1945

Oil on canvas, 20 × 24 in. Japanese American National Museum, Los Angeles, Gift of Ibuki Hibi Lee, 96.601.528

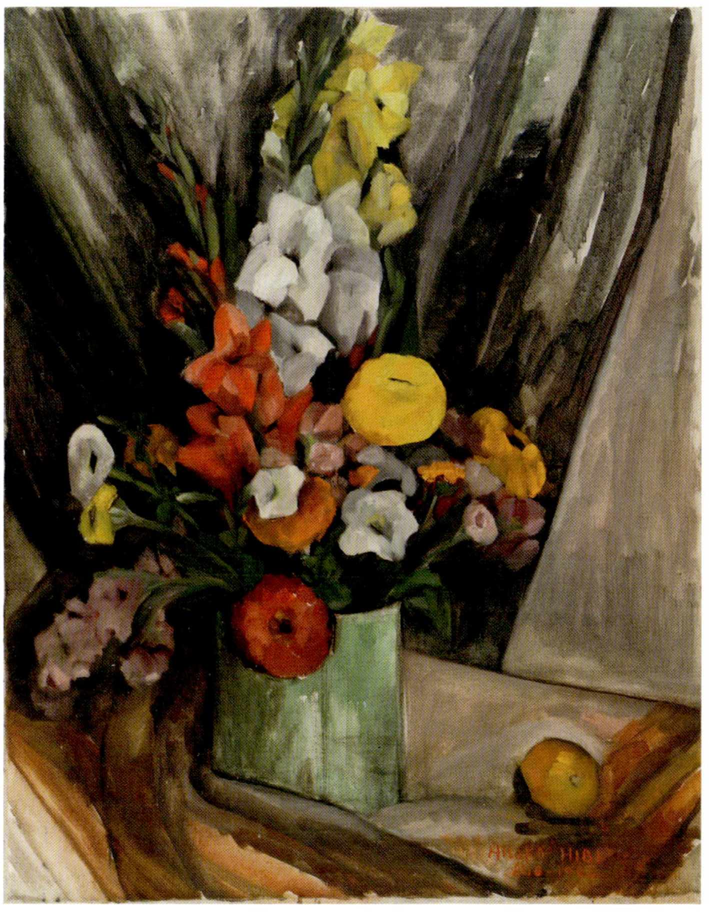

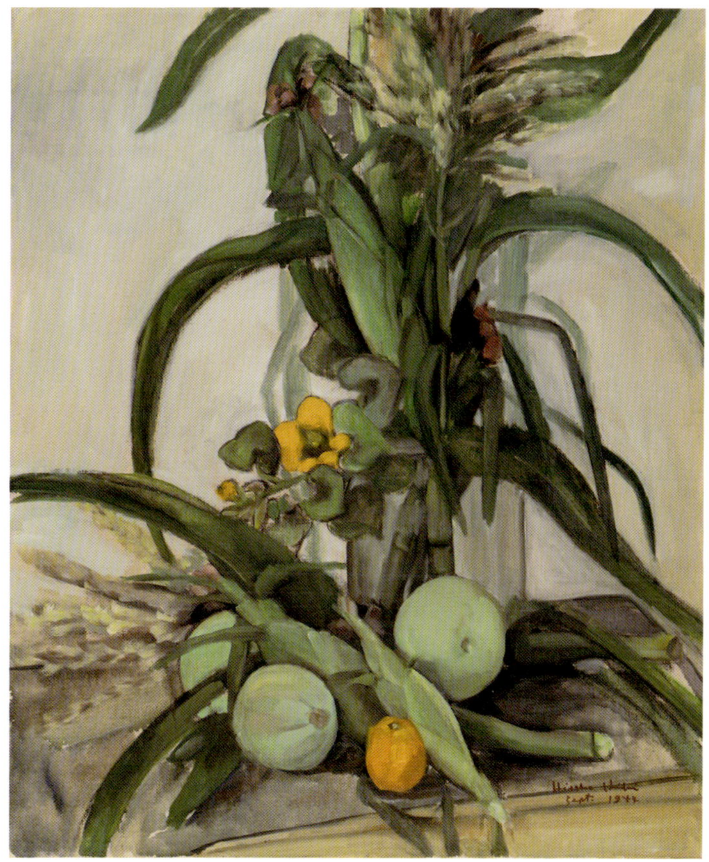

69
Hisako Hibi
*Flowers Grown in Tanforan*
August 1942

Oil on canvas, 25 × 20 in. Japanese American National Museum, Los Angeles, Gift of Ibuki Hibi Lee, 96.601.7

This painting was sent to the *Relocation Center Art Exhibit* held at the Friends Center in Cambridge, Massachusetts, in October 1943. The exhibition, sponsored by the Friends—Americans who helped the incarcerated Japanese and Americans of Japanese ancestry—included artworks from all ten camps. In addition to Hibi's painting receiving a special award in flower painting, Chiura Obata's *New Moon* (Topaz, Utah) won first prize; Paul Zaima's *Horizons Can Be Clear* (Heart Mountain, Wyoming), second prize; and Y. Tsuruda's *Lonely Country* (Amache, Colorado), third prize. Hibi's fellow Topaz incarceree Frank Taira won a special award in the portrait class with his *Bunny*.

70
Hisako Hibi
*Topaz Farm Products*
September 1944

Oil on canvas, 26 × 22 in. Japanese American National Museum, Los Angeles, Gift of Ibuki Hibi Lee, 96.601.32

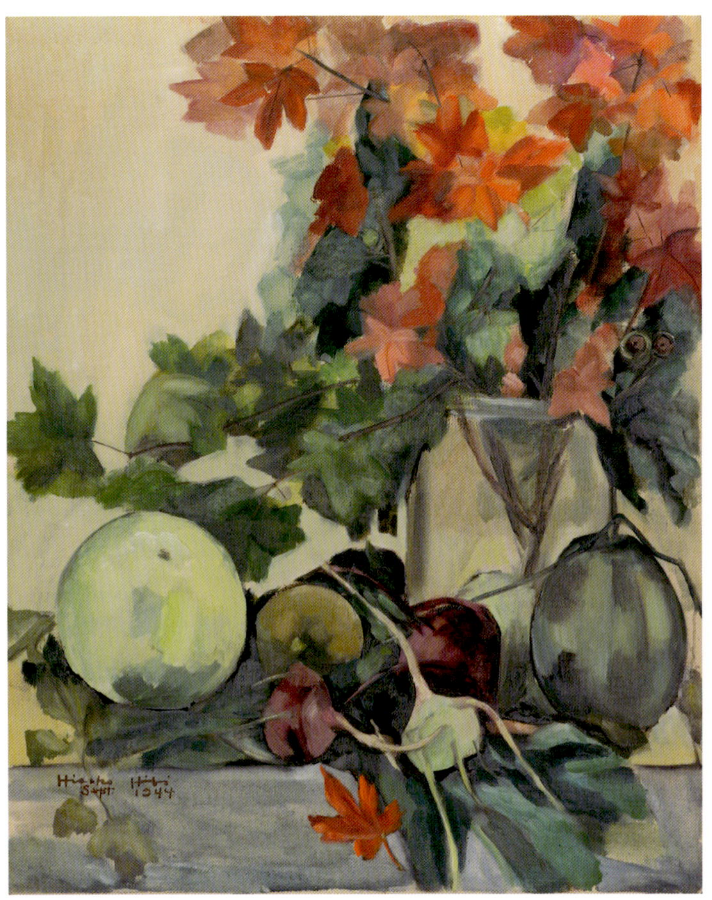

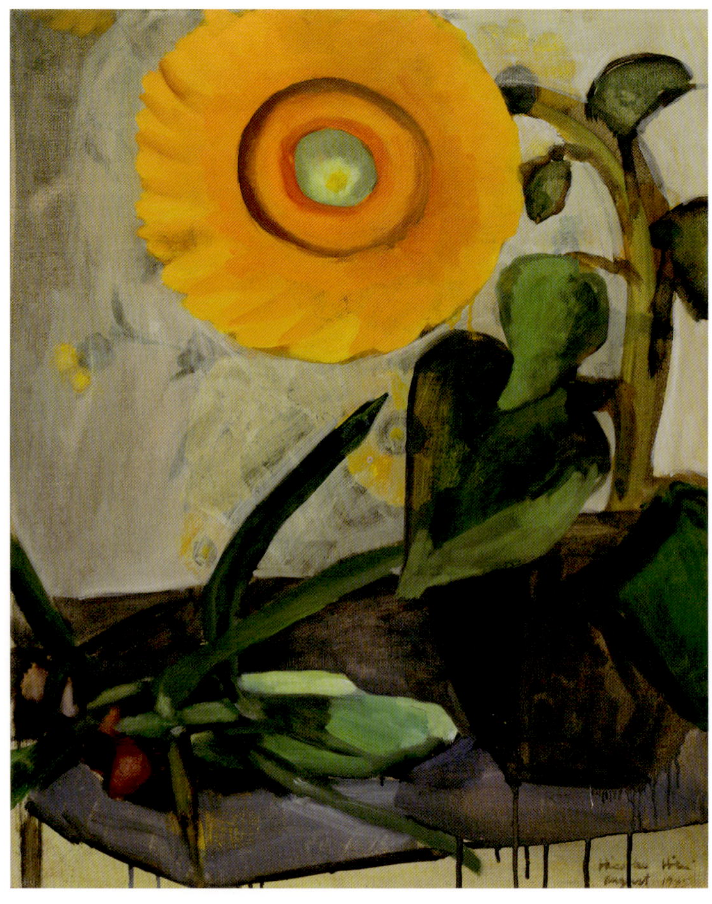

71
Hisako Hibi
*Autumn Leaves, Melons and Vegetables*
September 1944

Oil on canvas, 22 × 18 in. Japanese American National Museum, Los Angeles, Gift of Ibuki Hibi Lee, 96.601.30

72
Hisako Hibi
*Topaz Flower—Sunflower and Corn*
August 1945

Oil on canvas, 22 × 18 in. Japanese American National Museum, Los Angeles, Gift of Ibuki Hibi Lee, 96.601.55

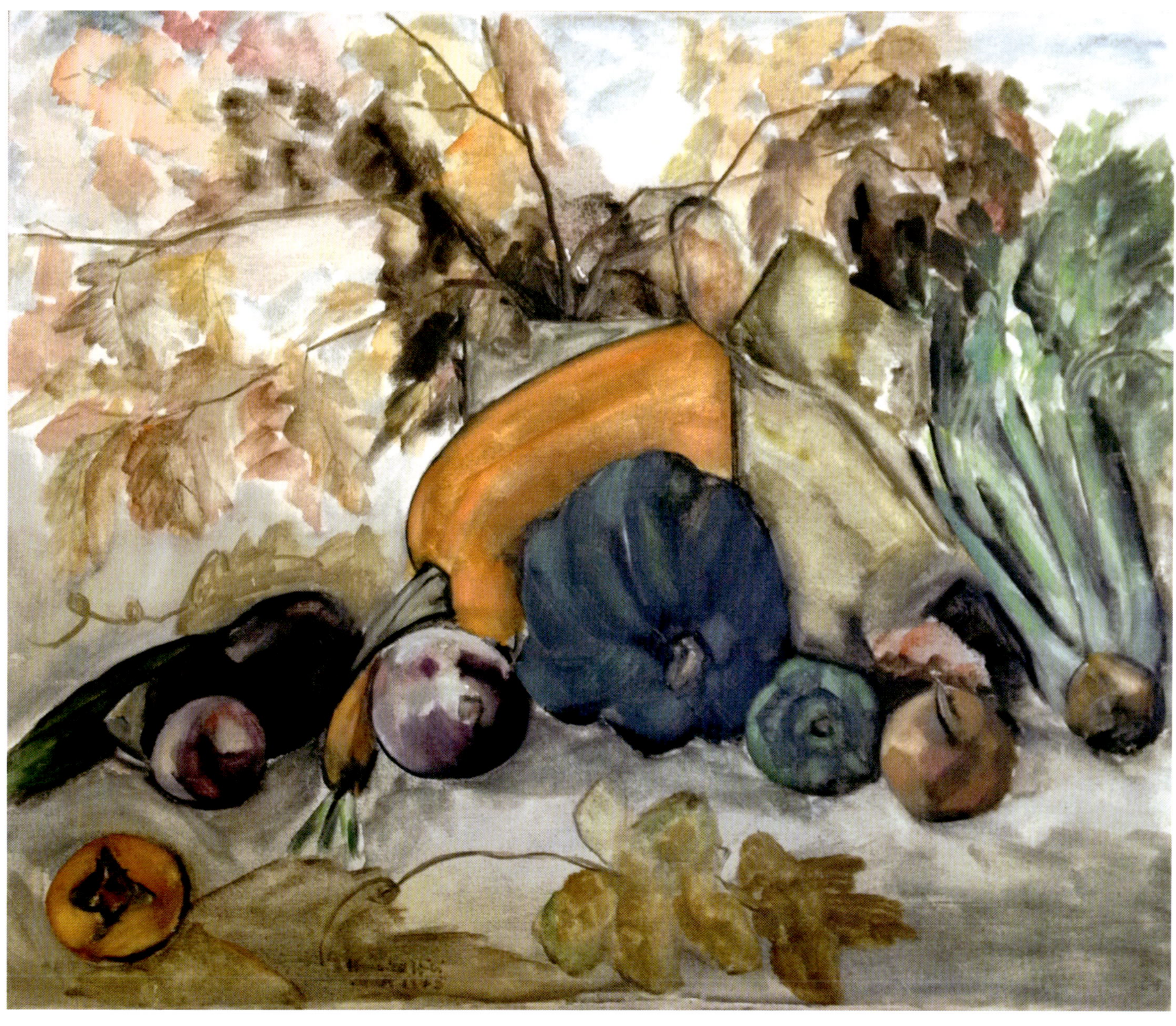

73
Hisako Hibi
*Still Life (Produce)*
New York City, 1945

Oil on canvas, 20 × 24 in. The Hibi Estate. Photo by ShiPu Wang

Cécile Whiting

# Hisako Hibi: Depicting Place and Displacement

When President Franklin D. Roosevelt issued Executive Order 9066 in the spring of 1942, Hisako and Matsusaburo George Hibi, along with their son, Satoshi, and daughter, Ibuki, were forced to leave their home in Hayward, California. Initially, they were sent to the detention center located at the former Tanforan Racetrack in San Bruno, California, and then, four months later, they were moved to the Topaz incarceration camp erected near Delta, Utah. Before leaving Hayward, the Hibis gave their paintings to neighbors to distribute to various public and civic institutions for safekeeping.[1] Only a handful of their prewar paintings survive, however. Hisako Hibi's extant paintings, depicting homes nestled in verdant, hilly landscapes in and around Mount Eden and Hayward, establish a poignant backdrop to the paintings she completed in the Tanforan and Topaz camps. Her small-scale paintings from the war, numbering around seventy, testify not to a bucolic environment but to the modern state's prison system. Identical barracks enclosed by barbed wire fences and guard towers stand in either a muddy racetrack or the desolate Utah desert. Nature provides only an occasional glimpse of beauty in a handful of these paintings. More often, it seems instead to join with the built environment to contain and oppress those imprisoned within the camps. Immediately after the war, Hibi and her family moved to New York City, where the urban landscape, absent virtually any evidence of nature, emerged in her paintings as a place of loss and fear. During the first half of her career, Hibi depicted scenes of people coexisting with, constrained by, or alienated from their setting, while remaining committed to a modernist visual language.

Hibi pursued a career in art within the possibilities and limits of a life history in which she was consistently marginalized by her ethnicity and gender. In 1920, at the age of thirteen, she moved with her parents from Japan to the United States. Five years later, she refused to return with the family to Japan, stating in retrospect that she knew she would have become the caretaker of her five younger siblings.[2] A strong spirit of independence enabled her to stay behind to complete her high school education and to undertake artistic training, starting in 1928 at the California School of Fine Arts (CSFA, later renamed the San Francisco Art Institute, now the San Francisco Art Institute Legacy

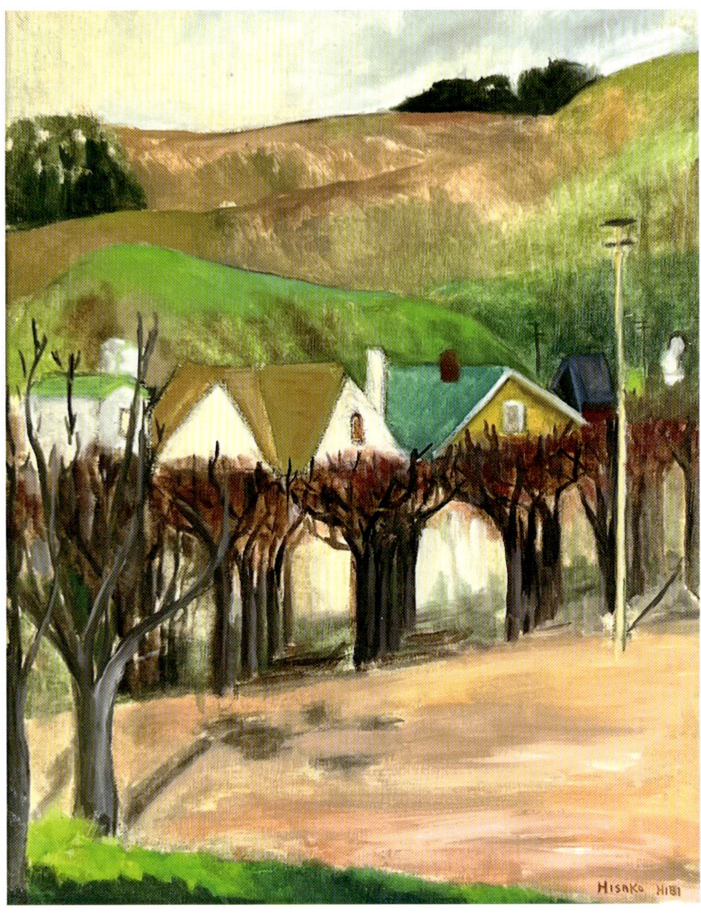


4.1

Foundation). At the CSFA, she met artist Matsusaburo George Hibi, whom she married in 1930, commenting later that she had many suitors but chose a man who understood art and would allow her to continue to paint after marriage.[3] The Hibis moved to Mount Eden in 1932 and then to Hayward, where Matsusaburo taught Japanese language and art classes, while Hisako continued to paint, exhibit her art, and raise their two children.

According to Hibi's recollections, she and her family found in Mount Eden and Hayward a thriving and welcoming Japanese American community. Japanese immigrants of various professions were attracted to the area by the low cost of living and availability of jobs. Hibi described a Japanese nursery near her home with many greenhouses filled with fragrant roses and carnations. Additionally, their house was flanked by an apricot orchard and, on the other side, a wide stretch of tomato fields cultivated by Japanese sharecroppers.[4]

*Spring II* (ca. 1940; Plate 56) exemplifies the type of idyllic landscapes Hibi painted when living in Mount Eden and Hayward. Exceptionally, this painting includes a figure: clad in work clothes, his face hidden by a broad-brimmed hat, a man bends to tend his small garden with a hoe. *Spring II* portrays a farmer coexisting peacefully with nature, cultivating his plot of land in a setting characterized by single-family homes ensconced in a pastoral landscape.

Hayward was no rural village in the 1930s but rather a small city, with municipal buildings, a thriving business district, and an urban downtown. Hibi's early paintings are, however, altogether untouched by modernity, save perhaps for the occasional presence of telephone poles. In *Spring II*, one such pole stands atop the hill at the far right, while in *Apricot Trees along Jackson Street, Hayward* (ca. 1930s; Fig. 4.1), one utility pole stands in front of the cherry orchard, obscuring the group of houses clustered at the bottom of some hills. Hibi's is an arcadian retreat removed from the modern city and its burgeoning technology.

Turning her back on urban life, Hibi adopted techniques learned in the classes in Impressionism and Post-Impressionism she had taken as a student at the CSFA. In the 1920s, Hibi had studied with Swiss American artist Gottardo Piazzoni, who took his students into Marin County to learn plein-air painting.[5] *Spring II* demonstrates that Hibi had absorbed her teacher's lessons and had aligned herself with the practice of landscape painting in Northern California. Note, for instance, how she relied on loosely applied, darker patches of brown paint to delineate the tree trunks and muddy ground in the foreground, and thinner dark lines to outline the simple geometry of the house. Striations of brown alternate with patches of green paint to indicate the plantings in the field; broad patches of green or white paint evoke the foliage of the trees. Dabs of thinned green paint build up the verdant hillside.

4.1

Hisako Hibi, *Apricot Trees along Jackson Street, Hayward*, ca. 1930s. Oil on canvas, 25½ × 17½ in. Courtesy of the Hibi Estate.

Beginning in the early twentieth century, the type of pastoral landscape Hibi painted, in a style derived from Impressionism and Post-Impressionism, replaced the bombast of mid and late nineteenth-century landscapes that had heralded the sublime wilderness of Yosemite and the Sierra Nevada. As many scholars have suggested, such pastoral landscapes contributed to an Edenic and peaceable vision of California, harkening to a past in which the rural landscape and coastline had yet to be developed by agribusiness, canneries, and shipyards.[6] By the time Hibi was painting and exhibiting her arcadian idylls in the 1930s and early 1940s, most farms functioned like large-scale factories rather than embodying the Jeffersonian ideal of the small-scale family farm. Moreover, the Alien Land Laws passed in 1913 and 1920 prohibited "aliens ineligible from citizenship"—immigrants such as the Hibis—from owning land; this legislation served as a means of forcing Japanese landowners to sell their land and preventing others from acquiring it. In the meantime, the Great Depression provoked mass migration from the Dust Bowl into California, where newcomers typically encountered legislation controlling their movement and depressed wages on corporate farms. Tensions flared in California over immigration, labor conditions, and land ownership during this period, as examined at the time by both social scientists and novelists.[7]

During this era, Hibi exhibited her landscapes, filled with small homes and farms, orchards and rolling hills, in art shows, including at the California State Fair, the Oakland Art Gallery, and the San Francisco Art Association annuals. Today, some of the titles of Hibi's landscapes include words identifying place: *Spring #2, Hayward* (1940; Plate 55) or *Apricot Trees along Jackson Street, Hayward*. However, when they were exhibited, Hibi's landscapes had generic titles such as *Early Spring* and *Spring*.[8] Few features in Hibi's paintings locate them specifically in Hayward, and none refer to the Japanese community settled in the region. The ethnicity of the figure appearing in *Spring II* is not discernable, making him a surrogate for any male farmer tending to his plot of land. Hibi's pastoral scenes depicting single-family homes and farms framed by flowering fruit trees did double duty: Inspired by Hibi's immediate local surroundings, they paid loving tribute to homes and gardens, which, while likely not owned by the Japanese immigrants in Hayward, nevertheless provided a place to which Hibi felt she belonged. At the same time, these paintings, as generic scenes of spring planting, contributed to an idealized and nostalgic vision of the family farm in California that had long ago disappeared.

Any illusion of peaceful belonging to a place was shattered on Evacuation Day, May 8, 1942. In her memoir, Hibi recalled that about a week earlier, a peddler had piled the furnishings of the Hibis' comfortable home—upright piano, radio, record player, rugs—on a cart and taken them away in exchange for a pittance.[9] Having packed some few remaining belongings in what suitcases they could carry, families such as the Hibis assembled in the Hayward City Park, mounted requisitioned Greyhound buses, and traveled to the Tanforan Assembly Center (Fig. 4.2). There, the Hibi family was housed in a whitewashed horse stall with two tiny rooms and four army cots. Only partial walls separated them from other families occupying adjacent stalls. Hibi recalls feeling nervous and irritable in Tanforan, her paintings becoming cloudy and gray.[10]

The few paintings that date from this four-month period reveal the harsh realities of detention. *Tanforan Assembly Center* (San Bruno, California, August 24, 1942; Plate 60) provides an overview of Tanforan from a slightly elevated perspective, as if Hibi had positioned herself in the grandstands, overseeing barracks packed tightly together near the bleachers and in the center of the racetrack. On the opposite side of the track, black vertical masses, perhaps trees or bushes, form a barrier, beyond which appear some small residences and barren mountains. There is no sign of life except for a bluebird flying overhead, now a symbol of freedom rather than of the bucolic pleasures of nature celebrated in *Spring II*. An obvious and dramatic shift in subject matter took

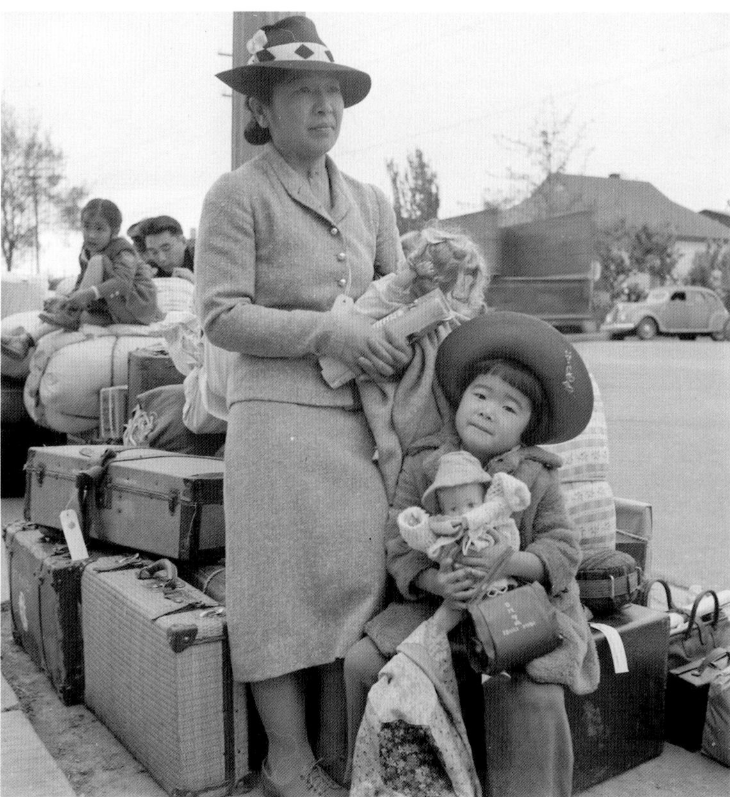

4.2

4.2

Dorothea Lange, "These people of Japanese ancestry are awaiting the special bus which will take them, and other evacuees, to the Tanforan Assembly Center. . . . ," Hayward, California, May 8, 1942. Records of the War Relocation Authority, Record Group 210, NAID 537522, National Archives at College Park, Maryland.

Lange did not note the names of her subjects: Hisako Hibi with her daughter, Ibuki. Another photo by Lange shows both Ibuki and her older brother, Satoshi, sitting on top of a pile of luggage.

place in Hibi's art at the time of her incarceration, from orchards, abundant fields, and single-family homes to the desolate prison barracks placed at the bottom of towering mountains.

The family reached Topaz on September 21, 1942, transported from California to Utah with other inmates by train and bus, and they remained imprisoned there for three years. The camp, still under construction when the Hibis arrived, was located on one square mile in the Sevier Desert, surrounded by barbed wire fences and watchtowers as well as mountains in the distance. Hibi recalled soldiers with bayonets at every gate.[11] Hibi's paintings from Topaz highlight the physical layout of the camp and the seasonal weather in the desert. Examined in chronological order, the paintings offer occasional insight into the development of the camp over time by naming and depicting new buildings, such as the high school or the auditorium. Overall, however, the paintings emphasize sameness: the imposed order of rectilinear barracks lined up in rows and surrounded by utility poles, barbed wire, and guard towers. Beyond the barbed wire, the angular gray and brown mountains provide a further natural barrier, and often share the same dark color and sharp diagonals as the barracks themselves, as seen in *Western Sky* (Topaz, Utah, July 1945; Plate 67). Titles bring attention to times of day (*Morning* [1942], *In the Evening* [1944], *A Night* [January 1944; Plate 65], *Sunset* [1944]); to seasons (*The Third Winter in Topaz* [January 1944; Fig. 4.3], *A Summer Day* [1943]); and especially to weather events (*A Stormy Day* [1943], *A Wind Brought a Storm* [1945], *White Heat* [June 1943; Plate 62], *Stormy* [1943]). Some of her titles contain gerunds—"waiting," "snowing"—to indicate states of suspension. Dramatic dust storms and snowstorms often engulf the buildings of the camp in her paintings.

Hibi's art stresses the ways in which the bleak environment constrained, depersonalized, and isolated the inmates. Dated by month and year, her paintings do more than depict a place: they also function as a kind of diary, providing snapshots of daily life within the camp. In fact, unlike the landscapes from the prewar era, Hibi's paintings completed at Topaz frequently include people contending with the prison setting and desert environment. Generally, however, when depicting her fellow detainees, Hibi eschewed portraits and instead included anonymous and frequently isolated figures, seen from a distance or behind, walking across empty foregrounds or navigating between barracks. These small staffage figures, sometimes nothing more than smudges of paint, as in the foreground of *Snowing* (January 1945; Fig. 4.4), appear bent by the wind, dust, and snowstorms. Created from one round patch of black paint on top of a diagonal stroke of gray-black paint, the figure in *Snowing* effectively evokes the force of the storm as it buffets the walker in the snow. On the one hand, these figures suggest Hibi was thinking of early Impressionism, when

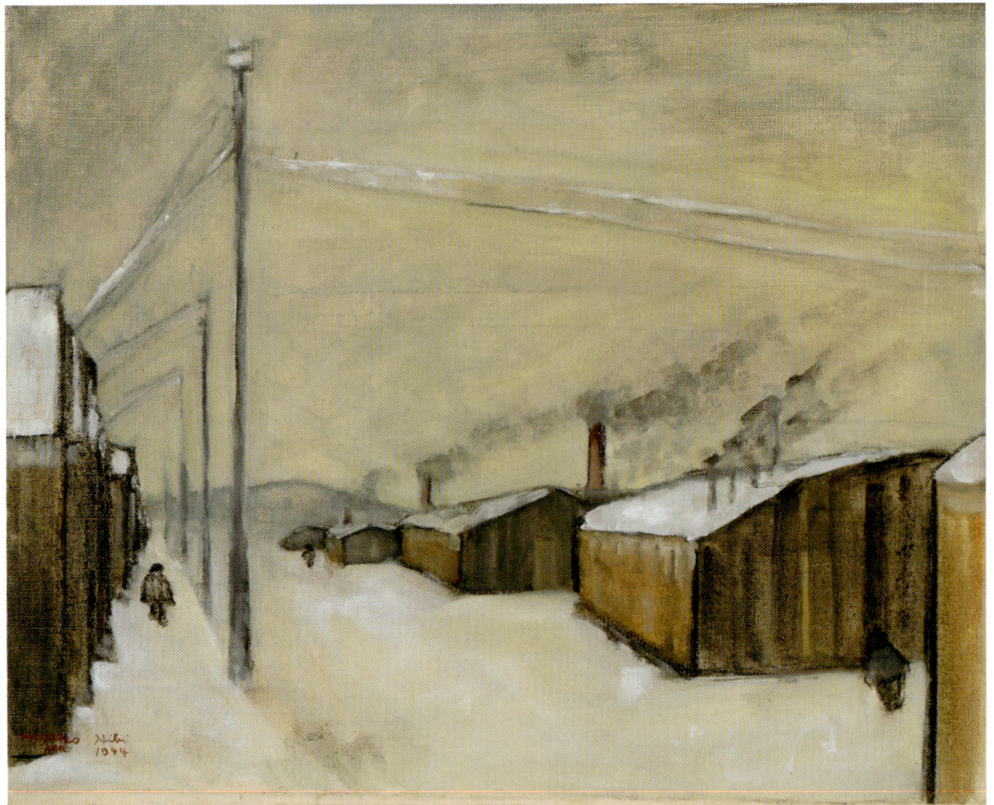

4.3

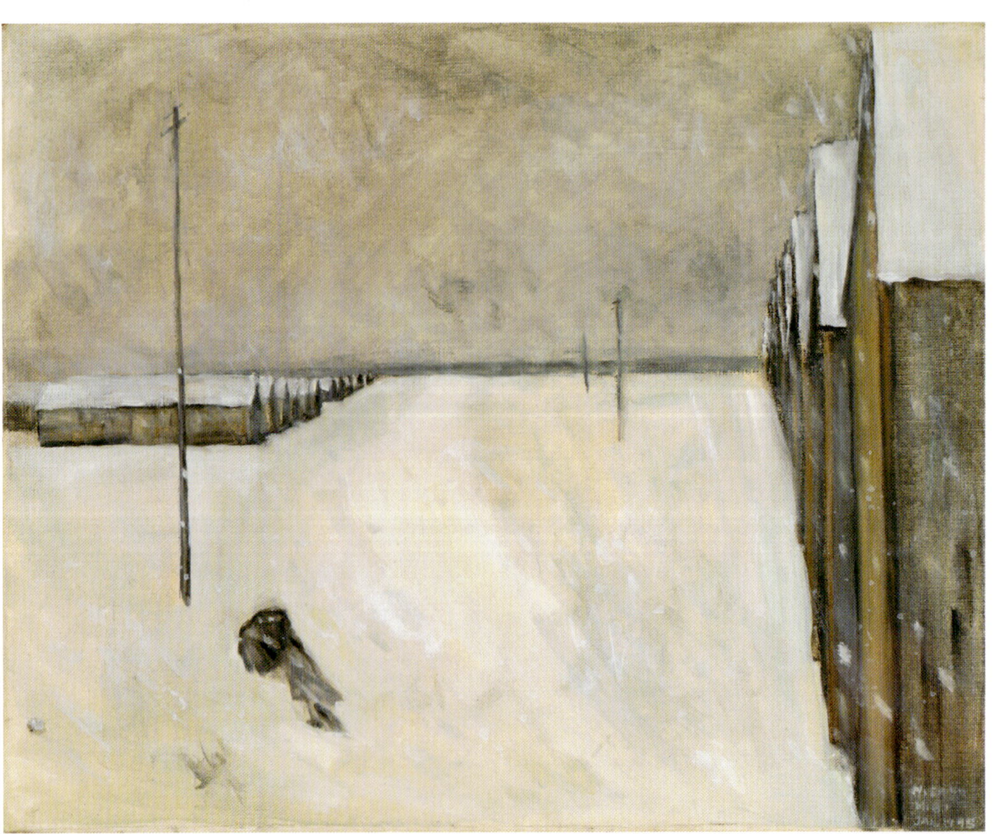

4.4

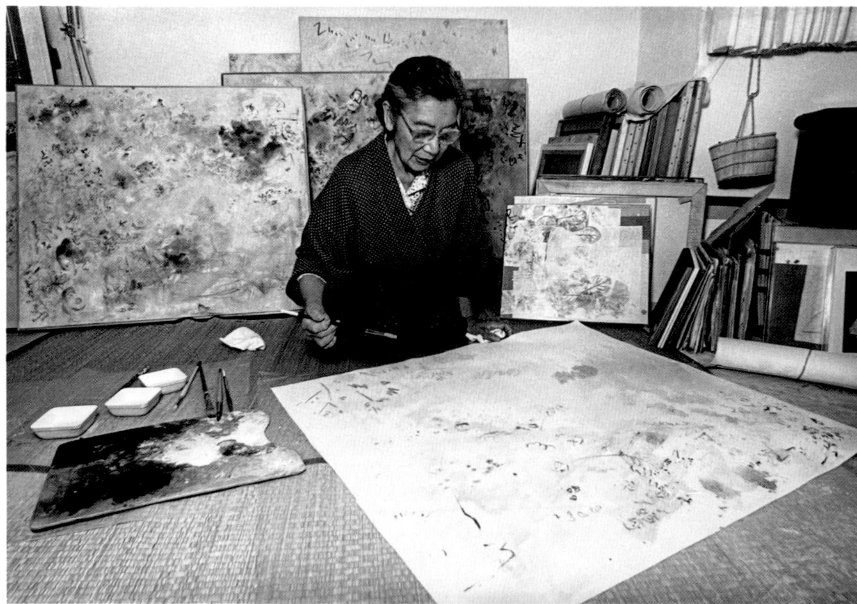

4.5

4.3

Hisako Hibi, *The Third Winter in Topaz*, January 1944. Oil on canvas, 16 × 20 in. Japanese American National Museum, Los Angeles, Gift of Ibuki Hibi Lee, 96.601.37.

4.4

Hisako Hibi, *Snowing*, January 1945. Oil on canvas, 16 × 20 in. Japanese American National Museum, Los Angeles, Gift of Ibuki Hibi Lee, 96.601.44.

4.5

Hisako Hibi painting in her one-room apartment in San Francisco's Japantown, 1985. Courtesy of the Hibi Estate.

artists such as Claude Monet reduced figures to dabs of oil paint, as seen in his *Boulevard des Capucines* of 1873. On the other hand, the small figures in Hibi's paintings emphasize the way in which camp life reduced all the prisoners to a visual uniformity that obviated the need to represent individual characteristics. Hibi later remarked that all women were forced to don cotton slacks or jeans and a bandanna, while the men had to wear army surplus khaki pants, caps, and oversized peacoats.[12] Such unvaried clothing was a far cry from the fashionable hat, jacket, and skirt in which Hibi was attired on Evacuation Day, as seen in the photograph taken by Dorothea Lange. The drab, often ill-fitting standard-issue clothes worn by the camp prisoners blurred sartorial difference between the sexes and generations.

Despite the bleak colors of the barracks and mountains, the evidence of extreme weather, and the emphatic isolation of figures, Hibi's paintings occasionally explode with joyous colors. Sometimes the scenes contain dabs of red paint to distinguish the clothing or scarves of women and children, as if to flaunt frivolity and fashion in the face of standardization and uniformity. More often, bright colors define the beauty and unpredictability of skies that extend beyond the confines of the camp, perhaps offering a source of hope and joy to inmates. In her memoir, Hibi recalled the uplifting beauty of nature—brilliant desert sunrises or sunsets, the stars at night, the infinite sky, clouds moving and changing.[13] In both *Western Sky* and *Eastern Sky 7:50 A.M.* (February 25, 1945; Plate 66), Hibi devoted over half the canvas to dramatic reds, oranges, and yellows sweeping across the skies, overwhelming the dark mountains and barracks below.

As the Topaz camp was closing, the Hibi family moved to New York City. Historian Greg Robinson suggests that the United States government actively discouraged Japanese Americans from returning to their prewar homes in an effort both to avoid racial violence on the West Coast and to encourage assimilation across the country. Given that New York already had a reputation as a gathering place for Japanese intellectuals, artists, and performers, it is not surprising that artists such as the Hibis would have moved there.[14]

Several works completed by Hibi shortly after the war, both before and after her husband's untimely death in 1947, depict the urban landscape of New York. Nature is generally absent in these paintings. In one of the most extreme examples of this shift, *Frightful NYC* (1946; Plate 75) depicts a backdrop of thin, darkly colored skyscrapers against an opaque sky (rather than the barracks and mountains of her previous paintings). The scene brings together a variety of people, including a man maneuvering a horse-drawn cart in the street and an elongated white woman attired in red on the sidewalk. Strange animals loom, such as the misshapen horse pulling a cart and the gargantuan cat peering out of a window. Two observers with dark hair, perhaps Hibi and her daughter, look out a window onto the scene. Despite Hibi's retrospective account of feeling free to explore a city filled with immigrants, her paintings of New York record a dark, claustrophobic space populated by uncanny creatures, both human and animal.[15]

In the final decades of her career, after she had returned to San Francisco in 1954 as an American citizen, Hibi's paintings moved away from traditional landscapes altogether to embrace abstraction (Fig. 4.5). She named two teachers who encouraged her shift away from Impressionism and Post-Impressionism: Victor D'Amico and Ann O'Hanlon. In 1952, she studied oil painting at the Museum of Modern Art, New York, with D'Amico, the director of art education there, who told her, "Cezanne [*sic*] is dead," and urged her "to paint your free expression your way. Your colors are the vocabulary for you."[16] In retrospect, she claimed she was not ready to embrace D'Amico's lessons fully at that time, but in 1965, she received further encouragement to explore abstraction when she attended classes with O'Hanlon and became a member of Sight and Insight/Perception Gallery at the Fort Mason Center for Art and Culture, in San Francisco.[17] O'Hanlon, who had studied at the CSFA and had also learned calligraphy in Japan, quoted the words of modernist artists while embracing the differences she perceived in artistic practice between the Japanese and European American traditions with the goal of encouraging students to explore self-perception, intuition, and abstraction.[18] Hibi noted that her colors became brighter, freer, and less representational in the mid-1960s.[19]

Actually, Hibi had been experimenting with abstraction on and off since the war, and she would continue to oscillate between abstraction and representation until the end of her career. But it was in the 1970s and 1980s that she first developed a consistent abstract vocabulary on a large scale that enabled her to revisit and rework some of the themes from the war years. At the time of her incarceration, she had already moved away from a romantic ideal in which humans coexisted harmoniously with nature, instead depicting small figures distorted and contained by the prison environment. The late abstractions, much larger in size than the earlier small-scale paintings, do not proffer a stable or coherent organization of space. Rather, any identifiable motifs—human head or figure, Japanese calligraphy, leaf, bird—are caught up in fulsome loops, dashes, and splotches of rich color that collapse the difference between the observing self and nature. These late paintings unleash dynamic, undulating layers of colorful paint, inspired by the seasons (*Eternal Seasons* [1983; Plate 103]), weather (*Storm* [1972]), or humans (*Pollution* [1974] and *War and Suffering* [1982; Plate 102]). Enveloping viewers in their swirling momentum and shifting moods, these paintings highlight a present and ongoing experience of the seasons, a storm, or war, rather than depicting a coherent space that captures an idyllic spring day or a horrifying prison ordeal from another time and place.[20]

Largely overlooked by the art world, Hibi nevertheless pursued professional development and experimentation in painting throughout her life. A prolific artist, she focused during the first period of her career on landscape painting in which the varying relationships of people to their environment often testified to her own life experiences. Of those paintings, the landscapes dating from the 1930s contributed to regional myths of California, while her subsequent landscapes from the early 1940s document a shameful episode in the history of the nation during World War II. It was not until the end of her career that Hibi solidified a visual vocabulary to depict not particular experiences or locations but broader phenomena that cut across cultural and even national differences.

Dr. Cécile Whiting is professor emerita and Chancellor's Professor of Art History at the University of California, Irvine. The winner of the twenty-first annual Charles Eldredge Prize for Outstanding Scholarship in American Art for *Pop L.A.: Art and the City in the 1960s* (University of California Press, 2006), she also received the 2018 Lawrence A. Fleischman Award for Scholarly Excellence in the Field of American Art History from the Smithsonian Archives of American Art.

NOTES

1 "Japanese Artist Leaves All Paintings to Hayward Groups," *Hayward Daily Review*, April 9, 1942, newspaper clipping, Hayward Area Historical Society.
2 Biographical information comes from the Japanese American National Museum Guide to the Hisako Hibi Collection and Hisako Hibi, *Peaceful Painter: Memoirs of an Issei Woman Artist*, ed. Ibuki Hibi Lee (Berkeley: Heyday Books, 2004).
3 Leonard D. Chan and Philip Chin, "An Interview with Ibuki Hibi Lee," *AACP Newsletter* (Asian American Curriculum Project) (July 2005): 2.
4 Hibi, *Peaceful Painter*, 7, 11. For a history of the area, see the Hayward Area Historical Society's website, https://www.haywardareahistory.org/.
5 Hibi, *Peaceful Painter*, 6.
6 On the relationship between California Impressionism and the growth of industry in Northern California, see Anthony Lee, *Painting on the Left: Diego Rivera, Radical Politics, and San Francisco's Public Murals* (Berkeley: University of California Press, 1999), 76–80. On California Impressionism, see Emily Neff, *The Modern West* (New Haven: Yale University Press with the Museum of Fine Arts, Houston, 2006); and Steven Nash, *Facing Eden: 100 Years of Landscape Art in the Bay Area* (Berkeley: University of California Press, 1995).
7 Colleen Lye, *America's Asia: Racial Form and American Literature, 1893–1945* (Princeton, N.J.: Princeton University Press, 2005), 141–203.
8 The title *Apricot Trees along Jackson Street* appears below the reproduction of the painting in Hibi, *Peaceful Painter*, 42. The titles *Spring* and *Early Spring* appear in catalogues for the 1939 Annual Exhibition of Paintings at the Art Gallery of the California State Fair, Sacramento, and the 1940 Annual Exhibition of Oil Paintings at the Oakland Art Gallery, respectively.
9 Hibi, *Peaceful Painter*, 11.
10 Transcript of speech presented by Hisako Hibi at the symposium "A View from Inside" at the Oakland Museum, co-sponsored by the UC Berkeley Asian American Studies Department, on October 16, 1976.
11 Hibi, *Peaceful Painter*, 20.
12 Hibi, *Peaceful Painter*, 24.
13 Hibi, *Peaceful Painter*, 21–22.
14 Greg Robinson, *After Camp: Portraits in Midcentury Japanese American Life and Politics* (Berkeley: University of California Press, 2012), 3, 54.
15 Hibi, *Peaceful Painter*, 29–36.
16 Hisako Hibi, interview by Eric Saul for the oral history project for the National Japanese American Historical Society, San Francisco, March 23, 1986, 9.
17 Hibi, *Peaceful Painter*, 37.
18 For more information on Ann O'Hanlon, see Ann O'Hanlon, *Seeing/Perception: Looking at the World through an Artist's Eye* (Sausalito, Calif.: Arctos Press, 2001); and Susi Martin and Elinor Severinghaus, *According to Ann . . . [Re-Imagined]* (Mill Valley, Calif.: O'Hanlon Center for the Arts, 2019).
19 Hibi, *Peaceful Painter*, 39.
20 The only substantive scholarly analysis on these paintings is Karin Higa, "What Is an Asian American Woman Artist?" in *Art/Women/California, 1950–2000: Parallels and Intersections*, ed. Diane Burgess Fuller and Daniela Salvione (Berkeley: University of California Press in association with the San José Museum of Art, 2002), 7–89.

Patricia Wakida

# The Remarkable and Resilient Lives of Hisako Hibi and Miné Okubo

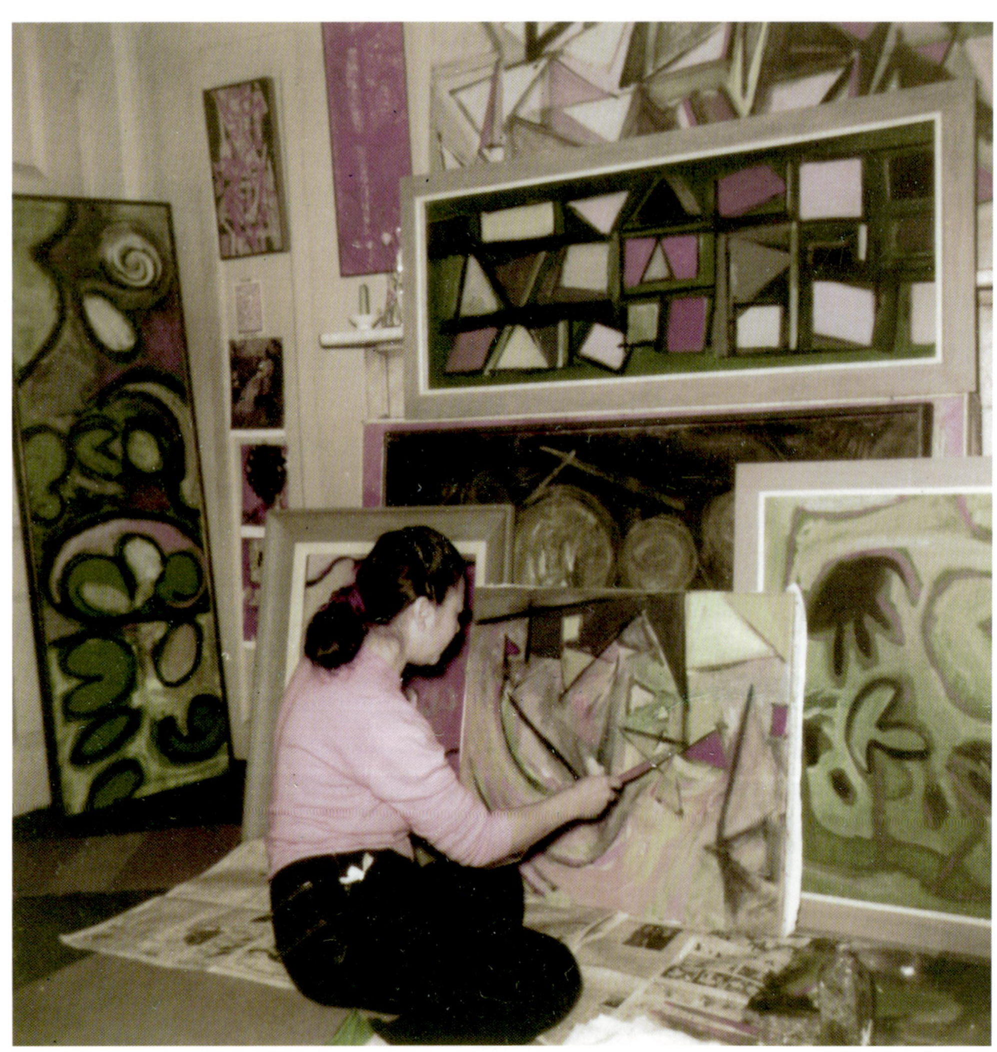

5.1

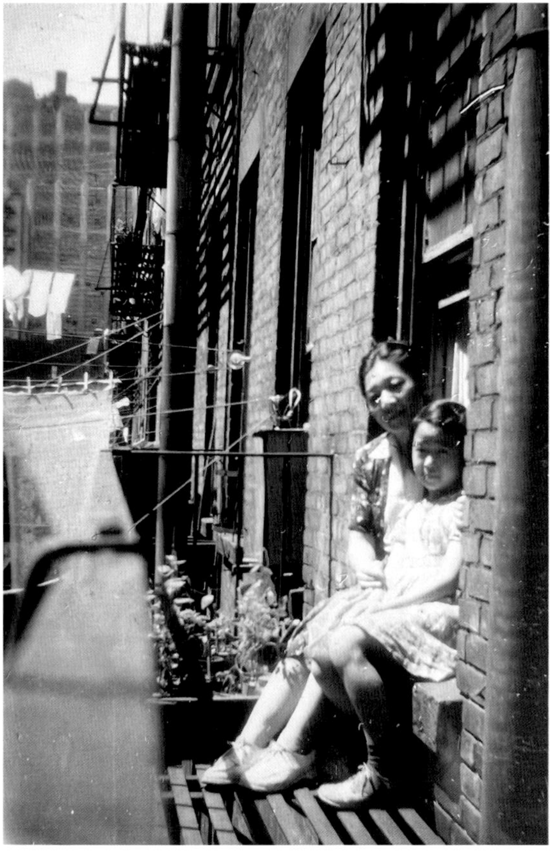

5.2

5.1

Miné Okubo in her studio, 1956. The Miné Okubo Collection, Center for Social Justice & Civil Liberties, Riverside Community College District, California, s-e-29-1a.

5.2

Photograph taken by Matsusaburo George Hibi of wife Hisako and daughter Ibuki sitting by the window of their New York apartment, ca. 1946. Courtesy of the Hibi Estate.

Eight decades ago, Hisako Hibi and Miné Okubo left an American concentration camp located in the salty desertscape of Utah, where they had been detained throughout World War II. They were swept up in the detention of 125,284 West Coast Japanese Americans and imprisoned at Tanforan, in San Bruno, California, and Topaz, near Delta, Utah. Prior to the war, Hibi and Okubo had achieved acclaim in California's mainstream art world and were part of a diverse San Francisco milieu, where Japanese and Chinese artists were active contributors. Despite the traumatic loss of their civil liberties, Hibi and Okubo used every opportunity to make art under incarceration. Okubo taught at the Tanforan Art School and served on the staff of the *Topaz Times* newspaper and *Trek* magazine,[1] all while recording her camp experience through over two hundred ink drawings on paper. Hibi, too, spent her days in exile creating art. In addition to raising two young children, she produced more than seventy oil paintings and a sheaf of sketches and taught at the Topaz Art School, which was founded by fellow artist Chiura Obata. Hibi's husband, artist Matsusaburo George Hibi, worked closely with Obata on the art school's curriculum and took over the school's directorship when Obata left Topaz.

Unlike Okubo, who was born in California and thus a Nisei, or second-generation American citizen, Hisako and Matsusaburo Hibi were Issei, or immigrants, which added additional stress to their predicament, since they were labeled wartime "enemy aliens" with no legal rights while the two countries were at war. Shame, repressed pain, and sorrow—in addition to the fear of rejection and the unknown—had a deep, lasting impact on the artists. This essay illuminates how Hibi and Okubo continued making art in the postwar decades and found new communities in which they thrived. They began their postwar lives in Manhattan, facing racism, poverty, and other hardships, but never gave up on their creative lives, persevering and growing into adventurous artists and inspiring models for successive generations.

In January 1945, the U.S. government announced that Topaz would permanently close by October 31; there were still 5,922 inmates living at the camp, mostly elderly Issei and families with young children with no place to return to. Okubo had been able to leave Topaz on January 19, 1944, with the assistance of a work sponsor, and moved to Manhattan's Greenwich Village (Fig. 5.1).[2] The Hibi family, on the other hand, were among the last detainees to leave. On September 19, 1945, they passed the Topaz gatehouse one final time and took trains from Utah to Chicago and then to New York City, where they relied on a network of Japanese American camp friends who faced the same dilemma of finding housing. When Matsusaburo inquired about a nightly room at the New Yorker Hotel on upscale West 34th Street and Eighth Avenue, he was flatly denied.[3] Long term, the family rented the third story "railroad" apartment at 458 West

37th Street for twenty dollars a month; the apartment, like camp, was heated by a coal-burning potbelly stove, but they had a private toilet (Fig. 5.2).[4] Matsusaburo held a number of temporary jobs, and Hisako found work in the garment industry: "A friend from Topaz was working at the shop of a top-notch Madison Avenue fashion designer, Charles James. She helped me get a job as an apprentice seamstress. Dress orders for evening gowns came from Washington D.C. and New York high society, and many young, aspiring designers were studying these."[5] Aside from the stresses of city life, the Hibis were surrounded by a dynamic Japanese American circle of artists such as Hideo Date, Henry Sugimoto, Lewis Suzuki, and Miné Okubo, all fresh from the camps, in addition to Issei and Nisei artists who had not been imprisoned due to their East Coast residency, such as Yasuo Kuniyoshi, Isamu Noguchi, and Michi Weglyn.

Dark shadows soon fell over the Hibis' new life when Hisako was admitted to St. Vincent's Hospital in 1946 for severe pain. Although she underwent a hysterectomy, the cancer would persist for years. In June, Matsusaburo began complaining of "unpleasant feelings from his right shoulder down to his ribs," but doctors couldn't find a cause and diagnosed it as possibly arthritis.[6] As Hisako recalled: "In the fall Matsusaburo consulted an Issei physician who immediately noticed his jaundice. The Caucasian doctor who had examined him before had not suspected jaundice because he said that he thought Asians naturally have yellowish skin. With still a great deal of hope for the future, Matsusaburo died of cancer in June 1947, just one year and nine months after coming to New York City."[7]

In marked contrast to Hibi's struggles, Okubo arrived in New York with a job and connections. While still incarcerated, she had submitted a drawing of a camp guard to the San Francisco Art Association's annual exhibition in 1943 and won a top prize (Plate 28). Impressed, *San Francisco Chronicle* editors featured Okubo's sketches, which attracted the attention of Deborah Calkins, associate art director of *Fortune* magazine. Calkins sent a telegram to Okubo at Topaz, inquiring about a commission for the magazine's year-end issue on Japan, in conjunction with Issei artists Yasuo Kuniyoshi and Taro Yashima.[8] This interaction led to a second invitation for Okubo to create work, this time for the April 1944 issue, titled "Japan and the Japanese: We Must Defeat, a Pacific Problem We Must Solve."[9] Okubo's commissioned illustrations were a sensation and were featured, alongside works by Kuniyoshi and Yashima, in a special exhibition at the San Francisco Museum of Art in August 1944.[10]

Once she arrived in New York, Okubo met with M. Margaret Anderson, editor of *Common Ground*, a magazine published in the 1940s by the Common Council for American Unity, which featured articles by and about Japanese Americans who had been incarcerated and their postwar resettlement. In March 1945, Okubo exhibited her camp imagery in an exhibit at the *Common Ground* offices, before it toured

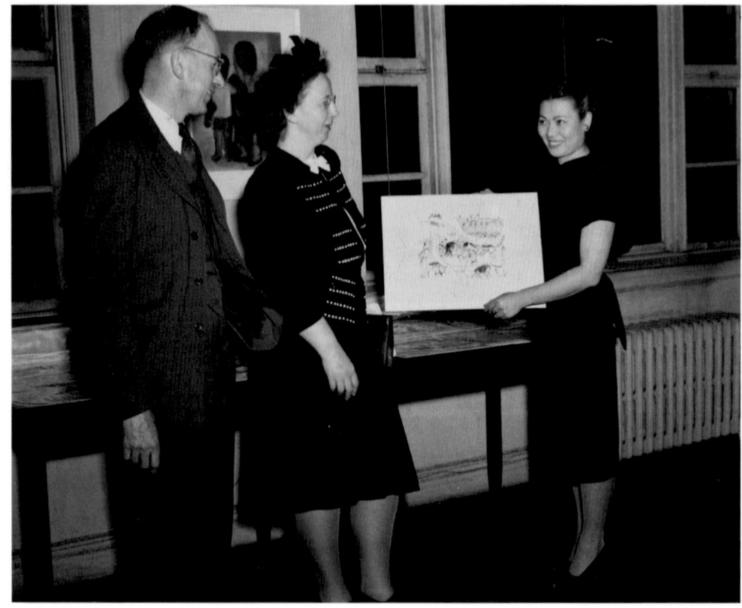

5.3

5.3
"Miss Mine Okubo, Nisei, who resettled to New York from the Topaz Center, is showing one of her drawings to Read Lewis, executive director of the Community Council for American Unity, and Miss M. Margaret Anderson, editor of the Council quarterly, *Common Ground*, at the opening of an exhibit of Miss Okubo's drawing and paintings of center life under the Council's auspices March 6, at the American Common," 1945. War Relocation Authority Photographs of Japanese-American Evacuation and Resettlement, 1942–45, BANC PIC 1967.014—PIC, The Bancroft Library, University of California, Berkeley, WRA no. G-829. Photo by Toge Fujihira. Courtesy of Wikimedia Commons.

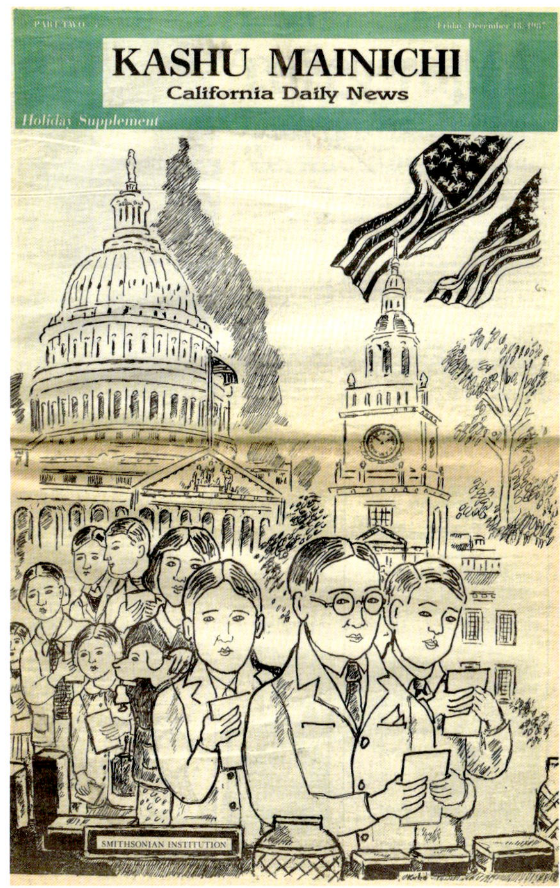


5.4

5.4

Miné Okubo's illustration for *Kashu Mainichi/ California Daily News*, December 18, 1987. The Miné Okubo Collection, Center for Social Justice & Civil Liberties, Riverside Community College District, California.

the West Coast (Fig. 5.3).[11] In September of the same year, her graphic memoir, *Citizen 13660*, was published by Columbia University Press. It was the first book on the camp experience written by a former incarceree and was widely lauded for its powerful visual storytelling and Okubo's biting wit, while introducing the physical and emotional toll of the concentration camps to the American public.

Okubo realized that she could not support herself through selling paintings alone and began accepting more commissions, including mural work and illustrations, which were featured in books and national periodicals (Fig. 5.4). However, by 1960, she knew it was time to return to her painting. Utilizing rhythm, line, and color, Okubo invented a vibrant, imaginative world populated with curious figures cavorting with cats and birds to "reaffirm the human qualities and the vital spirit"[12] in a steadfast pursuit of her own vision.

Hibi went through a metamorphosis as well. After Matsusaburo's death, she labored on as a single mother and seamstress, but still found time to enroll in a weekly class with artist Victor D'Amico at the Museum of Modern Art. D'Amico's advocacy for a return to the "child's mind, [to] go back to nothingness"[13] left an impact on Hibi, as seen in paintings that became increasingly abstract, emphasizing the effects of light and the application of short, deliberate paint strokes.

The 1952 Immigration and Nationality Act (also known as the McCarran-Walter Act) made foreign-born Asians eligible to become American citizens for the first time. Hibi, who had always loved the freedom allotted to women in the United States as compared to Japan,[14] seized the opportunity and was granted American citizenship in 1953. A year later, she and her daughter, Ibuki, left New York for San Francisco: "After a twelve-year absence from the Bay Area, many things had changed, but the beautiful scenery of San Francisco had not—the blue water and sky, the good weather, the hills of the city, the Golden Gate bridge, the clanging bells of the cable cars."[15] They stayed with Tom and Kazue Yamashita on Sutter Street, then moved to an in-law garden apartment on 21st Avenue, where they lived while Ibuki finished high school.[16] Hibi applied for a sewing machine operator's job at the San Francisco Dressmakers Union and worked a demanding job at the Lilli Ann and Betty Clyne Factories, sewing off-the-rack garments that sold at chic department stores such as City of Paris and I. Magnin. She reinvigorated her art practice by enrolling in a noncredit course, Painting with Ralph Putzker, at the California School of Fine Arts (later renamed the San Francisco Art Institute, now the San Francisco Art Institute Legacy Foundation), in the fall of 1958 and spring of 1959.[17]

Once Ibuki finished her undergraduate studies and moved to New York, Hibi retired from dressmaking and found employment as a live-in housekeeper for socialite artist Helen Salz, who was known for painting portraits of her bohemian friends (Fig. 5.5). Salz had also co-founded the Northern California chapter of the American Civil Liberties Union (ACLU) with Alexander Meiklejohn in 1934 and remained an executive board member for life. The Northern California ACLU was dedicated to challenging the wartime violation of Japanese Americans' civil rights, and Salz showed her support personally by offering refuge to a succession of domestic servants at her home.[18]

In 1972, Hibi permanently left the Salz household and went to live with Ibuki and her children in New York for an entire year, and from 1974 to 1975, she visited her parents and son, Satoshi, in Japan, while recording her experiences in paintings. When she returned from her sojourns, she moved to the studio apartment below the Lucien Labaudt Art Gallery at 1407 Gough Street, where she lived and painted for nearly a decade. The list of artists who exhibited during the Labaudt Gallery's tenure included a constellation of local talent, such as muralist Lucienne Bloch, painter Gottardo Piazzoni, and ceramicist Antonio Prieto, as well as important Asian Americans like Nobuo Kitagaki, Yun Gee, and Wilfred Wong.[19] Labaudt dedicated a posthumous exhibit to Matsusaburo Hibi in 1962 and staged Hisako's first solo show in 1970.

In a cultural environment that encompassed the Vietnam War, the birth of ethnic studies, and the coming of age of the Sansei generation,[20] interest in firsthand accounts of the concentration camps intensified, but it wasn't until the late 1960s that a national movement demanding that the U.S. government take accountability for the gross abuse of Japanese Americans' civil liberties commenced. As the redress and reparations movement gathered steam, Hibi's and Okubo's wartime art was being rediscovered.

The redress movement raised awareness of a broader history of Asian American oppression and resistance, and artist collectives such as Visual Communications, Kearny Street Workshop, and the I-Hotel Committee proliferated. In 1970, the artist collective Basement Workshop was founded by artists and urban planners in New York's Chinatown, and it went on to produce the seminal publications *Bridge: The Magazine of Asians in America* (1971–85) and *Yellow Pearl* (1972), host performances and readings, and mount exhibitions of artists such as Tomie Arai, Larry Hama, and Alan Okada. Executive director Fay Chiang struck a deep friendship with Okubo and hosted an exhibit of her work in 1985. By this time, Okubo's

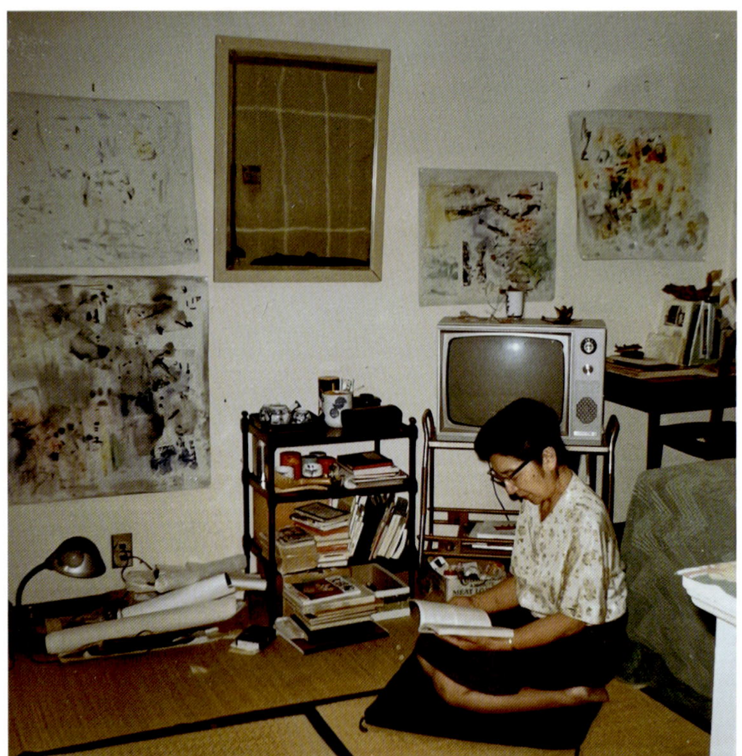

5.5

5.5 Hisako Hibi wrote on the back of the photo: "My room—a housekeeper of Mrs. Helen Salz, from June 1963–May 1972." Courtesy of the Hibi Estate.

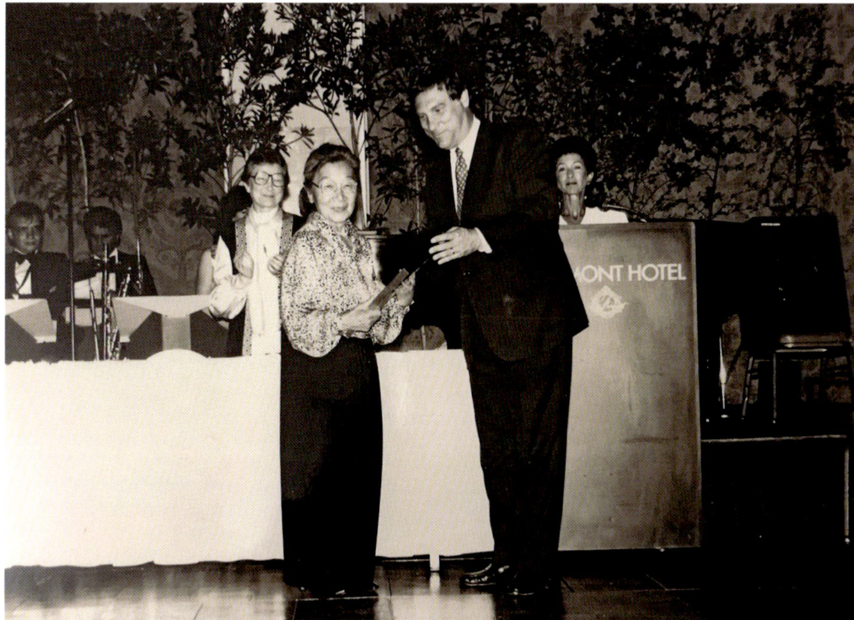


5.6

identity as a Japanese American and her understanding of what it meant to be Nisei was nationally amplified. She was featured in a 1965 CBS-TV documentary titled *Nisei: The Pride and the Shame*, and in 1972, *Miné Okubo: An American Experience*, her first major retrospective, opened at the Oakland Museum. Earlier that year, the first national exhibition of art created in the wartime concentration camps, *Months of Waiting, 1942–1945*, had opened in San Francisco, featuring work by six artists: Estelle Ishigo, Chiura Obata, Henry Sugimoto, Miné Okubo, Matsusaburo Hibi, and Hisako Hibi. A string of shows that included artwork by Okubo or one or both Hibis, and sometimes all three, followed.

Nearly forty years after leaving Topaz, Okubo told her story again, this time to the Commission on Wartime Relocation and Internment of Civilians (CWRIC), a Congress-appointed committee charged with reviewing the facts surrounding Executive Order 9066 and its impact. The CWRIC held public hearings across the country, including a one-day session on November 23, 1981, at the Roosevelt Hotel in New York, where other witnesses included Issei artist Henry Sugimoto. In her testimony, Okubo raised the issue of the failure to include the Japanese American incarceration in school curricula: "I believe an apology and some form of reparation are due in order to prevent this from happening to others. Textbooks and history studies on this subject should be taught to children when young in grade and high schools. Many generations do not know that this ever happened in the United States."[21] She ended by presenting a copy of *Citizen 13660* and displayed her sketches, drawings, and paintings at the back of the room. The CWRIC ultimately concluded that the U.S. government's policy of exclusion, removal, and detention of all West Coast residents of Japanese ancestry—with no evidence of espionage or sabotage—was the result of racial prejudice, war hysteria, and a failure of political leadership.[22] The commission recommended that Congress offer a public apology, provide appropriate funding for educational purposes, and award reparations of $20,000 to each of the surviving persons of Japanese ancestry incarcerated during World War II.[23]

Meanwhile, Hibi was also being recognized for her lifelong contributions to American art. The San Francisco Arts Commission presented her with an Award of Honor and a solo show, *Hisako Hibi, Her Path: 1935–1985*, at the Somar Gallery in 1985 (Fig. 5.6). A year later, the National Japanese American Historical Society recorded her oral history and mounted a retrospective titled *Floating Clouds*; at the show's opening, Rep. Robert T. Matsui delivered a Congressional Salute in Hibi's honor.

To mark the bicentennial of the U.S. Constitution in 1987, the Smithsonian National Museum of American History acknowledged the World War II American concentration camps with the exhibit *A More Perfect Union: Japanese Americans and the United States Constitution*, which again included artwork by Hibi and Okubo. Morale in the community was high, as redress was gaining momentum in Congress, when the Oakland Museum

5.6

Hisako Hibi receiving the San Francisco Arts Commission award, 1985. Courtesy of the Hibi Estate.

premiered *Strength and Diversity: Japanese American Women, 1885–1990*, presenting the relatively unknown stories of Japanese American women and featuring five of Hibi's camp paintings. The museum invited Hibi to a panel of Issei, Nisei, and Sansei women speakers, before an audience of college students.

In the early 1990s, a brilliant curator named Karin Higa, representing the visionary, soon-to-open Japanese American National Museum (JANM) in Los Angeles, visited Hibi and discovered an astonishing inventory of paintings stacked along the apartment walls. Higa was curating an exhibition of art produced in camps to commemorate the fiftieth anniversary of the signing of Executive Order 9066. In October 1992, *The View from Within*, featuring 130 pieces of artwork, opened in Los Angeles before traveling nationally. Higa wrote: "The biggest obstacle in organizing an exhibition of this kind is finding the art. For every painting or drawing saved, many others were lost. For every artist included in this exhibition, there must be others who have not been identified or acknowledged."[24] Higa's trailblazing effort not only brought many artists out of obscurity but also made an exhibition like *Pictures of Belonging* possible.

Hisako Hibi had donated most of Matsusaburo's camp paintings, sketches, and prints to the Japanese American Research Project at the University of California, Los Angeles, in 1962, but her own art stayed within the family after her passing in 1991. Higa returned to San Francisco in 1992, this time accompanied by JANM's senior historian, James Hirabayashi. These discussions between JANM and the Hibi family led to the donation to the museum of sixty-three oil paintings created at Tanforan and Topaz and resulted in the retrospective *A Process of Reflection: Paintings by Hisako Hibi*, on view at JANM from July 27, 1999, through January 30, 2000.

In her final years, Hibi moved into an apartment on Sutter Street, marking a return to Japantown, where she had once lived as a newlywed, and found solace at Hinode Towers, with its spectacular views and outpouring of natural light. Living in Japantown put Hibi in walking distance of the Buddhist Church of San Francisco, and she eventually gifted the church a painting she made at Topaz, depicting the Obon festival under a full summer moon; today, the painting still hangs in the church. Hibi died at age eighty-four on October 25, 1991; Hisako's and Matsusaburo's cremated remains are at the Japanese Cemetery in Colma, California. The marble tombstone at the site includes a rendering of an eagle, carved by Hibi, based on one of Matsusaburo's final paintings.[25]

Okubo remained in her Greenwich Village flat for more than fifty years, painting canvases on the floor while navigating the furniture as an afterthought. By the time of her death, at age eighty-eight, in 2001, she had amassed thousands of pieces of artwork. At her request, her art and archives went to numerous repositories, including the Riverside Community College District (RCCD), in California. In February 2006, RCCD officially named a street on campus Miné Okubo Avenue, and her collection was put on permanent exhibition in its Center for Social Justice & Civil Liberties, which opened on Okubo's one hundredth birthday, in June 2012.

Throughout their lives, Hibi and Okubo sought to discover what was possible by allowing themselves to transform, liberated by art and spirit. "But after all these years of struggle, it's coming into the wholeness of life, the wholeness of yourself again," Okubo once mused. "And you realize that you had nothing to learn—that you had it all from the very beginning. Once you make it good in one thing, all else will follow."[26]

Patricia Wakida is associate editor of the Densho Encyclopedia project and a contributing editor to the Discover Nikkei website. She formerly served as associate curator of history at the Japanese American National Museum and currently serves on the Topaz Museum Board of Directors.

## NOTES

1 *Trek* was a literary and art magazine produced at Topaz between December 1942 and June 1943. Three quarterly issues were produced in this period.
2 Deborah Gesensway and Mindy Roseman, *Beyond Words: Images from America's Concentration Camps* (Ithaca, N.Y.: Cornell University Press, 1987), 69.
3 Hisako Hibi, *Peaceful Painter: Memoirs of an Issei Woman Artist*, ed. Ibuki Hibi Lee (Berkeley: Heyday Books, 2004), 29.
4 Satoshi Hibi, interview by the author, April 14, 2022.
5 Hibi, *Peaceful Painter*, 32.
6 Hibi, *Peaceful Painter*, 32.
7 Hibi, *Peaceful Painter*, 32.
8 Deborah Calkins, telegram to Miné Okubo, October 5, 1943, Miné Okubo Papers, Center for Social Justice & Civil Liberties, Riverside Community College District, California.
9 Christine Hong, "Illustrating the Post-War Peace: Miné Okubo, the 'Citizen-Subject' of Japan, and *Fortune* Magazine," *American Quarterly* 67, no. 1 (March 2015): 120.
10 "Japanese Works to Be Shown," *Oakland Tribune*, August 6, 1944, 18.
11 *Topaz Times*, March 6, 1945.
12 Shirley Sun, *Miné Okubo: An American Experience* (Oakland, Calif.: Oakland Museum, 1972), 41.
13 Hisako Hibi, interview by Eric Saul for the oral history project for the National Japanese American Historical Society, San Francisco, March 23, 1986.
14 Ibuki Hibi Lee, email interview by the author, March 16, 2022.
15 Hibi, *Peaceful Painter*, 36.
16 Ibuki Hibi Lee, email interview by the author, March 15, 2022.
17 Hisako Shimizu file, California School of Arts/San Francisco Art Institute Office of the Registrar, accessed June 23, 2022.
18 Helen A. Salz, *Sketches of an Improbable Ninety Years*, oral history transcript, August 20, 1974, Bancroft Library, University of California, Berkeley.
19 "Honoring All Exhibitions, 1946–1966, Lucien Labaudt Annuals," broadside, Hibi Family Collection.
20 "Sansei" refers to third-generation Japanese Americans.
21 Records of the Commission on Wartime Relocation and Internment of Civilians, Record Group 220: Records of Temporary Committees, Commissions, and Boards, 1893–1999, National Archives, Unsolicited Testimony files, 1981–1982. For the full text of Okubo's testimony, see "Selected Artist Statements" in this catalogue.
22 Commission on Wartime Relocation and Internment of Civilians, *Personal Justice Denied, Part Two: Recommendations* (Washington, D.C.: U.S. Government Printing Office, 1983), 8–10.
23 H.R. 442, "An Act to Implement Recommendations of the Commission on Wartime Relocation and Internment of Civilians," approved August 10, 1988; PL 100-383; General Records of the United States Government, Record Group 11, National Archives.
24 Karin Higa, *The View from Within: Japanese American Art from the Internment Camps, 1942–1945* (Los Angeles: Japanese American National Museum, 1992), 16.
25 Ibuki Hibi Lee, email interview by the author, March 17, 2022.
26 Sun, *Miné Okubo*, 51.

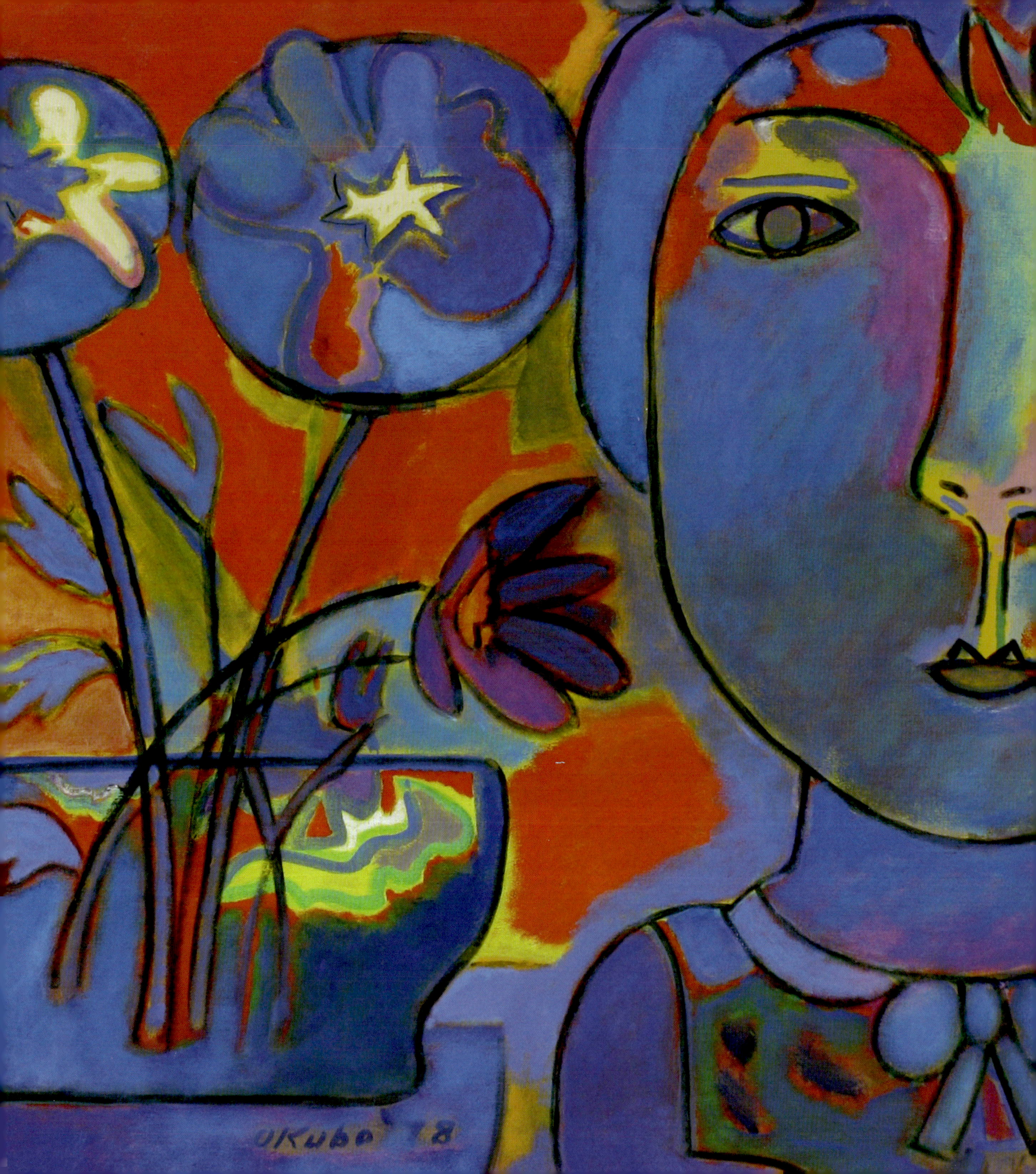
OKUBO '78

# III

# Explorations & Rediscoveries

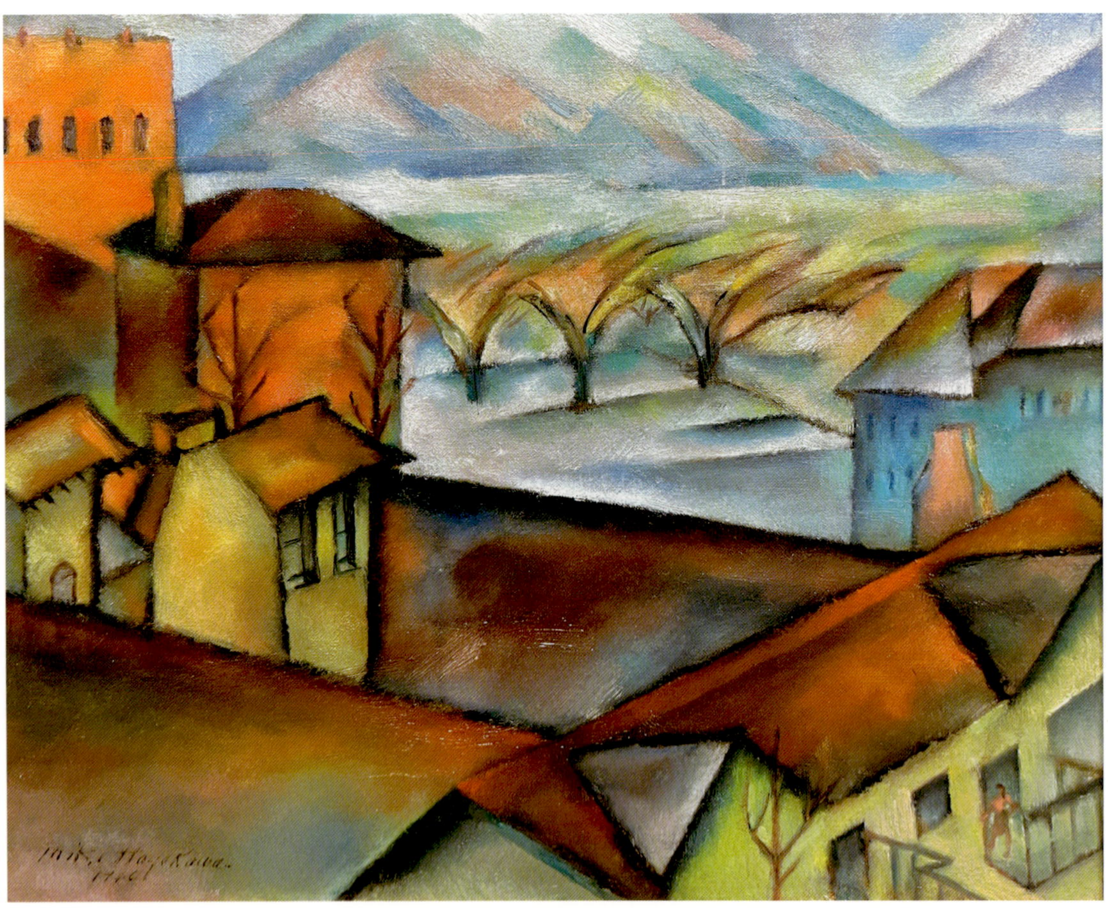

74
Miki Hayakawa
*Roof Tops*
1946

Oil on canvas board, 16 × 20 in. Collection of Richard Sakai. Photo by ShiPu Wang

75
Hisako Hibi
*Frightful NYC*
1946

Oil on canvas, 24 × 20 in. The Hibi Estate. Photo by ShiPu Wang

Hisako Hibi wrote on the verso: "From the internment camp, Topaz, Utah, with two children we relocated to New York City, Sept. 25, 1945. Frightful, devilish NYC. I felt at that time."

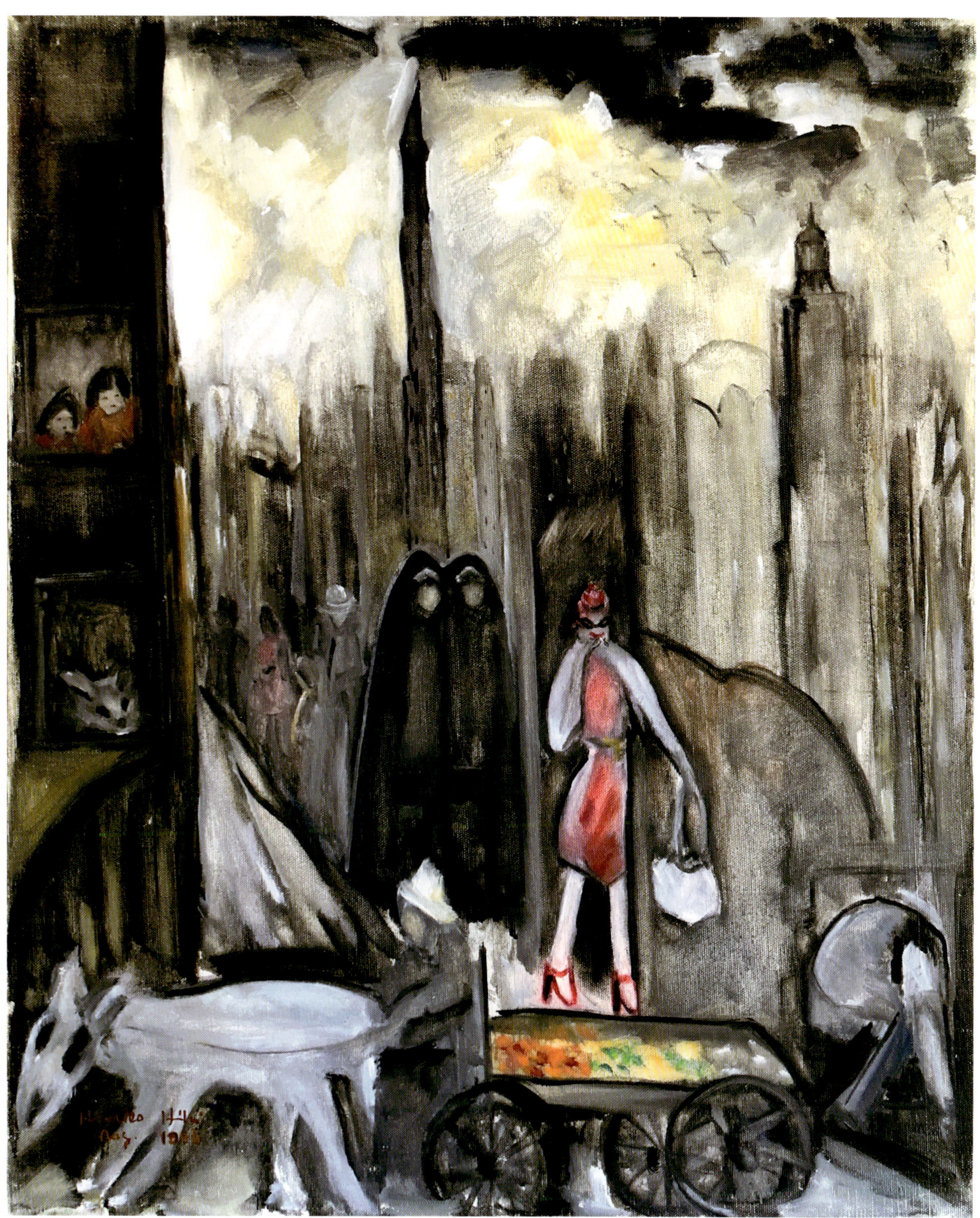

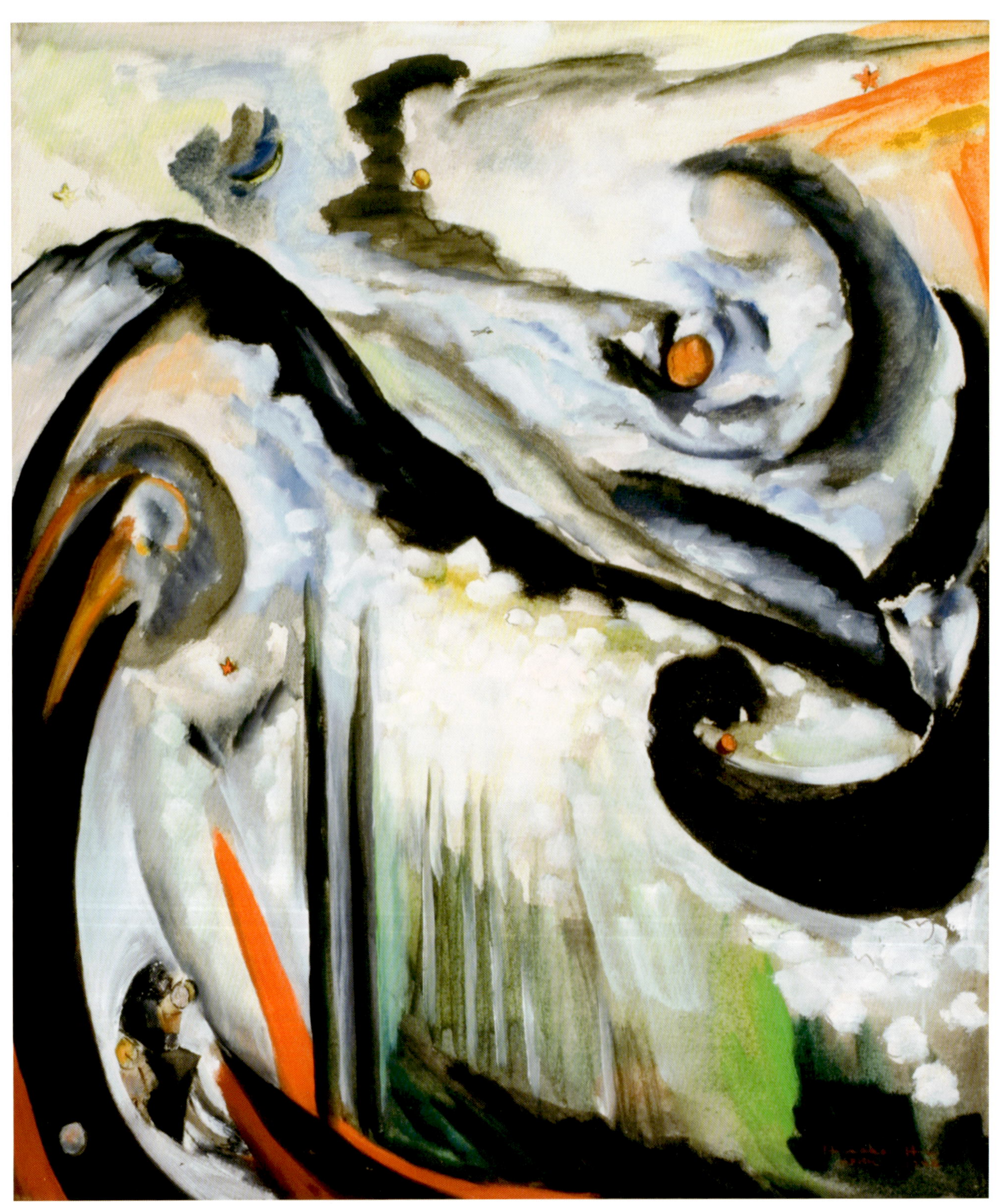

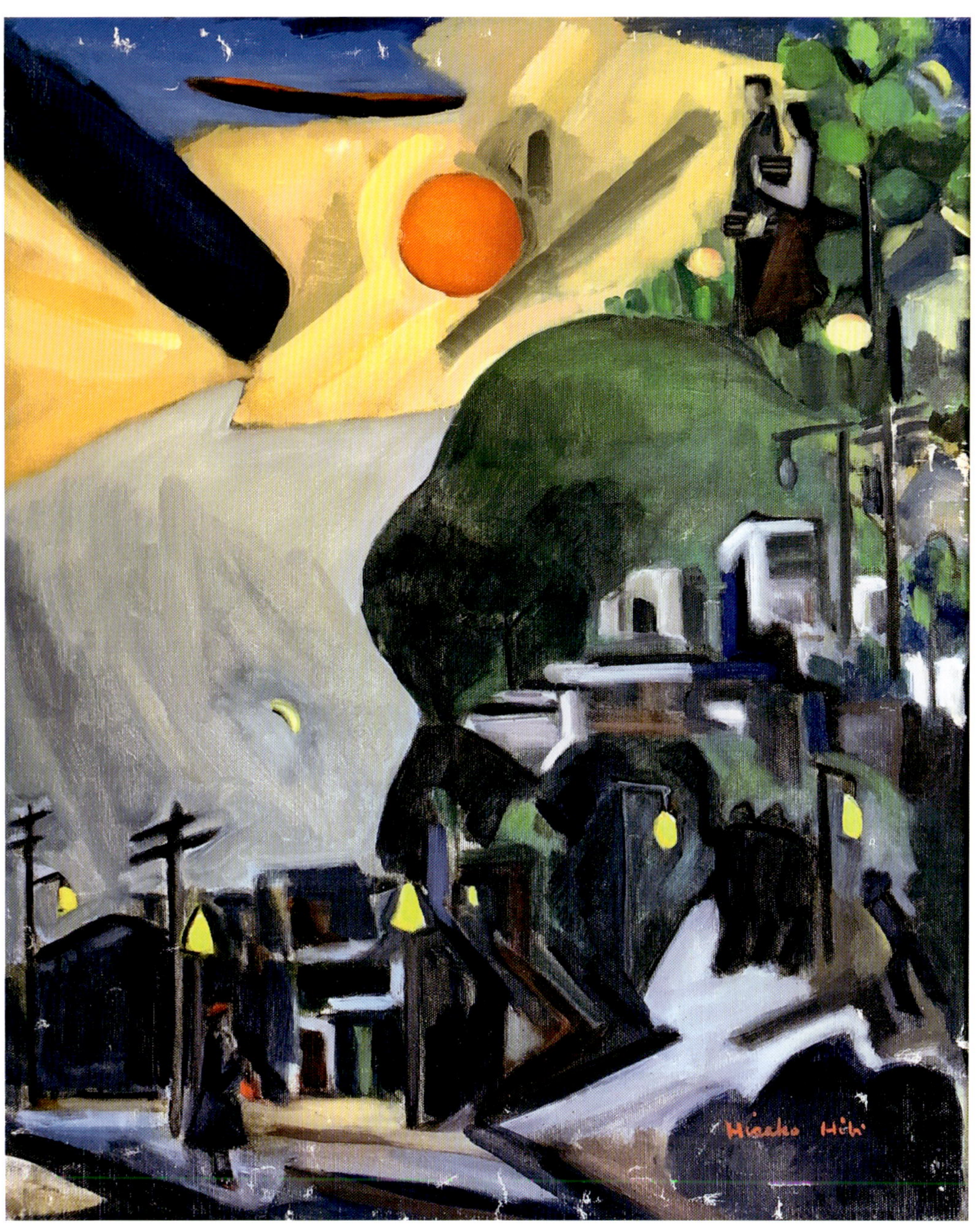


**76**
Hisako Hibi
*Fear*
1948

Oil on canvas, 25¾ × 22 in. (65.405 × 55.88 cm); frame, 27½ × 23½ × 2 in. (69.85 × 59.69 × 5.08 cm). Los Angeles County Museum of Art, Purchased with funds provided by Mr. and Mrs. Thomas H. Crawford, Jr., M.2005.115.4. Photo © Museum Associates/LACMA

**77**
Hisako Hibi
*Waiting for Bus to Work*
1955

Oil on canvas, 24 × 20 in. The Hibi Estate. Photo by ShiPu Wang

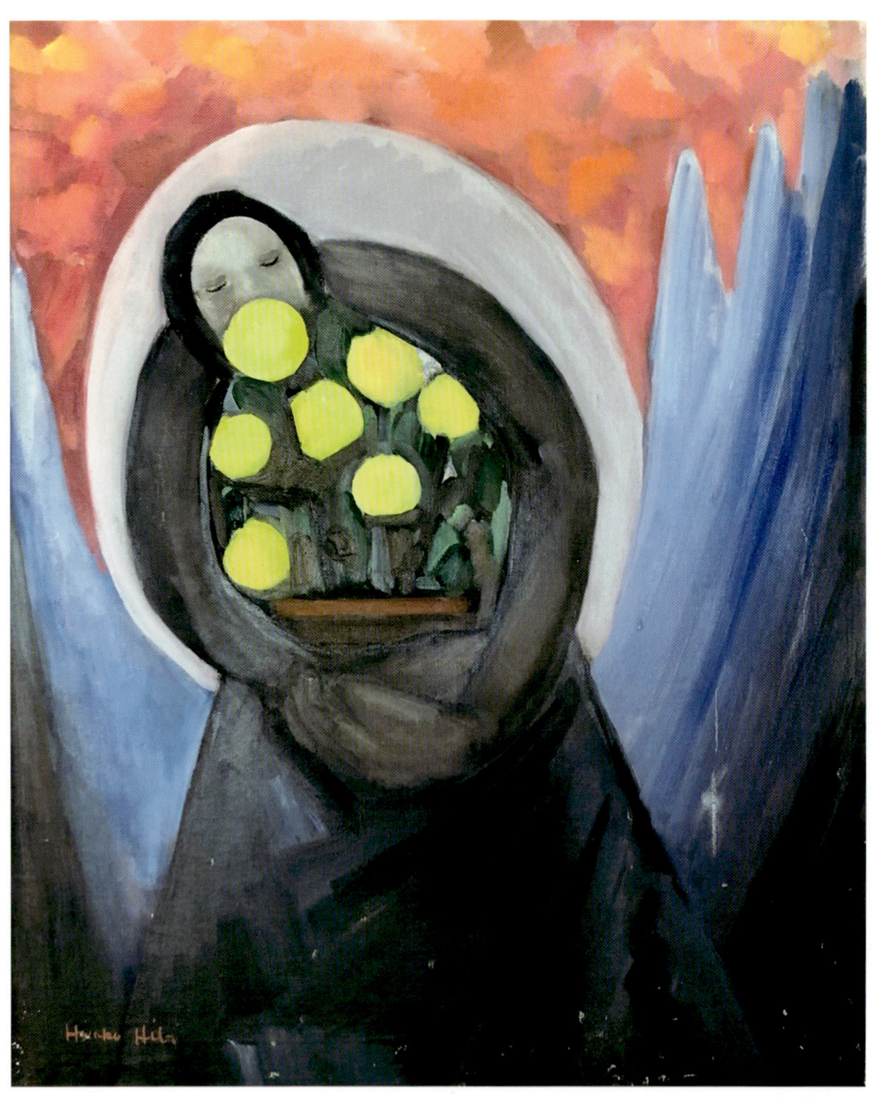

**78**
Hisako Hibi
*Mother's Day Present*
*(from Satoshi and Ibuki)*
1948

Oil on canvas, 25½ × 21½ in. The Hibi Estate. Photo by ShiPu Wang

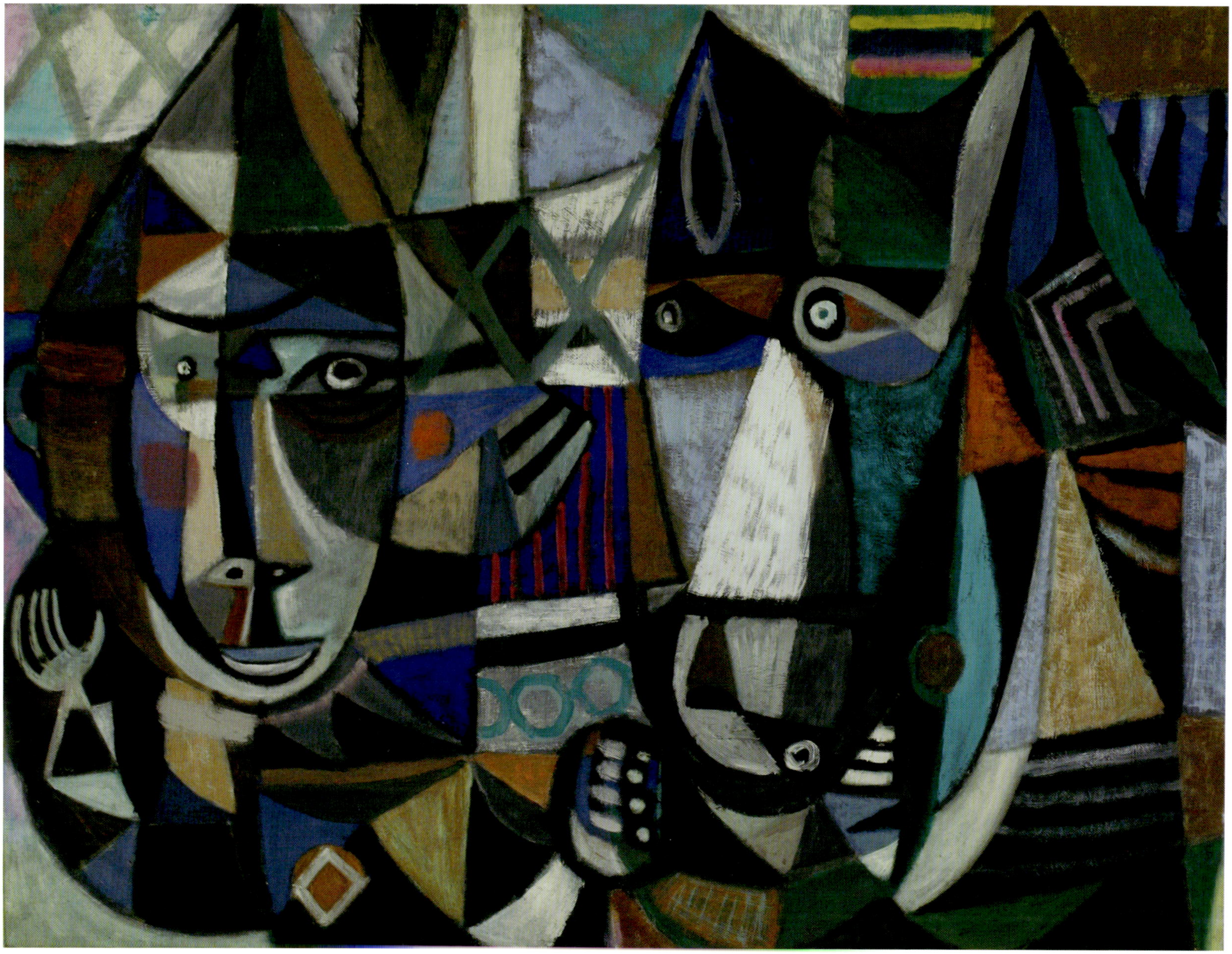

79
Miné Okubo
*Clown and Horse*
early 1950s

Oil on Masonite, 38 × 50¼ in. Riverside City College, Riverside Community College District, California, Gift of the Miné Okubo Estate, 2010.1.750. Photo by Tom Callas

80
Miné Okubo in front of *Clown and Horse* at her studio
early 1950s

Riverside City College, Riverside Community College District, California, Gift of the Miné Okubo Estate, 89-4-1

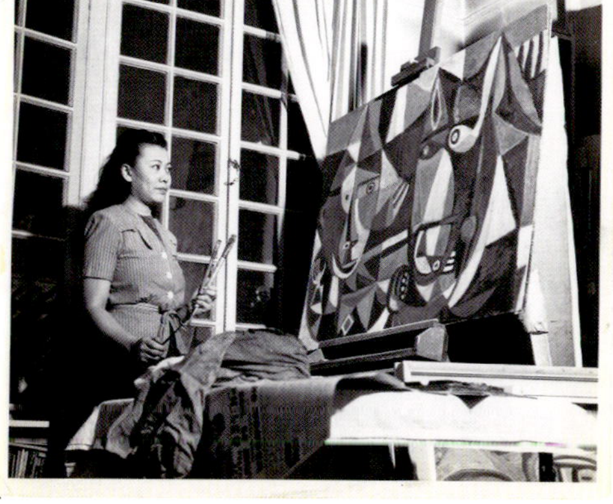

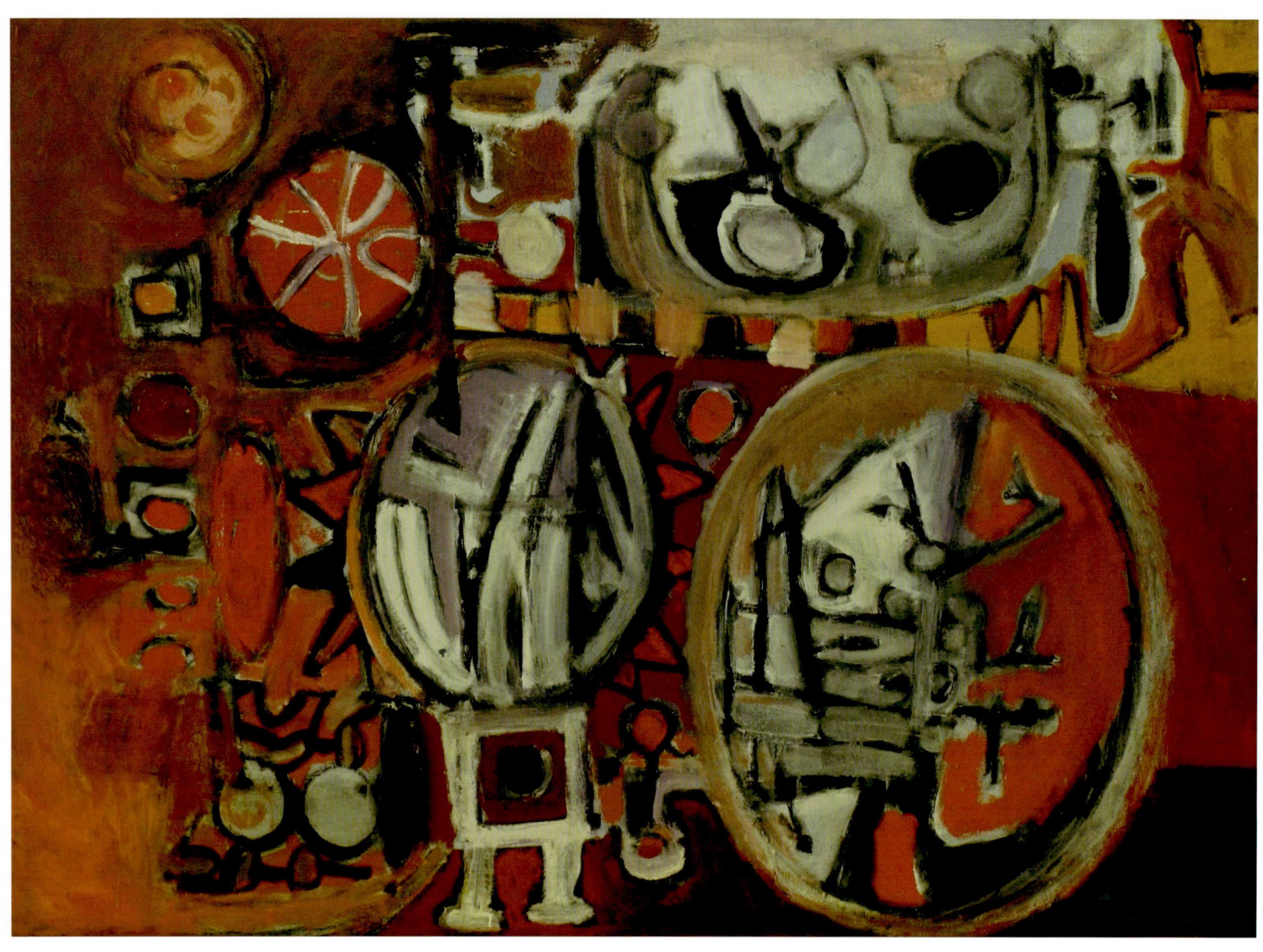

**81**
Miné Okubo
*Proverb*
early 1950s

Oil on canvas, 39¼ × 52½ in. Riverside City College, Riverside Community College District, California, Gift of the Miné Okubo Estate, 2010.1.789. Photo by Tom Callas

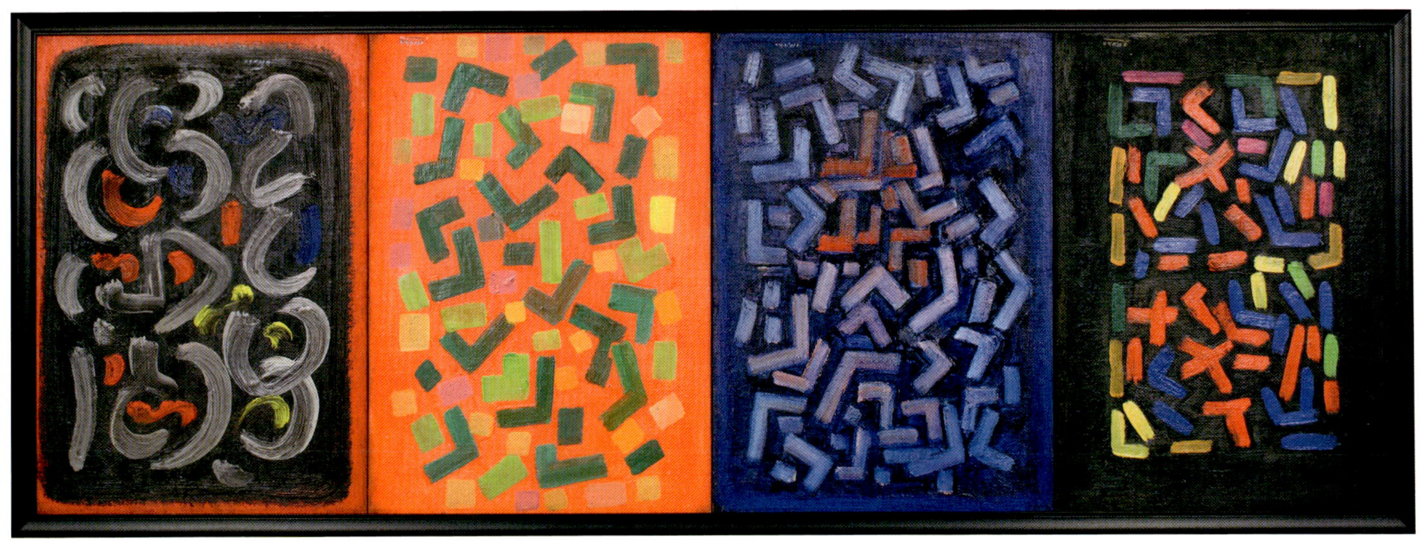

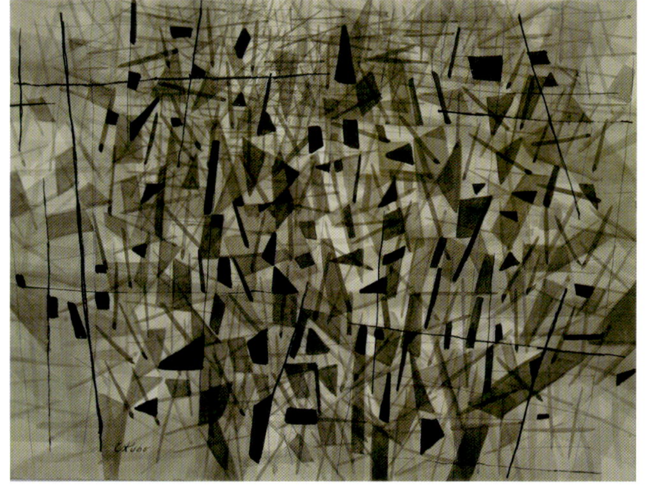

**82**
Miné Okubo
*Understanding of Order, Relation of Integrity*
ca. 1950s

Oil on canvas, 13 × 9 in. each; 15 × 41 in. with frame. Riverside City College, Riverside Community College District, California, Gift of the Miné Okubo Estate, 2016.1.44 A-D. Photo by Tom Callas

**83**
Miné Okubo
*Meadow*
before 1972

Ink on paper, 14⅞ × 19⅞ in. Riverside City College, Riverside Community College District, California, Gift of the Miné Okubo Estate, 2012.1.25. Photo by Tom Callas

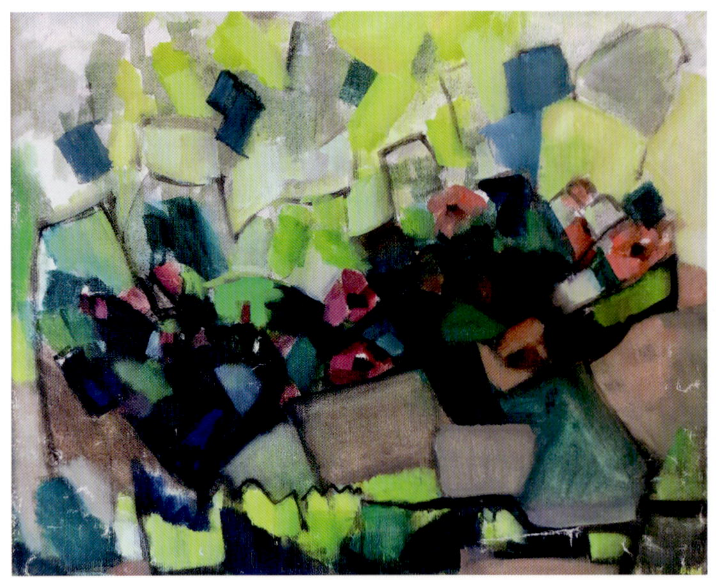

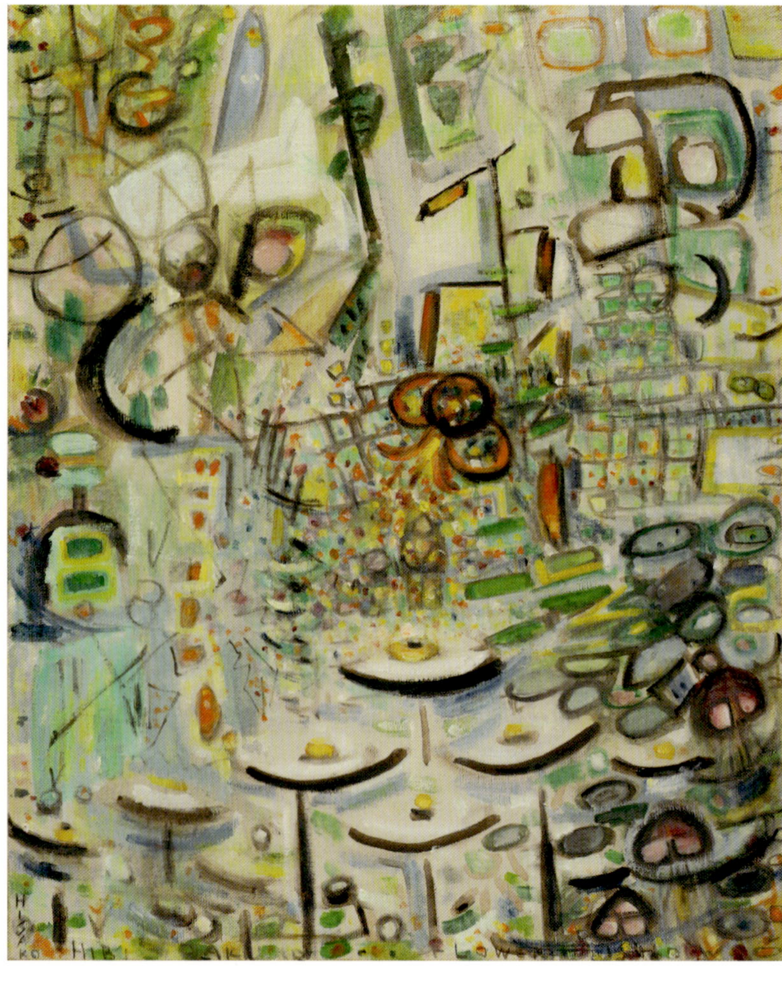

84
Hisako Hibi
*At Kazue-san's Garden*
1962

Oil on canvas, 17½ × 25½ in. The Hibi Estate. Photo by ShiPu Wang

Hisako Hibi lived in the back unit of Kazue (Kay) and Tom Yamashita's home for a few years after moving back to San Francisco in 1954.

85
Hisako Hibi
*Flower Garden*
1964

Oil on canvas, 24 × 20 in. Japanese American National Museum, Los Angeles, Gift of Ibuki Hibi Lee in honor of Karin Higa and Kristine Kim, 2000.401.2

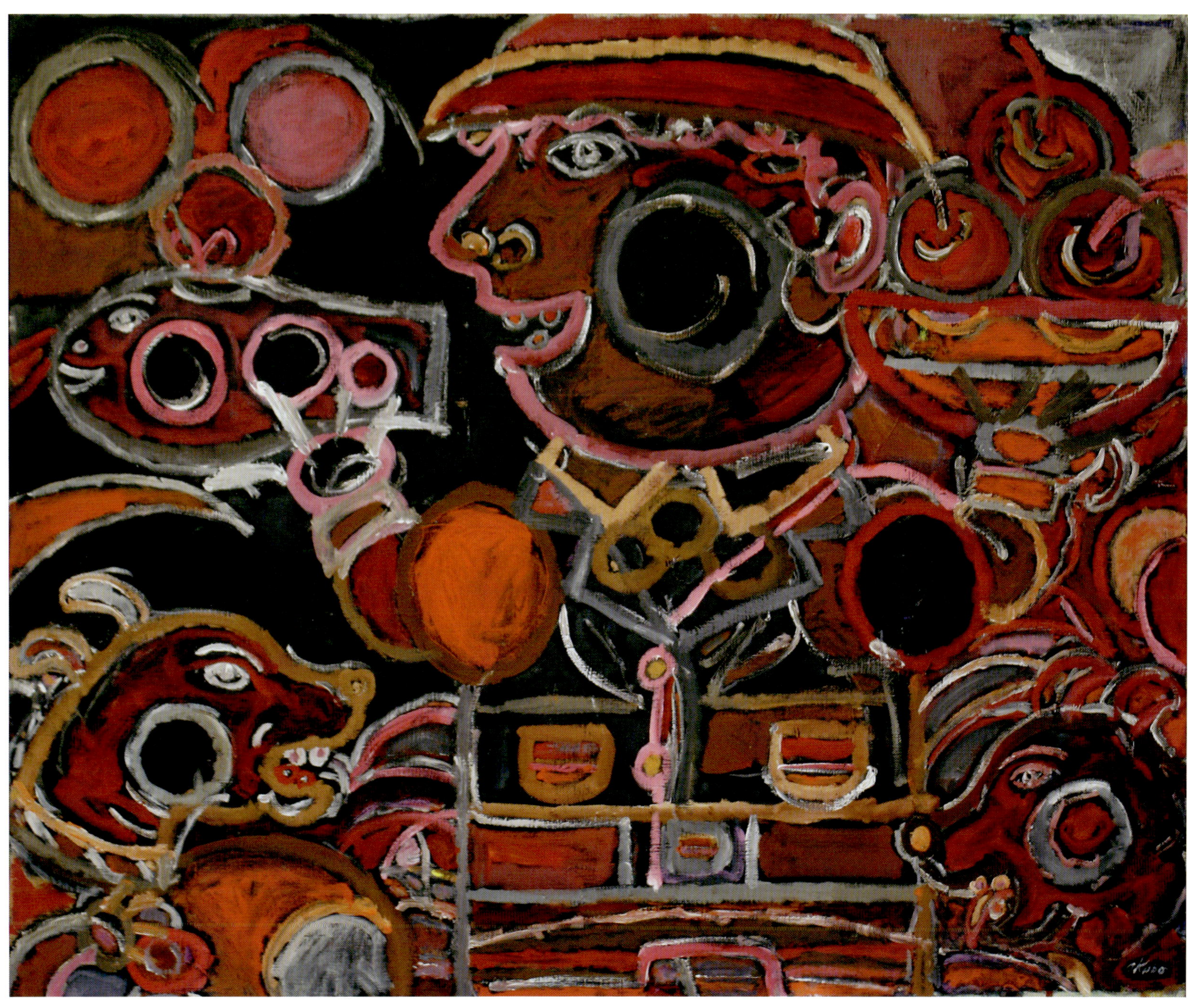

**86**
Miné Okubo
*Holiday*
1967

Oil on canvas, 42½ × 51¼ in.
Riverside City College, Riverside Community College District, California, Gift of the Miné Okubo Estate, 2010.1.805. Photo by Tom Callas

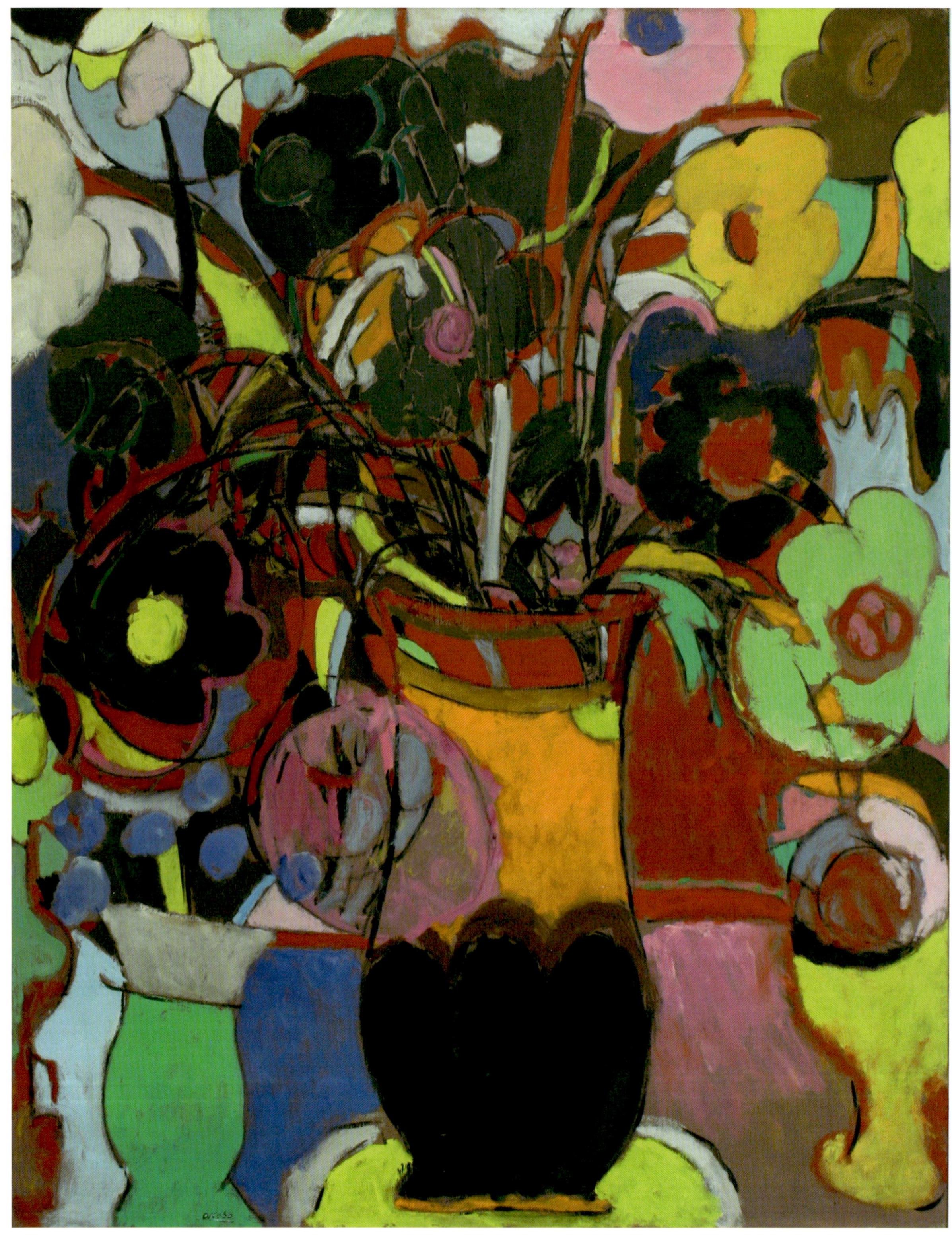

**87**
Miné Okubo
*Flowers*
1963

Oil on canvas, 49 × 39 in. Riverside City College, Riverside Community College District, California, Gift of the Miné Okubo Estate, 2016.1.143. Photo by Tom Callas

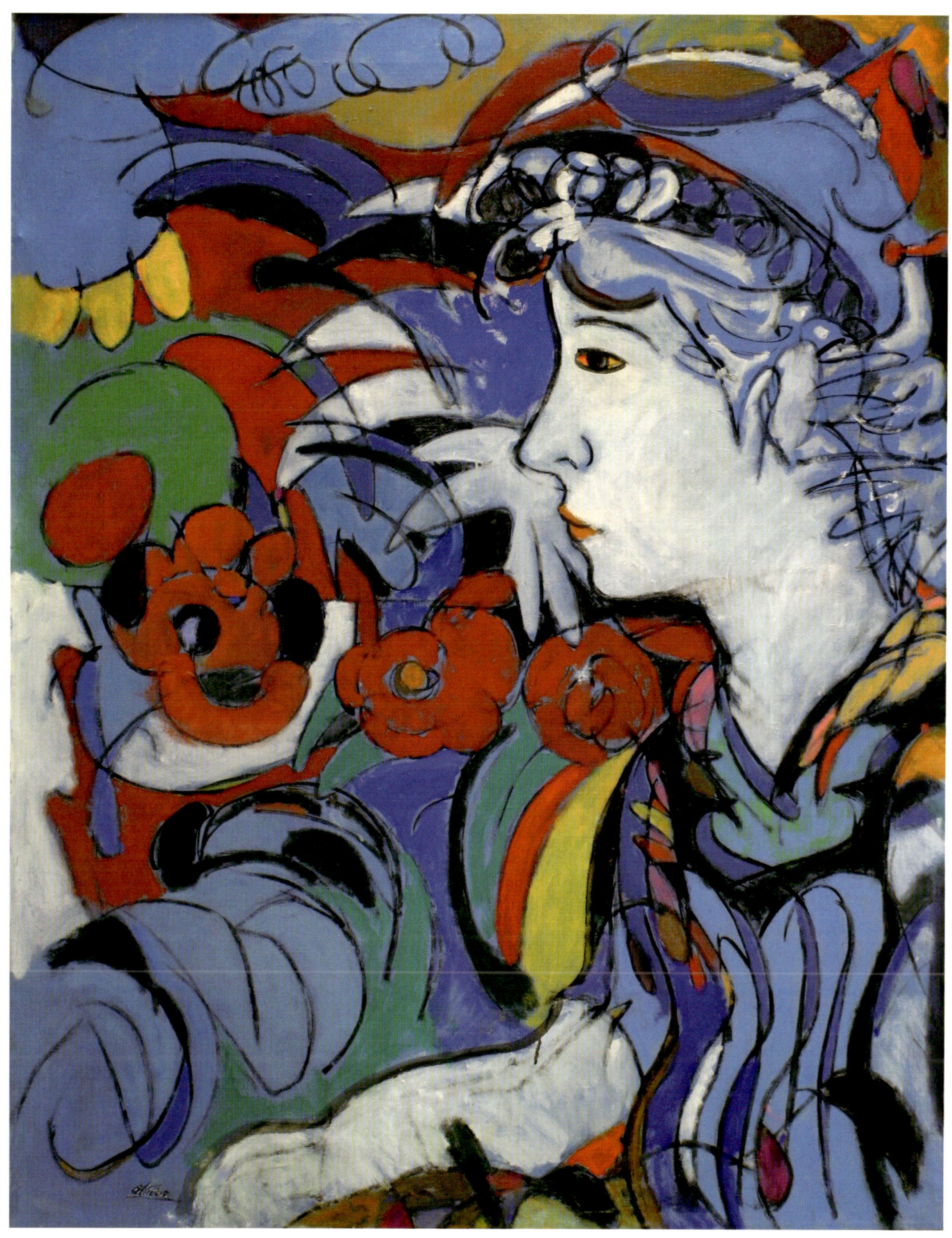

**88**
Miné Okubo
*Lady with Red Flowers*
1963

Oil on canvas, 50⅛ × 40⅛ in. (127.3 × 101.9 cm). Riverside City College, Riverside Community College District, California, Gift of the Miné Okubo Estate, 2016.1.42. Photo by Tom Callas

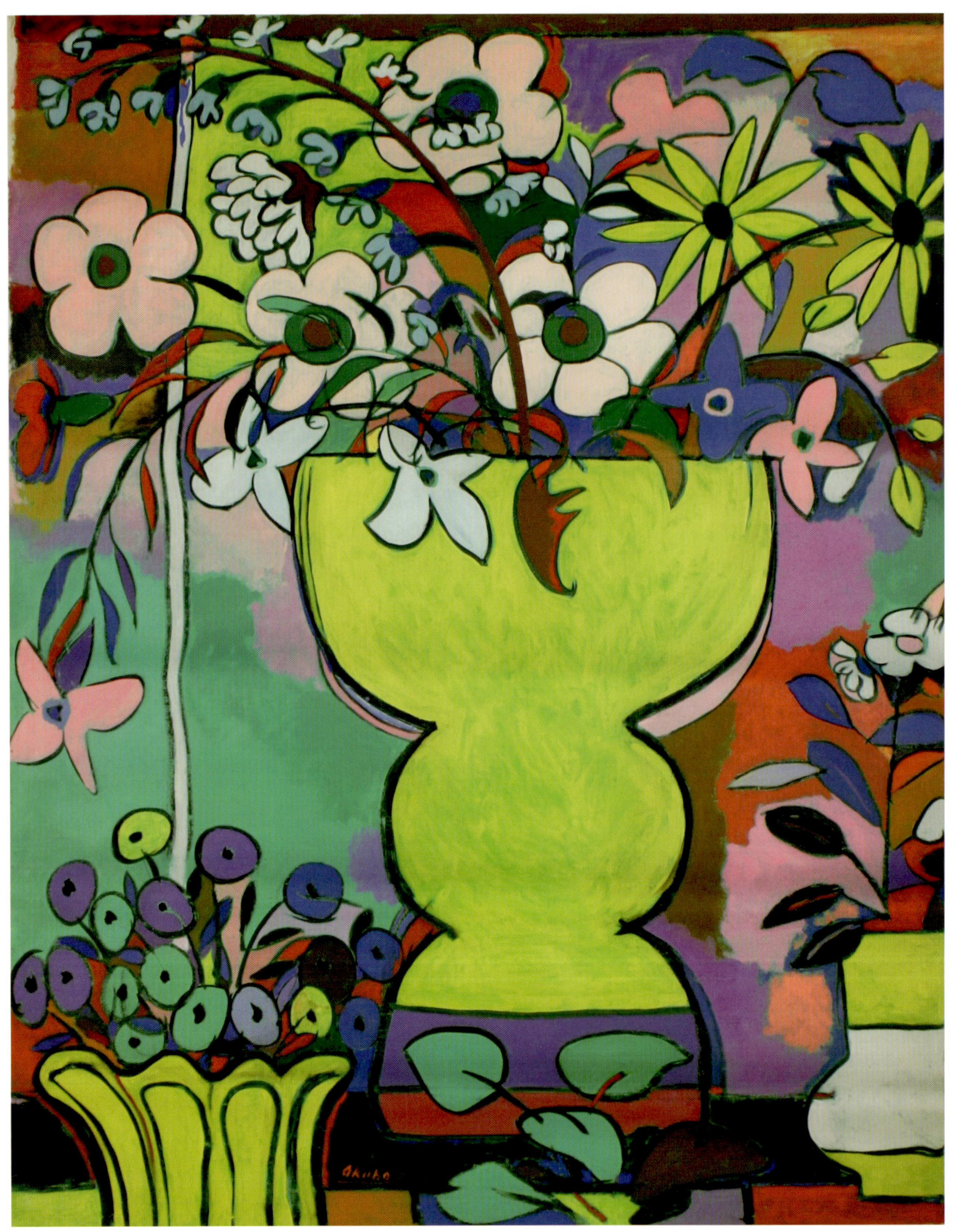
Okubo

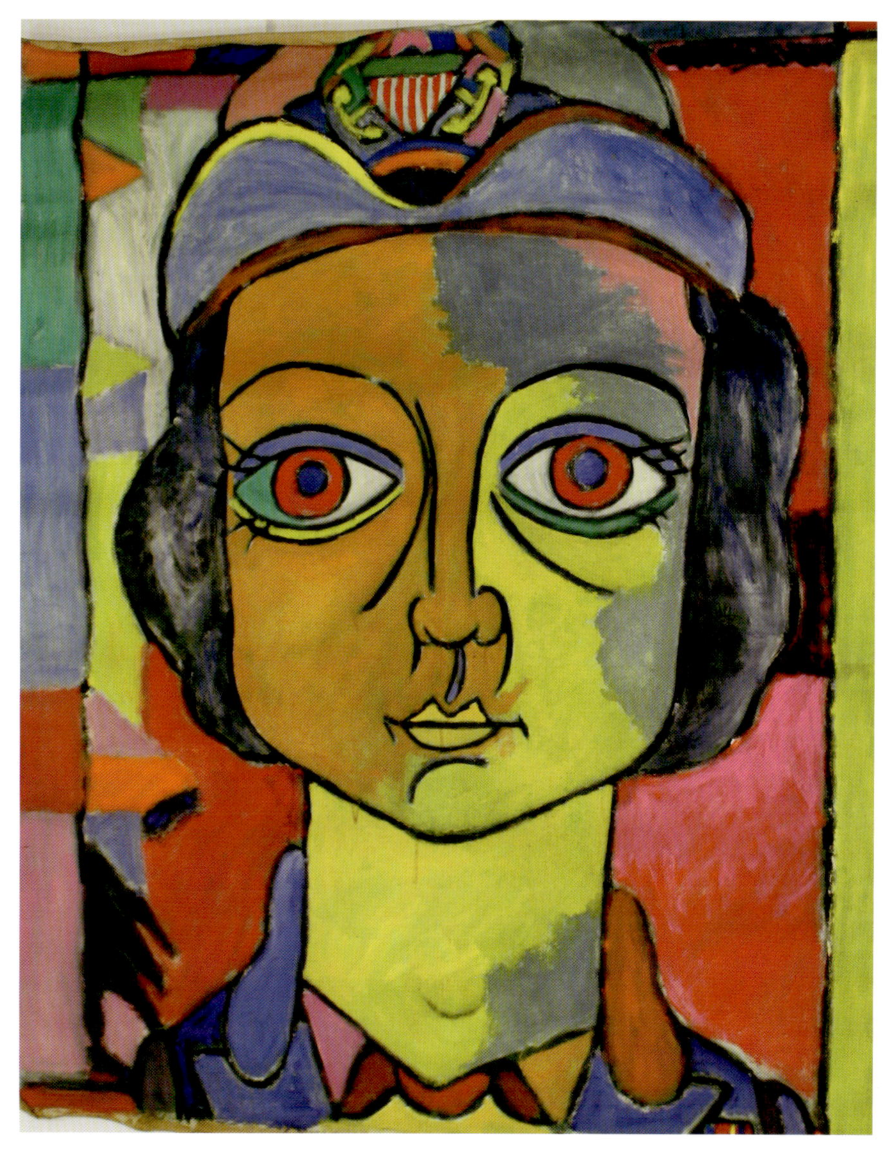

89
Miné Okubo
*Untitled*
ca. 1965

Oil on canvas, 52 × 42¼ in. Riverside City College, Riverside Community College District, California, Gift of the Miné Okubo Estate, 2012.1.148. Photo by Tom Callas

90
Miné Okubo
*Untitled (Woman Wearing a Naval Officer's Uniform)*
ca. 1960s

Oil on canvas, 53⅛ × 44½ in. The Miné Okubo Charitable Corporation, EL 2012.1.28. Photo by Tom Callas

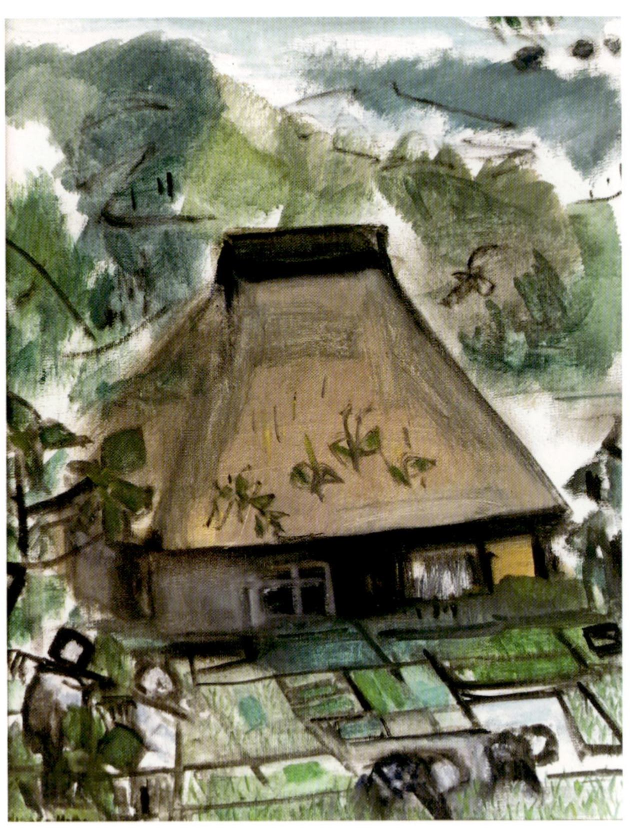

91
Hisako Hibi
*Thatched House*
ca. 1963

Oil on canvas, 21½ × 17½ in. The Hibi Estate. Photo by ShiPu Wang

Hisako Hibi was able to visit her relatives in Japan in 1963. This painting captures a traditional thatched house and a farmer in rural Japan, acknowledging her background as someone who came from a farming village in Japan's Fukui Prefecture.

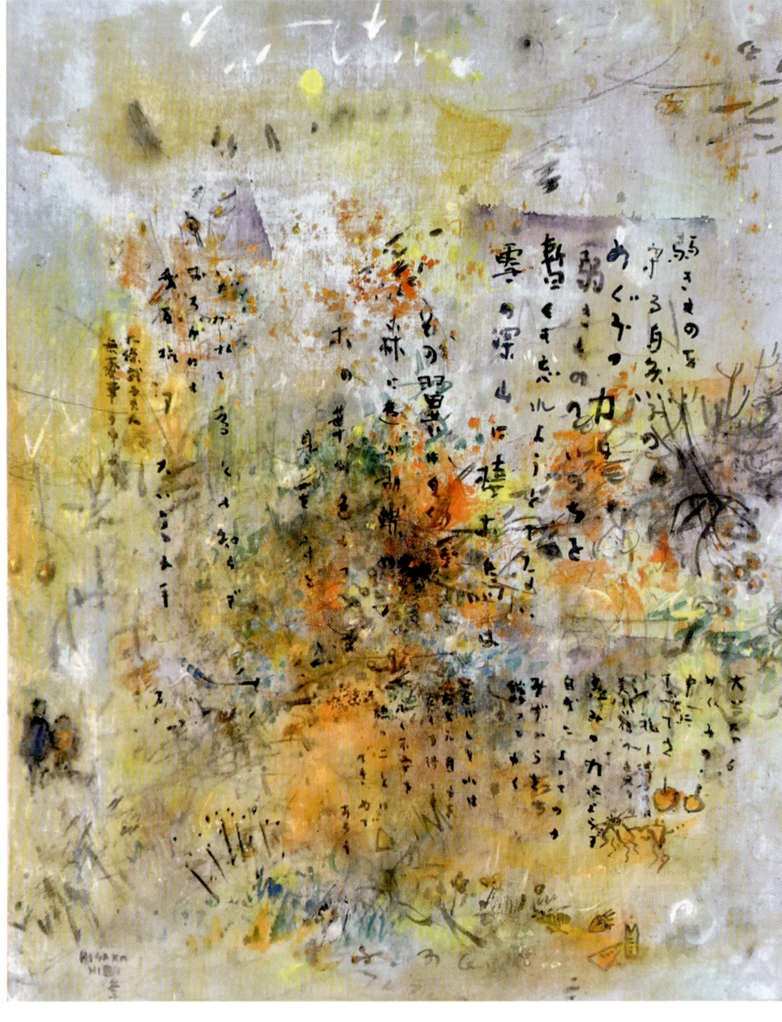

92
Hisako Hibi
*Poems by Madame Takeko Kujo*
1970

Oil on canvas, 28½ × 22½ in. The Hibi Estate. Photo by ShiPu Wang

Lady Takeko Kujo (九条武子, 1887–1928) was a noted educator, poet, and co-founder of the Buddhist Women's Association in Japan. Her teachings were influential in Japan and overseas, and Hisako Hibi, a lifelong Buddhist, was an admirer.

Hibi incorporated into this work her own version of an excerpt of Kujo's poem "Yowakiga mamani (as weak as you are)": "In nature, the weak birds and insects protect themselves naturally, such as having the same color with the snow or the leaves. The blessings of nature do not neglect the weak ones. On the contrary, human beings do not know how to protect themselves. They don't entrust themselves to the power of the blessings. They only can protect themselves with the power of their ego. It helps them maintain themselves, but they will never have the peace of mind" (translation courtesy of Ryuta Furumoto).

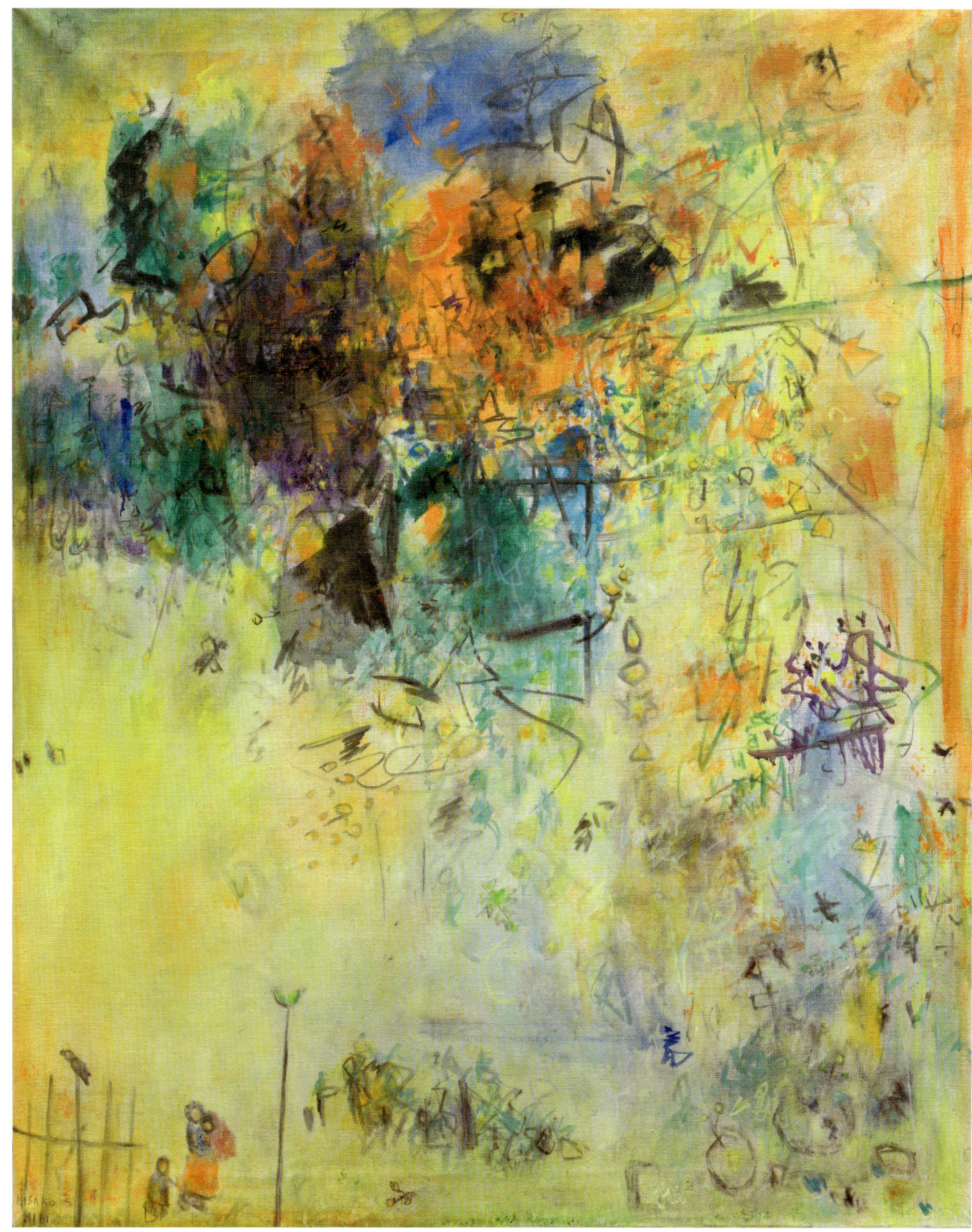

**93**
Hisako Hibi
*Autumn*
ca. 1967

Oil on canvas, 39⅛ × 32¼ × 1½ in. (99.4 × 81.9 × 3.8 cm). Smithsonian American Art Museum, Museum purchase through the American Women's History Initiative Acquisitions Pool, administered by the Smithsonian American Women's History Initiative

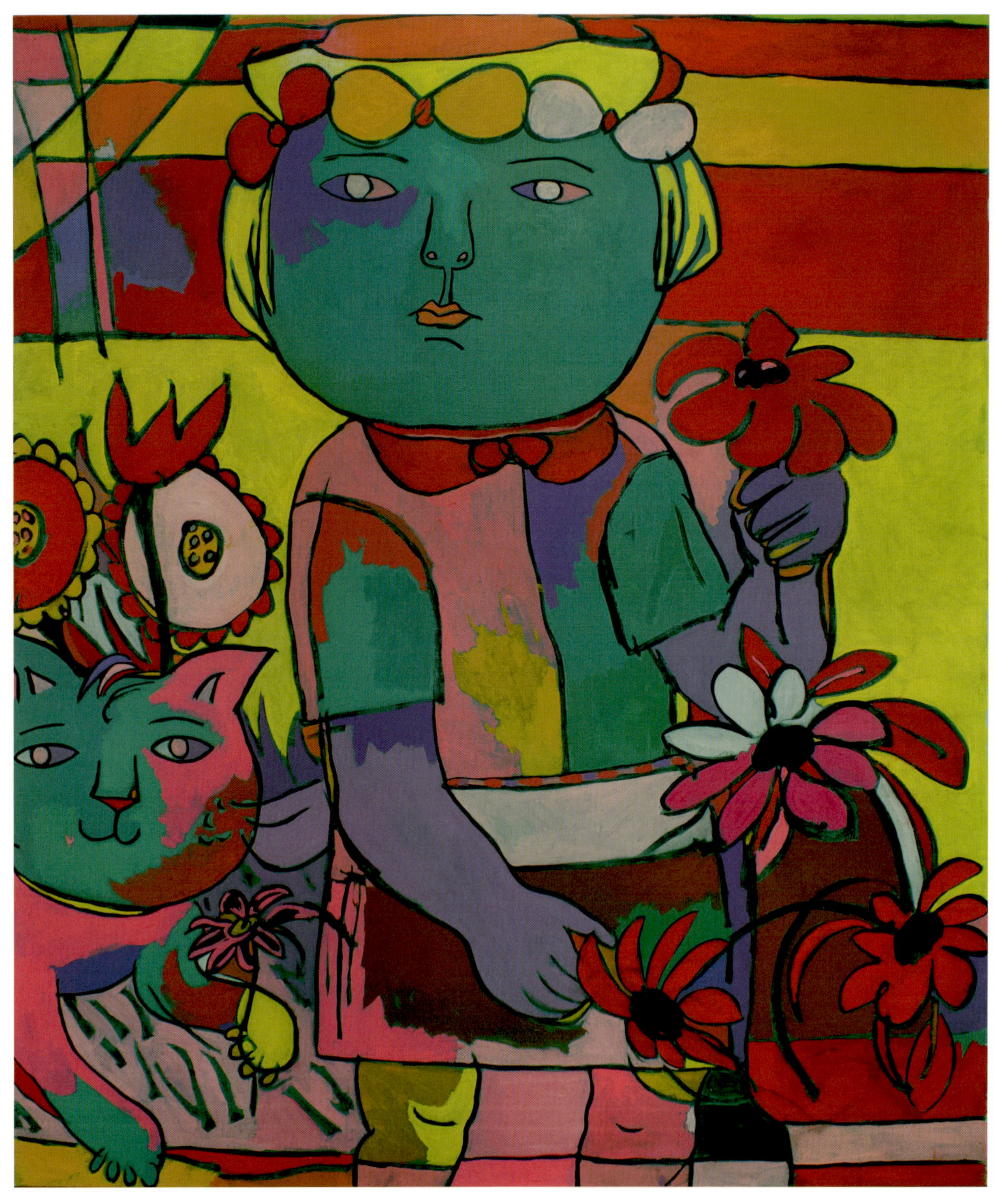

**94**
Miné Okubo
*Girl, Cat, Flower*
before 1972

Acrylic on canvas, 60 × 51¼ in. Riverside City College, Riverside Community College District, California, Gift of the Miné Okubo Estate, 2012.1.33. Photo by Tom Callas

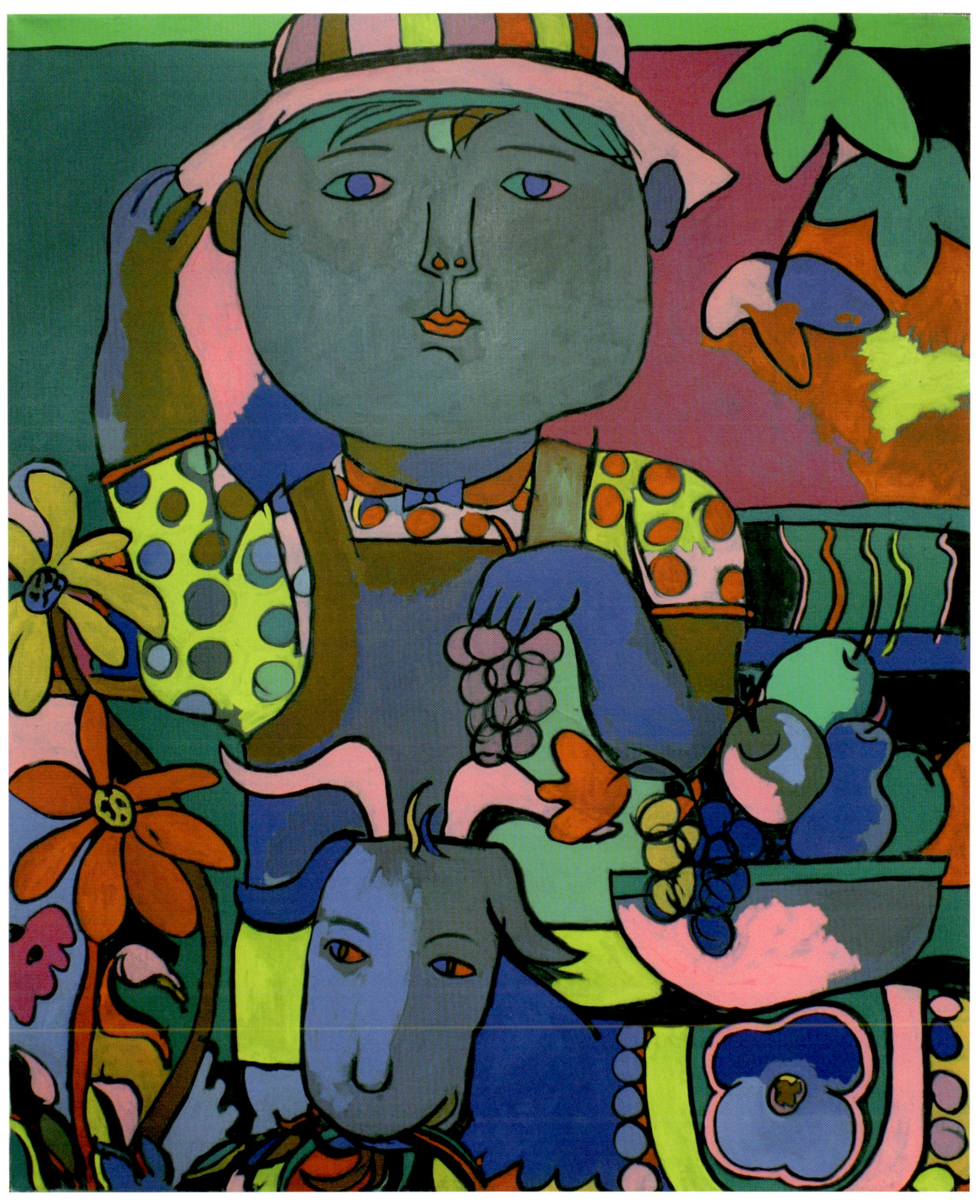

95
Miné Okubo
*Boy, Goat, Fruit*
before 1972

Acrylic on canvas, 60 × 51 in.
Riverside City College, Riverside Community College District, California, Gift of the Miné Okubo Estate, 2012.1.34. Photo by Tom Callas

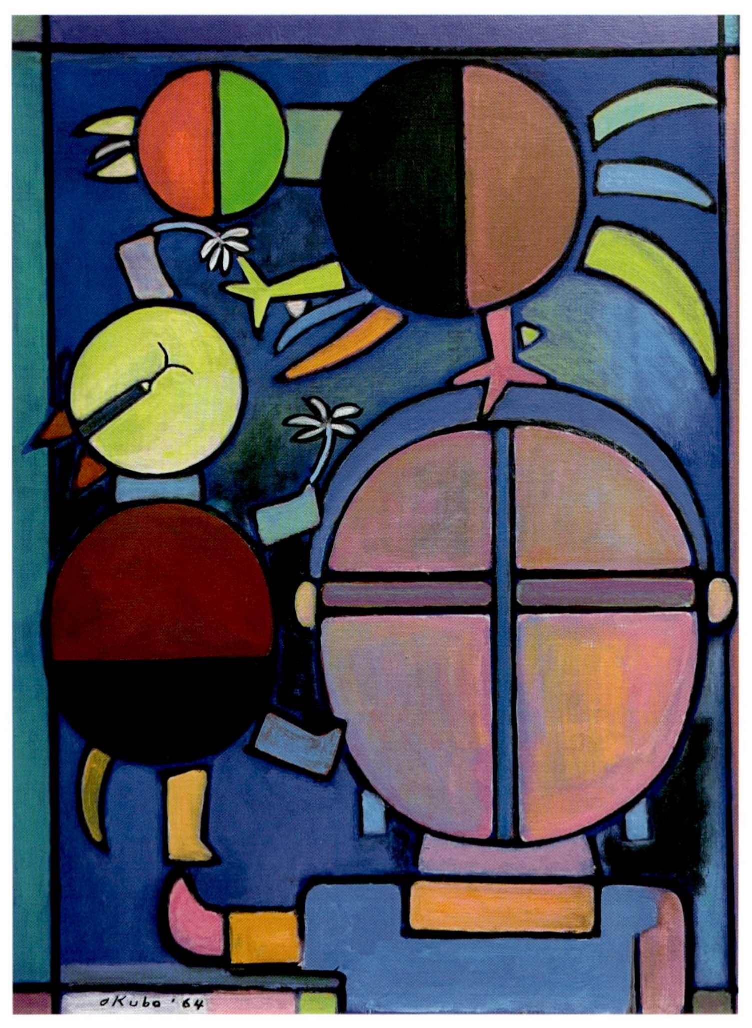


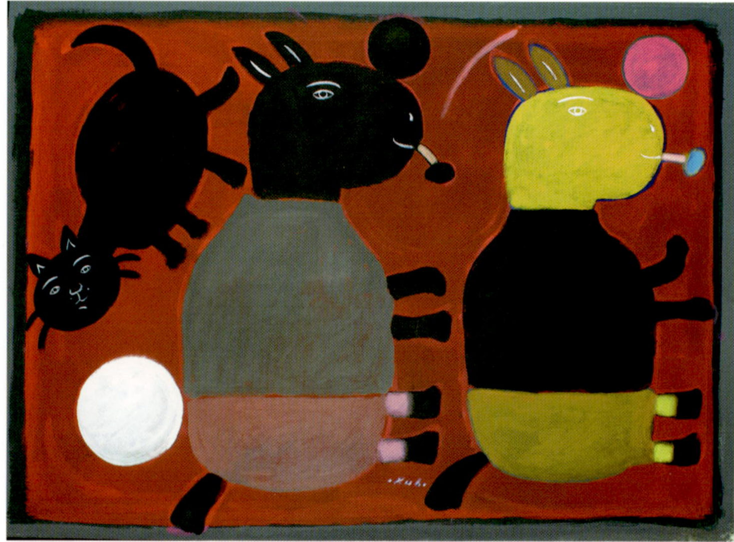

96
Miné Okubo
*Boy, Rooster, Cat*
1964

Oil on canvas, 32 × 22 in. Collection of Richard Sakai. Photo by ShiPu Wang

97
Miné Okubo
*Cat, Two Horses, White, Black, Pink Ball*
before 1972

Oil on canvas, 30½ × 42¾ in. Riverside City College, Riverside Community College District, California, Gift of the Miné Okubo Estate, 2016.1.49. Photo by Tom Callas

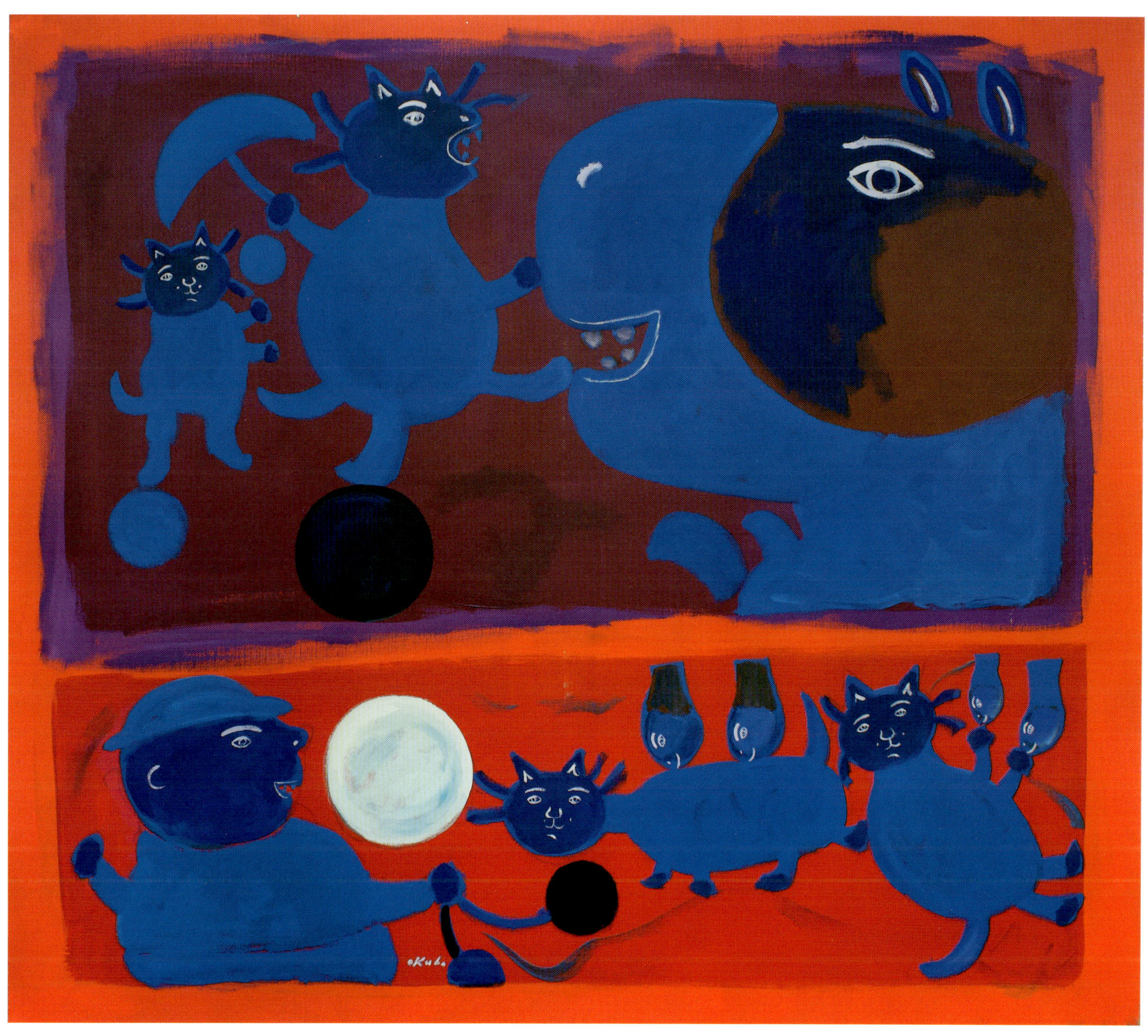

**98**
Miné Okubo
*Horse, Man, Two Cats and Four Fish*
ca. 1972

Acrylic on canvas, 52 × 60 in. Riverside City College, Riverside Community College District, California, Gift of the Miné Okubo Estate, 2010.1.805. Photo by Tom Callas

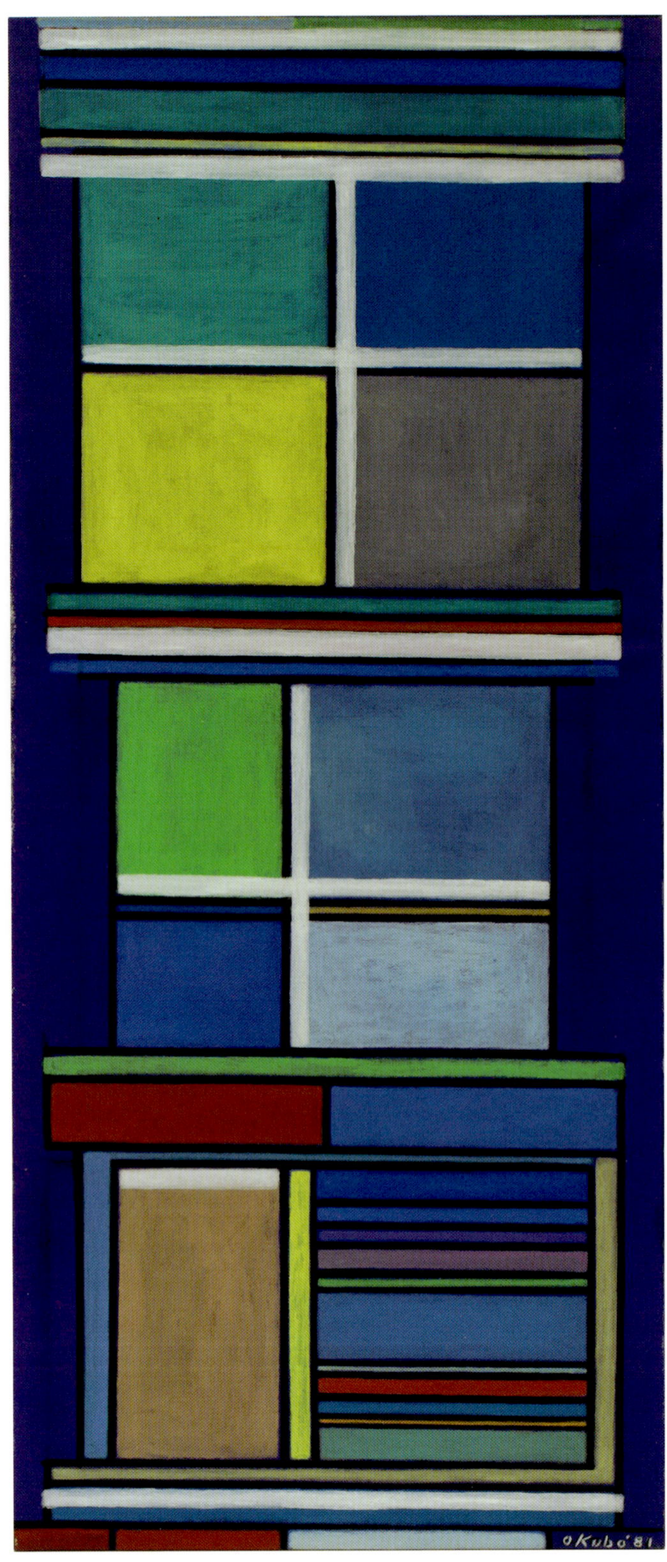


99
Miné Okubo
*Untitled*
1981

Acrylic on canvas, 57 × 25½ in. Riverside City College, Riverside Community College District, California, Gift of the Miné Okubo Estate, 2010.1.753. Photo by Tom Callas

100
Miné Okubo
*Festival Girl*
1980

Acrylic on canvas, 72 × 50 in. Riverside City College, Riverside Community College District, California, Gift of the Miné Okubo Estate, 2010.1.829. Photo by Tom Callas

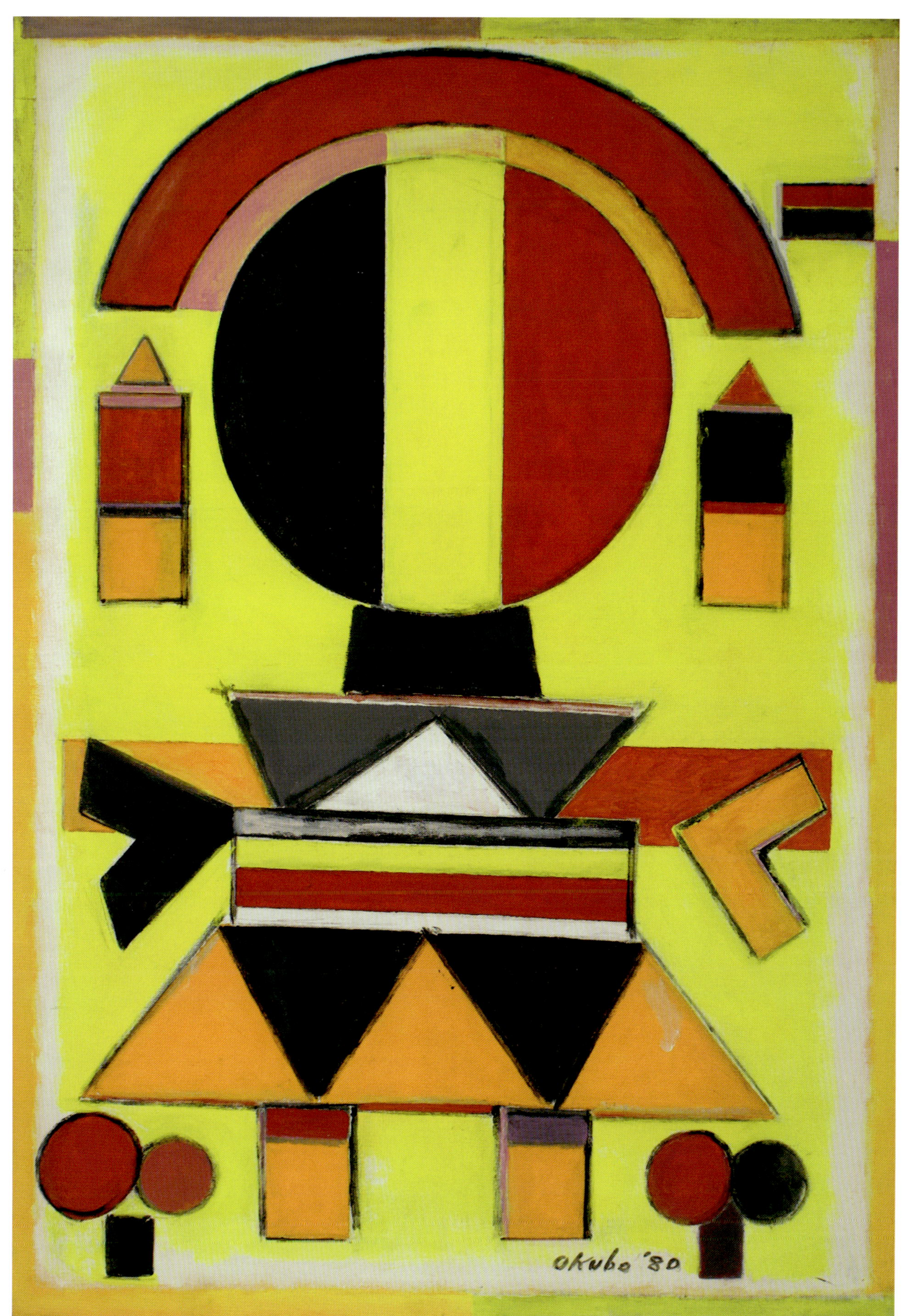
Okubo '80

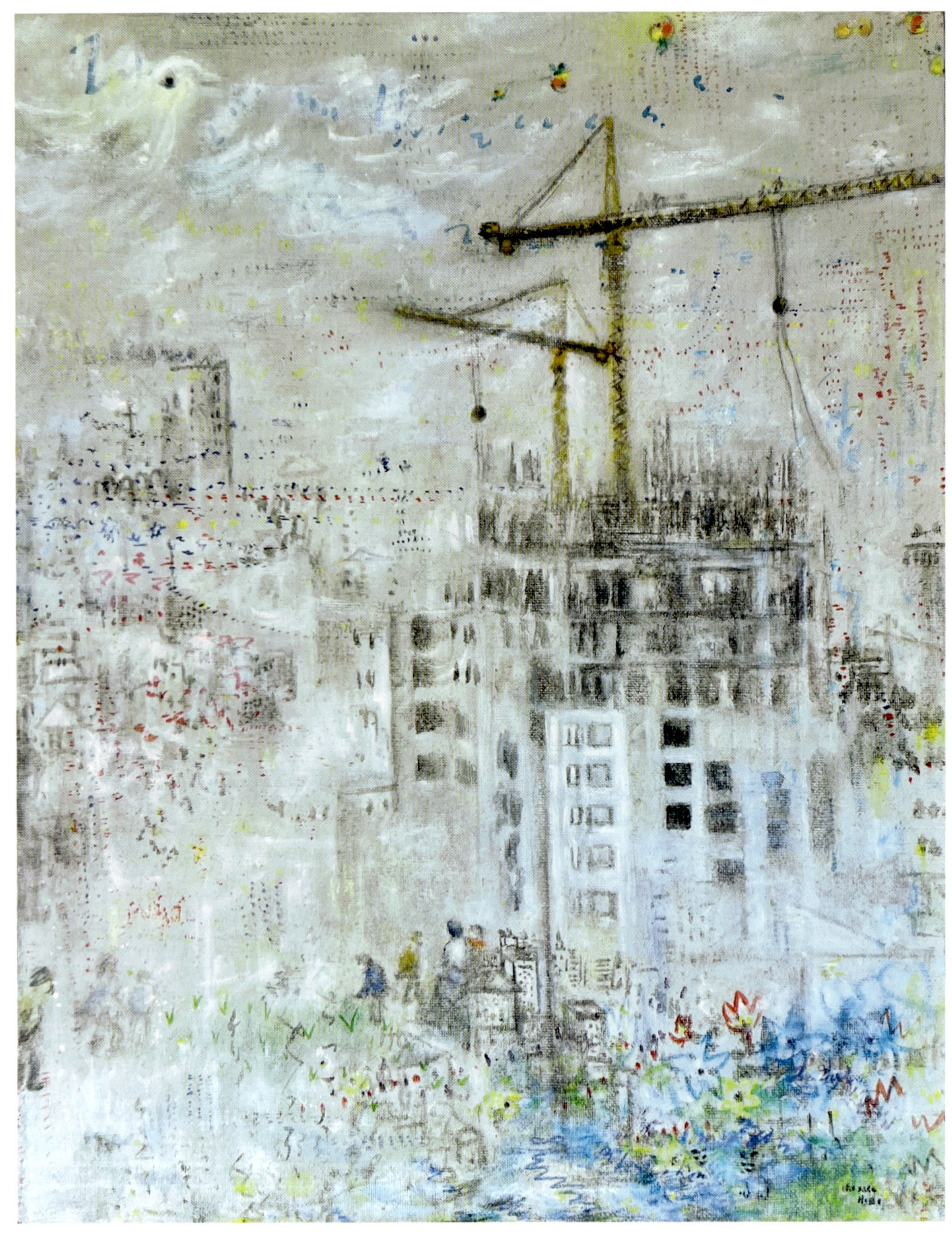

**101**
Hisako Hibi
*Construction*
1985

Oil on canvas, 41 × 33½ in. The Hibi Estate. Photo by ShiPu Wang

Hisako Hibi lived in a Hinode Towers apartment in San Francisco's Japantown. The painting captures the view from her window of a rising cityscape.

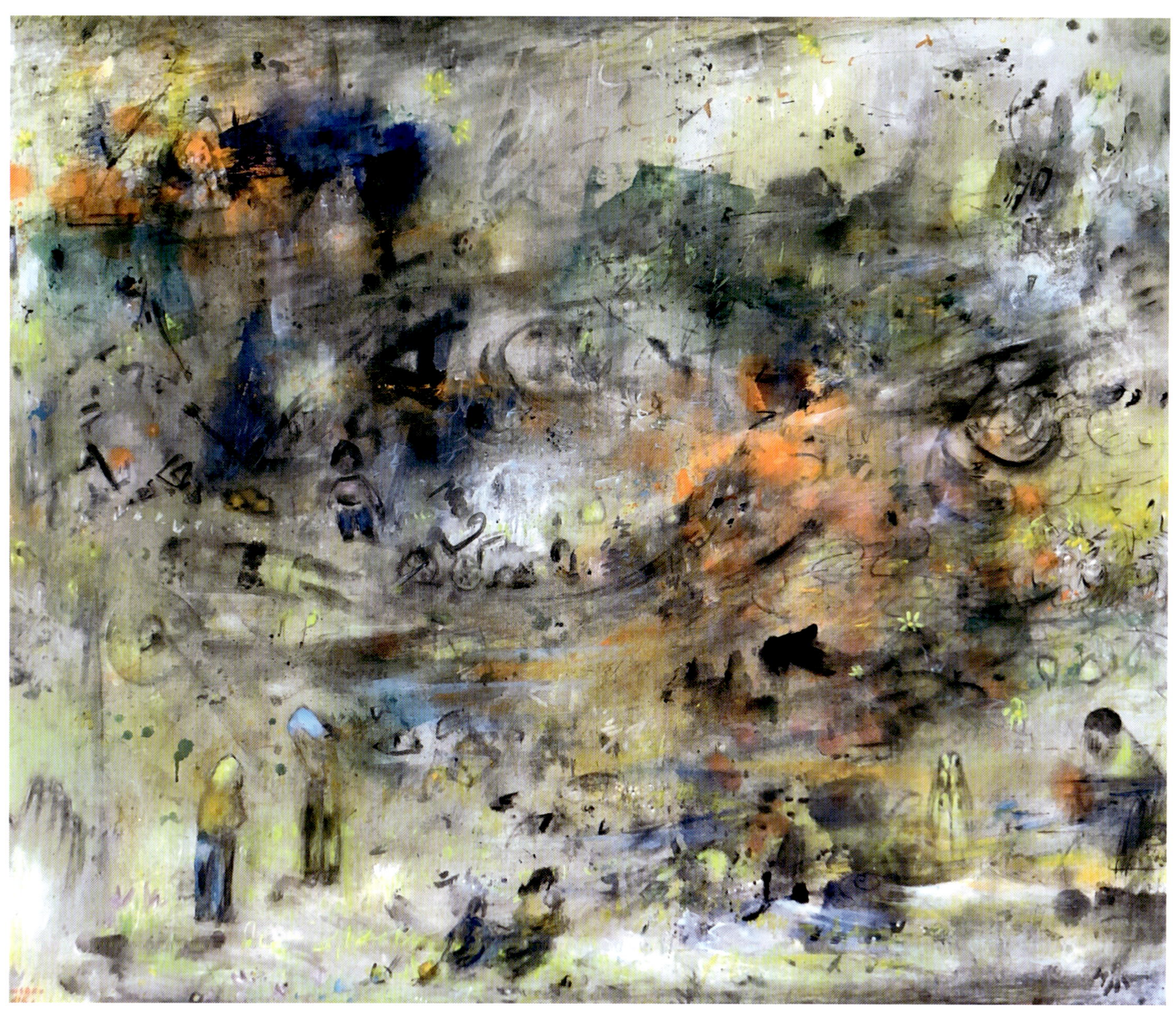

102
Hisako Hibi
*War and Suffering*
1982

Oil on canvas, 35¾ × 42½ in. The Hibi Estate. Photo by ShiPu Wang

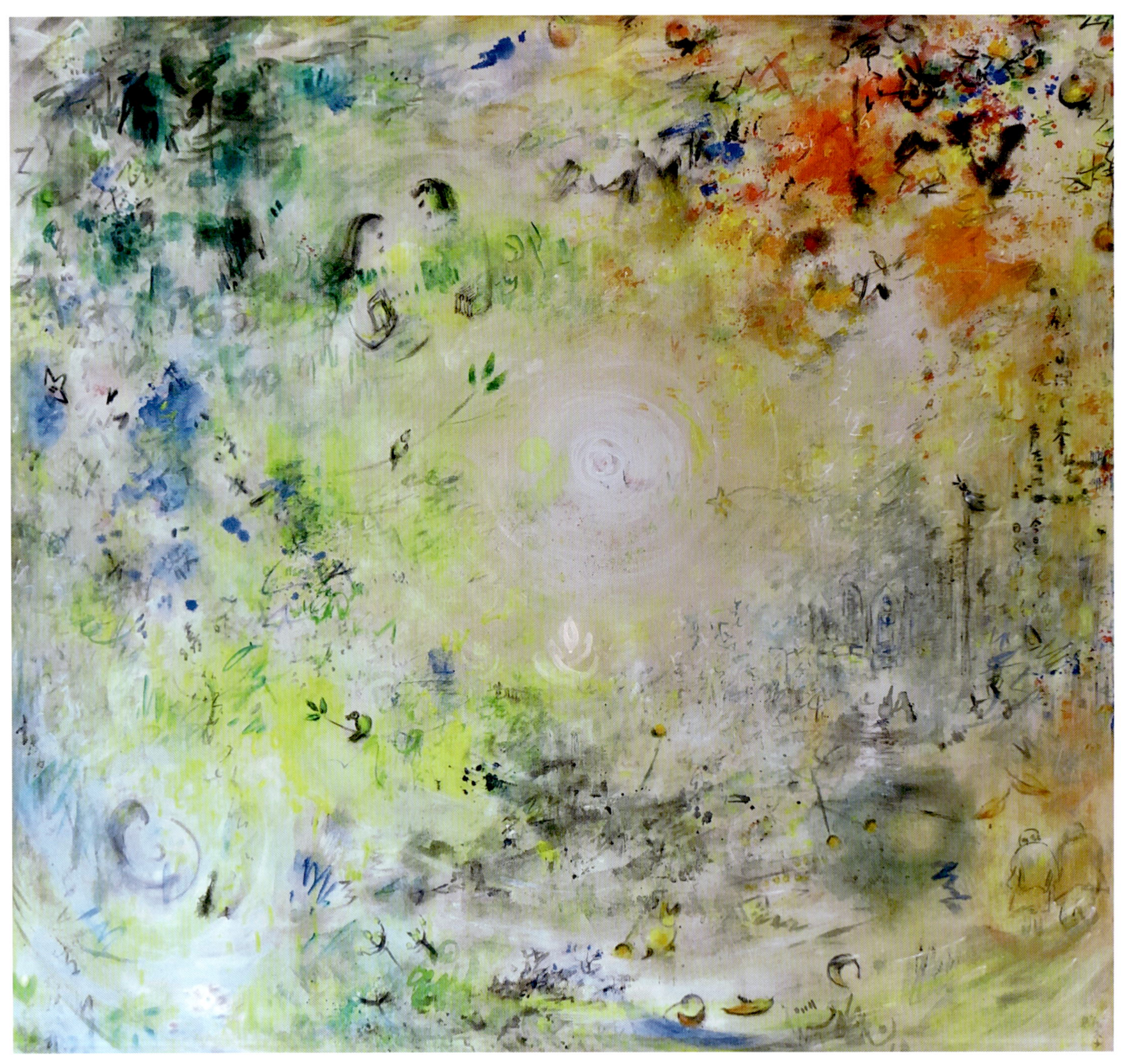

**103**
Hisako Hibi
*Eternal Seasons*
1983

Oil on canvas, 40 × 44 in. The Hibi Estate. Photo by ShiPu Wang

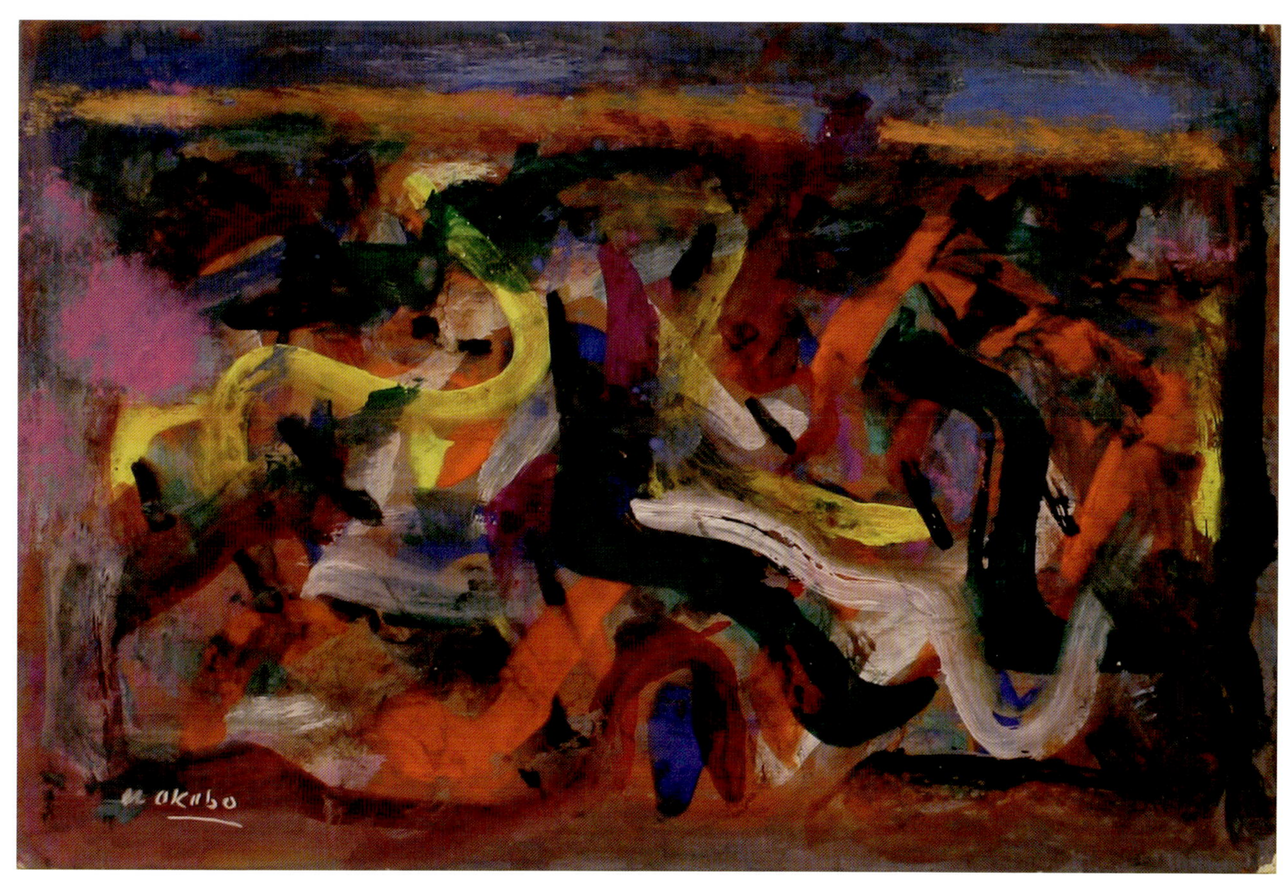

**104**
Miné Okubo
*Untitled*
ca. 1980s

Acrylic on paper, 15 × 22½ in.
Riverside City College, Riverside Community College District, California, Gift of the Miné Okubo Estate, 2010.1.1088. Photo by Tom Callas

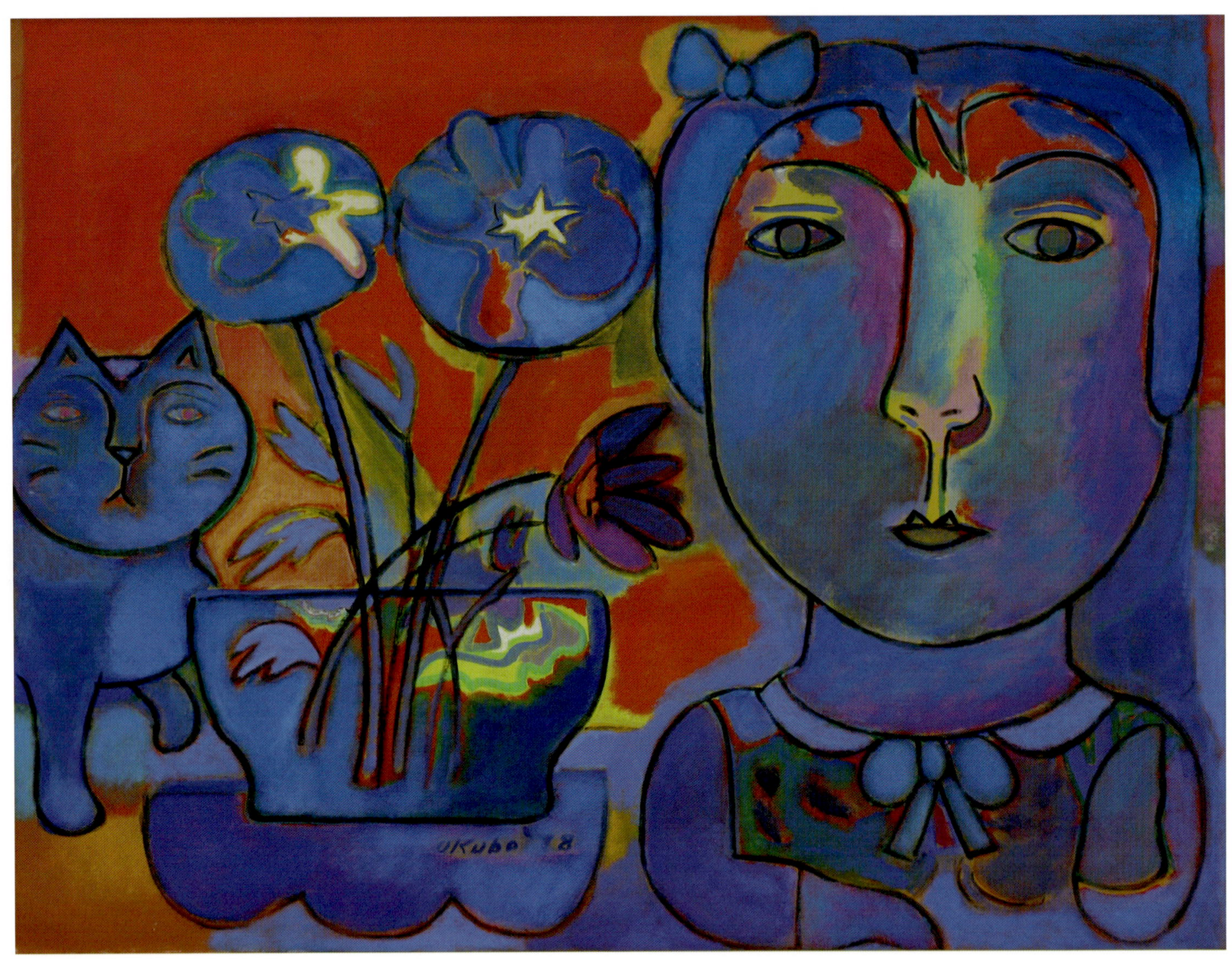


**105**
Miné Okubo
*Cat, Vase of Flowers, Girl—Blue*
1978

Acrylic on canvas, 35½ × 50⅞ in. Riverside City College, Riverside Community College District, California, Gift of the Miné Okubo Estate, 2010.1.777. Photo by Tom Callas

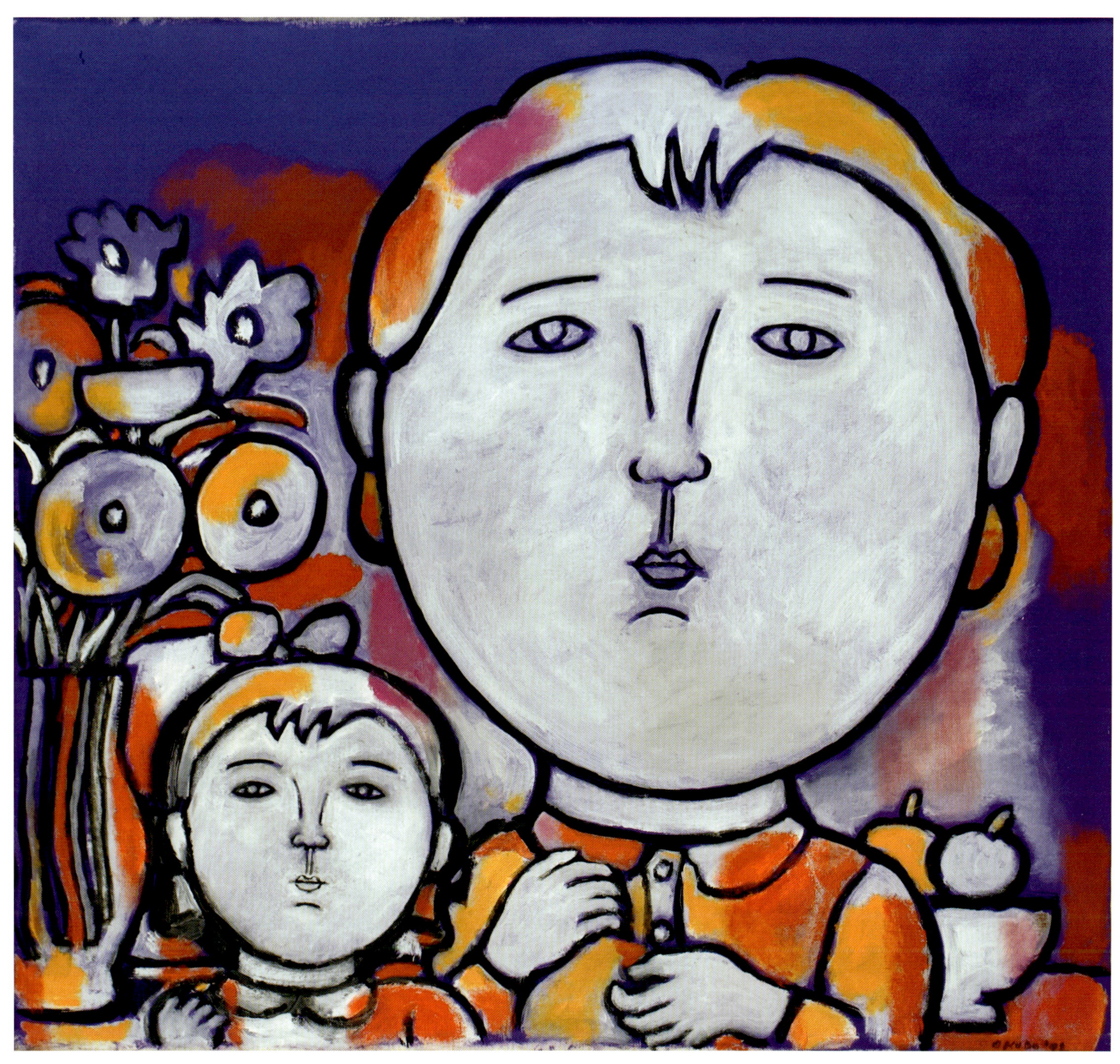

**106**
Miné Okubo
*Mother and Child*
1992

Acrylic on canvas, 43¼ × 47 in. Riverside City College, Riverside Community College District, California, Gift of the Miné Okubo Estate, 2010.1.777. Photo by Tom Callas

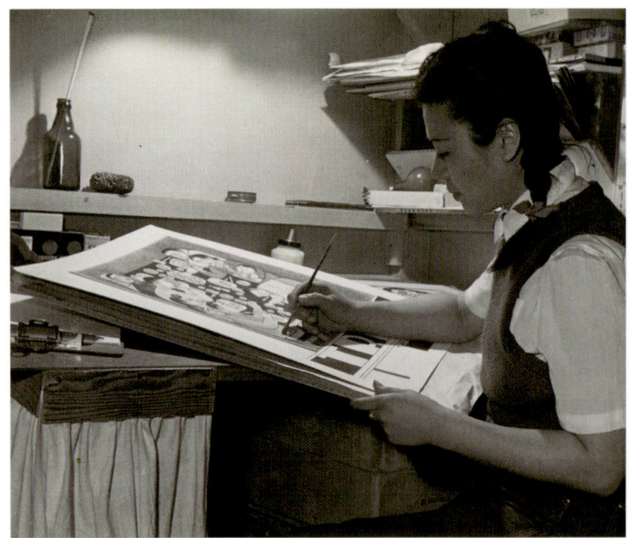

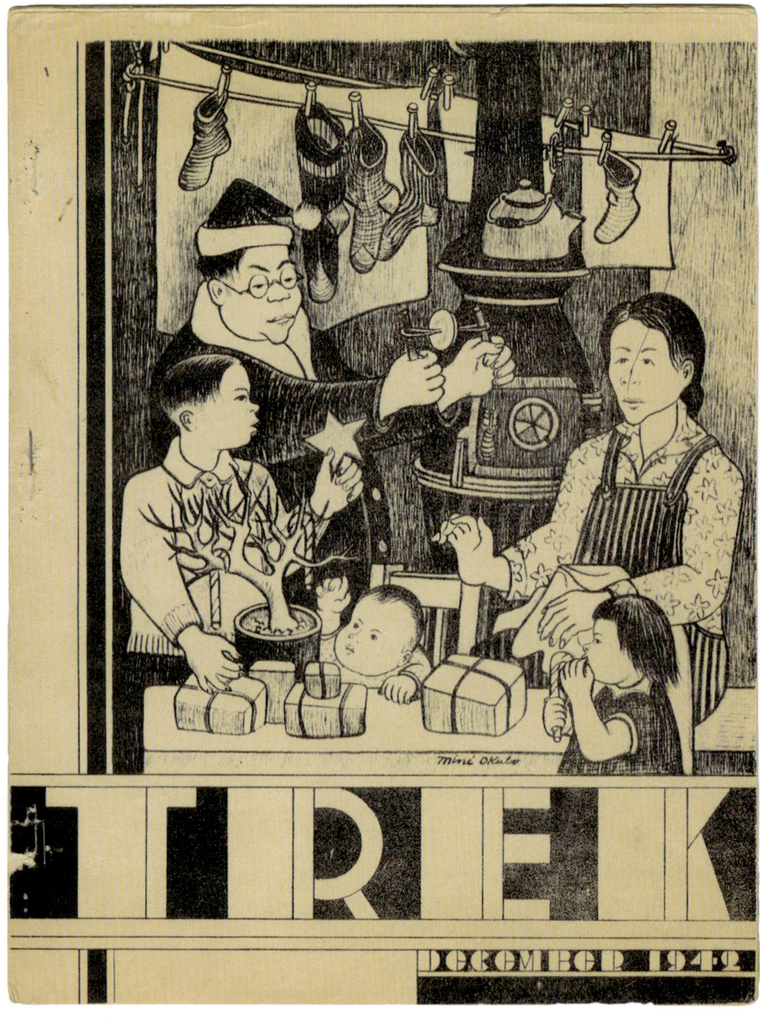


107
Miné Okubo creating the
*Trek* February 1943 cover

Japanese American National Museum, Los Angeles, Gift of the Miné Okubo Estate, 2007.62.549_5a

108
Miné Okubo
Cover of *Trek*
December 1942

Japanese American National Museum, Los Angeles, Gift of the Miné Okubo Estate, 2007.62.486

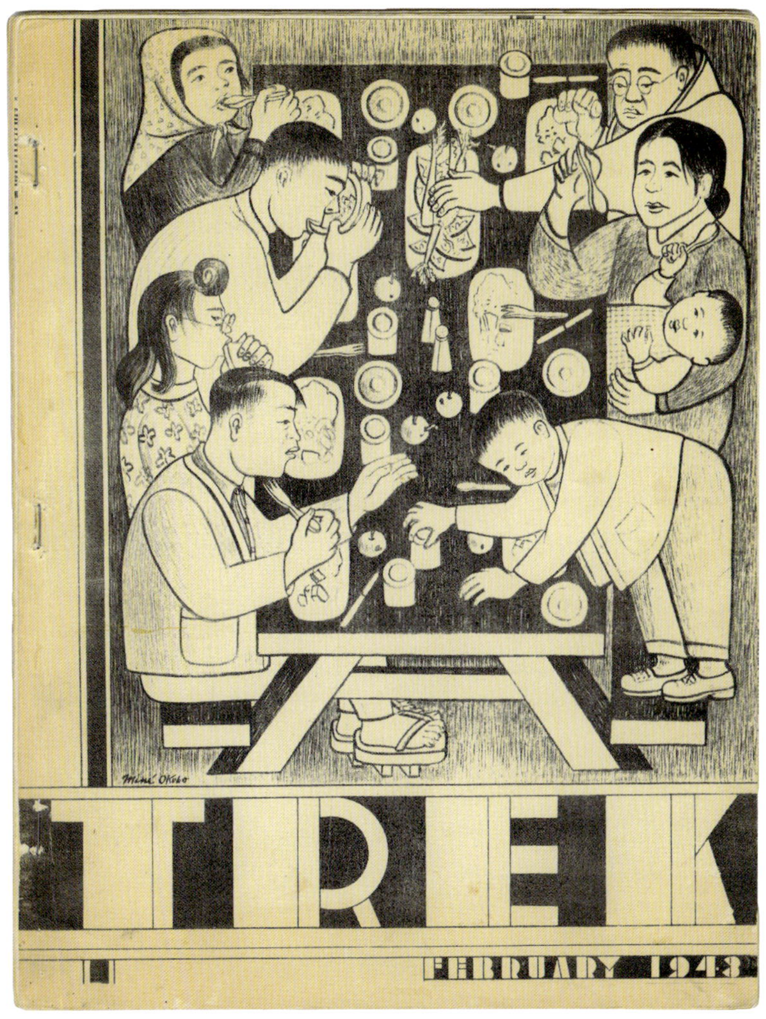


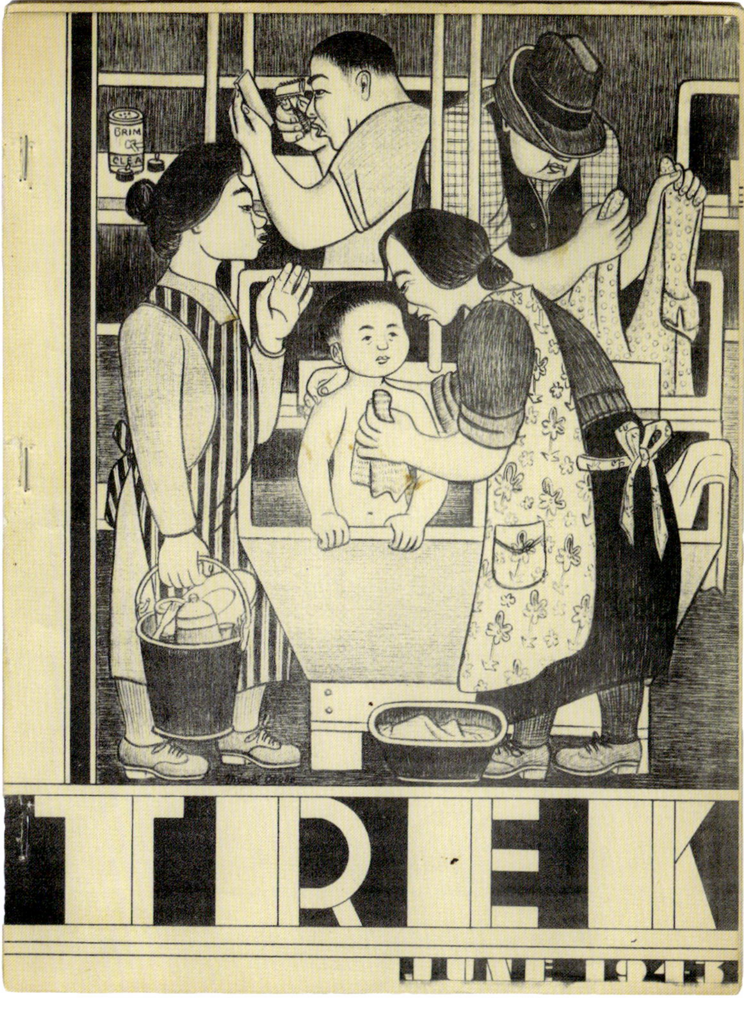


109
Miné Okubo
Cover of *Trek*
February 1943

Japanese American National Museum, Los Angeles, Gift of the Miné Okubo Estate, 2007.62.487

110
Miné Okubo
Cover of *Trek*
June 1943

Japanese American National Museum, Los Angeles, Gift of the Miné Okubo Estate, 2007.62.488

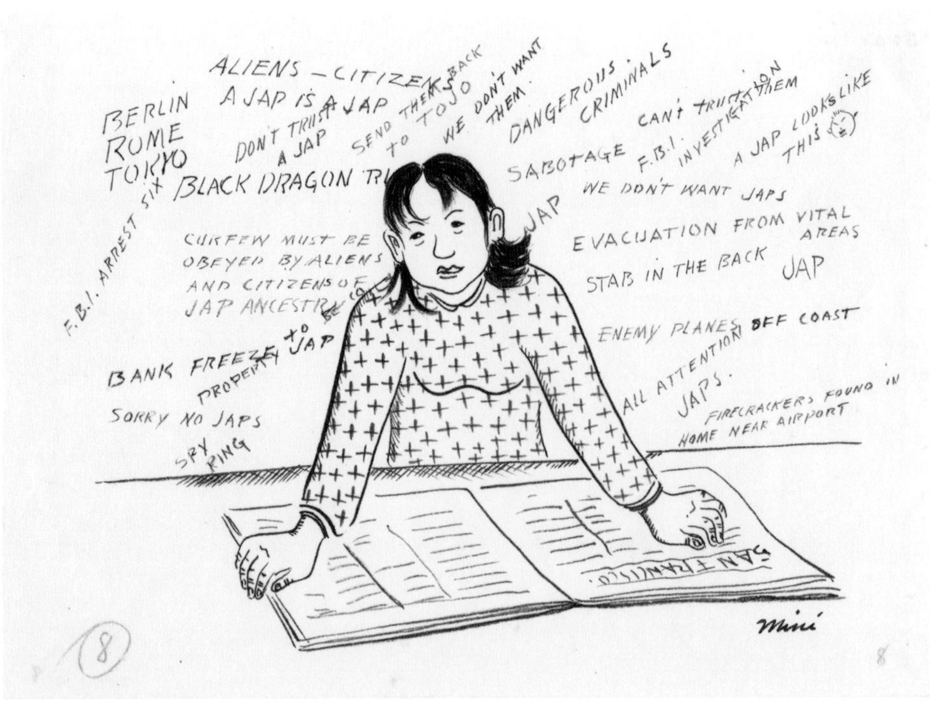


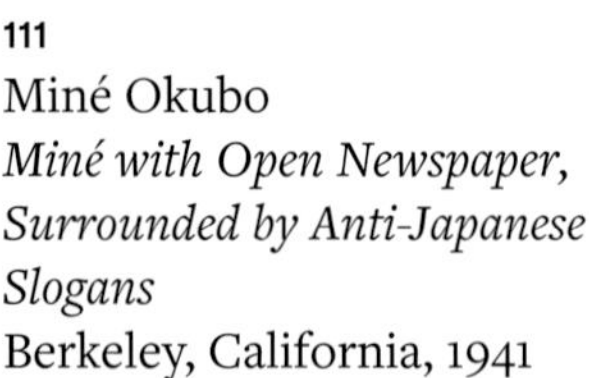

**111**
Miné Okubo
*Miné with Open Newspaper, Surrounded by Anti-Japanese Slogans*
Berkeley, California, 1941

Ink on paper, 9¼ × 13 in. Japanese American National Museum, Los Angeles, Gift of the Miné Okubo Estate, 2007.62.14

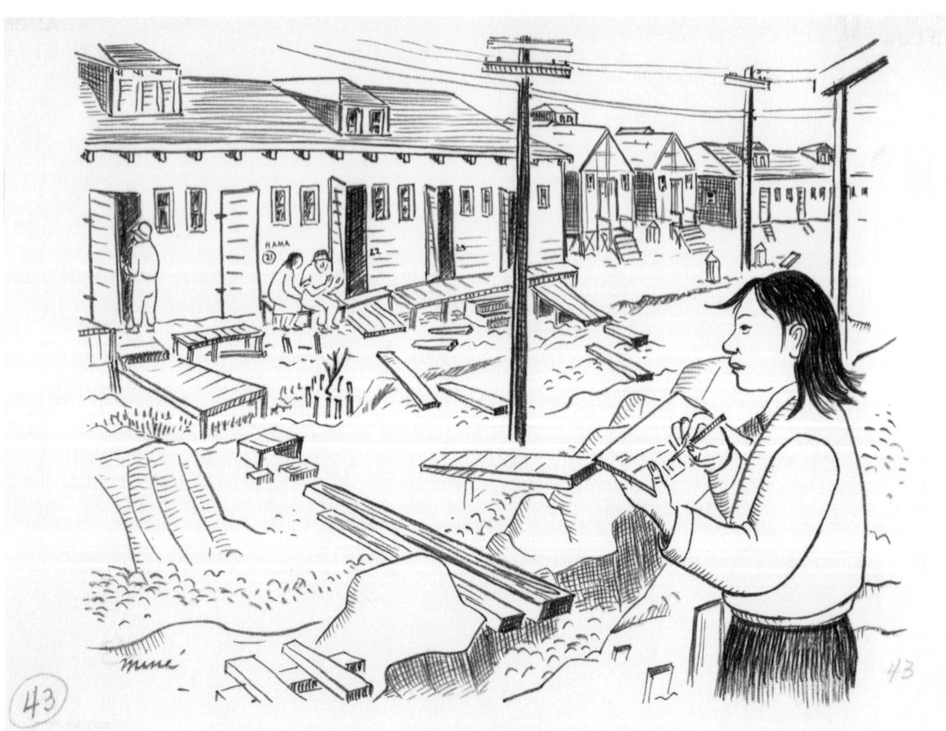


**112**
Miné Okubo
*View of the Camp*
Tanforan Assembly Center, San Bruno, California, 1942

Ink on paper, 9¼ × 13½ in. Japanese American National Museum, Los Angeles, Gift of the Miné Okubo Estate, 2007.62.49

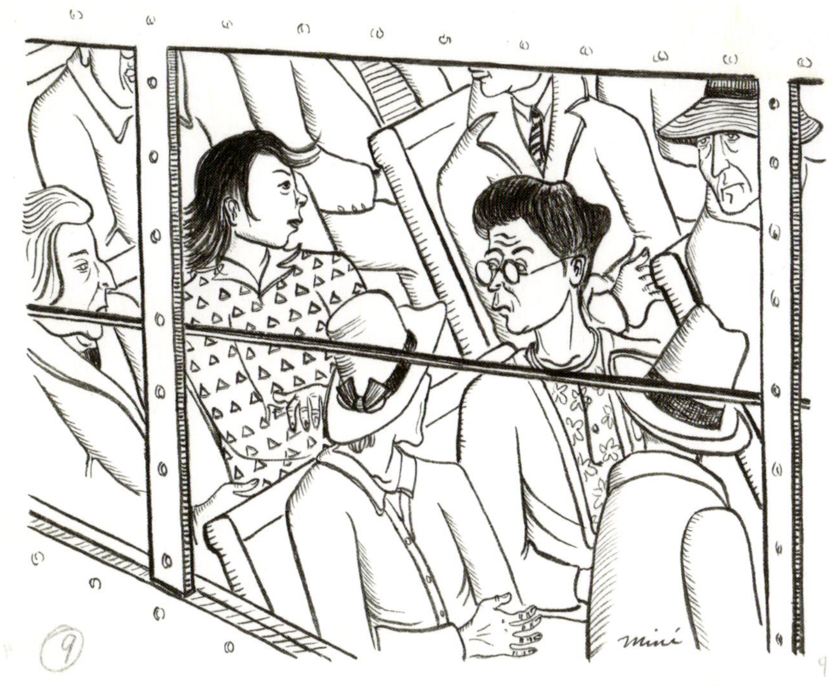

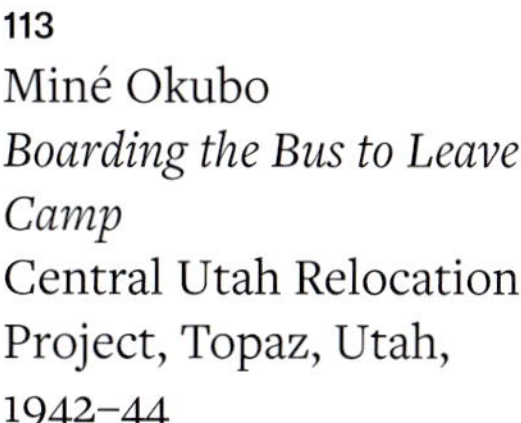

**113**
Miné Okubo
*Boarding the Bus to Leave Camp*
Central Utah Relocation Project, Topaz, Utah, 1942–44

Ink on paper, 9¾ × 14½ in. Japanese American National Museum, Los Angeles, Gift of the Miné Okubo Estate, 2007.62.205

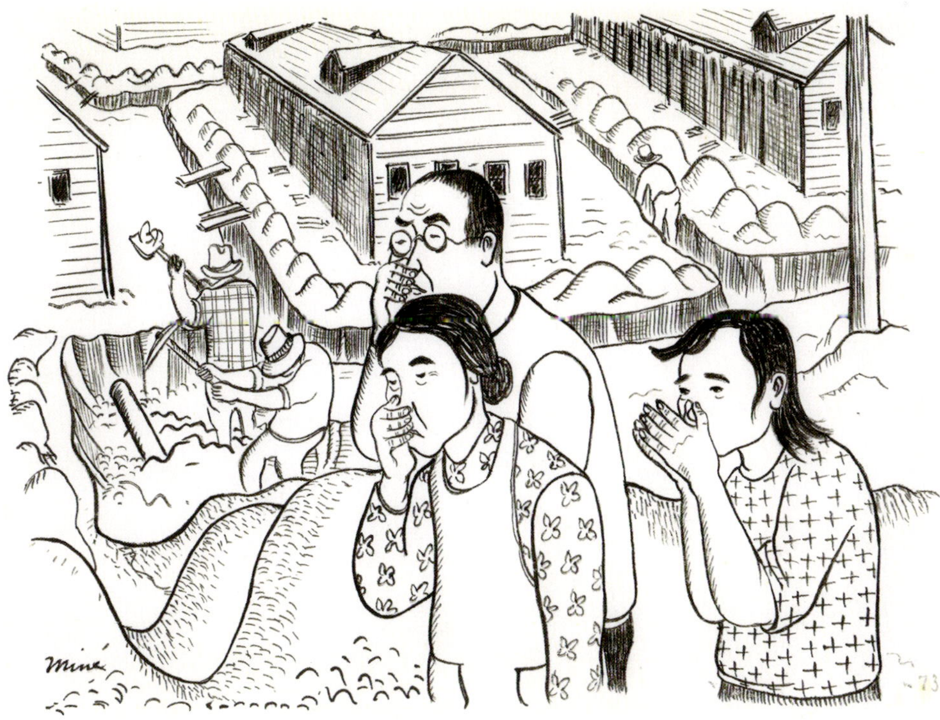

**114**
Miné Okubo
*Sewage System Repairs*
Tanforan Assembly Center, San Bruno, California, 1942

Ink on paper, 9¾ × 14½ in. Japanese American National Museum, Los Angeles, Gift of the Miné Okubo Estate, 2007.62.79

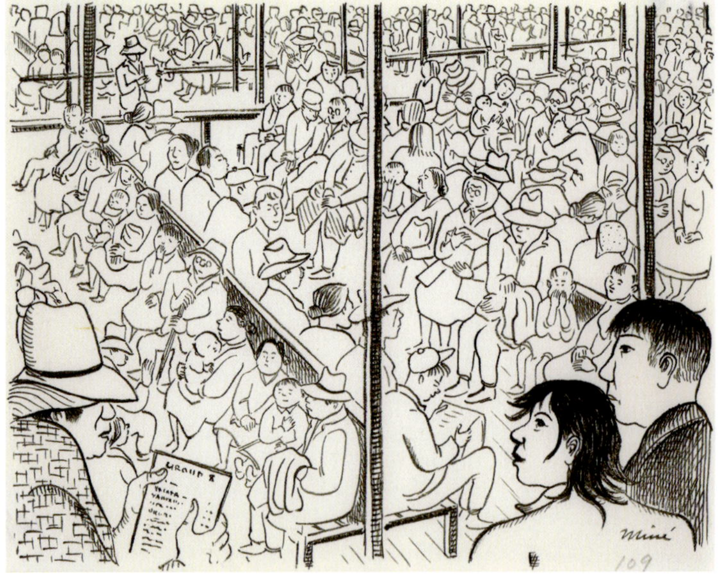

115

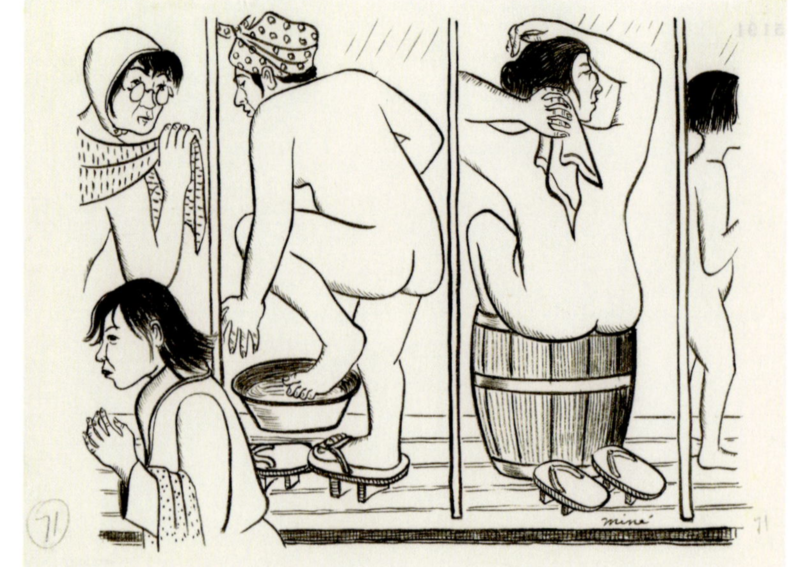

116

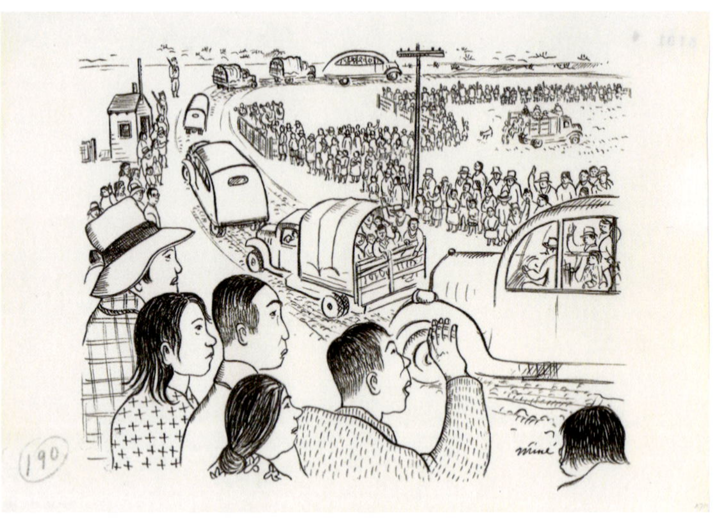

117

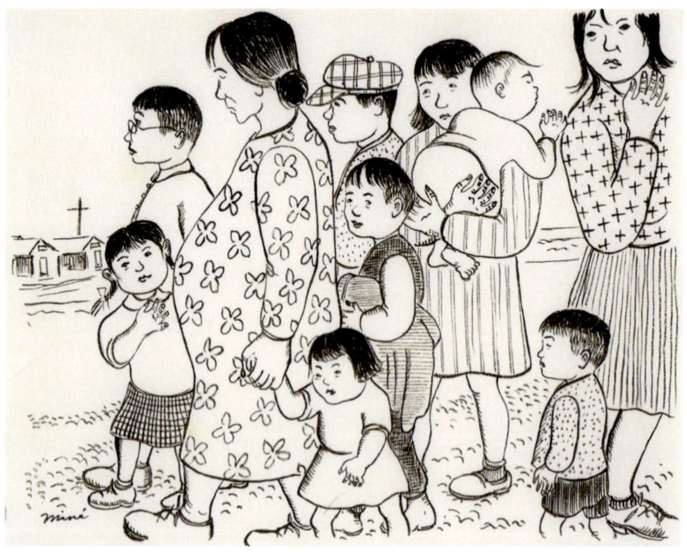

118

**115**
Miné Okubo
*Detention Room Filled with Departing Residents*
Tanforan Assembly Center, San Bruno, California, 1942

Ink on paper, 9¼ × 13 in. Japanese American National Museum, Los Angeles, Gift of the Miné Okubo Estate, 2007.62.115

**116**
Miné Okubo
*Bathing in Tubs*
Tanforan Assembly Center, San Bruno, California, 1942

Ink on paper, 9¼ × 13 in. Japanese American National Museum, Los Angeles, Gift of the Miné Okubo Estate, 2007.62.77

**117**
Miné Okubo
*Departure and Segregation of Pro-Japanese to Tule Lake*
Central Utah Relocation Project, Topaz, Utah, 1942–44

Ink on paper, 9¼ × 13 in. Japanese American National Museum, Los Angeles, Gift of the Miné Okubo Estate, 2007.62.197

**118**
Miné Okubo
*Families with Many Children*
Central Utah Relocation Project, Topaz, Utah, 1942–44

Ink on paper, 10 × 14½ in. Japanese American National Museum, Los Angeles, Gift of the Miné Okubo Estate, 2007.62.162

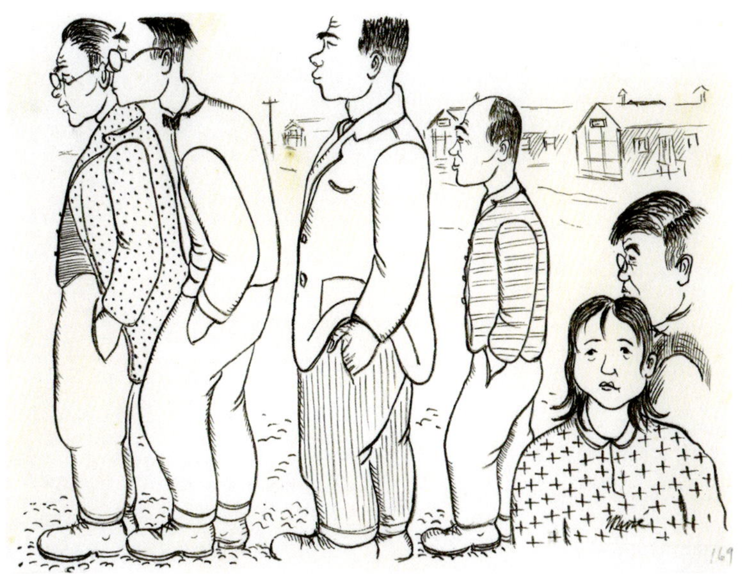

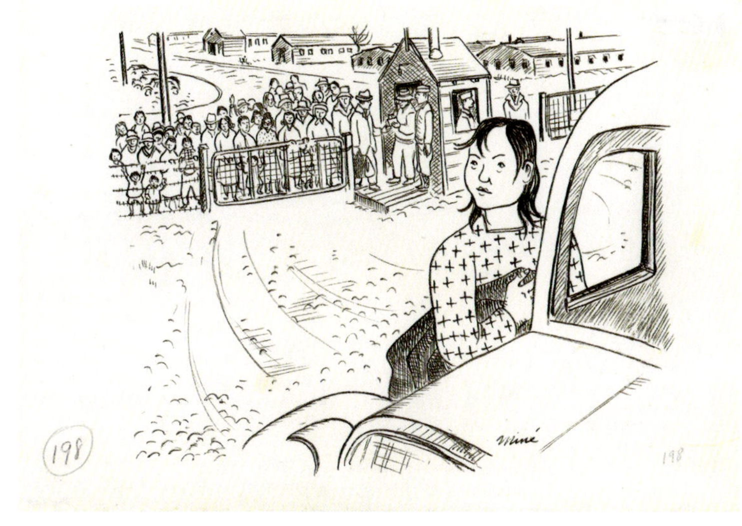

119
Miné Okubo
*Men Stand in Line to Volunteer for the Japanese American Combat Team*
Central Utah Relocation Project, Topaz, Utah, 1942–44

Ink on paper, 10 × 14½ in. Japanese American National Museum, Los Angeles, Gift of the Miné Okubo Estate, 2007.62.176

120
Miné Okubo
*Boarding the Bus to Leave Camp*
Central Utah Relocation Project, Topaz, Utah, 1942–44

Ink on paper, 9¾ × 14⅛ in. Japanese American National Museum, Los Angeles, Gift of the Miné Okubo Estate, 2007.62.205

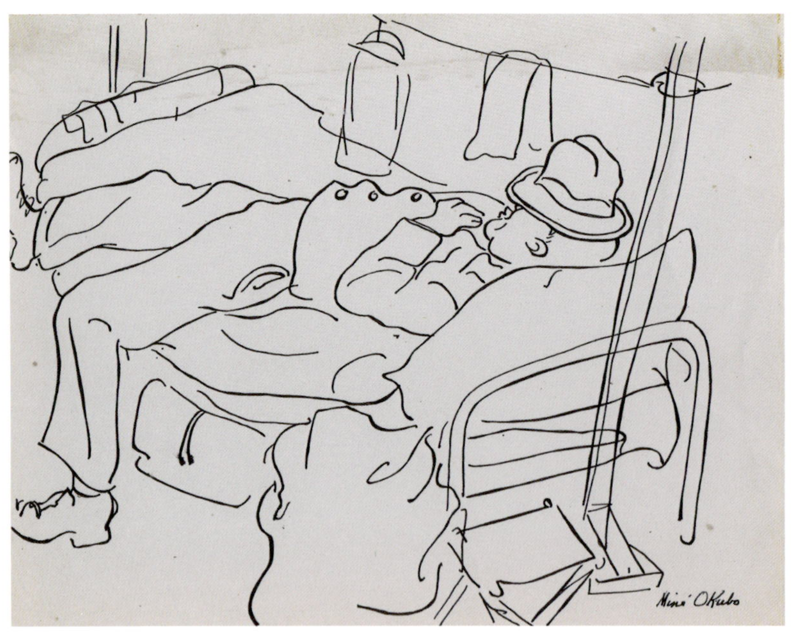


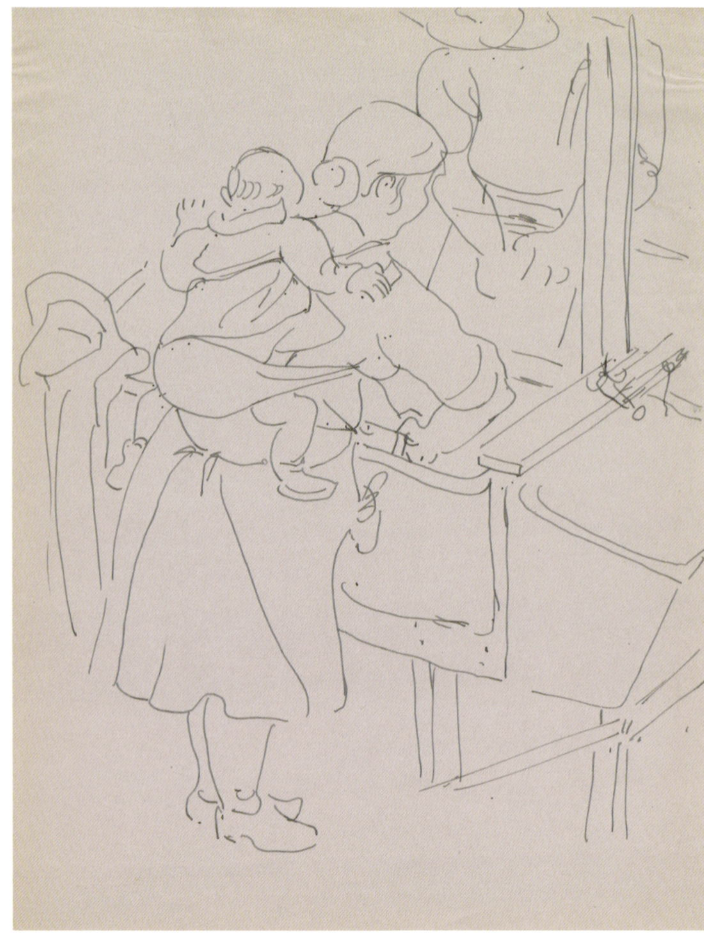

**121**
Miné Okubo
*Man Sleeps*
ca. 1942–43

Ink on paper, 9¾ × 14½ in.
Japanese American National Museum, Los Angeles, Gift of the Miné Okubo Estate, 2007.62.449_2

**122**
Miné Okubo
*Untitled (Mother with Baby Doing Laundry)*
ca. 1942–43

Ink on paper, 14½ × 9¾ in.
Japanese American National Museum, Los Angeles, Gift of the Miné Okubo Estate, 2007.62.450_2

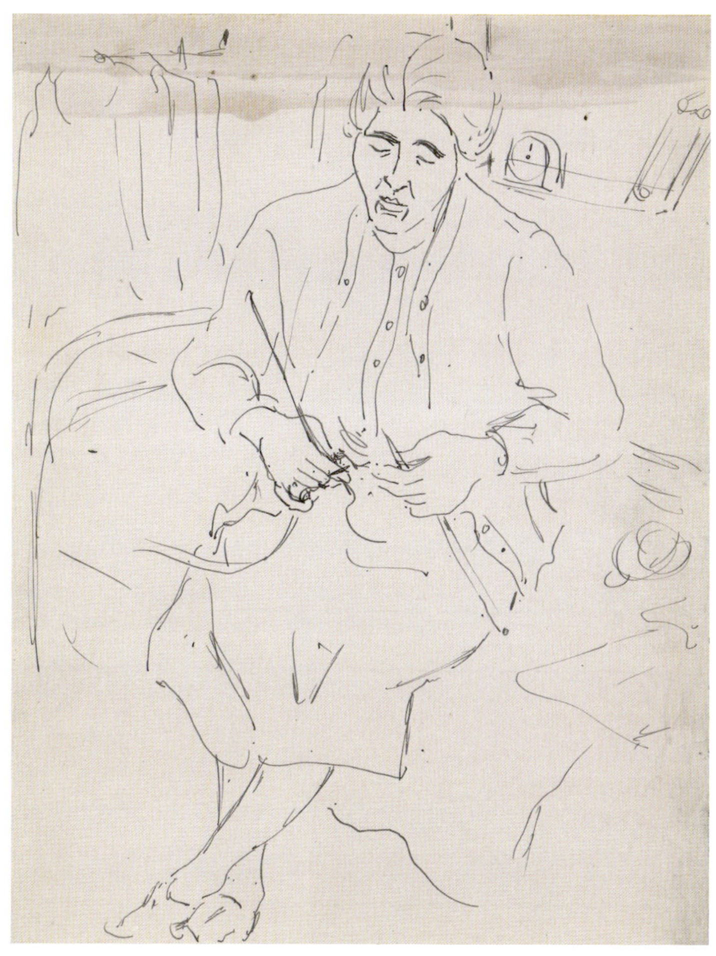

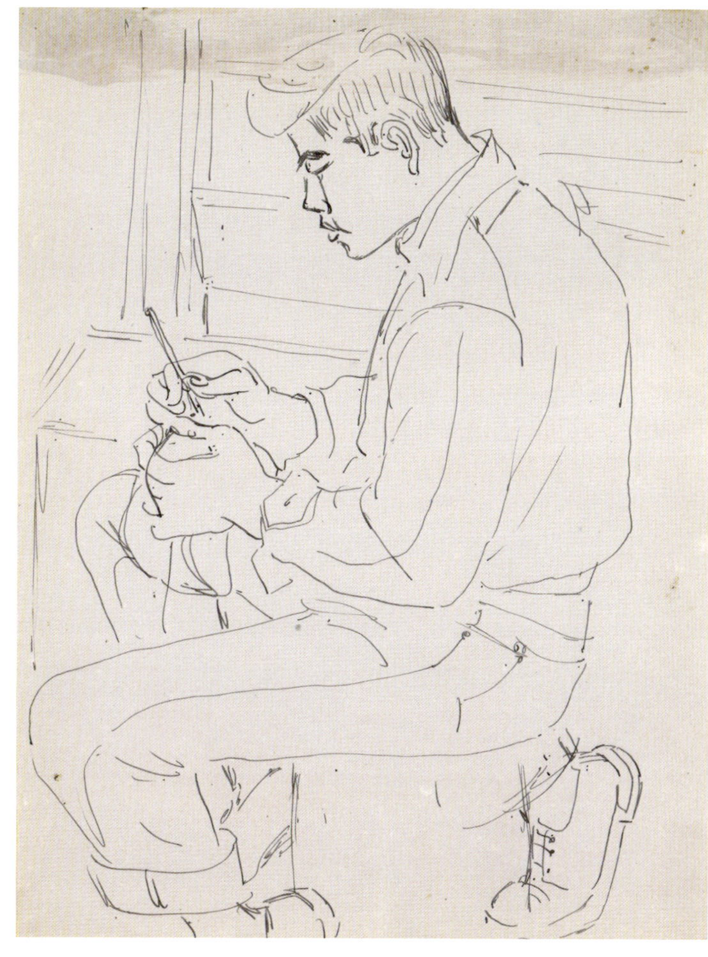

**123**
Miné Okubo
*Untitled (Woman Knitting)*
ca. 1942–43

Ink on paper, 14½ × 9¾ in.
Japanese American National Museum, Los Angeles, Gift of the Miné Okubo Estate, 2007.62.441_3

**124**
Miné Okubo
*Untitled (Young Man)*
ca. 1942–43

Ink on paper, 14½ × 9¾ in.
Japanese American National Museum, Los Angeles, Gift of the Miné Okubo Estate, 2007.62.450_1

Rihoko Ueno

# Unquiet Emotions: The Miné Okubo Letters at the Smithsonian Institution's Archives of American Art

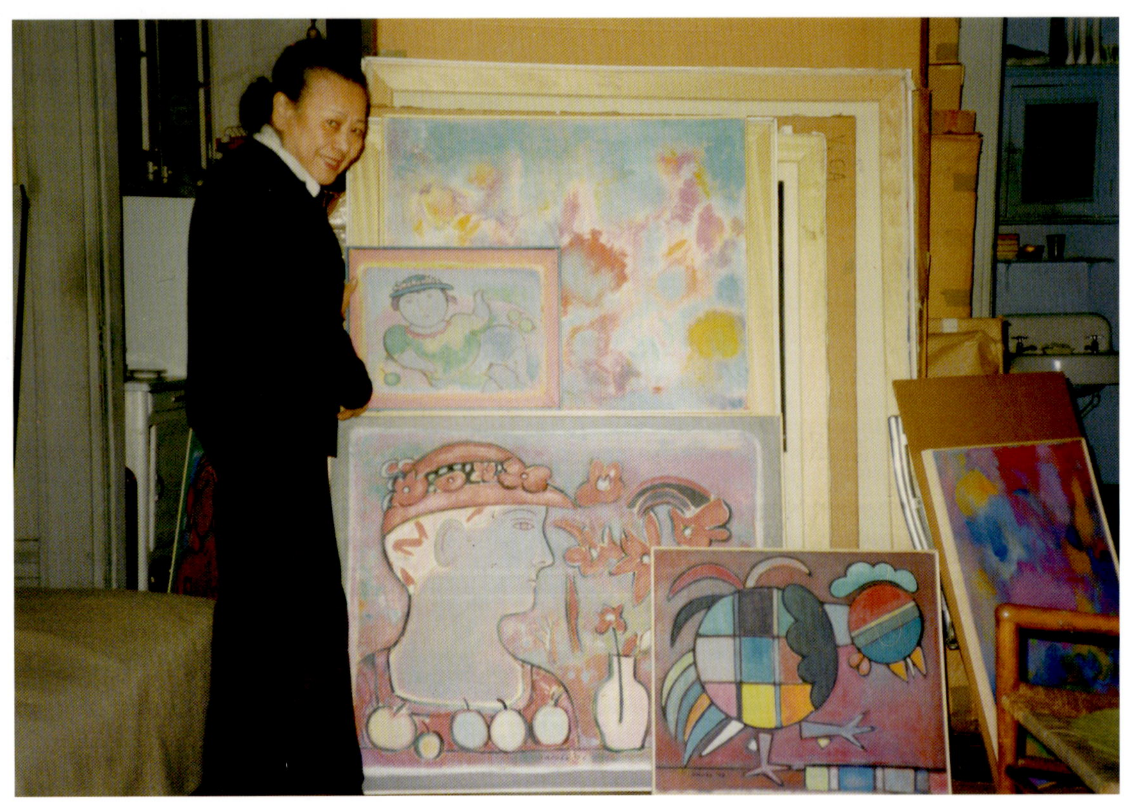

6.1

6.1

Miné Okubo with her numerous artworks in her Greenwich Village apartment, ca. 1980s. The Miné Okubo Collection, Center for Social Justice & Civil Liberties, Riverside Community College District, California, m-e-19-4.

Working as an archivist sometimes means crossing paths with an artist again and again, deepening one's knowledge with each encounter. I first became aware of Miné Okubo around 2015 through her letters in the Bob Stocksdale and Kay Sekimachi papers[1] while conducting research for a blog post.[2] Five years later, as I was preparing the papers of painter Chiura Obata for digitization,[3] Okubo's name repeatedly came up in relation to her role teaching art to children inside the Tanforan and Topaz incarceration camps for Japanese Americans. The two collections contain a sampling of the primary sources related to Okubo that are available at the Smithsonian Institution's Archives of American Art, where I arrange the personal papers of artists for use by researchers. Unlike the finished paintings framed and mounted on museum walls, the documents in the archives often catch artists in medias res, simply going about their lives and trying to figure things out like the rest of humanity. ShiPu Wang's generous invitation to contribute to this exhibition catalogue gave me the opportunity to see Okubo's work afresh, and revisiting her letters to Kay Sekimachi allowed me to appreciate her not just as an artist but as a woman striving against tremendous odds—resourceful, determined, and at times incandescent with anger. I'm altogether glad I (re)met her.

Miné Okubo's letters to Kay Sekimachi date from circa 1956 to 1998, spanning over four decades, continuing until three years before her death in 2001. During World War II, Sekimachi and Okubo were among roughly 120,000 people of Japanese ancestry who were forcibly removed to incarceration camps. The two would be sent to the same camps, Tanforan Assembly Center in California and Topaz War Relocation Center in Utah, during approximately the same period, 1942–44. Okubo's star was already on the ascendant before the camps, as she had found considerable success as an artist, as discussed in this exhibition catalogue's essays. Okubo was Sekimachi's art teacher at Tanforan and Topaz, where there were schools attended and run by fellow incarcerated Japanese Americans. Okubo went to New York City after obtaining early release from Topaz to illustrate a special 1944 edition of *Fortune* magazine on Japan,[4] while Sekimachi eventually returned to California with her family and became a respected fiber artist, whose works are in the Smithsonian American Art Museum and other major museum collections. But the letters find them reconnected eleven years after the war.

Through their correspondence, it is possible to see the portrait of a friendship, of New York City, and of the formidable personality of Okubo—her fiery spirit leaps off the pages. In an early letter to Sekimachi dated August 27, 1956, Okubo writes: "At this point in my decision to follow the <u>pure creative painting</u> I think I am <u>stark raving mad</u> but it's too late to turn back for I've put too much into the fight. . . . Creative dreamers need lots of [luck] to buck the tide of non-dreamers in this world."[5] Echoing this sentiment, one of the last letters to Sekimachi, from December 1996, states: "The mouse year was a very difficult year with everything gone wrong. It was very painful but great in self growth. Individual road is total odds road against the tide of everybody and everything because the search is for truth." It's safe to say that Okubo's pugnaciousness is a constant over the years, and she railed against many things without hindrance: conformity was the enemy; a lack of critical thinking and an apathetic mindset were the enemy; even the art establishment of museums and galleries was the enemy.

Okubo had legitimate cause for complaint, however, and her impassioned outbursts were useful, since, by her own admission, her emotions fueled her: "I guess this continuous anger and cussing is what keeps me going" (October 2, ca. 1984). Okubo seldom dwelled on the injustice of the forced removal and incarceration of Japanese Americans during World War II, and the letters mention it only in reference to her memoir *Citizen 13660* and the ongoing interest in her art from that period, since there was no shortage of other obstacles to deal with. "New York City Okubo"—as I have come to think of her in her letters to Sekimachi—was scrappy. Although Okubo was born in Riverside, California, she ultimately settled in New York's Greenwich Village, where she lived in the same rent-controlled fourth-floor studio on East Ninth Street for over fifty embattled years (Fig. 6.1). It was not an easy stay. She mentioned in her letters that her place was broken into and burglarized on at least three different occasions; but robberies were far from her only concern.[6]

As the Village became gentrified, several landlords tried to displace Okubo so they could rent out her place at a higher price, and there were years when her unit was deliberately neglected to induce her to move out, so she was plagued by maintenance issues.[7] In an undated letter from December 1956 or January 1957, she wrote that she was composing her letter under a tent of blankets because of boiler problems. On March 9, circa 1971, Okubo wrote about a leak from the ceiling: "I got the waterfall late one night. . . . Well [the plumbers] couldn't find where leak was coming from as they decided to break open my wall and man in here now. The stench was killing me. It is in such an awkward and conspicuous place. He will only do quick job of plaster and I will have to somehow [accurately] match paints and get it back to look okay. . . . Well life problems don't fail to cease." The challenges, as she mentioned, were constant, and the litany of apartment troubles continues even into the 1990s: "It's a hell road but I'm walking on—[illegible] eviction is a worry" (April 22, ca. 1992). Still, the landlords all learned their efforts were futile, for Okubo proved to be as fixed and unyielding as a barnacle. One forced relocation during a lifetime was enough.

What's remarkable is that these trials and tribulations did not tarnish Okubo's opinion of New York City in the least. She remained undaunted, and she loved New York in an all-encompassing way, much like countless artists before and after her. In an August 7, 1973, letter to friend and art collector Roy Leeper in response to his offer to rent a studio for her to paint in (presumably out in California, where he lived), she graciously declined: "For the present New York is the best base for me in every possible way. Here I am totally independent and free and I have a feeling of being able to come and go as I please. . . . Also I am able to step out the door at will and enter the pulsating whirl of people and life activities which is a delight and also a necessity to me . . . [I] wake up and

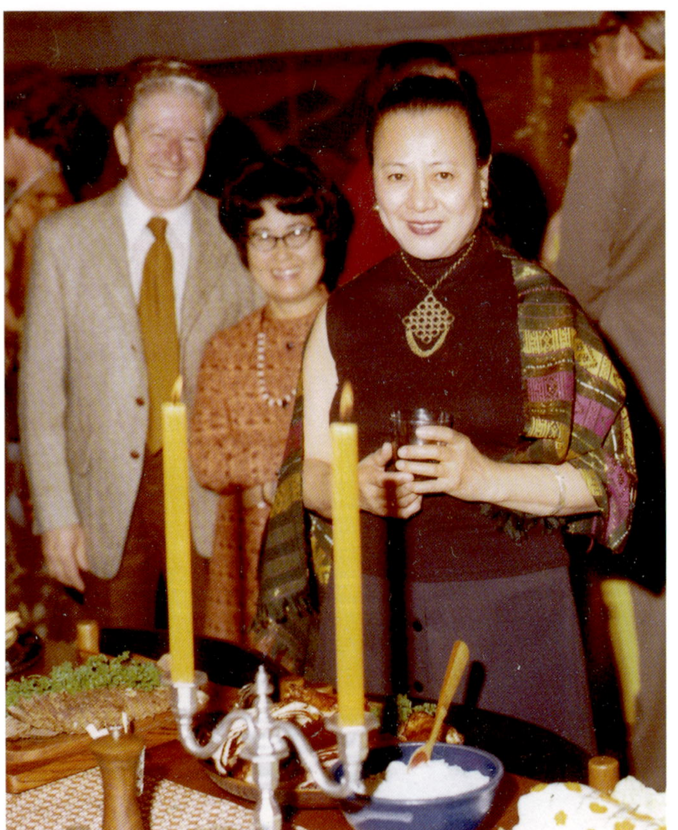

6.2

6.2
Bob Stocksdale, Kay Sekimachi Stocksdale, and Miné Okubo (left to right), ca. 1970s. The Miné Okubo Collection, Center for Social Justice & Civil Liberties, Riverside Community College District, California, s-e-29-1a.

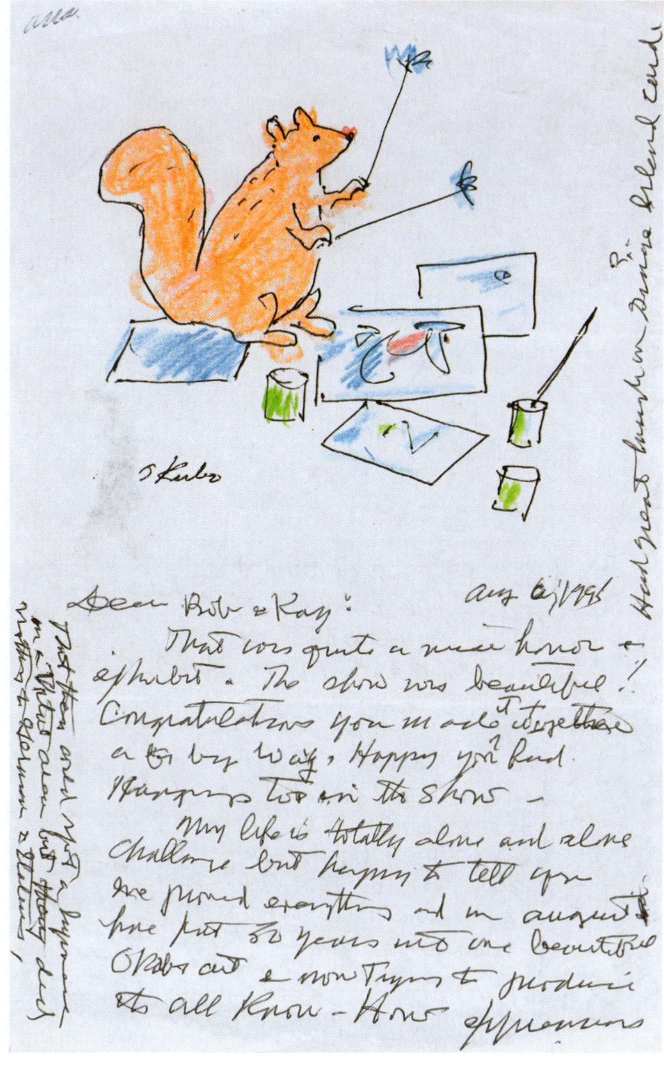

S Kubo

Dear Bob & Kay: Aug 6, 1995

That was quite a nice honor & exhibit. The show was beautiful!
Congratulations you made it together a big way. Happy you find
Happiness too in the show—

My life is totally alone and alone challenge but happy to tell you
I've proved everything and in August I have put 50 years into one beautiful
Okubo art & now trying to produce to all know—How expressions

6.3

6.3

Miné Okubo's letter to Kay Sekimachi and Bob Stocksdale, August 6, 1995. The Bob Stocksdale and Kay Sekimachi papers, Archives of American Art, Smithsonian Institution, Washington, D.C.

this room tower in the middle of people & life madness is perfect as I function on instincts and not plans."[8] She even seemed to feel a certain satisfaction in experiencing the 1977 blackout as proof of her status as a true New Yorker. There's a fanciful postcard that shows a line of human feet beneath a dark cloud of scribbles, as though the darkness were a centipede and people were nothing more than its limbs. Basically, she was home.

The letters are also a testament to abiding friendship, even as their relationship evolved over the years. Sekimachi had considered Okubo a role model ever since she was a student in Okubo's art classes at Tanforan. Okubo's generosity is apparent in these letters, which are sprinkled with gentle encouragement: "Keep weaving. Your work is beautiful original with quality. It will find its place" (June 14, 1970). Also: "After covering all the museums and being so nauseated coming to your show was enlightenment and hope. Your work is very original a monofilament is something new" (September 8, ca. 1970). I imagine her mentorship meant a lot to Sekimachi. And as Sekimachi became a successful fiber artist, the two became peers, attending each other's exhibitions and offering mutual support (Fig. 6.2). One clear indication of Okubo's regard is that several letters mention Sekimachi purchasing a painting, and the two even exchanged art. Okubo was notorious for hanging on to her paintings, rebuffing pleas from her visitors and friends to buy them when they visited her studio—but she made an exception for Sekimachi (Fig. 6.3).

In some ways, the rapport between Okubo and Sekimachi feels inevitable because of the similar trajectory of their lives as Japanese American women with shared experiences of forced removal and incarceration at Topaz and Tanforan, along with their pursuit of life as artists. While Okubo prided herself on her independence, it's clear that having friends who respected and understood her, who allowed her to fully express herself without judgment, was invaluable. Notably, Okubo, who was known for her uncompromising dedication to art, nonetheless expressed moments of wistfulness in her letters to Sekimachi. In one letter, she wrote, "Visitors came and yesterday I took in the 5 cents Staten Island Ferry. It was beautiful and the sea breeze—wow! I certainly thought I chose the wrong life. My thoughts were on ocean voyage and far off places. If I had chosen the normal road. Too late, stuck with the [path(?)] chosen" (June 26, ca. 1971). This vulnerability is touching because it is so rare. To me, these moments when Okubo confides in Sekimachi about her hardships feel like evidence that artists, even adamantly self-reliant ones, need support systems, and contradict the romanticized vision of suffering alone for one's art.

Okubo often describes herself in her letters as walking a solitary road in pursuit of "truth and beauty," but as an archivist, it's possible to see her life as embedded in a web of interrelationships. Before working at the archives, I knew about the World War II Japanese American internment, just as I was aware of Isamu Noguchi's time in the Poston Relocation Center. However, I was unfamiliar with Kay Sekimachi, who led me to Miné Okubo, who I later discovered had taught art alongside Chiura Obata. Combing through the letters again, I noticed that Okubo mentioned the death of Hisako Hibi, who also taught art at Tanforan and Topaz (November 10, 1991). While it isn't surprising that these artists all knew one another, sometimes the relationships are a little more circuitous. Processing the papers of painter and arts administrator Arthur Monroe, I was surprised to find photographs of Okubo's vivid paintings being uncrated, possibly for her 1972 retrospective at the Oakland Museum (Fig. 6.4).[9] I see the threads connecting these seemingly disparate lives and quietly marvel. There is a dialogue happening. Following the daisy chain of connections, serendipity sometimes yields profundity. There are always new revelations, although upon a moment's reflection, it's not surprising that many of the collections "speak" to or reference each other in this way, considering the vast holdings at the Archives of American Art. It is not luck that strings these artists' papers together, but the outcome of a deliberate process involving unsexy things like institutional mandates, collecting policies, and workflows.

The responsibilities of archivists include not just stewardship of the actual collections, but also advocacy. Joyce Davis, the archivist and reference librarian who dedicated years to arranging the immense Miné Okubo Collection at the Center for Social Justice & Civil Liberties

6.4

Photograph of two women holding up a painting by Miné Okubo, n.d. Arthur Monroe papers, Archives of American Art, Smithsonian Institution, Washington, D.C.

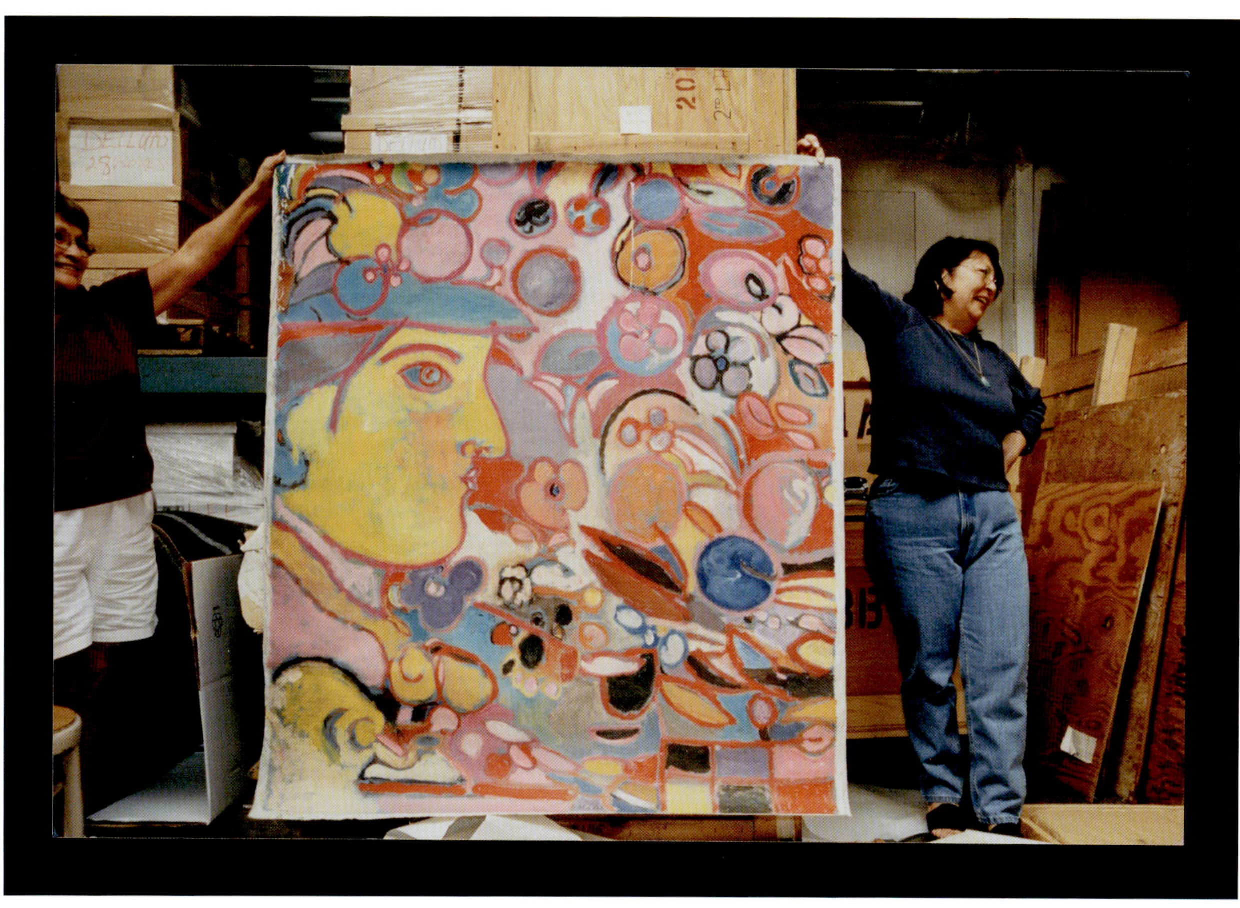

6.4

at Riverside Community College District, told me during a phone interview in 2022 that it has always been her goal to make the collection "available for anybody, anywhere." And while the collection is accessible to the public, it is primarily used by Riverside professors. So, to bolster its visibility, Davis, prior to her retirement, occasionally stood outside the building entrance and physically ushered in passersby, encouraging them to view the holdings, eager to share Okubo's art with others. Davis noticed that Okubo's paintings, especially the large canvases, really impressed children visiting with their parents: "When I pull out the drawers [with the paintings], the colors just hit you!"

I am not an art historian, but looking at Okubo's paintings—especially the ones from the 1970s and 1980s, in which simple outlines of children, flowers, and animals seem to float in luminous swaths of color—I see little indication of her difficulties; whereas her letters to Sekimachi provide a stark contrast, riddled as they are with observations about the lack of time, constant deadlines, nonstop visitors, and endless disruptions. Okubo wrote, "I think like a bird in my work—all reality, common sense, and true values" (November 21, 1968), but she often had to abandon this aerial view to deal with practical concerns, the daily complications on the ground. Mirroring this sentiment, Okubo's letters were often illustrated with birds, sometimes flying in their rightful place among the trees and other times lying on their backs at the bottom of the page with *X*'s for eyes, felled by exhaustion. Okubo's vitality, sense of humor, and commitment to her creative vision kept her buoyant, but her letters underscore the fact that her life had been an arduous journey. Hardship had taught Okubo a lot—"failure was the best thing that happened for life's learning can only be learned through challenges, conflicts and adversity" (January 11, 1994)—and notes of vindication gleam through her final letters, yet I wish she could have spent more of her life aloft.

The challenge of modern archives is to address certain deficiencies and biases in the art establishment's collective imagination and practices by striving for greater accessibility, diversity, and inclusivity. I can only speculate as to how much of the irascibility that courses through Okubo's letters came from feeling marginalized, but I hear the clarion call of her anger and I recognize it. The emotion will be familiar to anyone who has experienced and persevered against the nullifying effects of discrimination and injustice. While archives cannot fully rectify past wrongs, it is possible to preserve Okubo's papers alongside those of others who deserve to have their work and contributions acknowledged and remembered. Not that she needs much help in that department; Okubo would be the first to claim, and rightfully so, that her place in the canon is secure. Her story is still relevant today. In a December 1996 letter, she wrote, "I have proved everything. I am happy I stayed with my convictions and followed the values universal, timeless and ageless instead of the popular for the times," insisting on her own worth until the end. The audacity! (I love it.) While she might have bemoaned the lack of spare hours to dedicate to her art during her lifetime, the archives offers space and time in abundance. Welcome, Miné Okubo. There is room for you.

Rihoko Ueno is an archivist at the Archives of American Art, Smithsonian Institution.

## NOTES

1 All but one of the quotes from letters in this essay (see note 8) come from the Bob Stocksdale and Kay Sekimachi papers, ca. 1900–2015, Archives of American Art, Smithsonian Institution.

2 Rihoko Ueno, "An Epistolary Friendship: Miné Okubo's Letters to Kay Sekimachi," *Archives of American Art Blog*, May 26, 2016, https://www.aaa.si.edu/blog/2016/05/epistolary-friendship-min%C3%A9-okubo%E2%80%99s-letters-to-kay-sekimachi.

3 Chiura Obata papers, 1891–2000, bulk 1942–1945, Archives of American Art, Smithsonian Institution.

4 A copy of this *Fortune* magazine edition exists in the Roy Leeper and Gaylord Hall collection of Miné Okubo papers, ca. 1940–2001, Archives of American Art, Smithsonian Institution.

5 All of the quotes from the letters in this essay are direct quotes and reflect Okubo's original phrasing, grammar, and emphasis.

6 Letters from April 18, 1969; December 30, ca. 1970; and June 30, ca. 1972, mention Okubo's apartment being robbed. Bob Stocksdale and Kay Sekimachi papers, ca. 1900–2015, Archives of American Art, Smithsonian Institution.

7 Shirley Geok-Lin Lim, "A Memory of Genius," in *Miné Okubo: Following Her Own Road*, ed. Greg Robinson and Elena Tajima Creef (Seattle: University of Washington Press, 2008), 184, 186.

8 Roy Leeper and Gaylord Hall collection of Miné Okubo papers, ca. 1940–2001, Archives of American Art, Smithsonian Institution.

9 Arthur Monroe papers, ca. 1940–2019, Archives of American Art, Smithsonian Institution.

Melissa Ho

# New Acquisitions: Notes from an Expanding Field

I have been lucky in my professional life. The longer I work, the more I realize how much I don't know. As a curator of late twentieth-century art, the territory I survey continually shifts and extends beyond my grasp. It didn't always seem so. My earliest education in art history told a linear and contained story of modern art in the United States, one that began in the 1940s and more or less unfolded in New York. As my studies progressed, the story deepened, becoming more complicated and textured. But it was only when I landed my first staff position as a museum curator that I confronted a huge and troublesome category of art: the art that is *not* exhibited, *not* written about, *not* bought and sold. In short, the art that never entered or at some point fell out of the "canon."

Museum workers are painfully aware how much of this art exists, preserved in every long-standing collection. As a new curator trying to learn my institution's holdings, I spent hours perusing the database and squinting at racks in art storage. *What is this?* I would think, as I came across one unfamiliar work or artist name after another. *Should it be on view?* I was then at a museum of modern art with a forty-year collecting history and holdings of some twelve thousand objects. Given the volume, most works garnered little more than a quick look—never mind those that lacked photography or were hidden from easy view. Also challenging was the steady flow of inquiries from artists or their family members requesting consideration of their work. Such unsolicited offers of art were always reviewed by the curatorial team but rarely led to an acquisition or exhibition.

These everyday gatekeeping responsibilities made me very uneasy at first, and I still struggle with them. The limitations of time, labor, and space demand that museum workers set priorities that influence what art *is* or *is not* preserved, exhibited, and seen. Now, I am a curator at the Smithsonian American Art Museum (SAAM), the nation's oldest federal art collection, with more than forty-five thousand objects spanning virtually all media and periods of U.S. history. More than two million people visit our galleries in Washington, D.C., in a typical year. In this context, the stakes of curatorial decision-making are higher still: choices about what to collect and present have a canon-defining effect not only on "art," but also on who and what is considered "American." In this context, it becomes urgent to confront patterns of injustice and erasure, and to invest attention in makers who have been sidelined by virtue of who they were and where they lived.

*Pictures of Belonging* brings into the larger light of American art history the painters Miki Hayakawa, Hisako Hibi, and Miné Okubo. This multi-venue, cross-country exhibition marks the first time the artists will be celebrated on a national stage. As art historical figures, the three have in common their very uncommonness. All born before 1915, they forged distinguished artistic careers in the United States at a time when the social and legal constraints placed on them—as women and people of Japanese descent—were formidable. Although the Japanese were the first Asian immigrants to participate significantly in American modern art, their contributions have been overlooked in scholarly and public conceptions of U.S. art and culture. With only a few exceptions, Japanese American artists of the early to mid-twentieth century have been little valued in the art market and their work seldom exhibited in "major" museums. This is in part the lingering effect of anti-Asian and anti-Japanese U.S. public sentiment and laws of the twentieth century. Asian émigrés faced targeted economic barriers (such as being prohibited from owning land) and were denied the right of naturalized citizenship until 1952.[1] The issuing of Executive Order 9066 during World War II was especially devastating, resulting in the incarceration or displacement of the many Japanese American artists—both U.S. citizens and noncitizens—who previously thrived on the West Coast.[2] Thousands of lives and livelihoods, including those of Hayakawa, Hibi, and Okubo, were upended and countless works of art lost in this catastrophe.[3] It took years for individual artists to rebuild after the war, and not all succeeded. Cultural invisibility has been especially profound for female Japanese American artists, considering that few women from this period, regardless of ethnic background, were taken seriously in an art world dominated by restrictive, sexist ideas about creative genius and artistic worth.[4]

The national presentation of a special exhibition such as *Pictures of Belonging* is significant and necessary. But it is also vital that major works by Hayakawa, Hibi, and Okubo be permanently cared for—and therefore more broadly seen and studied—in art museum collections across the country. Since their work has so seldom appeared in publication and their estates lack gallery representation, barriers exist to curators locating pieces for acquisition. Most of the works by Hayakawa, Hibi, and Okubo that reside in museums today were donated years ago by the artists, their family members, or friends and are regionally clustered in California, where each of them once lived, and New Mexico, where Hayakawa moved to avoid incarceration after Executive Order 9066.[5] Okubo lived and worked in New York City for more than fifty years, beginning in 1944, when she was released from the Topaz concentration camp to take a job with *Fortune* magazine. Yet little of her art can be found in public collections on the East Coast.[6]

Art museums are increasingly rethinking their practices and striving to become more inclusive. The pursuit of a more equitable art history through collecting is not about demographic box-ticking. It is an effort to reveal a cultural inheritance that is richer, more deeply human, more meaningful and invigorating—and more honest. Contrary to what my earliest art history classes taught, American modern art has always been multistranded, taking place on numerous fronts and involving participants of many backgrounds. The exclusion from textbooks and museum displays of female artists, Asian diasporic artists, and other marginalized groups has a falsifying and limiting effect. When collections diversify, they not only more accurately reflect the dynamic and pluralistic nature of the country; they also multiply what is possible to think, imagine, and question through art.

Take the example of Hisako Hibi, whose paintings *Floating Clouds* (April 1944; Plate 63), *Peace* (1948; Fig. 7.1), and *Autumn* (ca. 1967; Plate 93) recently entered the collection of the Smithsonian American Art Museum.[7] These new acquisitions—purchased from the Hibi family—will make her work more accessible to researchers, fueling scholarship on the artist and the communities in which she grew and thrived. The writing of art history is a collective, multigenerational effort. By gathering key works, museums secure the primary material needed for future scholars to advance the field. In this case, concurrent with SAAM's acquisition of paintings, the Smithsonian's Archives of American Art received the generous donation of Hibi's personal papers, a rich trove of material that will now become publicly available for the first time.[8] The cataloguing and long-term preservation of these artworks and papers is ensured by a team of professional conservators, registrars, and archivists. And the potential impact of the acquisitions will be amplified by SAAM's Fellowship Program, which each year brings to the museum a cohort of art historians pursuing research often based in Smithsonian collections. I look forward to future fellows coming to SAAM expressly to dive into Hibi's art and life.

But most exciting, at least from this curator's perspective, is the expanded visibility that the artworks will enjoy. By entering the museum's collection, Hibi's paintings will be discovered by new generations of admirers—whether on display in SAAM's D.C. galleries, on the museum's website and social media, in open storage, or on loan to other institutions. The impact of such encounters is intangible yet significant. I am imagining, for example, a viewer discovering Hibi's *Floating Clouds*, from 1944. This is among the dozens of oil paintings Hibi created while incarcerated with her family at the Topaz War Relocation Center in Utah. Hibi's interest in landscape painting dates to her studies at the California School of Fine Arts (later renamed the San Francisco Art Institute, now the San Francisco Art Institute Legacy Foundation) in the 1920s.[9] At Topaz, she painted en plein air despite the harsh high-desert climate—searingly hot in summer and intensely cold in winter. The sky above Topaz is a recurrent motif in these works, and Hibi mentions it repeatedly in her memoir as well, recalling its expanse and changeability, its brilliant color at sunset and dawn, and the appearance of immense clouds forming and breaking apart.[10] *Floating Clouds* is both specific and universalized, grounded in observed reality yet transcendent in theme. While many of Hibi's camp paintings feature small figures in the landscape, here she omits the ground entirely, directing our gaze past the geometric rooftops of the barracks to the sensual—almost bodily—clouds above. The image is luminous with yearning. Indeed, Hibi later inscribed on the back of the canvas: "Free, free. . . . / I want to be free, as free as that cloud I see up above Topaz."[11] Trapped in an oppressive environment and surrounded by barbed wire and watchtowers, it is no wonder Hibi turned to the sky for solace and mental escape. In its boundlessness, the sky suggests freedom as well as *connection*—it is shared by everyone on earth. The sky Hibi looked at from Topaz was the same sky all Americans looked up to from across the vast United States.

A work of art previously unknown to the general public holds the potential of a revelatory perspective. It offers a window into another human being's experience and does so across great disjunctures of place and time. As exhibition curator ShiPu Wang eloquently argues in this catalogue, Hibi's pursuit of painting was a powerful assertion of her personal agency and a means of testifying to *her* American experience—as a modern artist, an immigrant, a diasporic Japanese, a Californian, a mother, a woman, a worker, and so much more. The three pictures now in SAAM's collection amply demonstrate this. Despite the racial injustice, financial insecurity, and personal loss she confronted during her life, Hibi created a lasting body of work in which beauty mingles poignantly with pain, hope, and joy.

7.1

Hisako Hibi, *Peace*, 1948. Oil on canvas, 26½ × 22⅝ × 1⅛ in. (67.3 × 57.5 × 2.9 cm). Smithsonian American Art Museum, Museum purchase through the American Women's History Initiative Acquisitions Pool, administered by the Smithsonian American Women's History Initiative.

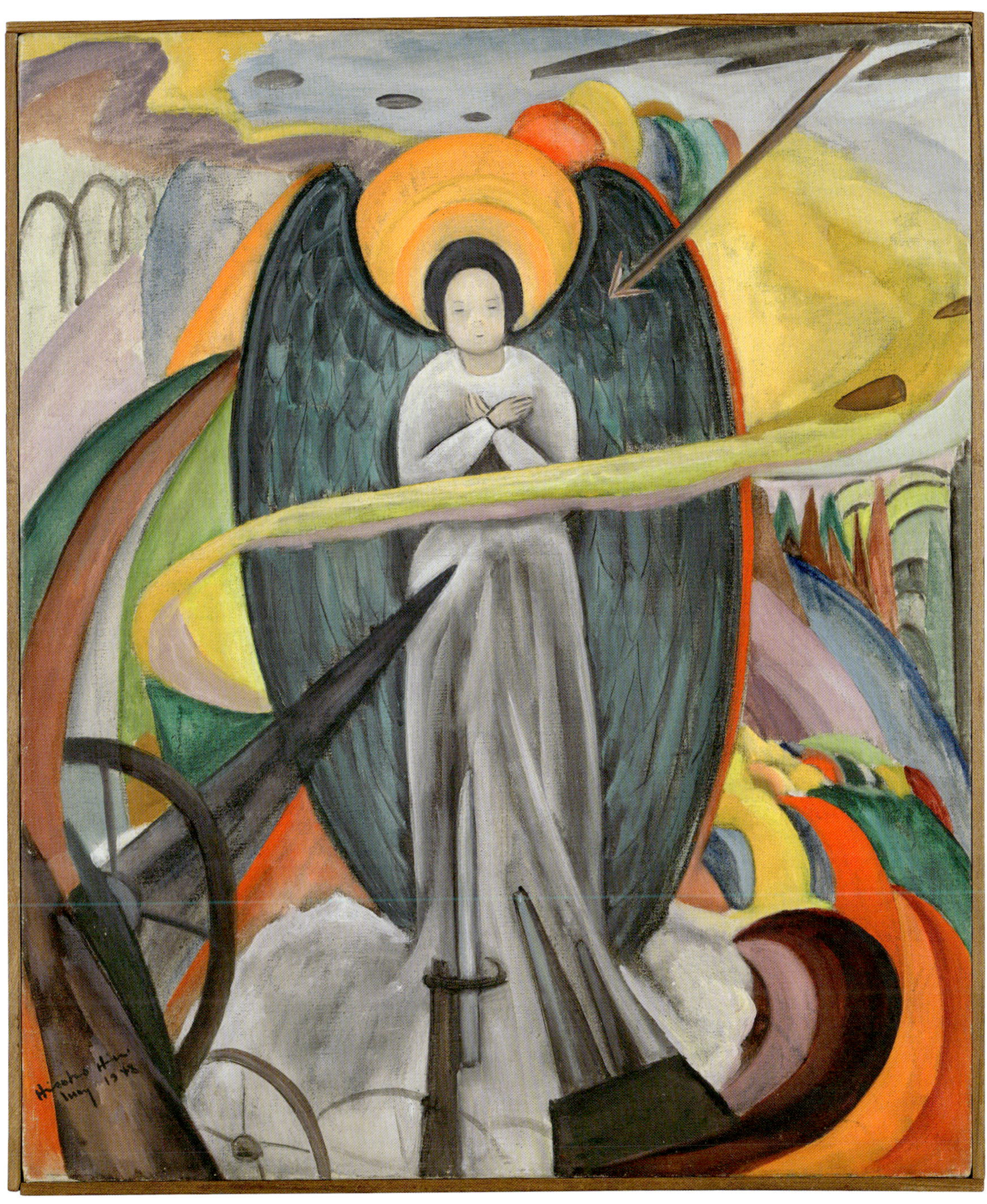

7.1

The rich human and historical insights that a single painting can unlock for viewers exemplify what is gained when art museums overcome a canon that is singular and static. By pursuing exceptional artworks by a wide array of artists, we better account for the diverse influences and life experiences that define artistic practice in the United States. Art is a realm of images, ideas, and stories—it provides a shared space in which difference can be recognized and community formed. The national focus of American art and overly restrictive conceptions of nationhood and citizenship have long suppressed the visibility of immigrant and transnational artists. But we can't afford to lose their voices and visions. Ultimately, a more complete examination of our cultural past is about shaping the future. The works of Hayakawa, Hibi, and Okubo reflect a country whose story is more complex, more fascinating, and sometimes far less ideal than some would like to remember. We must stake a claim for its place in American art.

Melissa Ho is curator of twentieth-century art at the Smithsonian American Art Museum, where she curated the major exhibition *Artists Respond: American Art and the Vietnam War, 1965–1975*. She formerly served as curator at the Hirshhorn Museum and Sculpture Garden, Smithsonian Institution, from 2011 to 2016.

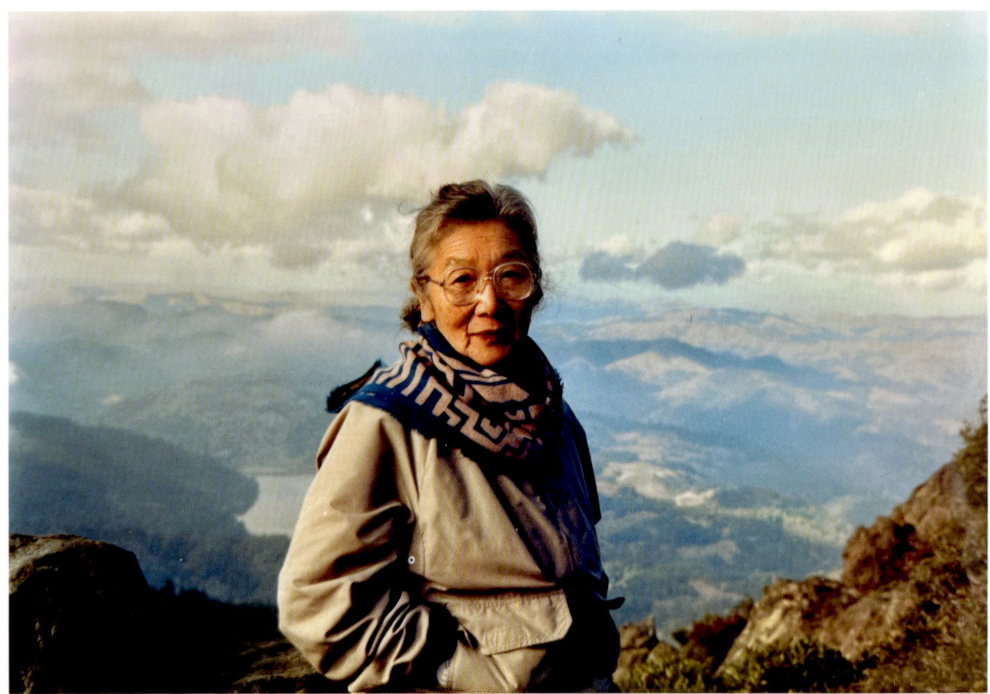

7.2

7.2
Hisako Hibi at Mount Tamalpais, ca. January 1988. Photo by Ibuki Hibi Lee. Courtesy of the Hibi Estate.

## NOTES

1 Hibi made her home in the United States for more than thirty years before gaining citizenship in 1953, and Hayakawa passed away from cancer the same year, having lived in the country for more than four decades without attaining citizenship. Only Okubo, born in California, was an American citizen throughout her life.

2 Artists of Japanese descent were well recognized in the mainstream of modern art on the West Coast before World War II. For more on the cosmopolitan, multicultural milieu of San Francisco's art scene in the 1920s and 1930s, see Becky Alexander's essay in this volume, as well as ShiPu Wang, *The Other American Moderns: Matsura, Ishigaki, Noda, Hayakawa* (University Park: Penn State University Press, 2017); and ShiPu Wang, *Chiura Obata: American Modern* (Oakland: University of California Press, 2018).

3 Before being removed to the camps, the Hibis donated paintings to community organizations in Hayward, California, and only a few of these works have resurfaced in the years since; these include Hisako Hibi's *Spring II* (ca. 1940; Plate 56), included in *Pictures of Belonging*, on loan from the Hayward Area Historical Society. "Japanese Artist Offers to Give Paintings Away," *Oakland Tribune*, April 7, 1942; Ibuki Hibi Lee, email to the author, August 29, 2022.

4 It is only after decades of feminist art historical work, for example, that Ruth Asawa's extraordinary woven sculptures have become widely valued by art institutions and private collectors. Like Hibi and Okubo, Asawa was incarcerated during World War II, though she was sixteen years old and not yet an exhibiting artist when she entered the camps, compared to the twenty-nine-year-old Okubo and thirty-four-year-old Hibi in April 1942.

5 One exception is Miné Okubo's 1940 painting *WPA*, recently purchased by the Phoenix Art Museum.

6 The Metropolitan Museum of Art and the Museum of Modern Art in New York each own one print by Miné Okubo. Both works entered these museum collections in 1943 via the Works Progress Administration. The prints were created by Okubo while she was employed by the Federal Art Project in San Francisco from 1939 to 1941.

7 Many thanks to Ibuki Hibi Lee, daughter of Hisako Shimizu Hibi and Matsusaburo George Hibi, and her children Amy Lee-Tai and Eric Lee for facilitating my research and supporting this acquisition. I also wish to thank ShiPu Wang for introducing me to the Hibi family. In addition to the three paintings by Hisako Hibi, SAAM acquired one painting, *Coyotes Came Out of the Desert* (1945), by Matsusaburo George Hibi.

8 The Smithsonian American Art Museum and the Archives of American Art are separate but related units within the Smithsonian Institution, with adjacent offices in Washington, D.C. The Hibi paintings and papers will thus reside in proximity, a convenience for researchers.

9 Hibi remembered with fondness her earliest experiences painting outdoors under the tutelage of the Swiss-born painter Gottardo Piazzoni. Hisako Hibi, *Peaceful Painter: Memoirs of an Issei Woman Artist*, ed. Ibuki Hibi Lee (Berkeley: Heyday Books, 2004), 6.

10 Hibi, *Peaceful Painter*, 21–25.

11 Omitting those words that have been struck out and are illegible, Hibi's inscription on the back of *Floating Clouds* reads: "Topaz Utah / April, 1944 / Hisako Hibi / Topaz sky / It was an interesting cloudy day / Floating clouds / フワリ フワリ フワリ [*fuwari, fuwari, fuwari*] / Free, free, freeforme [*sic*] in the spacious sky / I want to be free, as free as that cloud I see up above Topaz."

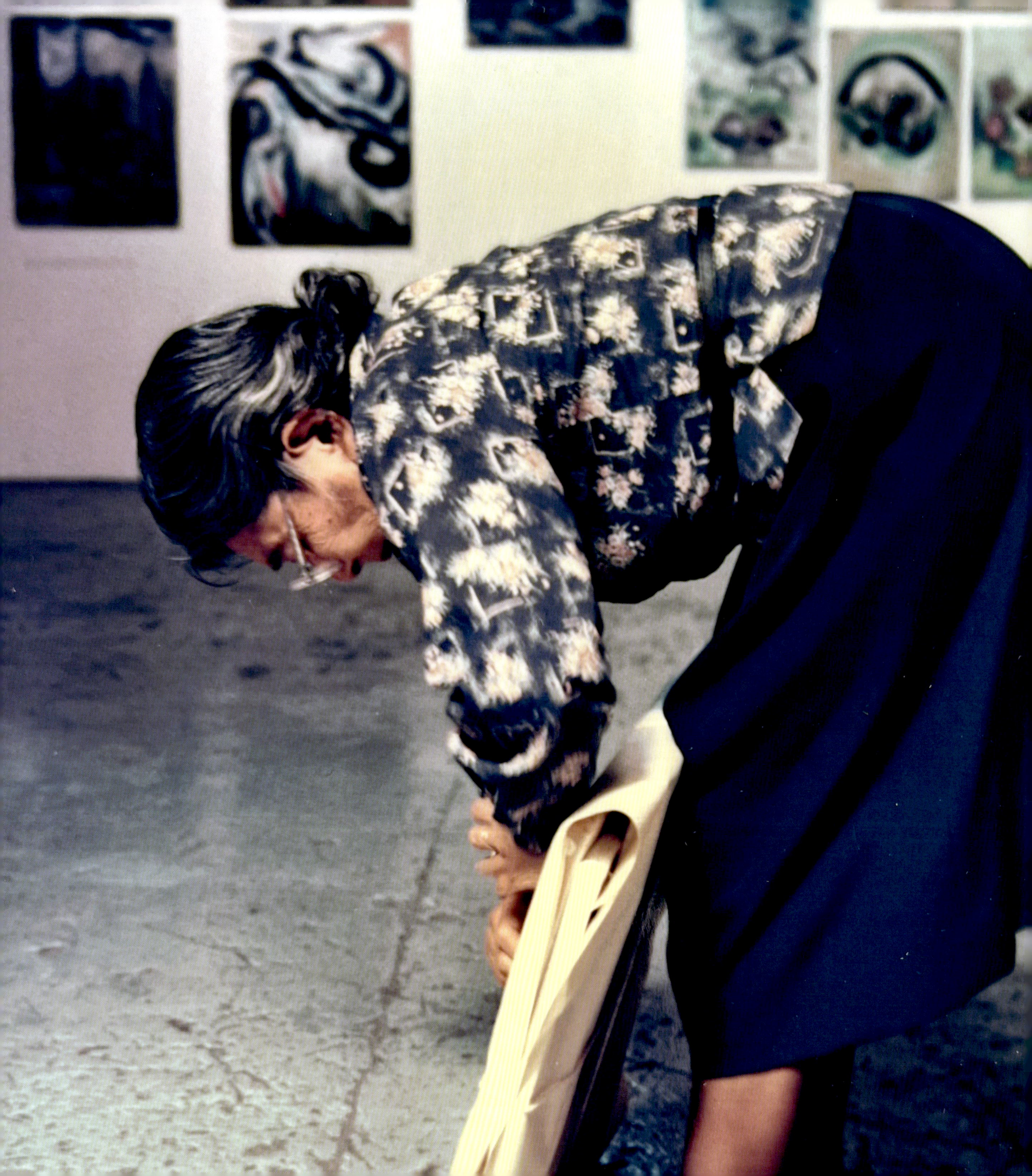

# Selected Artist Statements

Hisako Hibi handling a painting at her solo show *Hisako Hibi, Her Path: 1935–1985*, at the Somar Gallery, July 1985 (detail), with *Frightful NYC* (1946) and *Fear* (1948) on the wall, visible above her head.

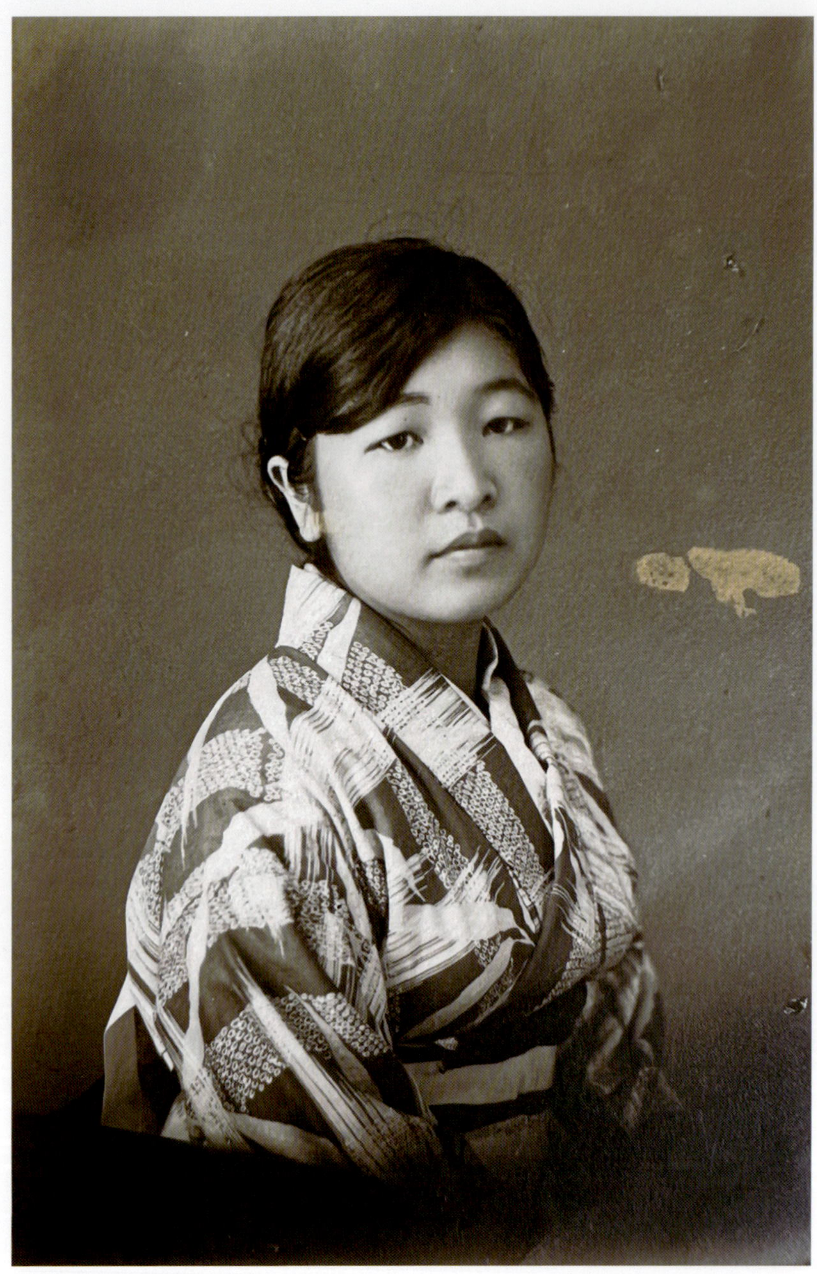

Hisako Shimizu (Hibi) in Japan, 1930. Courtesy of the Hibi Estate.

## Hisako Hibi, Speech Given on the Occasion of an Exhibition at the Oakland Museum Symposium "A View from the Inside," October 16, 1976

I am a grandmother, born in Japan, 1907. I have lived more than fifty years in the U.S.A. but do not yet speak English well. My Japanese [is] not good either. I hope that you will understand. I shall talk [about] some of my experiences.

Already thirty-five years have passed since the first shock of the Pearl Harbor news and the uprooting of Japanese and Japanese Americans from the Pacific Coast. We can hardly believe today that this kind of event had happened in Oakland and San Francisco.

"The ideas of men go buzz and die like gnats; men change their institutions and customs as they change their coats; the intellectual triumphs of one age are the follies of another"—by Clive Bell.

Truly, people's thoughts do change in time and condition.

We were sent to Tanforan to a horse stable and were put in humiliating conditions. My husband and I were born in Japan, and were told that we were the unnaturalized aliens, so that we had to endure whatever the condition might be. But for our children, five and ten years old, and all other Japanese Americans born in the U.S.A., it was their future we were concerned about the most. Fear, frustration, anxiety in the crowded horse stall—I was nervous. I was irritable. My voice rose high for nothing and down to the whispering low tone in fear.

Professor Chiura Obata from UC Berkeley; Miss Miné Okubo; M. Hibi, my husband; and many other associates of arts got together and established Tanforan Art School a few weeks after we started our life in the horse stalls. The music school opened, also. Soon the beautiful melodies of piano [and] violins flowed from the horse stables and highly spiritual *sumi-e*, watercolors, [and] oil painting[s] were also produced in the stable. The art materials were given by the Caucasian friends from outside and we bought more from Flax, San Francisco.

Looking over the barbed wire fences, the hills of South San Francisco were already changing colors from green to yellow ocher. The children played between the horse stables, and I felt sad.

My painting became cloudy, gray. One day I was sketching the dark green eucalyptus leaves behind the stalls with South San Francisco in the background. An internal officer came and confiscated my sketch without a word.

Hibi's script for her speech, along with many of her documents, notes, sketchbooks, and diaries, is now in the Smithsonian Archives of American Art's Hisako Hibi and Matsusaburo "George" Hibi Papers. Miné Okubo's 1944 letter to the Hibis is in the same collection.

At the time I was scared, afraid to ask him, "Why could I not sketch that scene?"

We stayed about four months in Tanforan and were sent to the inland camp at Topaz, Utah. Topaz Art School was an extension of Tanforan Art School and many residents, young and old, attended art classes. In the [open] desert land systematically were arranged forty-two blocks; one block consisted of twelve barracks, one mess hall, and one for shower, latrine, and washing, surrounded by the barbed wires and watchtowers. Here, too, I felt sad—heaven and earth, everything seemed gray—I used lots of gray color.

Although the nature was always beautiful! The desert sunrise and sunset, so brilliant and so magnificent, somehow I could not bring out the brilliant colors on the canvas. The stars at night were another beauty—clean and clear!

I entered California School of Fine Arts, now SF Art Institute, [in] summer 1926 to study Western-style oil painting. Thus, I was influenced by Impressionism and Post-Impressionism. My camp scenes in the exhibition were mostly painted on the canvas as I have seen them—objects seen. However, I did not paint purposely, nor consciously, but the paintings speak for themselves. For instance, "The children bathed in the washing-tubs," "A child almost blown off by some force," "An old couple walking aimlessly in the desert," and so on—they tell the social conditions at that time.

After three and a half years of confinement we walked out [of] the camp [in] September 1945. I was granted a naturalized U.S. citizenship [in] 1953. Since then, I have participated [in] the local and the national elections, and began to think of the society we live [in] and my heritage. What is Eastern mind-spirit?

I do not know exactly when nor how, perhaps 1964 or 1965, colors of my paintings became brighter and much freer expression[s] of objects on the canvases. I use more warmer colors now, and the paintings became less representational.

I noticed the differences in Eastern and Western civilizations. To construct a Japanese garden it says to start in asymmetry and within this area to build up beauty and harmony.

To arrange flowers it says to use irregular triangle lines, and here, too, to create a peace, [a] harmony of beauty by arranging the various flowers and branches in interesting ways.

Affinity with nature is our precious heritage. Our ancestors studied nature and learned . . . the movement of the universe, and teach us the way of life—that this life is not secured, balanced for symmetry—that nothing stays still, everything changes in time and condition—and that which included the human thoughts and behavior—love, hatred, anger, happiness, sadness, and so on—yesterday's enemy is today's friend, and reverse, often. It says, What does not change is changes!

Through sharing our bitter experiences of evacuation we may contribute something to the society we live [in]. The exhibition and the Forum are very significant and meaningful to me. To those young people of Asian American studies and Toni Mar of Oakland Museum, Department of Special Exhibit[s] and Education, I thank you very much for this opportunity you have given me.

Thank you all very much.

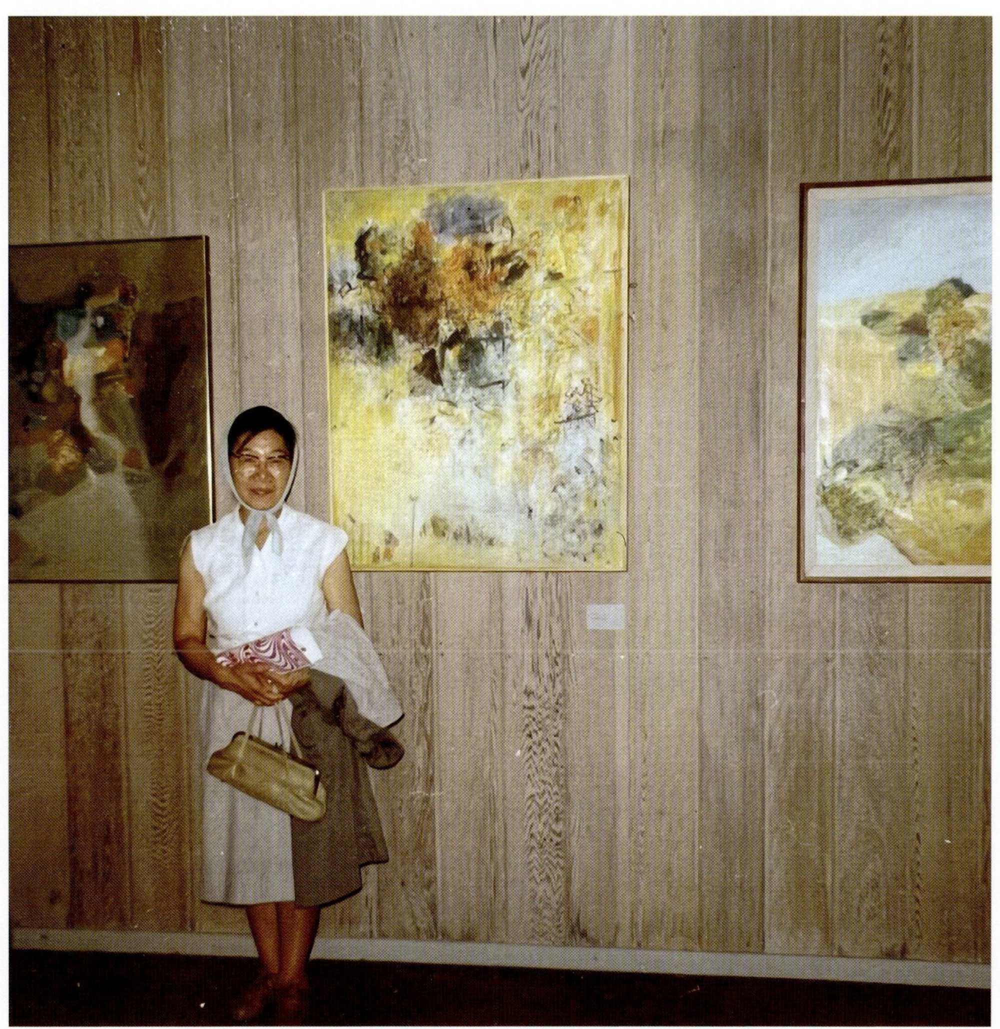

Hisako Hibi in front of her painting *Autumn* (ca. 1967) at the California State Fair in Sacramento, September 1967. Courtesy of the Hibi Estate.

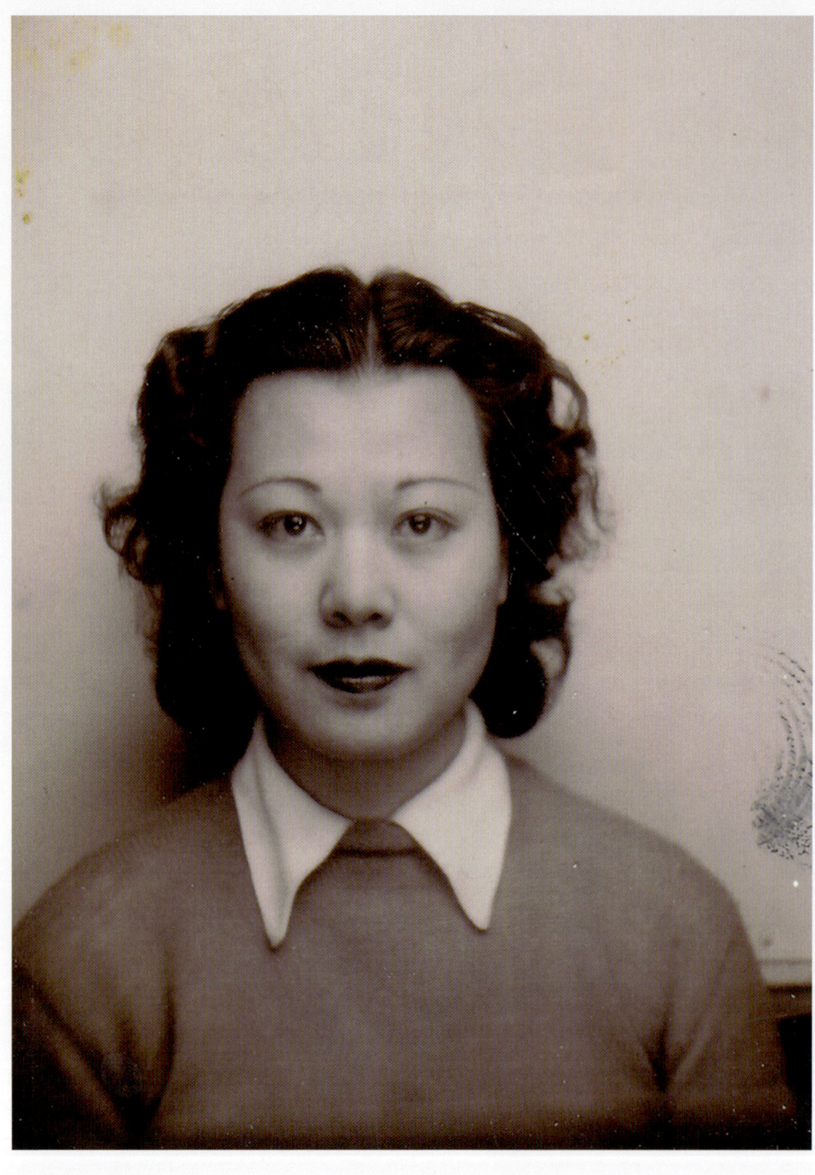

Miné Okubo in France, ca. 1938–39. The Miné Okubo Collection, Center for Social Justice & Civil Liberties, Riverside Community College District, California, box 92, s-e-2-11 600.

# Miné Okubo, Letter to the Hibis, March 1944

Dear Mr. & Mrs. Hibi,

I arrived in New York and went to work immediately for *Fortune* magazine on a special assignment. It was a rush order and I had to work day and night on the job—the work is finished now and I am able to hunt for a place to live. When I find a place to live I will go job hunting—living in New York is expensive but I think jobs will be plentiful—so you see there is no time to fool around[;] it's a mad existence. (My work will appear in [the] April issue of *Fortune*).

At this stage I feel as if I'm going to pitch a tent on one of these tall buildings—there is absolutely no apartments available. It is very discouraging but I think I'll find one someday—.

Busy as I am I keep wondering if the "Art News Magazine" comes to you. I have no way of knowing as all my mail does not reach me. I have no permanent forwarding address yet.

Please let me know on the enclosed card whether or not you receive the magazine. In case you do not, I'll go see the people in the Art News Magazine office here in New York—

It's a tough existence but I guess I'm happier to be on the outside—I'm meeting many important people and it is such a great joy to see art galleries again—New York is full of them—

Hoping that you are all well and painting lots of pictures. Might as well make use of the free hours at camp for it will be a battle for existence on the outside—good luck to both of you and the children—

Very sincerely yours,
Miné Okubo

## Miné Okubo, "Personal Statement," 1972

From the beginning, my work has been rooted in a concern for the humanities. Having traveled and studied both people and art in Europe, having experienced the commercial art world of New York, and having lived through the Japanese American Evacuation during World War II—I decided to follow an individual road of dedication to [my] own inner vision, instead of the popular arts of the times. By using all my technical ability and knowledge of art, I followed this difficult road of research and study for over 45 years.

In my painting, I took everything back to the basics of a workable and universal truth. In the process, I found my own identity, my handwriting, the simplest possible usage. In the process, beauty and statements of truth revealed themselves in the simple and the sensitives, and all that is conceited and false fell aside. I found myself working with and shaping definite "what's" and "how's." What appeared to be seemingly unimportant, minute, undefined areas, became form and color—and every act, a direct statement which related and interrelated.

To me life and art are one and the same, for the key lies in one's knowledge of people and life. In art one is trying to express it in the simplest, most imaginative way, as in the art of past civilizations, for beauty and truth are the only two things which live on timeless and ageless.

I stepped out of the establishment when I was very successful as an illustrator for leading periodicals, newspapers, and books—*Fortune*, *Time*, *New York Times*, and *Saturday Review* among them. Instead, I spent the last 45 years on this research. My earlier work covered subject and realism. I then wanted to show the simplicity of primitive art in the use of forms and color. My latest work is non subject, a spontaneous free-flow of forms and color which relate and interrelate in sensitive subtle beauty, and in endless movement and motion. I followed the French impressionists in their open use of forms and color, and in my final work, much of the simplicity and beauty represents a return to my Japanese ancestry.

This statement comes from box 3, folder 10, "Documents—Resumes and Personal Statements," Miné Okubo Collection, 2007.62, Japanese American National Museum, Los Angeles.

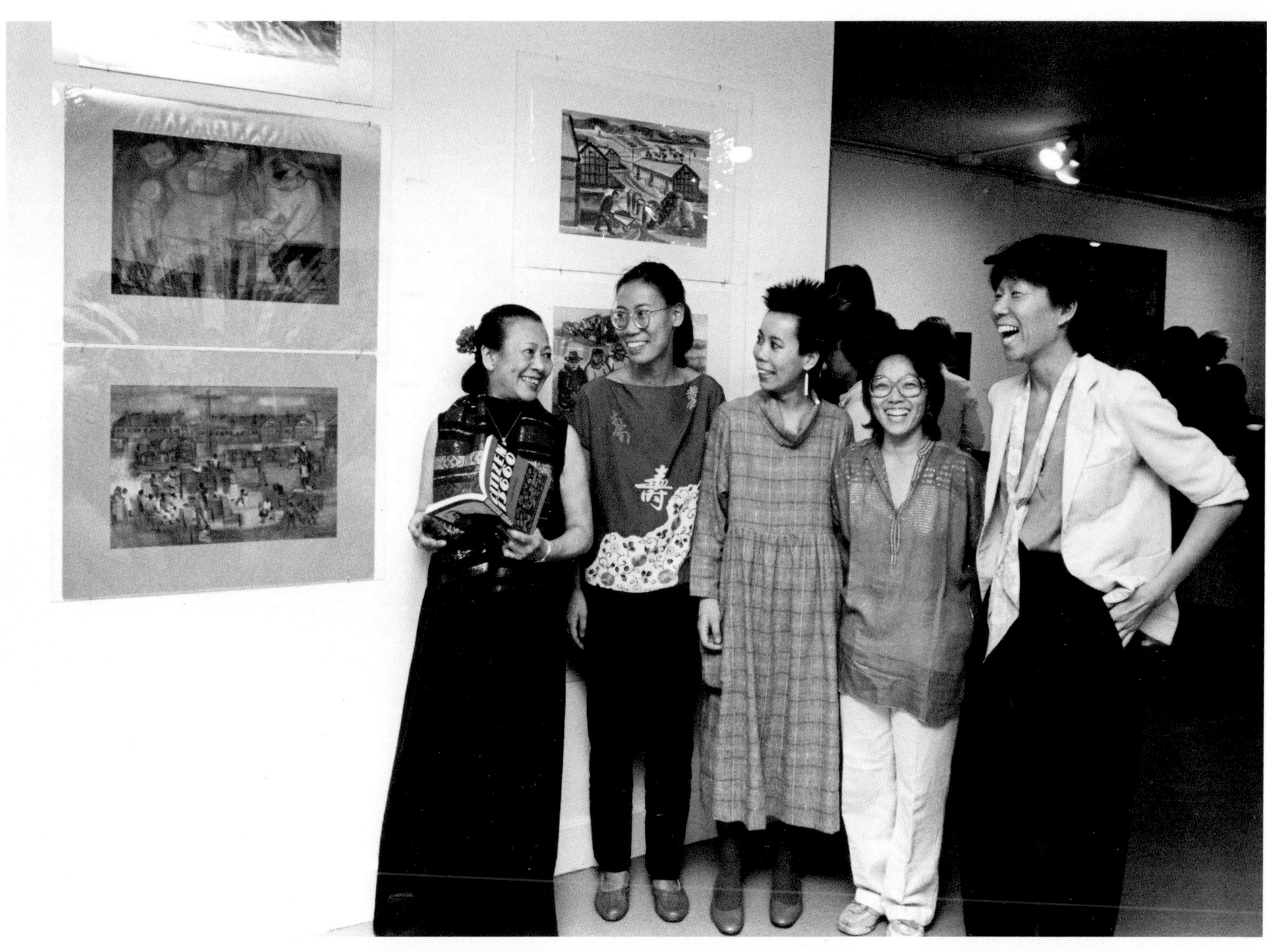


Miné Okubo (far left) at her forty-year retrospective at Basement Workshop's Catherine Gallery, accompanied by (left to right) the artist collective's longtime executive director, Fay Chiang, with Jean Chiang, Theodora Yoshikami, and Mary Lum, 1985. The Miné Okubo Collection, Center for Social Justice & Civil Liberties, Riverside Community College District, California, a2 p6-1.

# Miné Okubo, "Statement before the Commission on Wartime Relocation and Internment of Civilians," 1981

This is a new experience for me. My name is Miné Okubo. I am an artist. I was traveling and studying in Europe for almost two years on a fellowship from the University of California. I made the last American ship leaving Bordeaux, France.

When I returned to California, I worked on the Federal Arts [*sic*] Project. At the time of Pearl Harbor and the declaration of World War II, I had been commissioned to do several mosaic murals for the new Oakland Serviceman's Center and for Fort Ord by the Federal Arts Project for the Army.

Shortly after Pearl Harbor all American citizens and aliens of Japanese ancestry were restricted to an 8:00 p.m. to 6:00 a.m. curfew and were not allowed to travel outside a five-mile radius of their home. However, I received a special permit from the Government and those in authority to go to work every day from Berkeley to Oakland to complete these murals.

I finished the murals work, but I only had three days to prepare for evacuation. My brother was attending the University of California and lived with me, so it was a big help. We had to clean the house of everything quick and fast. We gave away almost everything and left our important things with our Caucasian friends and left a couple of bulky crates at some of our friends['] to store with the Government.

We were exhausted and weary from lack of sleep, no eating, and packing, but with friends picking us up in their station wagon, we managed to make the control station on time.

It was a pathetic sight to see mountains and mountains of number-tagged [bags] and hundreds and hundreds of people number-tagged of different ages. The buses were lined up for blocks on this quiet residential street. The First Congregational Church was our control station. Church people served us sandwiches and fruit. We marched to the bus with soldiers on guard. Our friends waved goodbye and people gawked. Our destination was Tanforan Assembly Center.

Cameras were confiscated. Photography was not allowed in any of the camps. Being an artist, I decided to record my whole camp experience. I had many, many friends on the outside and I thought this would be a good way to repay them for their kindness in sending letters and food packages and telling us that we were not forgotten.

This statement comes from transcripts in the Records of the Commission on Wartime Relocation and Internment of Civilians, Record Group 220: Records of Temporary Committees, Commissions, and Boards, 1893–1999, National Archives, Unsolicited Testimony files, 1981–1982; typed and handwritten copies in the archives at the Center for Social Justice & Civil Liberties, Riverside, California, and the Japanese American National Museum, Los Angeles.

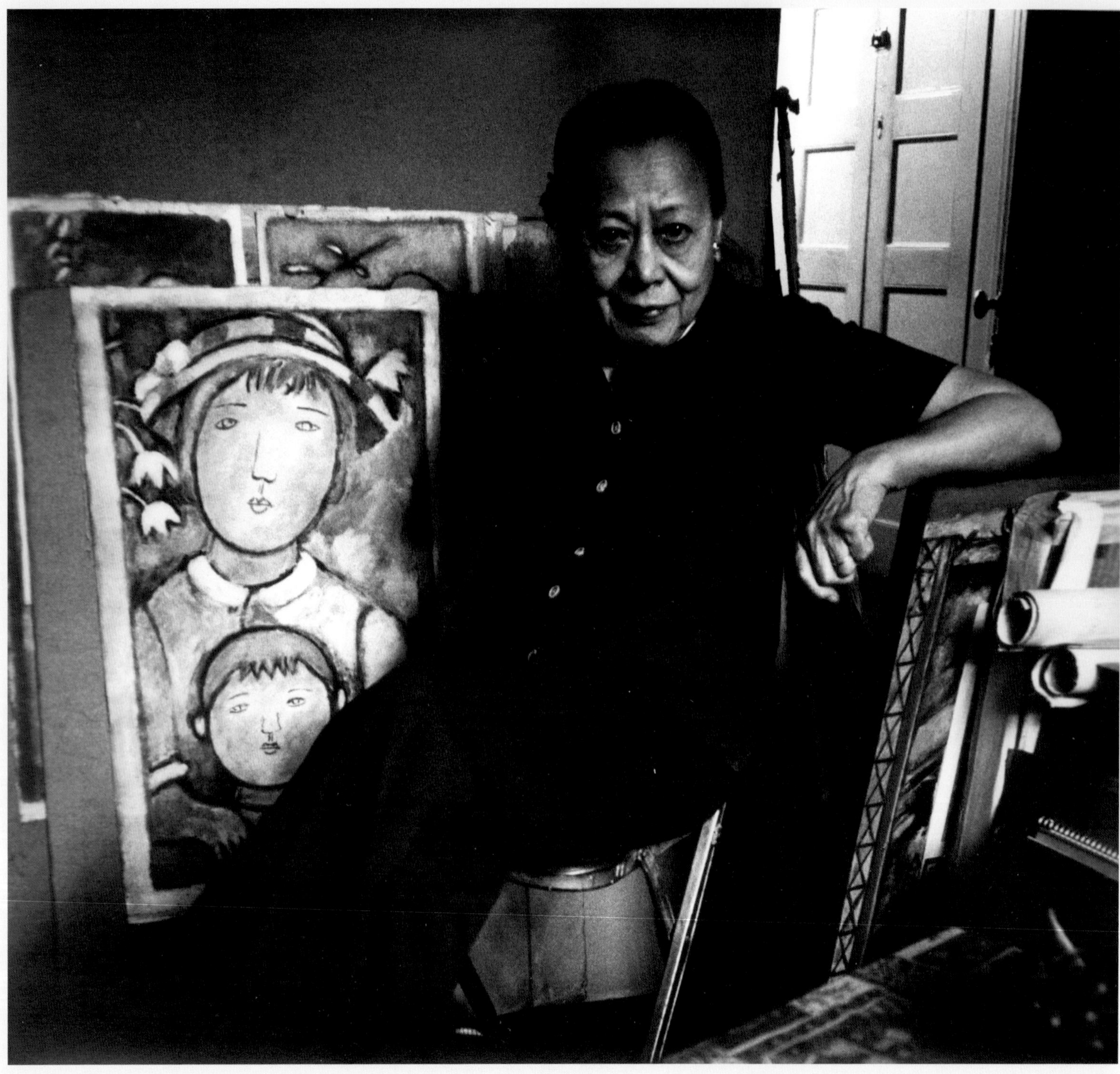

Irene Poon, *Miné Okubo*, 1996. The Miné Okubo Collection, Center for Social Justice & Civil Liberties, Riverside Community College District, California, box 95, 95-2-6.

I was interested in people and life, so the camp gave me an opportunity to study the human race from cradle to grave and to see what happens to people when they are reduced to one status and one condition.

I was all over the camp sketching everything from the very first day. There were untold hardships and sadness everywhere and humor because everything was so insane.

There were no plans or preparations for this forced evacuation. Everybody of Japanese ancestry was evacuated: the young, the old, the children, babies, pregnant mothers, sick—110,000 were evacuated in three months. One cannot know what it was like unless you lived it.

Since evacuees were not allowed to return to California and the West, and I knew nobody in the East, I decided to remain in camp until the gates closed, but in March 1944 *Fortune* magazine asked me to come to New York to help illustrate their special April 1944 Japan issue and I decided to stay in New York.

When the *Fortune* magazine people saw the vast collection of drawings that I had on the evacuation, they were surprised and excited, and when they learned that American citizens were evacuated, they were ashamed, and they decided to look into the matter more, and they wrote an article called "Issei, Nisei, Kibei."[1] It's one of the first illustrated articles that came out in one of the largest periodicals of the time, because anything Japanese was not quite known in the East yet.

These drawings were originally made for my friends on the outside, and the *Fortune* magazine people told me that I should continue and make it into a book. So the factual account of the Japanese evacuation and internment is in *Citizen 13660*, which was published in 1946 by the Columbia University Press. It was the first inside-the-camp documentary story of the Japanese evacuation and internment, coming out when the subject was not too well known in the East, and when everything Japanese was still unpopular. It was too soon after the war's ending.

I kept the drawings objective, and the brief text was not only to interest the reader but to record this tragic incident of the war.

I believe an apology and some form of reparation are due in order to prevent this from happening to others. Textbooks and history studies on this subject should be taught to children when young in grade and high schools. Many generations do not know that this ever happened in the United States.

Whenever I speak about evacuation, they think it happened in Japan.

I wish to present a copy of *Citizen 13660* to the Commission for the record.

I also have a copy of the *Fortune* article, "Issei, Nisei, Kibei," and for the public I have put together an exhibition of my sketches, drawings, and paintings for you in the back of the room.

1
"Kibei" refers to second-generation Japanese Americans, Nisei, who were born in the United States but educated largely in Japan.

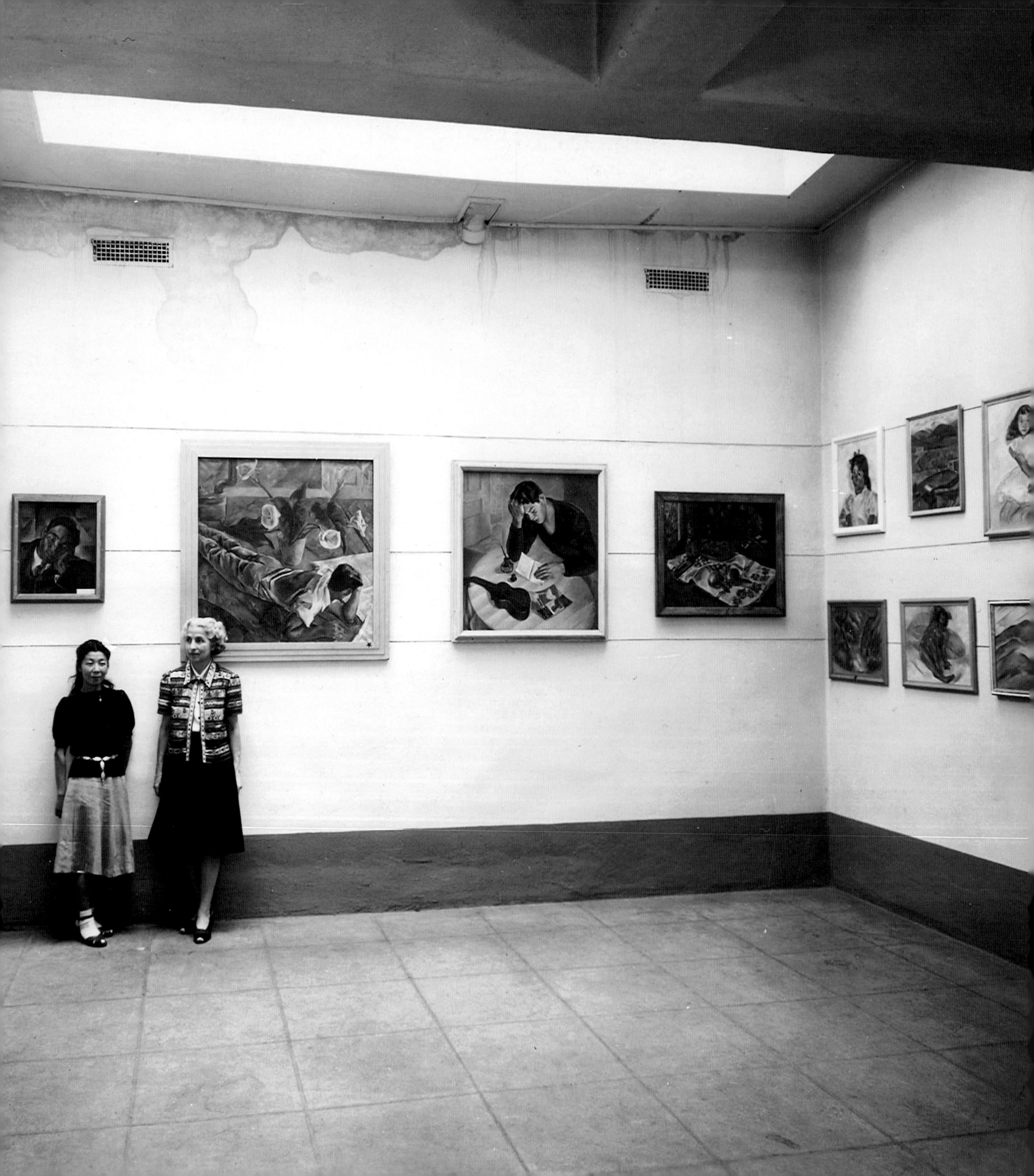

# Selected Exhibition Records, 1920–50

Researched and compiled by ShiPu Wang

Existing literature about Hisako Hibi's and Miné Okubo's oeuvres, such as *Peaceful Painter: Memoirs of an Issei Woman Artist*; *Miné Okubo: Following Her Own Road*; and *Miné Okubo: An American Experience*, includes records of the artists' exhibition activities in the postwar decades. Their prewar and wartime exhibition histories, however, are less known. Miki Hayakawa's exhibition records since the early 1920s have not been well documented, due to a scarcity of monographic studies. This list offers an overview of these artists' active participation in California's art scenes through 1950. It aims to serve as a basis, reference, and catalyst for more research in the future.

*Abbreviations*
MH: Miki Hayakawa
HH: Hisako Hibi
MO: Miné Okubo
SFAA: San Francisco Art Association
CSFA: California School of Fine Arts

Miki Hayakawa (left) at her Alcove Show at the New Mexico Museum of Art, November 1944 (detail). Courtesy of Shirley and David Astilli, Santa Fe, New Mexico.

**1920**
Poster Contest, California School of Arts and Crafts, Oakland — MH (First Prize)

**1924**
Forty-Seventh Annual Exhibition, SFAA — MH: *A Monster*; *Moonlight*; *Night*; *Wind*; *Silvery Moon* (all monotype)

**1925**
Forty-Eighth Annual Exhibition, SFAA — MH: *After the Rain*; *A Young Man*

**1926**
**No SFAA Annual Exhibition in 1926*
Annual Exhibition, Berkeley League — MH: *Japanese Tea House* (Third Prize)
Oakland Art Annual, Haviland Hall, UC Berkeley — MH: *Yakima Indian Girl*

**1927**
Forty-Ninth Annual Exhibition, SFAA — MH: *Lucille*; *Nude*; *Portrait*
*Painters and Sculptors of Southern California*, Los Angeles Museum of Art — MH: *Peggy*

**1928**
Fiftieth Annual Exhibition, SFAA — MH: *Landscape*

**1929**
Fifty-First Annual Exhibition, SFAA — MH: *Waldo*; *Park*
Annual Exhibition, Oakland Art Gallery and Oakland Art League — MH: *Landscape*
Student Art Show, CSFA, San Francisco — MH, in the "Third Painting Group"
Solo Exhibition, Golden Gate Institute (Kinmon Gakuen), San Francisco — MH

*Amateur and Professional Joint Painting Exhibition*, San Francisco Japanese Art Association — MH: *Pescadero*; *Summer of Waldo*; *View of Tamalpais from the Top of Mount Waldo*; *Hydrangea*; *Schooner of Mayor Rolph*; *Summer of Kentfield*; *Rest*; *Autumn*; HH (Hisako Shimizu in 1929): *Hill in Waldo*; *Late Spring*; *A Sketch*; *Solitary House*; *Summer*

**1930**

Second Exhibition, San Francisco Japanese Art Association — MH: *Late Autumn*; *A Ship Weighing Anchor*; *Magnificent Peak*; HH: *Still-Life, No. 1*; *Still-Life, No. 2*

**1931**

Fifty-Third Annual Exhibition, SFAA — MH: *Plant*

*Flower Show* — MH: *Waterlilies*; *Flower Composition*

Group Exhibition, San Francisco Society of Women Artists — MH: *Geranium*; *Plant*; *Portrait*

**1933**

**No SFAA Annual Exhibition in 1933*

Annual Exhibition of the Works of Western Artists, Oakland Art Gallery — MH: *Portrait*

**1934**

**No SFAA Annual Exhibition in 1934*

First Oriental Art Exhibit, Foundation of Western Art, Los Angeles — MH: *Tulips*; *Portrait of a Young Man*

Annual Exhibition of Paintings, California State Fair, Sacramento — HH: *Still Life*

**1935**

Annual Exhibition of Paintings and Sculpture, Oakland Art Gallery — MH: *Open Window*

Fifty-Fifth Annual Exhibition, SFAA (the opening exhibition of the San Francisco Museum of Art at its Civic Center location) — MH: *From My Window*; *One Afternoon*; *Portrait*; *Tulips*

**1936**

*Painters and Sculptors of Southern California*, Los Angeles Museum of Art — MH: *One Afternoon*

Annual Exhibition of Oil Paintings, Oakland Art Gallery — MH: *Boy Sawing*

**1937**

Fifty-Seventh Annual Exhibition, SFAA — MO: *Landscape*

Annual Exhibition of Paintings, California State Fair, Sacramento — HH: *My Nursery Chair*

*California Oriental Painters*, Foundation of Western Art, Los Angeles — MH: *From My Window*; *Boy Sawing*; MO: *Portrait Head*; *The Church*

Annual Exhibition of Oil Paintings, Oakland Art Gallery — MH: *Tulips*; HH: *Still Life*

*Painters and Sculptors of Southern California*, Los Angeles Museum of Art — MH: *From My Window*

Group Exhibition, Santa Cruz Art League — MH: *One Afternoon*

**1938**

Fifty-Eighth Annual Exhibition, SFAA — MH: *One Afternoon*; MO: *November*; *The Church*; *Portrait Study*

Annual Exhibition of Oil Paintings, Oakland Art Gallery — HH: *A Nursery Chair*

**1939**

*Art Exhibition by California Artists*, Golden Gate International Exposition, San Francisco — MH: *Portrait*; HH: *Landscape*

Annual Exhibition of Paintings, California State Fair, Sacramento — HH: *Spring*

Annual Exhibition of Oil Paintings, Oakland Art Gallery — HH: *Early Spring*

Seventh Annual Exhibition of Watercolors, Pastels, Drawings and Prints, Oakland Art Gallery — HH: *A Sea Monster*

**1940**

Sixtieth Annual Exhibition, SFAA — MO: *Mama y Felipe*; *Green Apples* (co-winner of the First Prize in Painting)

*Art Exhibition by California Artists*, Golden Gate International Exposition, San Francisco — MH: *From My Window*; HH: *Spring III*; MO: *Mother and Child*

Annual Exhibition of Oil Paintings, Oakland Art Gallery — HH: *Early Spring*

Eighth Annual Exhibition of Watercolors, Pastels, Drawings and Prints, Oakland Art Gallery — MO: *Ruins in Arles*

**1941**

Sixty-First Annual Exhibition, SFAA — HH: *Chicken Houses*; *Spring*; MO: *Chapel Hill*; *Miyo and Cat* (winner of the Anne Bremer Memorial Prize)

Annual Exhibition of Oil Paintings, Oakland Art Gallery — MO: *November*

Annual Exhibition of Drawings and Prints, SFAA — MO: *Study—Chapel Hill*

Fifth Annual Watercolor Exhibition, SFAA — MO: *Azar (La Bohéme)*

Ninth Annual Exhibition of Watercolors, Pastels, Drawings and Prints, Oakland Art Gallery — HH: *Mama Bocolini*

Solo Exhibition, SFAA Art Association Gallery at the San Francisco Museum of Art (Oct.) — MO

Sixteenth Annual Exhibition, San Francisco Society of Women Artists, San Francisco Museum of Art (Nov.) — MO: *Fishing Boats* (Honorable Mention)

"American Art Week" Exhibition, Japanese American Citizens League, San Francisco — MH, HH, and MO

**1942**

Sixth Annual Watercolor Exhibition, SFAA — MO: *Across the Street*; *Study*; *Wine to Drink* (Honorable Mention)

**The Sixty-Second SFAA Annual Exhibition included no artists of Asian descent.*

**1943**

Annual Exhibition of Drawings and Prints, SFAA — MO (from Topaz): *Evacues* [*sic*]; *On Watch* (winner of the Artist Fund Prize)

Seventh Annual Watercolor Exhibition, SFAA — MO (from Topaz): *Dust Storm*; *One Important Day*

*Thirtieth Annual Exhibition: Painters and Sculptors of the Southwest*, School of American Research, Museum of New Mexico, Santa Fe (Aug.–Sept.) — MH

Alcove Show, Museum of New Mexico, Santa Fe (Sept.–Oct.) — MH

**The Sixty-Third SFAA Annual Exhibition included no artists of Asian descent.*

**1944**

Annual Exhibition of Drawings and Prints, SFAA — HH (from Topaz): *Topaz City No. 1*

Fifty-Fifth Annual American Exhibition of Water Colors and Drawings, Art Institute of Chicago — MO (from Topaz): *Sunday*

*Thirty-First Annual Exhibition: Painters and Sculptors of the Southwest*, School of American Research, Museum of New Mexico, Santa Fe (Aug.–Sept.) — MH: *Hermana & Hermano*

Alcove Show, Museum of New Mexico, Santa Fe (Nov.) — MH

**1945**

Solo Exhibition of Camp Drawings and Paintings, Community Council for American Unity, American Common, New York (Mar.) — MO

Ninth Annual Watercolor Exhibition, SFAA — MO (from New York): *Strikers*; *Checkers* (winner of the Arthur and Anne Bailhache Purchase Award for Watercolor)

*Thirty-Second Annual Exhibition: Painters and Sculptors of the Southwest*, School of American Research, Museum of New Mexico, Santa Fe (Aug.–Sept.) — MH: *Snow on Atalaya*

Alcove Show, Museum of New Mexico, Santa Fe (Nov.) — MH w/ McCrossen

**1946**

*Thirty-Third Annual Exhibition: Painters and Sculptors of the Southwest*, School of American Research, Museum of New Mexico, Santa Fe (Aug.–Sept.) — MH: *Roof Tops*

Alcove Show, Museum of New Mexico, Santa Fe (Sept.) — MH w/ McCrossen

**1947**

*Thirty-Fourth Annual Exhibition: Painters and Sculptors of the Southwest*, School of American Research, Museum of New Mexico, Santa Fe (Aug.–Sept.) — MH: *Portrait*

Alcove Show, Museum of New Mexico, Santa Fe (Oct.) — MH w/ McCrossen

*The Japanese American Artists Group*, Riverside Museum, New York — MO

**1948**

*New Mexico Artist Series 1948: An Exhibition of Contemporary New Mexican Painting*, Santa Fe (Jan.–July) — MH

*Thirty-Fifth Annual Fiesta Exhibition: Painters, Sculptors and Craftsmen of New Mexico*, Museum of New Mexico Art Gallery, Santa Fe (Aug.–Sept.) — MH: *Little Angie*

**1949**

Sixty-Eighth Annual Exhibition, SFAA — MO: *Cat and Cradle* (winner of the Anna Elizabeth Klumpke Prize)

**1950**

*Thirty-Seventh Annual Exhibition: Painters and Sculptors of the Southwest*, Museum of New Mexico Art Gallery, Santa Fe (Aug.–Sept.) — MH: *Portrait*

Fourth New Mexico Exhibition of Prints and Drawings (Dec.) — MH

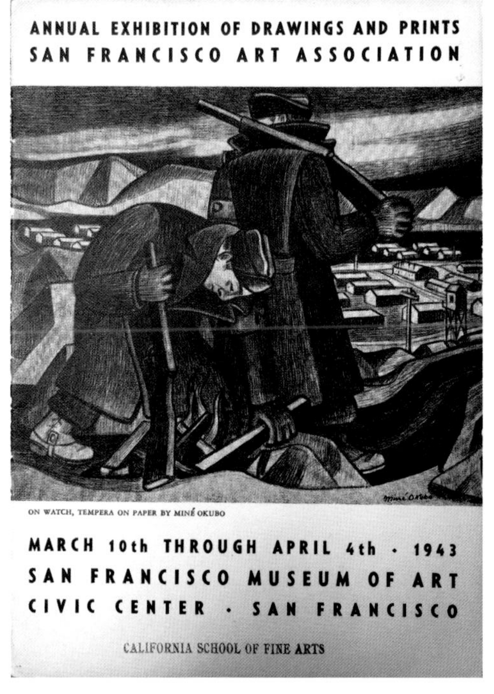


Miné Okubo's *On Watch* (Plate 28) on the cover of the SFAA Annual Exhibition of Drawings and Prints catalogue, 1943.

# Selected Bibliography

Compiled by ShiPu Wang with the assistance of Memphis Despain


**HAYAKAWA, HIBI, AND OKUBO**

Brown, Michael D. *Views from Asian California, 1920–1965*. San Francisco: Michael D. Brown, 1992, 24–26 (Hayakawa); 27–28 (Hibi); 50–51 (Okubo).

Chang, Gordon H., Mark Dean Johnson, and Paul J. Karlstrom, eds. *Asian American Art: A History, 1850–1970*. Stanford, Calif.: Stanford University Press, 2008, 190, 192, 322–24 (Hayakawa); 127–29, 328–29 (Hibi); 116–19, 407–8 (Okubo).

Series 1, California Artists Files (entry artists), California Asian American Artists Biographical Survey Records (SC0929). Department of Special Collections and University Archives, Stanford University Libraries, Stanford, Calif. "Hayakawa, Miki," box 5, folder 3; "Hibi, Hisako," box 5, folder 7; "Okubo, Mine," box 13, folder 9.

**HAYAKAWA AND HIBI**

Higa, Karin. "What Is an Asian American Woman Artist?" In *Art/Women/California, 1950–2000: Parallels and Intersections*, edited by Diane Burgess Fuller and Daniela Salvione. Berkeley: University of California Press in association with the San José Museum of Art, 2002, 85 (Hayakawa); 85–89, 92–94 (Hibi).

**HAYAKAWA AND OKUBO**

Hughes, Edan Milton. *Artists in California, 1786–1940*. San Francisco: Hughes Publishing Company, 1989, 203 (Hayakawa); 133 (Okubo).

Landauer, Susan. "Searching for Selfhood: Women Artists of Northern California." In *Independent Spirits: Women Painters of the American West, 1890–1945*. Berkeley: Autry Museum of Western Heritage in association with the University of California Press, 1995, 32, 35 (Hayakawa); 32, 34 (Okubo).

**HIBI AND OKUBO**

Albright, Thomas. *Art in the San Francisco Bay Area, 1945–1980: An Illustrated History*. Berkeley: University of California Press, 1985, 302 (Okubo); 285 (Hibi).

Gesensway, Deborah, and Mindy Roseman. *Beyond Words: Images from America's Concentration Camps*. Ithaca, N.Y.: Cornell University Press, 1987, 158 (Hibi); 66–75 (Okubo).

Higa, Karin M. *The View from Within: Japanese American Art from the Internment Camps, 1942–1945*. Los Angeles: Japanese American National Museum, 1992, 25, 27–28, 43–44, 75, 91, 96 (Hibi); 28–29, 76, 98 (Okubo).

Hirasuna, Delphine. *The Art of Gaman: Arts and Crafts from the Japanese American Internment Camps 1942–1946*. Berkeley: Ten Speed Press, 2005, 79, 127 (Hibi); 21, 128 (Okubo).

Niiya, Brian. *Encyclopedia of Japanese American History: An A-to-Z Reference from 1868 to the Present*. Updated ed. Los Angeles: Japanese American National Museum, 2001, 134, 192–93 (Hibi); 134, 324–25 (Okubo).

Taylor, Sandra C. *Jewel in the Desert: Japanese American Internment at Topaz*. Berkeley: University of California Press, 1993, 82, 128 (Hibi); 65–66, 69, 72, 81–83, 86, 88–91, 128, 140, 143, 145, 229, 250, 272 (Okubo).

**MIKI HAYAKAWA**

Bradbury, Ellen. "Two Women Who Went Their Own Way: Van Ness a Pleasing American Impressionist, Hayakawa a Santa Fe Painter with Presence." *Albuquerque Journal North*, February 8, 1986, 10.

Falk, Peter H. *Who Was Who in American Art: Compiled from the Original Thirty-Four Volumes of American Art Annual—Who's Who in Art, Biographies of American Artists Active from 1898–1947*. Madison, Conn.: Sound View Press, 1985, 270.

Hozumi, Toshiaki. "Miki Hayakawa and Japanese American Painters before the War in San Francisco." *Hokkaido Art Museum Studies* (2000–01): 107–24.

Kovinick, Phil, and Marian Yoshiki Kovinick. *An Encyclopedia of Women Artists of the American West*. Austin: University of Texas Press, 1998, 131–32.

Trenton, Patricia. "Before the World Moved In." In *The Not-So-Still Life: A Century of California Painting and Sculpture*, edited by Susan Landauer, William H. Gerdts, and Patricia Trenton. Berkeley: University of California Press; San Jose, Calif.: San José Museum of Art, 2003, 66, 192, 210n28.

Turner, Louise. "A Japanese American of the Cezanne School." *Southwest Profile* (1985): 19–24.

Wang, ShiPu. "In Search of Miki Hayakawa: A California Cosmopolitan." In *The Other American Moderns: Matsura, Ishigaki, Noda, Hayakawa*. University Park: Penn State University Press, 2017, 97–126.

Wang, ShiPu. "Miki Hayakawa: Portraying Interiority." In *The Unforgettables: Expanding the History of American Art*, edited by Charles C. Eldredge. Berkeley: University of California Press, 2022, 138–43.

### HISAKO HIBI

Hibi, Hisako. *Peaceful Painter: Memoirs of an Issei Woman Artist*, edited by Ibuki Hibi Lee. Berkeley: Heyday Books, 2004.

Hibi, Hisako, and Kristine Kim. *A Process of Reflection: Paintings by Hisako Hibi*. Los Angeles: Japanese American National Museum, 1999.

Jensen, Joan M. "Women on the Pacific Rim: Some Thoughts on Border Crossings." *Pacific Historical Review* 67, no. 1 (1998): 3–38.

Kano, Betty. "Four Northern California Artists: Hisako Hibi, Norine Nishimura, Yong Soon Min, and Miran Ahn." *Feminist Studies* 19, no. 3 (1993): 628–42.

Karolin, Alexis J. "'A Painter, a Very Poor Talker': Affective Experiences of Trauma and Coping Mechanisms in Hisako Hibi's Internment Artwork." *Atlantic Journal of Communication* (2022): 1–18.

Lee-Tai, Amy. *A Place Where Sunflowers Grow*. Illustrated by Felicia Hoshino. San Francisco: California Children's Book Press, 2006.

Selz, Peter. *Art of Engagement: Visual Politics in California and Beyond*. Berkeley: University of California Press, 2006, 131.

Wechsler, Jeffrey. *Asian Traditions/Modern Expressions: Asian American Artists and Abstraction, 1945–1970*. New York: Harry N. Abrams, Inc., in association with the Jane Voorhees Zimmerli Art Museum, Rutgers, The State University of New Jersey, 1997, 140–41, 154.

### MINÉ OKUBO

Carlson, Douglas. "The Citizenship Question: Mine Okubo, Margaret Anderson, Sensus Communis." *Georgia Review* 74, no. 1 (2020): 164–73.

Dowling, Sarah. "'How Lucky I Was to Be Free and Safe at Home': Reading Humor in Miné Okubo's *Citizen 13660*." *Signs: Journal of Women in Culture and Society* 39, no. 2 (2014): 299–322.

Hathaway, Heather. "Miné Okubo." In *That Damned Fence*. New York: Oxford University Press, 2022, 85–108.

Heller, Jules, and Nancy G. Heller, eds. *North American Women Artists of the Twentieth Century: A Biographical Dictionary*. New York: Garland, 1995, 542.

Hong, Christine. "A Blueprint for Occupied Japan: Miné Okubo and the American Concentration Camp." In *A Violent Peace: Race, U.S. Militarism, and Cultures of Democratization in Cold War Asia and the Pacific*. Stanford, Calif.: Stanford University Press, 2020, 79–106.

Hong, Christine. "Illustrating the Postwar Peace: Miné Okubo, the 'Citizen-Subject' of Japan, and *Fortune* Magazine." *American Quarterly* 67, no. 1 (2015): 105–40.

Kim, Hyung-chan. "Miné Okubo." In *Distinguished Asian Americans: A Biographical Dictionary*. Westport, Conn.: Greenwood Press, 1999, 276–77.

LaDuke, Betty. "Miné Okubo: An American Experience." In *The Forbidden Stitch: An Asian American Women's Anthology*, edited by Shirley Lim. Corvallis, Ore.: Calyx Books, 1989, 189–206.

LaDuke, Betty. "On the Right Road: The Life of Miné Okubo." *Art Education* 40, no. 3 (1987): 43–48.

McGavran, Grace W., and Miné Okubo. *Where the Carp Banners Fly*. New York: Friendship Press, 1949.

Okubo, Miné. *Citizen 13660*. New York: Columbia University Press, 1946; New York: Arno Press, 1978; Seattle: University of Washington Press, 1983/2014.

Okubo, Miné, and Esther Klotz. Esther Klotz Collection on Miné Okubo (MS 094). Special Collections & University Archives, University of California, Riverside.

Peacock, James. "'My Thoughts Shifted from the Past to the Future': Time and (Autobio)graphic Representation in Miné Okubo's *Citizen 13660*." *Journal of Postcolonial Writing* 52, no. 4 (2016): 445–63.

Ravela, Christian. "Citizenship in the Racial Break: Japanese Incarceration and Racial Subjectivity in Miné Okubo's *Citizen 13660*." *Twentieth Century Literature* 67, no. 3 (2021): 293–316.

Roberts, Brian. "Miné Okubo." In *Asian American Literature: An Encyclopedia for Students*, edited by Keith Lawrence. Santa Barbara, Calif.: Greenwood, 2021, 262–65.

Robinson, Greg. "Birth of a Citizen: Miné Okubo and the Politics of Symbolism." In *After Camp: Portraits in Midcentury Japanese American Life and Politics*. Berkeley: University of California Press, 2012, 5, 6, 59, 69–72, 74–84, 86, 261nn8–9, 263n19, 263n20, 264n27, 264n33, 265n44.

Robinson, Greg, and Elena Tajima Creef, eds. *Miné Okubo: Following Her Own Road*. Seattle: University of Washington Press, 2008.

Robinson, Greg, and Elena Tajima Creef, eds. "A Tribute to Miné Okubo." Special issue, *Amerasia Journal* 30, no. 2 (2004).

Roy Leeper and Gaylord Hall collection of Miné Okubo papers, circa 1940–2001. Archives of American Art, Smithsonian Institution, Washington, D.C.

Shin, Yihyun. "Graphic Deconstruction of Spatially Marked Race in Miné Okubo's *Citizen 13660*." *Studies in British and American Language and Literature* 146 (2022): 291–310.

Stanutz, Katherine. "Inscrutable Grief: Memorializing Japanese American Internment in Miné Okubo's *Citizen 13660*." *American Studies* 56, no. 3 (2018): 47–68.

Sun, Shirley. *Miné Okubo: An American Experience*. Oakland, Calif.: The Oakland Museum, 1972.

Westphal, Ruth, and Janet Blake Dominik. *American Scene Painting: California, 1930s and 1940s*. Irvine, Calif.: Westphal, 1991, 173, 176.


For the sake of space and balance among the three artists, this bibliography includes only a portion of the existing literature that focuses mainly on analyzing Okubo's *Citizen 13660*. It is my hope that seeing the paucity of substantial studies of Hayakawa's, Hibi's, and Okubo's oeuvres will engender more research projects in the future. Thanks to Memphis Despain at the University of California, Merced, for assisting me in compiling the bibliography.

This book is published in conjunction with the exhibition *Pictures of Belonging: Miki Hayakawa, Hisako Hibi, and Miné Okubo*, organized by the Japanese American National Museum.

**Exhibition Dates**
Utah Museum of Fine Arts, Salt Lake City
February 24 through June 30, 2024

Smithsonian American Art Museum, Washington, D.C.
November 15, 2024, through August 17, 2025

Pennsylvania Academy of the Fine Arts, Philadelphia
October 2, 2025, through January 4, 2026

Monterey Museum of Art, California
February 5 through April 19, 2026

Japanese American National Museum, Los Angeles
Late 2026

This exhibition is made possible through support from the Terra Foundation for American Art. In addition, this project is supported in part by the National Endowment for the Arts.

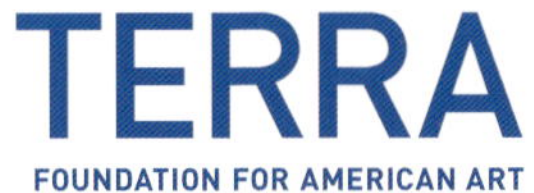


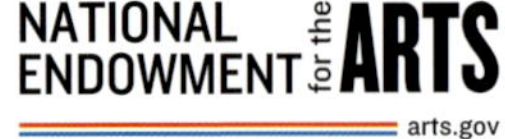




Library of Congress Cataloging-in-Publication Data
Names: Wang, ShiPu, editor. | Japanese American National Museum (Los Angeles, Calif.), organizer, host institution.
Title: Pictures of belonging : Miki Hayakawa, Hisako Hibi, and Miné Okubo / ShiPu Wang.
Description: Los Angeles : Japanese American National Museum, [2023] | Includes bibliographical references.
Identifiers: LCCN 2023019352 | ISBN 9780520394674 (hardcover)
Subjects: LCSH: Japanese American art—California—20th century—Exhibitions. | Hayakawa, Miki, 1899–1953—Exhibitions. | Hibi, Hisako, 1907–1991—Exhibitions. | Okubo, Miné—Exhibitions.
Classification: LCC N6538.J32 P53 2023 | DDC 704.03/956073—dc23/eng/20230524
LC record available at https://lccn.loc.gov/2023019352

Published by the Japanese American National Museum
100 North Central Avenue
Los Angeles, CA 90012
www.janm.org

Published in association with University of California Press
www.ucpress.edu

Produced by Marquand Books, Seattle
www.marquandbooks.com

Edited by Kristin Kearns
Designed by Jayme Yen
Typeset in GT America and Freight
Proofread by Janice Lee
Color management by I/O Color, Seattle
Printed and bound in Singapore by Pristone

**Image Credits**
Page 2
Miné Okubo, *Lady with Red Flowers* (detail), 1963.

Page 4
Hisako Hibi, *Topaz Flower—Sunflower and Corn* (detail), August 1945.

Page 18
Miki Hayakawa, *Untitled (Young Man Playing Ukulele)* (detail), ca. 1934–36.

Page 76
Miki Hayakawa, *From My Window* (detail), 1935.

Page 116
Miné Okubo, *Cat, Vase of Flowers, Girl—Blue* (detail), 1978.